MAX

A BIOGRAPHY BY

DAVID CECIL

CONSTABLE
LONDON

First published in 1964
by Constable and Company, Ltd
10–12 Orange Street, London, WC2
Copyright © 1964 David Cecil
Printed in Great Britain
by Butler and Tanner, Ltd
Frome and London

MAX

Also by David Cecil

Biography:

THE YOUNG MELBOURNE
(And the Story of his Marriage with Caroline Lamb)

LORD M.
or the Later Life of Lord Melbourne

TWO QUIET LIVES
Dorothy Osborne and Thomas Gray

THE STRICKEN DEER
or The Life of Cowper

Criticism:

POETS AND STORY-TELLERS

EARLY VICTORIAN NOVELISTS

Essays in Revaluation of Dickens,
Thackeray, the Brontës, Trollope,
George Eliot and Mrs Gaskell

HARDY THE NOVELIST

THE FINE ART OF READING

MAX BEERBOHM

To

JOAN DROGHEDA

*with affection and
admiration*

CONTENTS

PART I

Chapter I CHILDHOOD AND CHARTERHOUSE   *page* 3

II OXFORD   43

III THE 'YELLOW BOOK'   64

PART II

IV 'THE WORKS OF MAX BEERBOHM'   113

V THE 'SATURDAY REVIEW'   168

VI LOVE   218

VII 'YET AGAIN'   242

VIII MARRIAGE   269

PART III

IX THE VILLINO   303

X LONDON REVISITED   324

XI THE FIRST WAR   334

XII 'SEVEN MEN'   346

XIII ITALIAN DAYS   360

XIV 'AND EVEN NOW'   379

XV 'A VARIETY OF THINGS'   405

XVI ON THE AIR   430

XVII THE SECOND WAR   445

PART IV

XVIII LATTER DAYS   469

XIX THE END   494

INDEX   499

ILLUSTRATIONS

MAX BEERBOHM   *frontispiece*
From the portrait by Sir William Nicholson in the
National Portrait Gallery

HERBERT BEERBOHM TREE   *page* 8
From *Caricatures of Twenty-five Gentlemen*

MAX AT CHARTERHOUSE   31
From a photograph in the possession of Lord David Cecil

REGINALD TURNER   53
From *A Book of Caricatures*

THE YOUNG ROTHENSTEIN   65
From a caricature in Merton College, Oxford

OSCAR WILDE   72
From a caricature in the Ashmolean Museum, Oxford

CISSEY LOFTUS   81
From a photograph in the possession of Mrs Reichmann

MAX BEERBOHM AND WILLIAM ROTHENSTEIN AT
     OXFORD   94
From a photograph in the possession of Rupert Hart-Davis

SOME PERSONS OF THE NINETIES   106
From *Observations*

GRACE CONOVER   118
From a photograph in the possession of Mrs Reichmann

WILLIAM NICHOLSON   132
From *A Book of Caricatures*

AUBREY BEARDSLEY   138
From *Caricatures of Twenty-five Gentlemen*

EDMUND GOSSE   153
From a caricature in the possession of Lord David Cecil

FRANK HARRIS   165
From *Caricatures of Twenty-five Gentlemen*

ILLUSTRATIONS

MAX ON A HOLIDAY, SELF-CARICATURE *page* 185
In the Ashmolean Museum, Oxford

GEORGE MOORE 203
From *Caricatures of Twenty-five Gentlemen*

GEORGE MEREDITH 210
From *Max's Nineties*

HENRY JAMES 216
From *Max's Nineties*

CONSTANCE COLLIER 222
From a photograph in the possession of Mrs Reichmann

FLORENCE KAHN 230
From a photograph in the possession of Mrs Reichmann

MAX BEERBOHM 243
From a photograph in the possession of Mrs Reichmann

MAX BEERBOHM AND HERBERT BEERBOHM TREE 255
From a caricature in the possession of Mr Robert Taylor

FLORENCE IN ITALY 311
From a drawing in the possession of Mrs Reichmann

MAX BEERBOHM AND FRANK HARRIS 327
From a caricature in the possession of Lady Jones

FLORENCE ON THE TERRACE AT THE VILLINO 357
From a drawing in the possession of Mrs Reichmann

MAX BEERBOHM, SELF-CARICATURE 393
At Charterhouse

DORA BEERBOHM 403
From a photograph in the possession of Mr Ivan Moffatt

ELISABETH JUNGMANN 416
From a photograph by Germaine Kanova

MAX BEERBOHM, SELF-CARICATURE, 1952 471

MAX BEERBOHM 481
From a photograph by Cecil Beaton

PREFATORY NOTE

IN the autumn of 1956 I was visited by Lady Beerbohm, widow of Sir Max, who told me that her husband had wished me to write his biography. I look upon this as the finest compliment ever paid me; and I have been correspondingly anxious to show myself worthy of it. Mine has been a delightful task; but not an easy one. For Max's life was so uneventful that it is almost impossible to make a story of it. I have, therefore, concentrated less on the story than on the man; and sought, making use as far as possible of Max's own words and of those who knew him well, to compose, as it were, a succession of detailed portraits of him and his mind during the successive phases of his life. With this purpose in mind, I have decided not to give references for the phrases and passages from the books, letters and journals quoted in my text. If I mention any, I should have had to mention all: and this would have been to overweigh an already heavy volume. For it is of such quotations that the texture of my book is woven.

The reader will also note that I have not included any extensive criticism of Max's works. This is deliberate. Lengthy passages of criticism are out of place in a biography: they dissipate its atmosphere and interrupt its narrative flow. I have, therefore, not discussed Max's art except briefly, and then mainly in so far as it throws light on his character and opinions. I should, however, feel ungrateful for the extreme pleasure his works have given me if I did not take this opportunity to express my extreme admiration for them. No doubt they are airy and light-hearted productions. But what matter? So are *The Rape of the Lock* and *A Sentimental Journey*; and these are unfading masterpieces. *And Even Now* and *Seven Men* are not their inferiors. As for *The Poets' Corner* and *A Christmas Garland*, they must be a source of wonder and delight so long as the taste for parody and caricature endures. For Shaw was right to speak of 'the incomparable Max'. On his own chosen ground he is unrivalled; England's supreme parodist and caricaturist, her most exquisite master of satiric fantasy.

It remains for me warmly to thank the many people who have

helped me by lending me papers and pictures, or by telling me their reminiscences of Max, in particular: Mrs Reichmann, Miss Iris Tree, Lady Cory-Wright, Mr and Mrs Selwyn Jepson, Sir John Rothenstein, Mr Gordon Craig, Mr Robert Speaight, Mr Siegfried Sassoon, Mr S. N. Behrman, who has kindly allowed me to quote from his book *Conversation with Max* (published by Hamish Hamilton), Dr Riewald, Mr Douglas Cleverdon, Lady Jones, Dr Roger Highfield, Mrs Hendrey, Signor Oscar Pio, the Headmaster of Charterhouse, the Warden and Fellows of Merton College, Oxford. And also: Mr Cecil Beaton, Mr Oliver Brown, Mr Vyvyan Holland, Freiherr von Hutten, Mr Michael Lloyd, Sir Compton Mackenzie, Mr Somerset Maugham, Mr Moray McLaren, Mrs Charles Morgan, Dr Rau, Mrs Richardson, Mr Cecil Roberts, Mrs Ellis Roberts, Sir Sydney Roberts, Mr Wayland Young.

I must also acknowledge the kindness of the British Broadcasting Corporation for allowing me to listen to records of Max's broadcasts, the Ashmolean Museum, Oxford, the Universities of California, Harvard, Yale and London, the Brotherton Library, Leeds, Messrs William Heinemann and the Proprietors of the *Daily Mail*, for their assistance. Finally, I must thank Miss Phyllis Jenkinson for her valuable help, and Mr Rupert Hart-Davis for the information, advice and encouragement he has given me throughout my task.

DAVID CECIL

PART I

CHAPTER ONE

Childhood and Charterhouse

(1)

MAX BEERBOHM in his later years, turning the pages of some contemporary memoirs, came upon the following sentence: 'Posterity will be puzzled what to think about Sir Edmund Gosse.' Max noted in the margin, 'Posterity, I hope, will be puzzled what to think about anybody. How baffling and contradictory are our most intimate and contemporary friends! And how many of us can gauge even himself!' If Max did not understand himself, his biographer is likely to understand him even less—as he quickly discovers when he gets to work. Max would seem a straightforward enough subject; for he had such a marked and remembered personality. Across the pages of Edwardian social history he steps, a demure, dandified figure, with a big round head and heavy-lidded protuberant blue eyes, amusedly contemplating the world and from time to time letting fall a whimsical or ironic comment on it. Moreover, this personality is more fully displayed in his art. Max is a character in his own tales, a subject of his own caricatures: in his essays he addresses us directly in his own unique unmistakable voice.

Unique, unmistakable! Yet how much in fact does he tell us about himself? His talk, for all its ease, is not intimate, still less indiscreet; his art is designedly an art of the surface, disclosing little of its author's deeper feelings. Nor do the Edwardian social chronicles in which he makes a figure help us to elucidate him. They are full of anecdotes about his wit, his dress, his demeanour. But they say nothing to reveal the inner man, they never catch him making a confession or giving himself away. The facts of his history are equally unrevealing. His life was for the most part uneventful. But such events as do occur in it—his long-delayed marriage, his self-imposed exile to Italy—are mysterious enough to make us curious to know more about them, and, in particular, what Max felt about them. Our curiosity is baffled: he does not tell us. At once reserved and extrovert, he shrank from confession and was bored by self-analysis. He never could understand, he said, how anyone managed to keep a diary: his private letters—with rare exceptions— are as discreet as his essays. The result of all this is that the biographer, though he may permit himself to guess a little, can never be quite sure that he has found the key to his hero's mystery. Max remains for posterity a puzzle. Luckily the puzzle is a delightful one and a man of genius as well.

(2)

The genius was his own, the delightfulness partly inherited. He was born at 57 Palace Gardens Terrace, Kensington, on 24 August 1872, and christened Henry Maximilian. His father, Julius Ewald Beerbohm, was not an Englishman by birth, but the son of a prosperous merchant family established for several generations at Memel on the shores of the Baltic—romantic region of pine trees and amber—but themselves of mixed blood, Dutch and Lithuanian and German. It has often been suggested that they were Jewish too; and the notion gains colour in Max's case from his brains, his taste for bravura and his propensity to fall in love with Jewesses. It would have pleased him to think that he was of their kin. 'I would be delighted to know that the Beerbohms had that very agreeable and encouraging thing, Jewish blood,' he once said, 'but,' he added, 'there seems no reason for supposing it.' In fact the Beerbohms were an Aryan family themselves, nor, as far as we can trace their previous history, did any of them marry a Jewess. For several generations before Max, indeed, it would have been impossible. The Beerbohms belonged to the cream of Memel's upper bourgeoisie. They had even achieved an occasional connection with the court and aristocracy; one Beerbohm daughter married no less a personage than General Baron von Unruh, Military Governor to the Crown Prince of Germany. There could have been no question of her making such a marriage had she been suspected of harbouring a drop of Jewish blood in her veins.

As the youngest member of a large family, Julius Beerbohm had his own way to make in the world and decided, while still a boy, to make it abroad. After a short sojourn in France, he arrived in England somewhere about 1830, as a young man of twenty, and went into business as a corn-merchant: in due time he became a naturalized Englishman, and at the age of forty married an English-woman. His business modestly prospered and he was generally liked. This was to be expected. His handsome person, elegant clothes and beautiful manners—his French friends nicknamed him 'Monsieur Su-Perbe Homme'—were the outward expression of an amiable, honourable, cheerful nature, with strong scholarly interests which led him, in the rare intervals of a hard-worked life, to teach himself seven languages and even to take up the study of Anglo-Saxon when he was over sixty. He had also a pleasant streak of scholarly eccentricity. His clerks were amused one morning to see him arrive at the office with his bedroom slippers crammed absent-mindedly in his pocket by mistake for the newspaper: on another occasion, at a party where he was not enjoying himself, he was found by one of his daughters-in-law groping vaguely about the room. 'Are you looking for something?' she asked. 'The door!' gasped out Mr Beerbohm. Unlike his youngest son, he was not a man of outstanding gifts. But he was not ordinary either.

Nor were the women he married. His first wife, Constantia Draper, was the daughter of a clerk in Lloyds Bank, pious and unambitious, whose chief pleasure was in literature. Packets of yellowing letters of his still remain, written to his children in an old-fashioned, eighteenth-century style, florid and formal, expatiating on the beauties of Gray's poems and Milton's. Constantia Draper herself was pretty, charming, and dreamily out of touch with the workaday world. A stranger noticed her wandering down a London street with her shoelaces untied; he called her attention to this fact. 'I like it so,' replied Mrs Beerbohm serenely. Too unpractical to run a household, she early resigned the task to her more effective sister, Eliza. It was not for long; she died at thirty-two, leaving four children to her husband, and to later generations the memory of something at once comic and romantic.

In general Mr Beerbohm was conservative and cautious. But Constantia's death before long produced a crisis; at this crisis he acted boldly and unconventionally. He and Eliza wanted to marry. It was for the advantage of the children, and, besides, they seem to have loved each other. But the laws of England then forbade a man to marry his deceased wife's sister. Mr Beerbohm therefore took Eliza to Switzerland and married her there. Back in England, they settled calmly down to found another family. Possibly because they took the affair so calmly themselves, it seems to have created little scandal. The respectable Victorian circles in which they moved continued to receive them.

The second Mrs Beerbohm was plainer than her sister but a more considerable personality. Small, keen-eyed, and dressed usually in a lace cap and trailing silk skirts over which she was apt to stumble, she suggested to one witness a fairy-godmother, to another Queen Victoria. She had strong affections and the family charm, combining demonstrative sweetness with a mischievous, *gamine* humour; and, though not intellectual, she possessed a literary sense which showed itself both in her judgement of books and in the crisp amusing turns of phrase with which she adorned her letters—'I feel older than any hills,' she will exclaim; or describe a walk in Rotten Row where she saw Mrs Merton 'looking yellow and eager on a spirited bay'. Finally, she was a woman of will. Her stepchildren in particular noticed that, adroit and smiling, she got her way, however the others might oppose it. Though they responded to her charm, they were not always sure how much they trusted her.

There were four of them—three boys, Ernest born in 1850, Herbert born in 1852, Julius born in 1854, and one girl, Constance, born in 1856: Eliza herself gave birth to five children of whom three survived, Agnes and Dora, born in 1865 and 1868 respectively, and one boy, Max. The Draper and Beerbohm strains proved an unusual and successful combination. All seven children were in their different ways and degrees clever, charming and odd. The boys were the oddest; they were made more so by their education. Eliza Beerbohm—possibly because she thought three young boys a lot to manage when she wished to give her best attention to her own children—suggested that they should go to a boarding-school. Unluckily for them, Julius Beerbohm was attacked by one of those failures of imagination that can overtake the most affectionate parents. He recalled with piety the educational institutions of his fatherland and packed them off to a ferociously strict military school in Germany. They were homesick and furious; indeed, Herbert, the second boy, left school permanently convinced that education of any kind was in itself evil. However, suffering did not break his spirit or that of his brothers. On the contrary, it seems to have confirmed an innate determination to strike out on a line for themselves in life. They all started their careers in their father's corn-selling business; but, one after another, they soon gave this up. Their subsequent careers showed that they asked more colour and adventure from life than a London city office could provide.

Ernest, the eldest, left for the Antipodes and ultimately settled down as a sheep-farmer in Cape Colony, where he was later reported to have married a coloured lady. Malicious friends teased his stepmother and sisters about this new and exotic addition to their family: 'Is it true that Ernest has married a brunette?' asked one of them. Herbert, the second brother, stayed in England. But his career there was in its own way equally adventurous and more sensational. He wanted to be an actor. This was so unconventional an idea for anyone with his social background that his father opposed it for some years; with the result that Herbert did not get on to the stage till he was twenty-six. It did not matter. Within nine years, under his stage name of Herbert Beerbohm Tree, he was a leading actor-manager with a theatre of his own; before many more had passed he was the undisputed king of the contemporary stage. It was not that he was a great actor. The tall lanky figure with the carroty hair, restless pale eyes and soft purring voice, was completely suited only to fantastic roles; moreover, too impatient for the drudgery needed to acquire a solid technique, he remained to the end a brilliant amateur, capable of wonderful flashes of imaginative impersonation but rarely giving a sustainedly good performance. Nor, unmethodical, changeable and incapable of understanding figures, was he what is generally meant by an efficient stage director and producer. But to an original intelligence rare among actors and an exuberant, romantic imagination, he added a demonic energy that drove him irresistibly up to the top of his profession. Fastidious critics were contemptuous of his successes, flamboyant spectacles on a Wagnerian scale that were liable to overwhelm the plays Tree had designed them to illustrate—as when he sent the witches flying in a covey over Macbeth's blasted heath, or cut the text of *A Midsummer Night's Dream* in order to give time to build a wood on the stage with real rabbits in it. But even these aberrations were somehow imaginative; and they evinced an intense unquestioning belief in the world of Shakespeare's creating, which is often lacking in more scholarly presentations. Anyway, Tree did not take his productions over-seriously. If one failed, or

HERBERT BEERBOHM TREE

even if he found that acting in it bored him, he took it off at once and put on another. All this meant financial risk. But he was a natural gambler who thrived on risks. As a matter of fact he generally survived them. Again and again up to the last minute he seemed likely to fail. Rehearsals were a chaotic whirlwind with Tree at the centre, his red hair on end, gesturing, perorating, fooling. But on the night mysteriously all had fallen into place: Tree had imposed his purpose by sheer dynamism of personality.

It was as a personality, indeed, rather than as an actor that he made his unique impression on the imagination. It flowered even more outside the theatre than in it. For the stage was not enough to use up his energy. He lived a brilliant, helter-skelter social life, sitting up till three or four every morning at the Garrick Club or at huge supper parties given by himself at the theatre where he entertained the great world—famous artists, cabinet ministers, reigning beauties. More exhausting still, his private life was frequently disturbed by love-affairs, with all the dramatic scenes of rapture, jealousy and reconciliation attendant on them: 'He could say no to few women,' it was observed, 'and few women could say no to him.' Amazingly, he does not seem to have felt such an existence a strain. 'How are you, Mr Tree?' a friend asked him. 'I?' replied Tree, gazing round him absently. 'I? Oh! I'm radiant.' And though, like other artists, he could flare up in an explosion of temperament, his prevailing mood was of sanguine radiance over which played Puckishly a continuous sparkle of jokes ranging from the shamelessly facetious to Wildean witticisms—'He is an old bore,' he said of an acquaintance, 'even the grave yawns for him'—from witticisms to magnesium flashes of Marx Brothers crazy comedy. It was in these last that Tree's characteristic genius showed itself most agreeably. Once, walking down the street, he saw a workman staggering under a grandfather clock: 'My good fellow,' said Tree, concernedly, 'why not carry a watch?'; or, unsmiling and in dreamy tones he thus unexpectedly addressed a new acquaintance: 'Never neglect an opportunity to play leapfrog,' he said. 'It is the best of all games and, unlike the serious and conscientious pastimes of modern youth, will never become professionalized.' It is hardly surprising that Tree's talk bewildered ordinary people. Was he 'clever', they asked each other, or was he plain silly?

The third brother, Julius, was an equally striking though less successful figure. Outwardly the two differed: Herbert untidy, restless, histrionic; handsome Julius, an impassive exquisite dandy, his straw-coloured hair smooth as satin, a fresh gardenia always in his buttonhole, and never raising his low-pitched expressionless voice. Underneath, however, they had much in common. For Julius too was gifted and dynamic and fascinating; Julius too was a gambler; Julius too was a romantic, intoxicated by grandiose day-dreams. These last were his trouble. Unluckily he tried to realize them, not, like Herbert, on the stage, but in life where they clashed with the hard facts of the real world. He started his career promis-ingly enough. His first idea was to be an explorer; he therefore went on an expedition to Patagonia and wrote a book about it which had some success. Shortly afterwards he married, as her third husband, a rich and attractive lady called Evelyn Young-husband. This, however, was his last successful enterprise. Though he occasionally wrote some pleasing verses in the Swinburnian mode then fashionable, he did no more regular literary work, but spent his days wandering gaily and inconsequently round the Continent, losing money at casino after casino, only breaking off now and again to try to retrieve his financial position by some fantastic project of his own devising. At one time we hear of him arranging to dredge the mud of the Nile in search of the lost jewels of the Pharaohs; at another proposing to set up as a luxury hotel-keeper at Marienbad. This last was a short-lived effort. For, after paying the deposit for the hotel, Julius left Germany and clean forgot about the whole transaction till reminded of it by his credi-tors. Living like this, he soon lost all his money and most of his wife's as well, and could only finance his schemes, or indeed support life on anything like what he considered a civilized standard, by borrowing from others. It seems surprising that he could find any-one to lend to him. But the Beerbohm charm, combined with an infectious unshakable confidence in his own luck, made him ex-traordinarily persuasive, so that hard-headed businessmen found themselves giving him cheques without any sure guarantee that they would ever be repaid. If he failed to get a loan, Julius simply let his goods be sold up. A friend describes calling on him and finding the brokers on the ground floor and Julius lying in bed up-stairs serenely translating a lyric of Heine's. He never let his mis-fortunes ruffle his dandy's imperturbability or alter his dandy's habits. Faced by impending ruin, he yet continued to keep cabs waiting for him all day at the door, to send his shirts every week to be washed specially in Paris, and, immaculate as ever, to attend supper parties where he would sometimes entertain the company by reciting one of his poems.

Constance, the only female member of Mr Beerbohm's first family, lacked her brothers' conquering qualities. On the contrary, plain, unselfish and excessively tender-hearted, she was only too liable to be victimized. Her stepmother did victimize her a little. She preferred her own daughters and showed this clearly enough for Constance, when she grew up, to leave her and set up for herself. She did not like it; nor did her stepmother. One afternoon she came to call. Before entering the house she hid a paper parcel containing her things among some laurel bushes in the drive. She lingered till near supper-time: 'You had better stay to supper,' said Mrs Beerbohm. After supper, she lingered till near bedtime: 'You had better stay the night,' said Mrs Beerbohm. Constance fetched her parcel from the bushes. She stayed for the rest of her life. Mrs Beerbohm, while surrendering no essential power, was later glad to let Constance take on the practical management of the household. In the intervals of ordering meals and doing the accounts, she sought to add to the family's income by writing—comediettas for amateur acting societies and articles for the humbler kind of woman's journal on subjects like cooking, of which she knew little, or the Royal Family, of which she knew less. She also interested herself in charities, notably those in aid of distressed gentlewomen. Distressed gentlewomen were sometimes a nuisance in Constance Beerbohm's life; one, in particular, haunted the house, wearing a hat surmounted by nodding cherries and boring the rest of the Beerbohm family. She may well have bored Constance too, who had her share of the family's high-strung nerves and would now and again burst out in fits of exasperation quickly followed by abject apologies. All this combined with the articles and the accounts and the fact that she was not very strong to make Constance's life a strain. Yet she was not to be pitied. For she was much loved. Even Mrs Beerbohm grew very fond of her, and her other relations spoke of her as 'an angel'. Indeed, she seems to have been very lovable; for to warmth and sympathy she added her own brand of the Beerbohm–Draper imagination, flooding her view of the world with its comic and fantastic light. Nothing seemed too odd to her to be true. 'Mr X tells me he has a wonderful parrot,' she once informed her surprised relations. 'It can judge the years of wine vintages. I want to write an article about it for the papers.' She had misheard Mr X who had said 'palate' not 'parrot': Constance accepted the statement as quite probable. Yet she was far from being a fool, especially where people were concerned. Her talk, wandering inconsequently about, would casually let fall a remark revealing a delicate appreciation of the human comedy. 'I do love to talk to her,' she writes once of Mrs Patrick Campbell, 'for she has a devil. I now know why she always interested me so much: as long as a person is nice-looking and clever, a devil is a tremendous advantage.'

Constance's character, like that of her brothers, was pretty well formed by the time Max was conscious of her. His own sisters, on the other hand, were children with their dispositions still fluid. Already, however, each had begun to show individuality. Agnes, the budding beauty of the family; round-headed, amused Dora; each contributed an individual note to the characteristic harmony of the home. It was the Beerbohm ladies who set the tone of this harmony. The sons had left and gone out into the world too early and Mr Beerbohm was away all day at his office. The atmosphere, therefore, in which Max grew up was created by his mother and sisters. It was a very distinctive atmosphere, blending two diverse strains. On the one hand was the strain that came from its period and position, Victorian, feminine, ladylike: for the girls, unlike the boys, were in no way bohemian. The family life centred round the drawing-room: and this drawing-room, cosy rather than grand, with its well-worn, well-kept velvet curtains, its accumulation of family miniatures and mementoes, and the old convex gilt mirror over the chimney-piece, was the appropriate setting for a sheltered, stable, refined domesticity, enlivened by family jokes, warmed by family feeling, easily agitated, anxiously tactful, shrinking from any hint of coarseness or vulgarity, and with a tendency to hypochondria. The Beerbohm ladies were always asking one another, and anyone else, if they felt tired.

All the same, its atmosphere was not at all like that of the typical Victorian drawing-room, for through it throbbed the foreign intensity of the Beerbohm temperament, making its agitations more violent than normal, its high spirits more uninhibited, its affections more extravagantly demonstrative; and over it quivered the trans-figuring light of the Beerbohm imagination, gleaming out some-times in romantic fantasy, sometimes in flights of impish gaiety, puns, rhymes, comic imitations—the Beerbohms were all good mimics—which were the feminine equivalent of their brother Herbert's vein of crazy comedy. This power of enjoyment was child-like. Indeed, all the Beerbohms—male and female alike, stage-struck Herbert as much as home-keeping Constance—did retain more of the child in them than do most people. None of them was ever to seem quite grown-up. With the child's love of fun they kept also his power of make-believe, his habit of living in a world of his own fancy, his pleasure in cutting a figure. All this helped them to enjoy each other's company. They took as much pains to enter-tain each other as if they were talking to visitors. In the evenings, especially, they loved to sit round the fire talking lightly or gravely —but more often lightly—of people and books and life, now mischievously mocking their acquaintance, now breaking off to elaborate, amid peals of laughter, some nonsense game. 'Everyone at home in my young days,' related Max, 'could be perfectly agreeable. Members of the same family could practise conversation.' Indeed, the Beerbohm ladies had made use of the leisure and privacy of their mode of living to cultivate a natural gift for agreeability till it blossomed, a delicate fine flower of nineteenth-century civilization, whose perfume mingles a Thackerayan sharp-eyed humour with the whimsical nonsense of Edward Lear and a dash of dewy Pre-Raphaelite sweetness. This perfume pervaded the Beerbohm home.

(3)

This home, first at Palace Gardens Terrace and later at Clanri-carde Gardens, was a place in which any child was likely to be happy. Max especially; for, as the youngest of a large family and a boy as well, he was an especial object of love. His parents and his brothers and sisters united to make much of him. In addition to these advan-tages he had been born with a naturally happy disposition. Not that there was anything of the conventional, jolly, high-spirited boy about him. Rather had he the characteristics usually associated with the youngest child of elderly parents, conceived when their vitality was waning and brought up among people older than himself. Very small for his age, in a sailor suit and his hair cut in a fringe, he was what used to be called an 'old-fashioned' child, mentally precocious, but physically languid, unadventurous, polite and self-contained. This last quality was intensified by circumstance: since he was the youngest by five years of his family, his position was half that of an only child, and he early learnt to cultivate the pleasures of solitude. He had a great gift for pleasure; quickly knew what he enjoyed and how to enjoy it to the full. This was one chief reason why it was natural for him to be happy.

These pleasures were chiefly imaginative. His days passed delightfully in a dream world of his own invention, peopled by figures that appealed to his fancy, notably soldiers and policemen. He used to draw them and make believe to be one of them.

'Although, like my coevals, I wore a sailor suit, my heart was with the land forces; insomuch that I insisted on wearing also, out of doors, a belt with a sword attached to it, and on my breast a medal which, though it had merely the Crystal Palace embossed on it, I associated with the march to Kandahar. I used to watch with emotion the sentries changing guard outside Kensington Palace; and it was my purpose to be one of them hereafter. . . . But somehow, mysteriously, when I was eight years old or so, the soldiery was eclipsed for me by the constabulary. Somehow the scarlet and the bearskins began to thrill me less than the austere costume and calling of the Metropolitan Police. Once in every two hours a policeman came, on his beat, past the house of my parents. At the window of the dining-room I would await his coming, punctually behold him with profound interest, and watch him out of sight. It was not the daffodils that marked for me the coming of the season of Spring. It was the fact that policemen suddenly wore short tunics with steel buttons. It was not the fall of the leaf nor the swallows' flight that signalled Autumn to me. It was the fact that policemen were wearing long thick frock-coats with buttons of copper. But even more than in the day-time did policemen arrest me, as it were, in the watches of the night. The dark lantern was the truly great, the irresistible thing about them. More than once, from the window of my night-nursery, I had seen that lantern flashed at opposite front doors and through area-railings. My paintings of policemen were mostly nocturnes—a dim, helmeted figure with a long white ray of light. Although I possessed, of course, a dark lantern of my own, and used it much, I preferred my occasional glimpses of the genuine article, and looked forward impatiently to being a member of the Force.'

There is nothing very surprising in this; many little boys have played at being soldiers or policemen, but Max did it with a difference. His imaginary games were unlike those of other children in two notable respects. For one thing, they were neither romantic nor heroic. With precocious self-knowledge he realized it was the uniform that attracted him about the idea of being a soldier or a policeman; even in imagination he had no desire to emulate their more dangerous exploits. So little, in fact, that though he liked watching policemen on night duty, he never liked imagining himself as one of them. But let him speak for himself.

'I was not a strongly imaginative child,' he writes, 'I disbelieved in fairies, was not sure about knight errants, was glad to hear that the sea had been cleared of pirates and that Indians were dying out. I was a timid child on the side of law and order—a predilection that accounts for my having chosen to imagine myself a policeman. But even that prosaic office I followed only in day-time. Night beats as tending to the possibility of conflicts with ferocious burglars I eschewed. After dark I was simply a man-of-the-world. Very tall with a large blonde moustache and a pair of those small side-whiskers, a relic of the hirsute 'sixties, in my eye a monocle, in my button-hole a gardenia, in my shirt-front a jewelled solitaire. I dined at my club on chicken and cherry tart and went to a party . . . I had a contempt for professional beauties and aesthetes and also for mashers, because though I looked like one of them, I was tremendously clever. I cannot imagine what happened at the party except that I stayed late and was the guest of someone I had heard of in grown-up conversation.'

The child is father of the man here all right. It is curious to see how early Max's imaginative life had begun to take its mature shape. Already, though he may not have learnt the word, he is in love with the idea of the dandy, the artist in dress and demeanour whose sole and perfect creation is himself. Already, too, he has

given evidence of the scepticism which interweaves itself so unexpectedly with his taste for fantasy: even in the nursery Max did
not believe in fairies. And he shows finally that absorbed, minute
observation of the world of his own time and place which under-
pins all his subsequent achievement. He loved as a little child to
stand at the nursery window watching the people coming and
going in the houses opposite; such an activity was prophetic of his
attitude through life. For it was thus his imagination acquainted
itself with the kind of material it liked to work on. Max's fantasies,
even as a child, were always fantasies on an observed reality. He did
not want to play at being a pirate or an Indian, he preferred some
figure from the London he knew—the policeman, the man about
town. With sharp little eyes he noted the typical details of their
appearance; the copper buttons on the policeman's winter great-
coat, the man about town's monocle and solitaire and beautiful
blonde moustache. As he grew older, his imagination opened to
include a larger prospect: a new set of figures occupied the centre of
his dream world. These were ever more conspicuously topical and
contemporary than their predecessors had been.

'By the time I was eleven years old I despised the Force. I was
interested only in politicians—in Statesmen, as they were called at
that time.

I had already, for some years, been aware of them. I had seen
them, two-dimensionally and on a small scale, every Wednesday, in
the pages of *Punch*, and had in a remote and tepid way revered
them. I had not thought of them as actual, live men. Rather, they
were, as portrayed in the cartoons of the great John Tenniel, nobly
mythical to me. Sometimes they wore togas; but more often they
wore chitons and breast-plates, and were wielding or brandishing
swords. Their shins were protected by greaves, and their calves
were immensely muscular; and in the matter of biceps they were
unsurpassable. They were Ajaxes and Hectors and Achilleses. Now
and then they rose to greater heights, becoming Herculeses, Vulcans,
Marses and the like. *Punch* was firmly Gladstonian in its politics;
and therefore the Prime Minister was always more muscular than
any of his enemies, redoubtable though they too were; and
the attitudes that he struck were more striking than theirs. I
didn't quite like this. For my father was a Conservative, and so,

accordingly, was I. I wished—though I didn't care enough to pray —for the downfall of Gladstone. Some time in the year 1883 I read a speech delivered in the House of Commons by Lord Randolph Churchill. I felt that here was the man to compass the downfall; for he was so very rude. Even the best-behaved little boys rejoice in the rudeness of other people. Lord Randolph's rudeness in a good cause refreshed my young heart greatly; nor ever did his future speeches disappoint me. But, much though I delighted in him, I didn't quite think of him as an actual person. I thought of him as Phaeton. Tenniel—or was it Linley Sambourne?—had depicted him as Phaeton, standing ready on the ground while old Sir Stafford Northcote (the leader of the Opposition, here depicted as Phoebus Apollo) was driving the chariot of the sun. I resented the cartoonist's analogy. But the physical image abode with me.

It was the London Stereoscopic Company that first opened my eyes to the fact that Churchill and Gladstone, Northcote and Harcourt, Chamberlain, Hartington and all those others were actual, mortal, modern men. Not until I was nearly twelve did I inspect that great long double window on the eastern side of Regent Street, famous for its galaxy of photographs of eminent personages. The place of honour was accorded of course to members of the Royal Family. But precedence over Archbishops and Bishops, Generals, Admirals, Poets, Actors and Actresses, was taken by the Statesmen. . . . They were not perhaps Gods, but they certainly were Titans, in the public eye. And here they all were in *my* eye, tailored and hosier'd as men. With luck, I might some day see one of them in the street. I studied the portraits keenly. I fixed the features in my mind. I stayed there long. And on my way home I saw a man who was unmistakably—Mr Childers . . . he was at that time Chancellor of the Exchequer. It was a great, a throbbing moment.

Of Mr Childers I made several drawings—very unpromising little drawings—when I reached my home. And thereafter, in the course of my holidays from school, I drew many of his colleagues. When a Cabinet Council was to be held, the fact was usually announced by the morning papers of that day. And there at the hour appointed, there on the pavement of Downing Street, opposite to No. 10, would be I, awaiting breathlessly the advent of the Giants. The greatest and most awful of them all would of course be invisible. Mr Gladstone was somewhere behind those brown brick

17

walls. But the others would be vouchsafed to me, one of them coming perhaps from the direction of Parliament Street, another from the courtyard of the Government Offices behind me, another up the flight of steps from St James's Park.'

In fact he did at last contrive to get a glimpse of Gladstone himself. He had persuaded someone to take him to listen to a debate in the House of Commons at which Gladstone spoke in 1884: and again, crossing Parliament Square in 1886, he had seen him on his way to introduce the Home Rule Bill.

In all this appears another characteristic typical of the mature Max: his imaginative response to the great world of power and fashion and glory, his enjoyment at the spectacle of its august inhabitants. They did not rouse his sense of reverence. On the contrary, they appealed to him because, besides being grand, they were also laughable. He delighted in the sight of a great man, largely because it could make him smile. Here we come to the second outstanding feature of the child Max's daydream world. It was a comic world. Here once more it differs from that of most imaginative children. Children often have a sense of fun, but it is very rare for them to take a predominantly humorous view of life, still less an ironical pleasure in the spectacle of human folly. If humour comes into their daydreams at all, it is as comic relief to thrills and romance. None of these generalizations applied to Max. He was the most humorous of all the humorous Beerbohms; born liking jokes of all kinds, broad and subtle, practical and intellectual, hoaxes and grotesques and puns and comic songs. His favourite pictures were caricatures, his favourite reading was *Punch*; his childhood heroes had to be in some degree figures of fun. The Never-Never-Land of his fancy in which he spent so much of his time was a region of comedy. He portrayed it in his drawings. For, like his imaginative life, his talents showed themselves precociously in their mature form. From his earliest years Max loved drawing: by the time he was eight or nine his pictures were always caricatures, mostly of important public men of the day.

A sophisticated child? Yes—Max's humorous side was extremely sophisticated. This appears also in his pleasure in complicated plays on words. On his tenth birthday his brother Herbert gave him a glass of champagne: he asked for more. 'Max,' said Herbert, 'it is bad to be tipsy at ten.' Max replied, 'How can one be tipsy, when we are conscious they are not.' Herbert laughed. The brothers delighted in each other. Here was another element in Max's nature making for happiness; pleasure in other people. For all that he was self-contained, company and conversation and friendly intimacy were an especial pleasure to him: and where he was pleased he grew fond. He had an affectionate nature made more so by the atmosphere of love surrounding him. It is the loved who grow loving. As a child Max's love was for his family. Julius and Herbert—Ernest had left England too early—were flesh and blood heroes to him. Each in his different way, it will be noted, was like Max's dream heroes. Julius was a dandy; Herbert was associated with the great world and was haloed with its glamour. From the time that Max was four years old, Herbert loomed before his eyes, a very tall figure with bright red hair to whom he looked up with interest. Within a few years Herbert returned the interest.

'In 1879, or thereabouts, I had acquired a habit of drawing pictures; and what I liked about Herbert, whenever he came to see us, was that *he* could draw pictures, too. I think I liked him all the better for that our styles did not clash. I drew *and* painted—especially painted. Herbert used pencil only. The subjects I chose were soldiers, policemen, cottages, and knights in armour. These subjects he would sometimes assay, but only to please *me*: they did not really interest him, and his handling of them was (I still think) inferior to mine. What he excelled me in was Mr Gladstone and Lord Beaconsfield. He could draw either of them equally well in profile or in full-face, and as the features of both of them were very familiar to me in *Punch*, whose cartoons I was fond of colouring week by week, I was in a position to appreciate his skill. I was a Conservative, and Herbert (to my wonder and grief) was a Liberal. Yet his Lord Beaconsfield amused me not less than his Mr Gladstone. My mother, too, was very fond of watching him draw, and for her he used to draw all sorts of people—people whom he had recently met. "This is Whistler, the painter," he would say, or "This is E. W. Godwin," or "Here's Oscar Wilde, the poet." Henry Irving, however, was his favourite theme. And I remember him saying, one day, with some importance: "The Routledges have asked me to dine on Sunday night, and Irving is to be there." Whereat I communed with myself: "Dinner? On *Sunday* night?" Mr Edmund Routledge had the house opposite to my father's, and on the following Sunday, at my bedtime, I looked out at those lit windows, looked long at them. I was fascinated, in spite of myself, and, much as I pitied Herbert for being so unlikely now to go to Heaven, I was also envying him not a little, too.

I wanted to grow up quickly and belong (on week-days) to the great world in which Herbert was moving. And of that world I was soon to have a closer, more inspiring glimpse than had been vouch-safed by the Routledges' lit windows. I think the date of this glimpse was in March, 1882. Herbert nobly invited me to spend a Saturday morning with him. He had rooms in Maddox Street, sharing them with his friend A. K. Moore. I did not know that he had greatly distinguished himself at Oxford, and that he was destined to write very brilliant leading articles for *The Morning Post*. And even had I known these things I should still have regarded him as the man who smoked that pipe and stared at me and laughed again and again at the notion that Herbert had so small a brother. Herbert himself went on writing at a table by the window; but this preoccupation I excused, for he told me he was writing something for—*Punch*! And he told me that in a few minutes he was going to take his manuscript—and me!—round to Bouverie Street and show us both to Mr Burnand. At about this time Herbert wrote several skits for *Punch*. One of them, I know, was on the "interviews" given to reporters by Oscar Wilde during his American tour . . . I remember A. K. Moore looking through the manuscript and laughing, but doubting (which seemed to me just like him) whether Mr Burnand would put it in.

There were no marble columns even in the office of *Punch* itself; but there was, and I saw him with my own eyes, Mr Burnand; and he seemed to me the more greatly a prince of men because he was not smoking, and because he sat in a chair that swung round to-wards us in a most fascinating manner, and because he did not laugh at me. I liked also Mrs Bernard Beere, the famous actress, to whom, after another drive in a hansom, I was presented as she lay, in the middle of a large room somewhere, on a sofa of crimson velvet, with a great deal of lace around her head, and an enormous bunch of hothouse grapes on a small table beside her, and a com-pany of important-looking men standing and sitting around her. I liked her for giving me so many of her grapes; but my enjoyment of these was somewhat marred by the more-than-A.-K.-Mooreish mirth of one gentleman at the smallness of "Beerbohm Tree's brother". This gentleman was of immense height and girth; and I was just old enough to think of saying, and just too well-brought-up to say, that *I* might as well laugh at the bigness of "Beerbohm Tree's friend". I did but look fixedly at the striped shirt-collar that he wore; and later, when, in another hansom, Herbert told me that the gentleman was Mr Edmund Yates, I merely said that I did not like his striped collar.

The greatest event of that great day was yet to come: we were to lunch at Herbert's club. Was it the "Arundel", perhaps? The "Savage"? I know not. I cared not. It was Herbert's club, and I lunched in it, and was presented to the great Mr Godwin in it. At first I thought he must be "a conspirator", for he wore a large black cloak and a large soft black hat. But he had the most charming manners, and treated me as an equal, and I quite agreed with the opinion, so often expressed by Herbert in those days, that Godwin was a Master. I left the club in company with these two, and Herbert, after hailing a hansom for me and paying the driver, gave me a ten-shilling piece. To have gold seemed to me at that time hardly less wonderful than it would seem in this age of paper. That gold piece soon became some mere silver; that silver, vanishing copper; but the memory of those hours with Herbert was a treasure to be jealously hoarded.

Herbert was (then and always) a hero to me. But, let me add, Julius was a god. And he was not so because he had explored Patagonia (remote and savage things had no magic for me), nor because he had written a much-praised book about Patagonia (I was not literary) but because he was so cool and calm and elegant. Herbert seemed always to be in a hurry, Julius never. Herbert would overpay and dismiss his hansom whenever he came to see us, and at his departure would whistle frantically and piercingly for another. Julius always kept *his* hansom waiting, hour after hour. And *his* hansom was always one of that new and lordly kind, padded throughout with black leather, and fitted with two little looking-glasses, and drawn by a spirited horse, and driven by a not tipsy driver. . . . Also, he had a moustache. Not to have that when one was grown up seemed to me to argue a deficiency in sense of fitness. I knew that Herbert, being an actor, had to be clean-shaven. But I felt that I myself, if hereafter I had to choose between being an actor and having a moustache, should not hesitate. Not in virtue of his acting, but rather in virtue of himself, was Herbert a hero to me. More than once, schoolfellows of mine had said to me: "Your brother's an actor, isn't he?" They had not said this in a tone implying actual condemnation. But——

In some early month of '82 my classification of the two brothers underwent a sudden change. Herbert became a god, Julius sank to the level of a hero. For Herbert was engaged to be married; and being married had always seemed to me an even finer thing, a thing even more essential to the full glory of that adult state, than having a moustache. My father and mother, my sisters and I, were all of us equally enthusiastic about Miss Maud Holt. She and Herbert used to come and lunch in Clanricarde Gardens every Sunday, and these Sundays were great days. Miss Holt was so charming and amusing. Also, she used to play and sing to us; and I can see Herbert now, hanging over the piano, rapt, in devotion. A goddess, decidedly.'

Max was to play a part in the ceremony uniting these two deities. It would have been natural for Julius to be Herbert's best man: but shortly before the wedding took place it was made known that Julius, as usual unreliable, would be in Spain at the time. The ten-year-old Max was called in to take his place.

'Of the preparations for that day, I recall especially the two triumphal arches of flowers and branches, one at the gate of the garden, the other at the gate of the little church hard by. These were conceived and erected by the gardener and his brother; and I remember the surprise I felt when the gardener's brother said to me: "They're not what you might call awful grand, but they're what you might call rustic." To me they appeared awful grand. Under the garden-gate's arch, on the Sunday morning, I "posted myself a full hour before Herbert was expected to arrive. . . ." When at last he appeared, I was glad to see that his hat was of almost Julian splendour; but he looked so pale and excited that I gasped out instinctively: "Have you lost the ring?" However, all was well. The wedding was conducted as smoothly as the most exacting "best man" could wish. And at the wedding-breakfast there were silla-bubs, my favourite dish. I remember Herbert saying that they sounded Biblical—"And Sillabub, the son of Sillabub, reigned in his stead," a remark which shocked but amused me.'

Herbert often amused Max. Max amused Herbert too. This was why he took such an interest in him. He loved to regale his fellow actors in the Green Room with tales of the extraordinary little elf who was his brother. Indeed, the fellow actors noticed that if Herbert was in one of his rare gloomy moods and someone asked him 'How's Max?' his face would change. 'Oh, he's Maxing along,' he would reply, and would launch smiling into some new anecdote illustrating Max's wit and cleverness. Soon the Green Room was cheerful again; 'All because of Max!' said the actors to one another.

Though Herbert was his hero he did not occupy the first place in little Max's heart. Perhaps no one did! It was characteristic of Max to love all his family, but none obsessively. Mr Beerbohm, indeed, was unlikely to obsess anybody: there was nothing of the formidable Victorian father-figure about him. Max loved him warmly, respected him sufficiently, but viewed him with detachment: 'My father,' he wrote in later life, 'was not a remarkable man; but he had a beautiful character.' Max's mother inevitably played a more important part in his life. He was thought to be her favourite: certainly she was inclined to spoil him. But she cared too much for her other children morbidly to concentrate on Max. With the result that, though he loved her, he was not tempted to concentrate too much on her either.

Besides, Mrs Beerbohm had to share Max's tenderer affections with his sisters, and more especially with Dora. If Max had a favourite in his family, it was Dora. There was reason for this. She was the nearest to him in age, so that he saw the most of her: and she was the most like him; with the same round head and tilted nose and heavy-lidded eyes—though Dora's lashes were paler—the same turn for fantasy, pleasure in words and, above all, the same delight in the same kind of joke. Dora was the gayest of the family; always laughing, with her head flung back and throwing up her pretty hands. She had also something of Max's quick ironical intelligence: 'The cleverest of all my clever children,' Mrs Beerbohm called her. This is to be doubted; Dora's mind was a lightweight affair compared to her brother's. But she was in one sense the most exceptional of her family. For, mingled with the qualities she shared with

Max and the childlikeness and warm heart she shared with the whole family, ran a strain in her to be found in no other of them; a sense of forces unseen and unearthly, a capacity for selfless dedicated love that no human object could ever wholly satisfy, that instinctively sought some divine fulfilment.

This search was to mould Dora's destiny in time to come— taking her away to regions far from the secular gaiety of the Beerbohm home. But as yet no shadow of this future touched her and Max playing in their nursery or under the green or leafless trees of Clanricarde Gardens. They did not play quite on equal terms, for Dora was five years older than Max, a great difference at that age. This meant that she took the lead. She might have done so anyway, for she was the more adventurous child of the two. Max watched awestruck the dash and speed with which she swung herself to and fro on a trapeze in the nursery; himself he swung slowly and carefully. We get another glimpse of them playing at Robin Hood and his Merry Men, dressed in green velveteen tunics with huntinghorns slung over their shoulders and shooting arrows into the air. Max noticed with relief that the arrows were blunted: he suspected Dora would have been pleased to find that they were not.

Not that there was any risk of her treating his fears unsympathetically. As a child she lavished her power of devotion largely on him; and all the more because he was younger: she was always concerned to give him pleasure and spare him pain. On his side, Max found Dora's company a continuous pleasure; a pleasure mixed with amusement, for she was more romantic than him and he sometimes found this comic. Two or three years later, when she was about thirteen or fourteen, he writes,

'her free spirit happened upon another phase. "The Aesthetic Movement" had begun, and Dora accepted with ardour the Pre-Raphaelite influence, with the Kate Greenaway influence thrown in. She gravitated to sage-green and terra-cotta and "greenery yallery" hues, and puffed sleeves and short waists and (I think) sandalled shoes. I liked the effect very much, but was Philistine enough to laugh when, one morning, as she and I were looking at the window of a music-shop, she devoutly said, "What a graceful instrument an harp is!" And Dora, though she did rather like that "an", joined whole-heartedly in the laughter.'

This anecdote illustrates how close was the affinity of spirit between the two. An aesthete in embryo, Max liked Dora's aestheticism; but, since he was also a born humorist, he liked it all the more because it made him laugh. She in her turn liked him all the more for his laughter and herself found it infectious.

The relation between brother and sister can be peculiarly close and delightful. They are of the same generation; and, growing up together, have all the same terms of reference, so that they need hardly explain anything to one another. Further, the fact that one is a boy and the other a girl enhances the relation with a slight whiff of romantic charm, softened when the sister is older by an element of the maternal. Dora and Max's relationship as children was in some ways the most harmoniously agreeable either was ever to know. Circumstances kept them apart in later life; but people noticed that when they did meet—even when both were over sixty—they both changed. Their eyes danced, they seemed to be sharing some delightful, laughable secret. Max's attitude to women was strongly influenced by his boyish relation to Dora. Max was never a 'mother's boy' and did not grow up into the kind of man who is always looking for a substitute mother: he was too self-dependent for that. But he can be described as a 'sister's boy'; that is to say, he loved feminine company, feminine charm, feminine solicitude, but he preferred them in someone with whom he could feel on easy equal terms and who did not try to dominate or make violent emotional demands upon him. In fact, his ideal was someone who would be to him as Dora was, when he was a child.

(4)

Time passed and in 1881 Max started his formal education, at a day-school kept by Mr Wilkinson in Orme Square. It seems to have been a mild little institution with only fifteen to twenty boys in it—twenty-one, said Max, if you included the headmaster himself; for Mr Wilkinson seems to have been a striking example of that well-known English type, the man who becomes a schoolmaster because he has remained a schoolboy. He cared and thought only of two things, classics and cricket: 'Kingdoms may wax and wane,' he said, 'but what I want to know is what did Surrey do at the Oval yesterday!' Max did not want to know this in the least;

even at nine years old he took no interest in games. All the same, Mr Wilkinson pleased him very much. He started with the advantage of having a large blond moustache which fluttered in the wind when he played touch-last with the little boys at the end of afternoon school. Unathletic though he was, Max liked playing touch-last with Mr Wilkinson. Still more did he like learning Latin from him. 'He was far the best teacher I ever had,' he said in later life. 'Wonderfully interesting and "enthusing". He was so very sympathetic with the mind of a small boy . . . he gave me my love of Latin and thereby enabled me to write English well.' Under Mr Wilkinson's inspiration Max's sense of style precociously awoke, and when, later, he started to compose in his own language, consciously he applied the lessons and standards he had learnt at his first school. In consequence his lightest passages have always a classical substance and precision. Max had his first lessons in his other art at Orme Square too. Mrs Wilkinson taught him drawing; she was, in fact, the only drawing teacher Max ever had. He did not learn much from her; but he liked her. The Wilkinsons seem to have liked him too. He was a friendly, willing pupil, and law-abiding. An old schoolfellow remembers him standing up in class after he had broken some rule and beginning anxiously, 'Please Sir, I ought to tell you . . .'. The same boy also describes playing with him at Clanricarde Gardens. They broke a piece of china. 'We will now go and own up,' said Max. He did not say this from priggishness, still less from fear; Max was far too kindly treated to be frightened of his family. But he desired to please and knew how to do so. This was as true of him at school as at home. In consequence he was happy there. Life at Mr Wilkinson's establishment at Orme Square possessed a charm for him which he was always pleased to recall. Mr Wilkinson survived to be very old; and forty years later he and Max sometimes lunched together at the Savile Club. Time had reversed their roles. With amusement, the middle-aged Max would sit listening to his former headmaster still rattling boyishly on about Surrey's latest score at the Oval.

Such a master and such a school—especially since Max only attended it by the day—was not of a kind to divert the peaceful current of his life or change the colour of his experience. This had an important result. It meant that the transition from child to boy, which happens to most men when they are at their first school, was for him delayed longer. Not only did Max have an unusually happy child-hood but it lasted till he was thirteen. Up till then home was still the unquestioned centre of his existence, the people that counted in his life were still his loving relations; and, except that he learnt Latin and grew to think politicians more romantic than policemen, his chief interests and pleasures were still those he had enjoyed in the nursery. As a consequence he was an unusual mixture of the childish and the precocious. In mind, in taste, in humour, he was ahead of his age, partly because he was born clever, and partly because he had lived so much with older people. In other respects he was younger than his years. The childlike strain characteristic of all Beerbohms had been increased in Max by circumstances. It was not only that he had not gone away to school. At home, the fact that he was the beloved youngest child meant that though he was brought on mentally he was physically kept young, indulged, caressed, looked after; so that, like a child, he combined physical dependence with mental self-sufficiency. He liked to be loved and looked after and left to play by himself when he wanted. More important, in his play he retained the imaginative power of child-hood. Here his upbringing was a great advantage to him. The English middle-class system of education has its merits but it tends to check imagination; for it forces a child very early to live a com-munity life and to share community interests. Such children as enjoy games of solitary make-believe can go on playing them well into their teens. But they do not have much time to do so in the classroom or on the football field. In consequence, their power of imagination atrophies through lack of use. No doubt it would have needed more than a boarding-school to check such an imagination as Max's. But the fact that he was the youngest child living at home till he was thirteen, save for the few hours a day spent in the gentle atmosphere of Mr Wilkinson's school, enabled him to develop his imaginative life so that it flowered and spread and grew stronger with every year that passed.

All this was to the good, and the fact that he was loved and spoilt was to the good too. It usually is. Along with his prolonged child-hood Max kept the child's confidence in the possibility of happiness. Unlike so many sensitive artists, he suffered no premature disil-lusionment, was not brought up against the brutality and ugliness of life before he was old enough to stand it. In consequence, he did not suffer from any of those inner wounds and hidden resentments that lead people unhappy in childhood to set up later as outsiders and rebels. Thirteen years of happiness had given him a basic faith in life which was to be like a sort of spiritual bank balance on which he could always draw for reassurance when things went wrong.

(5)

He was soon to need it: for his idyllic existence was at last interrupted. In the Michaelmas term of 1885 he went to Charterhouse, first to Robinson's House and, a year later, to Girdlestone's, where he stayed till the end of the summer term of 1890. Life there was a sharp contrast to life at home. Thirteen years before, the school had been removed from London to a new site in Surrey: where now, amid a group of gaunt buildings in the semi-ecclesiastical, mock-Gothic style which the nineteenth century thought appropriate for seats of learning, four hundred representatives of male middle-class English youth were subjected to a Spartan regime of discomfort, athleticism and classical learning. This was not little Max's idea of an agreeable existence. To the end of his time there, he found going back to school a painful ordeal:

'. . . the impotent despair of those drives—I had exactly fifteen of them—I hope that I shall never experience a more awful emotion. Those drives have something, surely, akin with drowning. In their course the whole of a boy's home-life passes before his eyes, every phase of it standing out against the black curtain of his future. . . . I think, in saying that all boys, of whatsoever temperament, are preys to it. Well do I remember how, on the last day of the holidays, I used always to rise early, and think that I had got twelve more whole hours of happiness, and how those hours used to pass me with mercifully slow feet. . . . Three more hours! . . . Sixty more minutes! . . . Five! . . . I used to draw upon my tips for a first-class ticket, that I might not be plunged suddenly among my companions, with their hectic and hollow mirth, their dreary disinterment of last term's jokes. I used to revel in the thought that there were many stations before G—— . . . The dreary walk, with my small bag, up the hill! I was not one of those who made a rush for the few cabs. . . . The awful geniality of the House Master! The jugs in the dormitory! . . . Next morning, the bell that woke me! The awakening!'

Not for him, if he could have chosen it, the cold and the noise and the jostle, the bleak echoing passages pervaded by a stale smell of countless past unappetizing meals, and the battered chocolate paint of his cubicle with its hard little iron bedstead, surmounted by a rough, red, military-looking blanket! Not for him the rushed mornings and the strenuous afternoons!

'As I hovered, in grey knickerbockers, on a cold and muddy field round the outskirts of a crowd that was tearing itself limb from limb for the sake of a leathern bladder, I would often wish for a nice, warm room and a good game of hunt-the-slipper. And when we sallied forth, after dark, in the frost, to the swimming-bath, my heart would steal back to the fireside in Writing School and the plot of Miss Braddon's latest novel.'

Hunt-the-slipper and Miss Braddon's novel—these two preferences are significant and characteristic. The one a childish and the other a precocious taste for his age reveal Max as out of step with the average boy, and so ill-adapted for a life designed for him. 'In some respects I was too young, in others too old, for a perfect relish of the convention,' he said. Added to this, he was not at home in an hierarchical system. He was too individualistic and he disliked the responsibility it involved. For these reasons he resented fagging and got little satisfaction in making others fag for him.

'When I became a schoolboy, I greatly disliked being a monitor's fag. Other fags there were who took pride in the quality of the toast they made for the breakfasts and suppers of their superiors. My own feeling was that I would rather eat it myself, and that if I mightn't eat it myself I would rather it were not very good. Similarly, when I grew to have fags of my own, and by morning and by evening one of them solemnly entered to me bearing a plate on which those three traditional pieces of toast were solemnly propped one against another, I cared not at all whether the toast were good or bad, having no relish for it at best, but could have eaten with gusto toast made by my own hand, not at all understanding why that member should be accounted too august for such employment.'

Lack of hierarchical sense went with lack of community sense. Uncooperative and uncompetitive, he was unmoved by the incentives that made other boys throw themselves energetically into school activities. His school career was undistinguished. He never got any colours or won any prizes: he was never made a Head Monitor. He did not even, solitary as he was, make any close friends. It is no wonder that he left school without any very tender memories of it. Three years after leaving, he visited Charterhouse.

'I went down to Charterhouse,' he wrote to an Oxford friend, 'the other day, putting up at an Inn in the town. After a solitary dinner I walked up the hill and peered through the windows of my house where boys were sitting at "preparation" with rough hair on long forms giggling covertly—just as when I was among them. I suppose if I went there twenty years hence I should see just the same thing. Isn't school an awful place?'

In fact he had not minded the awful place all that much. Max's life at Charterhouse is no dreadful tale of misery. He cannot even be said to have been actively unhappy there. For one thing, his innate gift for enjoying himself did not desert him. He also now revealed himself as possessing another equally valuable talent, a power of manipulating circumstances in such a way as to get as much opportunity for pleasure and as little for pain as was humanly possible. Max even at thirteen was too sensible to waste his time repining or rebelling. Instead, adroit, purposeful and sure-footed, he set to work to cut himself a smooth pathway through the prickly jungle of public-school life. With considerable success: 'He always had the air of knowing where he was going and what he wanted and getting it,' said an observer. He adds that Max was usually alone. To be alone was in fact an important part of what he wanted. For at school he maintained the solitary and self-sufficient imaginative life of his childhood. This saved him from feeling forlorn and homesick. Imaginative children are often less homesick than others; for they carry their universe with them, their fantasies exist independent of places or people. Max might regret Dora and his mother and the comforts of Clanricarde Gardens, but he could still retire into his delightful inner fantasy world—full of jokes and statesmen and men about town, Lord Salisbury, Lord Randolph Churchill, Lord Rosebery, Mr Gladstone—and then recall their characteristics and

MAX AT CHARTERHOUSE

draw their portraits. Soon we find him adding another figure to his gallery. It was at school that Max began to caricature the Prince of Wales. He draws him as he draws Gladstone, with hostility. This is interesting and another sign of how early his mature dislikes showed themselves. It is also strange. Gladstone was a natural object of dislike to a Tory-bred child: but when and how did the boy Max acquire a perception of the future Edward VII's weaknesses.

Max made a fantasy figure of himself too. As a child he had dreamt of being a dandy; now it was his pleasure to set up as one in fact. Still unusually small for his years, he went on till he was seventeen wearing short jackets and Eton collars. But no one in the school wore an Eton collar so fashionably broad and dazzlingly white, no jacket was so well brushed as his, no trousers so smoothly pressed. 'My new black trousers are beautifully stripey and well made, perhaps a little loose about the knee but *very* nice,' he writes to his mother: and he rejoices to tell her that the buttonhole with which he had returned from his holidays is still unfaded. 'You do not appear to have written last night to this elfin child,' he remarks. 'I am still wearing my flower which has lasted wonderfully.' Elfin was the right word for his appearance. School group photographs show us a minute and immaculate sprite gazing inscrutably out at us through dark-lashed, foreign-looking eyes, melancholy beneath a head of smooth black hair divided by a parting of meticulous regularity. Max's hair was an object of his particular attention: it was said that, for fear of ruffling it, he never pulled his school cap full on to his head but pinned it with a hairpin to the back. His concern for his appearance did not come from vanity. Max never thought himself particularly good-looking, nor did he wish others to think so. Rather was he romantically dramatizing himself as a dandy to take part in his fantasy world.

Ironically too: humour was the chief ingredient of his imaginative life and as much at Charterhouse as at home. He looked round at the masters and the boys searching for what was comic in them. When he found it, down it went in his drawing-book. Every blank page of his school-books, was scrawled over with caricatures. His favourite books, too, were most of them humorous. Vaughan Williams, a contemporary of his, remembers his first sight of Max; he was coming out of the school library enthusiastically reciting some of Lear's nonsense poems. He also read and re-read *The*

Bab Ballads and the squibs and skits of Thackeray. Thackeray was a special object of Max's admiration. He read most of his books while at school. All his life he maintained *Vanity Fair* to be the greatest English novel. It was Thackeray's style, too, that first opened his eyes to the possibilities of English prose. Its mixture of the familiar and the elegant was exactly to his taste. He was always to try to blend the same ingredients in his own writing. Equally were his drawings influenced by Thackeray's.

Reading and drawing provided the higher satisfactions of solitude. But Max also liked taking more carnal pleasures alone.

'In my school, as in most others,' he said, 'we received now and again "hampers" from home. At the mid-day dinner in every house, we all ate together; but at breakfast and supper we ate in four or five separate "messes". It was customary for the receiver of a hamper to share the contents with his mess-mates. On one occasion I received, instead of the usual variegated hamper, a box containing twelve sausage-rolls. It happened that when this box arrived and was opened by me there was no one around. Of sausage-rolls I was particularly fond. I am sorry to say that I carried the box up to my cubicle, and, having eaten two of the sausage-rolls, said nothing to my friends, that day, about the other ten, nor anything about them when, three days later, I had eaten them all—all, up there, alone.'

These solitary enjoyments were procured, as it were, in spite of school and apart from it. But Charterhouse also provided Max with positive pleasures. For all its outward air of Sparta, it seems to have been an unusually civilized institution for the period. It tolerated some eccentricity, had a taste for humour, and, though encouraging games, did not make them compulsory. Max took full advantage of this last freedom. No one ever saw his bare knees, he boasted, at least not after his earliest years at school. He was equally selective about his work. Since he disliked French, algebra and science, he spent as little time over them as he could without risking getting into trouble. On the other hand, he retained the taste for Latin implanted in him by Mr Wilkinson. He enjoyed doing Latin prose and verses; ingenious pattern-making in words appealed to him. His masters at Charterhouse noticed this and encouraged it. One, Mr Alexander Todd, was particularly sympathetic. Inspired by him, Max in his last term composed *Carmen Becceriense*, a fourteen-line poem in Latin elegiacs making fun of the recitals given by Mr Becker, the music master, complete with mock notes in English, parodying the kind of note he must have seen in school editions of the classics; as, for example:

'6. *Innumeras k.t.* Needless difficulties have been made over this line. Some suggest we take it thus: "he scatters up and down his unnumbered hands". But seeing that this theory depends upon the absurd supposition that Beccerius possesses more hands than other people, I dismiss it instantly. By far the simplest and most straight-forward way of rendering it is "he shakes on every side innumerable hands", i.e., he shakes hands all round. Cf. the custom among pugilists of shaking hands before an encounter.

By the sudden and unusual transition of sense at the end of the pentameter the poet evidently suggests something or other; what, we are not quite sure, but the idea is none the less skilfully suggested.'

This is the first example we have of Max as a parodist. It is also his first printed literary work: for on Mr Todd's suggestion it was privately printed. He was grateful to Mr Todd, and to most of the other masters; he liked them all. They liked him in return.

The boys liked him too. Here was a second reason why Max was not very unhappy at school. Dandified, detached and unathletic, he might well have been an object of dislike and derision to his schoolfellows. But though, we are told, the boys thought him a freak, they never teased him. On the contrary, in a quiet way he was popular. This was not so surprising as it might seem. School-boys, like other primitive people, ill-treat those who scorn them and those who shrink from them. Max did neither. He was too shrewd openly to shrink, even if he had felt so inclined. In fact he did not: he felt friendly towards others. Nor, for all his sophistication, was there anything of the superior person about him. He did not take himself or his tastes so seriously as to expect others to respect them. Cheerfully he accepted the fact that most of his school-fellows, unlike himself, preferred football to Latin verses: and if they laughed at his concern for his hair he was not offended. He thought it rather comic himself. Moreover, Max was a born citizen of the world, who was interested to learn the customs of any society in which he found himself and was ready to conform to them sufficiently to avoid arousing antagonism: all the more easily because he was not so different from other boys as he liked to make out. On the contrary, he had some things very much in common with them. As much as most boys Max liked shirking his work, gossiping about the masters, eating, and discussing what he ate; and, of course, he enjoyed pranks and hoaxes and any other kind of joke. Here was common ground indeed. Public-school boys—unlike those who write about them—seldom take life very seriously; and their appetite for jokes is insatiable. Max was of their mind in this, and here he had something of his own to offer them. Not only did he share their amusement, he added to it. The boys, it was noticed, first took an interest in him because he was the brother of the famous actor Herbert Tree. This interest was increased and confirmed when they found he drew caricatures. Gradually the fame of these spread. From fifteen years old he was contributing cartoons to the school magazine: notably a series entitled 'Charterhouse Types', and another 'Exeat Sketches'. This last is amusing and vivid. The cheerful boy off home is contrasted with the gloomy boy forced to stay at school; we see some big boys at first dingy in their school uniforms and then transformed into fashionable young swells of the period to go away. Dress was always an inspiring theme to Max.

Not that he always saw it decoratively. Like his master, Thackeray, Max looked at schoolboys with an unflattering eye, portraying them as urchins and hobbledehoys, scruffy, spectacled, and with large ears and noses. He caricatured individual boys as well; but more often individual masters. Once again a distinctive characteristic of Max's maturity shows early. He enjoyed making fun of people more if he revered them or was supposed to revere them. Thirty years later we find him writing:

'The schoolmaster to his pupils, the monarch to his courtiers, the editor to his staff—how priceless they are! Reverence is a good thing, and part of its value is that the more we revere a man, the more sharply are we struck by anything in him (and there is always much) that is incongruous with his greatness.'

The Charterhouse masters took this mockery very well. So far from resenting it, they were amused and encouraged him. In his formal letter of farewell to Mrs Beerbohm when Max left, the headmaster even congratulates her on her son's drawings.

May 14, 1890

Dear Mrs Beerbohm,

I do not like the prospect of parting with your son. During his time here he has maintained so high a character that his absence will be a loss to the School. His artistic power will be much missed by many whose portraits he has often drawn and among these I may reckon.

Yours most faithfully

W. Haig Brown

Such a letter is a tribute to the general tolerance of Charterhouse masters. It also witnesses to Max's own charm and adroitness. He was so friendly and polite and respectful it was impossible to think of him as impertinent. The boys were less magnanimous. One of his subjects, it is reported, seized the offending paper from Max's hands and tore it up. Such an incident, however, helped to make Max popular with the other boys who were amused to see their schoolfellow discomfited. Only one of his old schoolfellows speaks of him with dislike. 'There was something sarcastic about him even as a boy,' he said, sourly. This 'something sarcastic', since it was kept well under the control of his good nature, made Max all the more entertaining.

He amused by word as well as by his drawings. His mother visited him on some day of school festivity. Max pointed out to her his housemaster's wife who was wearing a new pearl necklace. 'Do you see that necklace?' Max said. 'Every pearl represents a boy's empty stomach.' This remark got round the school and caused general amusement. As he got higher in the school Max was elected to the debating society, where he found scope for his wit. On one occasion the society was debating—as school debating societies are prone to do in every period—the advantages and disadvantages of a Channel tunnel. One speaker recommended the tunnel in a tedious speech: 'I am sure it might be quite well easily bored,' he urged. 'Like this society!' interposed Max in mild tones.

Altogether Max got enough fun out of life at Charterhouse to be able, by middle age at any rate, to look back on it with some benevolence. It was a good school as schools go, he supposed, and he himself had got some good out of being there.

'I have a power of getting outside myself. That is a very useful power. And it is a power which a shy and sensitive little boy learns better at a public school than he could anywhere else. A private tutor might have made me proficient in French, in Algebra, even in Science. Of these subjects (partly, but only partly, because I had no natural bent for them) I knew next to nothing when I left Charterhouse. The main thing that I had learnt there, and have not yet forgotten, was a knack of understanding my fellow-creatures, of living in amity with them and not being rubbed the wrong way by their faults, and not rubbing them the wrong way with mine.'

This was true: but less than the whole truth. Charterhouse had indeed given Max some valuable lessons in the art of getting on with his fellows. He had also managed to do so without swerving from his own independent path. This in its turn helped him to know exactly what this path was. He had already some idea by the time he went to school. But school made it clearer. Surveying for the first time a corporate competitive form of life, Max became sharply aware that such a life could never be his, that he was born to be an onlooker not a participant. Moreover, forced to retreat into the world of his imagination, he learnt more thoroughly to explore its nature and its extent.

All the same, there was never any question of his schooldays being the happiest of his life. He summed up his feelings about them many years later:

'My delight in having been at Charterhouse was far greater than my delight in being there. . . . I ought to have been very happy but—oh, how I always longed to be grown-up! Boys are mostly not cursed with a strong instinct towards independence; nor men mostly for the matter of that. I, alas, was. My lips duly said adsum for me at the right moment, on the appointed spot, but my heart was always out of bounds.'

For good or ill, his home remained the centre of his thoughts and his affections: he lived to the full only in the holidays.

Summer holidays were partly spent travelling. We hear of Max in Brighton in the summer of 1886 and in that of 1889 at Dinard. Some sketches of boulevard types indicate that in the same year or another he also visited Paris. But when he was not at Charterhouse he was mostly in London, till 1887 at Clanricarde Gardens and after that at the new house in Hyde Park Place. There he relaxed with relief into his old mode of life; drawing in his room, laughing and talking in the drawing-room with parents and sisters, sauntering down to Westminster to get a glimpse of some famous public man as he crossed Parliament Square or turned into Downing Street.

For Max's interest in politicians had only increased with the years. Politicians, not politics: he read the debates, and his letters home are full of comments on them. But though he professed himself a Tory like his father, his interest was not in political issues but in the drama of political life, the up and down of the party conflict, the clash of picturesque personalities.

In the Christmas holidays of 1888 he was lucky enough to get a sight of the political drama at its tensest. Someone gave him a ticket for a seat at the Parnell Commission, where with absorbed attention he watched the Irish leader, as with pale countenance and burning eyes he defended himself against his unrelenting cross-examiners. This, Max noted, is what a man looks like who feels himself driven into a corner.

There was the pleasure of the legitimate drama too. Herbert was as fond of Max as ever and used to let him come and sit in his dressing-room at the Haymarket Theatre during the entr'actes. These were when the actor-manager received visitors. Max sat silently observing the famous men and women of the stage and the arts and noting their idiosyncrasies. After he was fifteen Herbert sometimes enabled him to investigate them more fully at supper parties when the play was over. Herbert also gave him a seat to watch the play whenever he wanted one. He wanted one very often. In 1887 Max saw *The Red Lamp* seventeen times. With undiminished rapture too: surely, he thought, it was the best play ever written! No wonder, with such distractions and delights, Max found it hard to absorb himself in school life. 'Even in term when my body was at Charterhouse,' he said, 'my soul was at the Haymarket Theatre.'

Certainly it was somewhere in London; and this meant that school was a much less important influence in his life than it is to many boys. Hardly more than Mr Wilkinson's academy did Charterhouse alter the course or determine the direction of his development. Max said that his character remained there 'in a state of undevelopment'. It would have been truer to say that at Charterhouse his character remained undisclosed because, from caution or indifference, he never displayed it there. In fact, and especially during these years, he was maturing with abnormal speed. We have very little information about the actual process—no more than can be gleaned from a handful of letters—but these are enough to show that Max's development took a leap forward between the ages of thirteen and fifteen. At thirteen he was still a little boy, an odd, clever little boy, and precocious in some respects; but a little boy all the same. His early letters show it. Here is a typical one:

'I arrived safely at the Old Station and reached Duckites per waggonette which cost me one shilling. I was shewn into a room where I had tea and Duck soon came in and asked what sort of weather I had had and if I'd been to many theatres, etc. etc. Then Strode that boy whom you saw at Robinites—the lame one you know. Then Duck came in and talked to him and left us again. Soon we went to a room—drawing room, I think, and found Skinner and three new boys. After some time we had supper with Duck—chicken, cold beef, jelly, mincepies, etc. etc. After this we went back to the drawing room and stopped there till we went up to our cubicals [sic].'

Almost any thirteen-year-old schoolboy might have written this. Two years later, however, he is writing like a clever undergraduate in his second year at the university. Sagely and in the manner of an experienced journalist he will discuss the prospects of the Tory party at the next election; or sardonically he will describe a school ceremony:

'The band of the 2nd Life Guards made up the entertainment last night. Old General Marshall had been invited up to hear them play; they are said to be his old regiment. The real object of his invitation was to present him with a silver bowl, richly embossed and bought by shillings wrung from an unwilling school. The raison d'être being simply that he did not keep the lease of a field, which the school has purchased for cricket.'

His growing mastery of words fired him with a new ambition. It was at fifteen that Max first thought seriously of becoming a professional writer. He got some work published too. Not, indeed, under his own name.

'Thirteen years ago,' he wrote in 1899, 'when the writing-instinct first stirred in me, one of my relatives was writing a weekly "London Letter" for a well-known journal in Scarborough. I implored that I might be allowed to write it for him, claiming no reward. He assented. I well remember that the first paragraph I wrote was in reference to the first number of *The Star*, which had just been published. Mr T. P. O'Connor, in his editorial pronunciamento, had been hotly philanthropic. "If," he had written, "we enable the charwoman to put two lumps of sugar in her tea instead of one, then we shall not have worked in vain." My comment on this was that if Mr O'Connor were to find that charwomen did not take sugar in their tea, his paper would, presumably, cease to be issued. I believe the paragraph had a great success, in Scarborough. Recalling it, I do not think much of it.'

He may have been right not to: his contribution to the Scarborough journal may not have been very amusing. All the same, it does not sound as if it were the work of a schoolboy.

For, by the time he wrote it, he himself was not like a schoolboy. Starting to mature earlier than most people, he had finished earlier too. It was not just that his interests were precocious or that he showed precocious talents. These things are true of many clever boys. Where Max was unusual was that he had so early found himself. At an age when most clever boys still uncertain of their true bent are imitating other writers and following other thinkers, he had discovered the range of imaginative experience within which his creative power could operate: before ever he went to a public school he had settled for fantasy and satire and dandyism and the contemporary world. During his time at Charterhouse he began to concern himself with manner as well as matter, with searching for an appropriate personal style. And he had gone some if not all the way to finding one. His drawings grew gradually more original in manner and less Thackerayan: in the tone in which he teases T. P. O'Connor there is a hint of that easy graceful impertinence which characterizes the work of his prime.

Nor was his self-awareness exclusively intellectual. His tastes were grown-up and he knew it. He did not like romping or roughing it or rushing about in a herd: he did enjoy comfort and conversation and going about on his own. Further, experience at Charterhouse had taught him how to relate himself comfortably to society, made him skilful at following his bent without friction with his fellows. Now and again he wondered what figure he would cut in the larger world he must enter when he was a man. In a cartoon, also drawn when he was fifteen, he pictured himself as he might appear ten years later—as lawyer, student, artist, man about town. In all these roles he portrayed himself as ridiculous; a shrimp-like figure with a huge head, looking worried and consciously inadequate. Max—and here too he is wonderfully unillusioned for his age—viewed himself as well as others with detachment.

Intellectually and morally, then, he left school at eighteen already in some essentials his grown-up self. But how grown-up was this? Human beings have only a certain amount of energy for growth within them. Children old for their age in one way are often proportionately young in another. So it had been with Max when he was thirteen; so it was now. Mind and sense of values might have ripened but, for the rest, he remained strangely childlike. His mature emotions were unawakened and his attitude to life was that of a sensible, sweet-tempered, well-mannered child, fond of his elders and anxious to do right by them, but who, with the innocent egotism of childhood, is content to be looked after, so that he may be free to play, and who is able to play with a wholeheartedness possible only to one who has retained a child's imaginative vitality. When Max said he longed to be grown-up, he was not quite accurate. He longed, it is true, for the pleasures of the grown man, to be able to get up and go to bed and frequent theatres and restaurants when and wherever he wanted. But he shrank from the responsibilities involved in full practical independence. No more than Peter Pan himself did he want to be grown-up in the graver sense of the word. Did it not involve plunging into the battle of the world? What he had seen of the battle of the world at Charterhouse disposed him to avoid it. Nor, so far as we can tell, did he show any signs of that spirit of adolescent rebellion that leads many boys to break away from home. He never seems to have been adolescent. With characteristic adroitness, he contrived either to by-pass that uncomfortable phase of human development—or to stop short of it. At eighteen, in so far as he was not a finished man of the world,

Max was still a child looking down at mankind with curiosity and amusement out of his nursery window.

Meanwhile, it was time to leave school for Oxford. Should he go to Merton or New College? Mrs Beerbohm—for it was she rather than his father who seems to have occupied herself with the question—consulted a friend who told her that life at New College was likely to be the more expensive. At the beginning of the Michaelmas Term 1890, therefore, Max went up to Merton.

CHAPTER TWO

Oxford

(1)

IN 1899, from the mature age of twenty-seven, Max turned to survey his past:

'I was a modest good-humoured boy,' he said mischievously, 'it is Oxford that has made me insufferable. . . . Often since have I wondered whether a Spartan system be really well for youths who are bound mostly for Capuan Universities. It is true certainly that this system makes Oxford or Cambridge doubly delectable. Undergraduates owe their happiness chiefly to the consciousness that they are no longer at school. The nonsense which was knocked out of them at school is all put gently back at Oxford or Cambridge.'

The ironic mock-modesty with which he speaks only enhances the overwhelming sense of gaiety and glory associated in his mind with his memories of Oxford. The years he spent there were some of the happiest in his history: and some of the most important. For, after his home, Oxford was the chief formative influence in his life. It was there that his personality completed its development: there it was that he flowered. The flower was tinged indelibly with the hue of its environment. Never was bloom more exquisitely Oxonian.

Indeed, Oxford life might have been devised to suit Max. It was a grown-up life, in the sense that he approved of the word grown-up: he was free there to spend his day exactly as he wanted. On the other hand, the child in him was comfortable there too; for he was sheltered from the struggle of existence, freed from the pressure of responsibility. So long as he was in college by midnight, and could manage to produce some work for his tutor once a week, Max had done all that was required of him: and even if once in a way he failed to fulfil these obligations, nothing very bad could happen. Further, he felt immediately, instinctively, an affinity with the tone, the spirit of the place. No wonder! Oxford in 1890 was extraordinarily agreeable. Half antique monastery of learning, half playground for aristocratic youth, it partook of the charm of each; was on the one hand scholarly, sequestered, picturesquely traditional, on the other, stylish, exuberant, and in touch with the great world. For Oxford, though monastic, was not provincial. The dons were aware of London, though they might look down on it a little; the leading undergraduates hoped to make name and fame there when they left the university. Not that they valued London fame more than Oxford fame! The son of the Prime Minister himself was heard to say, 'I always feel when I leave Oxford that I am leaving the centre of things.' He meant the centre of anything that mattered, the centre of the life of ideas and ideals. The life of pleasure too: for, as always in aristocratic societies, pleasure and its arts were regarded as an important and integral aspect of existence. Wine parties played as much part in Oxford life as did lectures: the sound of hunting-horns mingled nightly with the clanging of medieval bells to awake the echoes of her venerable quadrangles.

These festive sounds and others like them were louder than ever in 1890. Though the old Queen was still alive, the Victorian age was over, and the reaction against its gravity and strenuousness was in full swing. Among the undergraduates of Oxford, especially, seriousness was out of fashion. The robust among them rode to hounds and roistered, the less robust smoked cigarettes and talked flippantly. Sometimes, in poetical mood, they also tried to talk beautifully. For these were the days of the aesthetic movement; and Oxford was its centre and birthplace. It was in his rooms at Brasenose College that Walter Pater had in the epilogue to his book on the Renaissance first defined its ideal, calling mankind to a life dedicated to the fastidious cultivation of aesthetic experience. He had roused the severe disapproval of the Master of Balliol; but he found plenty of response among undergraduates. All over the university, on college lawns or pacing moonlit cloisters, young men could be heard murmuring the magical names of Botticelli and Fra Angelico, Burne-Jones and Whistler, or rhapsodizing about 'delicate joys' and 'exquisite sorrows' and the importance of experiencing as much as possible of both of them. Aestheticism was in tune with the general reaction against Victorian puritanism. In it the cult of pleasure assumed its most refined and imaginative form.

Max came in for all this and enjoyed it thoroughly. He also enjoyed the cigarettes and the flippancy; and was far from objecting to the roistering huntsmen. His heart went out sympathetically to every manifestation of life in 'the little city of learning and laughter' as he called it. The phrase sums up what he found so uniquely attractive about Oxford, its blend of culture and gaiety. But, indeed, he liked everything about it; the idleness and the tradition, the modishness and the antiquity, the tranquillity and the whiff of the great world. Of course, he saw that Oxford had its weaknesses. It was full of eccentricity and affectation, and there was something ludicrous about its calm imperviousness to the claims of what the philistine outside world was pleased to call 'reality'. But Max was on Oxford's side about all this. Besides, he always liked things better if he could laugh at them. Simultaneously he loved and mocked the spirit of his university. Many years later this mingled emotion, 'recollected in tranquillity', inspired him to write a passage which is at once a supreme triumph of his art and the fullest expression of his sense of Oxford.

'Over the meadows was the usual coverlet of white vapour, trailed from the Isis right up to Merton Wall. The scent of these meadows' moisture is the scent of Oxford. Even in hottest noon, one feels that the sun has not dried *them*. Always there is moisture drifting across them, drifting into the Colleges. It, one suspects, must have had much to do with the evocation of what is called the Oxford spirit— that gentlest spirit, so lingering and searching, so dear to them who as youths were brought into ken of it, so exasperating to them who were not. Yes, certainly, it is this mild, miasmal air, not less than the grey beauty and gravity of the buildings that has helped Oxford to produce, and foster eternally, her peculiar race of artist-scholars, scholar-artists. The undergraduate, in his brief periods of residence, is too buoyant to be mastered by the spirit of the place. He does but salute it, and catch the manner. It is on him who stays to spend his maturity here that the spirit will in its fulness gradually descend. The buildings and their traditions keep astir in his mind whatsoever is gracious; the climate, enfolding and enfeebling him, lulling him, keeps him careless of the sharp, harsh, exigent realities of the outer world. Careless? Not utterly. These realities may be seen by him. He may study them, be amused or touched by them. But they cannot fire him. Oxford is too damp for that. The "movements" made there have been no more than protests against the mobility of others.

They have been without the dynamic quality implied in their name. They have been no more than the sighs of men gazing at what other men had left behind them; faint, impossible appeals to the god of retrogression, uttered for their own sake and ritual, rather than with any intent that they should be heard. Oxford, that lotus-land, saps the will-power, the power of action. But, in doing so, it clarifies the mind, makes larger the vision, gives, above all, that playful and caressing suavity of manner which comes of a conviction that nothing matters, except ideas, and that not even ideas are worth dying for, inasmuch as the ghosts of them slain seem worthy of yet more piously elaborate homage than can be given to them in their heyday. If the Colleges could be transferred to the dry and bracing top of some hill, doubtless they would be more evidently useful to the nation. But let us be glad there is no engineer or enchanter to compass that task. *Egomet*, I would liefer have the rest of England subside into the sea than have Oxford set on a salubrious level. For there is nothing in England to be matched with what lurks in the vapours of these meadows, and in the shadows of these spires—that mysterious, inenubilable spirit, spirit of Oxford. Oxford! The very sight of the word printed, or sound of it spoken, is fraught for me with most actual magic.'

This passage, at once ecstatic and ironical, is itself an expression of the Oxford spirit as Max conceived it.

He acquired it gradually. During his first few terms Max was a hesitant, inconspicuous figure. His college servant reported that he was so shy when he arrived that he seemed hardly able to give an order. His first letter to his mother, too, is a naïve enough document, much like those he wrote to her when he first went to Charterhouse; and, like them, much concerned with what he ate.

My dearest Mamma

I hope you arrived safely at home and that your throat is all right. I went to Scott last night about going in for honours and he arranged what books I should take up and what lectures I should attend. He also asked me and another person there to breakfast tomorrow morning. I went to a short service at Merton Chapel (where there is a fine stained-glass window!) at 8.30 and then there is not another service till 5.0, which I went to. It seems that it is also a Parish

Church and there was a Parish Service in the afternoon. I will write again this week. I said I would go in for boating when two men called this afternoon and I shall go to the river tomorrow—whether I shall keep it up I do not know, perhaps after a time I shall drop it. Dinner was at 6 today and on week-days is at 7. Today there were rissoles (is that the way to spell them?) and other things of the kind and also boiled fowl and roast beef and something else to choose from—also blancmanges and pastry and batter-pudding. I have lunch in my own room. . . .

He liked the place at once. It was pleasant that the dons should address him as 'Mr Beerbohm' and not 'Beerbohm' as a schoolmaster would have done; and he delighted in the fact that his room should once have been Lord Randolph Churchill's, who had cut his name in the writing-desk. Moreover, from the first Max showed signs that he was not quite the ordinary undergraduate. One of these signs is mysterious. Though he had been christened Maximilian, he signed himself Maxwell in the book in which undergraduates were required by the Warden to inscribe their names. Was this some whimsical, now meaningless, joke? Or was Maximilian in those days thought to be a ridiculous name, rather as Marmaduke is now; so that Max, already intent on creating himself as a personality, wished to shed it?[1] Another anecdote indicates specifically aesthetic aspirations. When his tutor, G. R. Scott, asked him whose lectures he wanted to attend, he replied, 'Mr Pater's.' Scott laughed scornfully. He might have done so with less confidence had he known how soon or how often Max was going to draw caricatures of him. This became such a habit that inadvertently he let Scott see them. 'The impudent fellow even shows up essays to me with caricatures of myself scrawled in the margin,' said Scott.

Scott was not the only don Max caricatured. Before long all the leading figures at the High Table had fallen victims to his pencil; especially Thomas Bowman, the chief disciplinarian of the college, represented by Max as a policeman pointing with his podgy finger,

[1] Max seems to have found his own name an unfailing subject for enigmatic private jokes. Years later he told Sir Owen Morshead that he had assumed the name Max at his confirmation: 'I owe my name to a bishop,' he said. If this were so, it is singular that his relations, prophetically, had called him Max all his life.

and the Warden, the Hon. George Brodrick. Brodrick was an ex-hilarating personality, at once an eccentric and a man of the world, who liked filling his house with distinguished visitors and asking undergraduates to meet them. To listen rather than to talk: once an undergraduate insisted on taking a large part in the conversation, whereupon Warden Brodrick, seizing a large bushy plant in a pot, interposed it between him and the company. Max ran no risk of incurring such a penalty. As at Herbert's supper parties, he enjoyed silently watching the company, and especially Warden Brodrick himself—whiskered, dressed in the fashion of 1850, and uttering, in slow high tones, Johnsonian sentences. Just what the head of a college should be, thought Max, and an appropriate subject for his art! The undergraduates were less so; Merton at that time was a small, self-sufficient college of about ninety young men, for the most part more gentlemanlike than interesting. However, it suited Max better than a more famous or fashionable college would have done. Always he preferred watching the spectacle of the world from the security of some quiet window outside it. He says too that he thought Merton the most intimate college: Max set a peculiar value on intimacy.

As at Charterhouse, he devised and followed his own individual pattern of living. Hard work formed no part of it. At first he sampled the lectures, but only enjoyed one course, that given by Merry on Aristophanes. During the others he spent the time drawing caricatures of the lecturers. His tutor turned out to be right about the lectures of Pater. Apart from anything else, they were inaudible. 'Giving lectures for him,' Max remarked, 'was a form of self-communion. He *whispered* them.' Pater the man was equally a disappointment. One morning soon after Max arrived in Oxford, he went into Ryman's print shop, where he noticed 'a small, thick, rock-faced man', wearing dogskin gloves and with a bristling military-looking moustache. 'I nearly went down when they told me this was Pater,' says Max.

Within a short time he had given up going to lectures altogether. As at Charterhouse he had taken a pride never to be seen with bare knees, so now he took pride never to be seen in academic dress. In these circumstances it was not to be expected that Max should distinguish himself academically. In fact when, in March of 1892, the examinations were impending, he began to feel nervous lest he might fail. However, good fortune and good teaching at Charterhouse enabled him to get a Third in Honour Moderations.

All this did not mean that his intellect lay fallow. At Oxford, as at school and at home, he continued to live his inner solitary life of thought and fancy. This was fed by reading. Some of this was academic: though Max did not bother to study the classics thoroughly for examination purposes, he was expert enough both at Greek and Latin to get a great deal of enjoyment out of reading them, notably the works of Plato and Herodotus. There is less information about what he read in English and modern languages. Himself he denied always that he read much at Oxford or at any other time. This is a paradoxical pose manifestly unjustified. His critical articles are full of literary allusions only to be learnt from reading. Besides, he was at nineteen already interested in parody. It is impossible to parody authors if you have not read their works. His own style, too, was on the way to becoming a highly accomplished one, making frequent use of devices learnt from other authors and resonant with echoes of their voices. Contemporary voices mostly: just as Max was primarily interested in the contemporary world, he preferred both now and later to read contemporary or near-contemporary books. 'The only writers who give me any pleasure are my contemporaries,' he was to tell his wife. 'I cannot go with pleasure further back than Matthew Arnold; he, in small doses, pleases me and inspires me with a sort of affection. Had I never been at Oxford, I don't suppose even Arnold would waken anything in me.' This is a slight exaggeration. Max could go back further than Arnold. Did he not enjoy Boswell's *Life of Johnson*? But it is true that, in general, for him enjoyable literature, other than the ancient classics, began with the nineteenth century; and, like most clever young men, he turned naturally to the up-to-date *avant-garde* writers of his own time, Meredith, Henry James, Ibsen, Maeterlinck —and, of course, the presiding spirits of the aesthetic movement, Pater, its god, and his florid young prophet Oscar Wilde. It was on such authors and the aspects of life revealed by them that the youthful Max desultorily meditated in his rooms in the medieval Mob Quad of Merton or wandering beneath the lime trees and chestnuts of the college garden.

He had plenty of time to do so. His mode of life was leisurely. If he was not a scholar, still less was he an athlete. After his first letter to his mother we hear no more mention of his rowing, though in the summer terms he did enjoy floating idly down the river in a canoe with a friend. He also avoided the big university societies, and, for his first two years at any rate, only attended the Union now and again to listen to some celebrated man down from London or a distinguished undergraduate speaker like Hilaire Belloc or Hugh Cecil. He made no attempt to speak himself.

There was no question, however, of his being a recluse. The fact that he was Herbert's brother got him introduced to undergraduates with theatrical connections. George Bancroft, son of the famous actor Squire Bancroft, asked him to breakfast with him in his first term to meet the son of the still more famous actor Henry Irving. Young Irving was a formidable youth. 'A brother of Beerbohm Tree, aren't you?' he asked, examining Max through his pince-nez. 'A half-brother,' Max faintly replied. 'Ha!' exclaimed Irving enigmatically. However, Max made a sufficiently good impression for Irving to ask him to lunch alone with him. But in general Max did not at first venture outside Merton College. There he was happy and at ease: and, unobtrusively sociable, was soon well in the gentle swim of Merton life. He did not mind raising his voice in the homely atmosphere of college gatherings, used to speak at the Merton Debating Society and was also a member of the smaller and more serious Essay Society. This was a short-lived body: with irony Max relates the story of its decline.

'There was in my college at Oxford a little "Essay Society", to which I found myself belonging. We used to meet every Thursday evening in the room of this or that member; and, when coffee had been handed round, one of us would read an essay—a calm little mild essay on one of those vast themes that no undergraduate can resist. After this, we would have a calm little mild discussion . . . "It seems to me that the reader of the paper has hardly laid enough stress on . . .". One of these evenings I can recall very distinctly. A certain freshman had been elected. The man who was to have read an essay had fallen ill, and the freshman had been asked to step into the breach. This he did, with an essay on "The Ideals of Mazzini", and with strange and terrific effect. During the exordium we raised our eyebrows. Presently we were staring open-mouthed. Where were we? In what wild dream were we drifting? To this day I can recite the peroration. *Mazzini is dead. But his spirit lives, and can never be crushed. And his motto—the motto that he planted on the gallant banner of the Italian Republic, and sealed with his life's blood, remains, and shall remain, till, through the eternal ages, the universal air re-echoes to the inspired shout—*"GOD AND THE PEOPLE!"

The freshman had begun to read his essay in a loud declamatory style; but gradually, knowing with an orator's instinct, I suppose, that his audience was not "with" him, he had quieted down, and become rather nervous—too nervous to skip, as I am sure he wished to skip, the especially conflagrant passages. But, as the end hove in sight, his confidence was renewed. A wave of emotion rose to sweep him ashore upon its crest. He gave the peroration for all it was worth. *Mazzini is dead.* I can hear now the hushed tones in which he spoke those words; the pause that followed them; and the gradual rising of his voice to a culmination at the words "inspired shout"; and then another pause before that husky whisper "GOD AND THE PEOPLE". There was no discussion. We were petrified. We sat like stones; and presently, like shadows, we drifted out into the evening air. The little society met once or twice again; but any activity it still had was but the faint convulsion of a murdered thing.'

It may have been one of these last and unsuccessful meetings which he describes in a letter home:

'I went to a meeting of the Essay Society last night, to hear a paper on "Totemism", read by a common little recluse—a Fellow of Merton—in his rooms: the whole thing was rather pathetic as hardly anyone came to sit on the large number of chairs that had been put out or drink coffee out of the innumerable cups on the table and the little man had to hover humbly round with a small packet of cigarettes whilst the President tried to account in a loud voice for the small attendance.'

Mazzini and totems were hardly Max's kind of subject: he is unlikely to have regretted the demise of the Essay Society. He was much more at home with the Myrmidons. This was a small and very select dining club drawn from the gilded youth of the college whose members met once or twice a term dressed in purple evening coats to enjoy a magnificent dinner. Now and again this was followed by an entertainment given by a professional; more often the members entertained each other, singing, making comic speeches, playing roulette and in general joyously disturbing the college. It is a measure of Max's social success at Merton that he became a Myrmidon soon after he arrived there. He delighted in the purple evening coat, he delighted in the uproarious evenings on which he wore it. Forty-seven years later, writing to another old member, Eric Parker, he lingers with pleasure on every detailed recollection.

'I divert my eyes very often from the present, and think about such things as S.C.S.[1] parties and Myrmidon dinners, and of Costa saying "G-hood game, isn't it?" Of you and Pita singing "Rahnd the Tahn", of you singing "And I was there as well", and "Where did you get that hat?" and of Pita reciting the tarpaulin story, and of Reggie singing "Hextra Speshul" or preaching one of his sermons (of those sermons I remember especially the one that was to be preached by young Bassett, the hair-dresser's eldest son, and a professional cricketer, who had taken Holy Orders . . . "An' we takes our stand at the wicket, which is 'Oly Writ, and it's the Devil that is bowling against us, and 'Eaven 'elp us if we 'aven't a second innings . . . And as we return to the Pavilion, which is Paradise, we 'ear the plaudits o' the spectators, an' we take off our cap, an' we look inside our cap, and we see the name o' the Maker, an' the name o' the maker is Gawd." '

The name Reggie introduces us to a very important figure in Max's life, Reginald Turner. Like many other people Max made his first close friendships at the university. They were mainly Merton men: Eric Parker, to whom he wrote the letter, Alfred Birnbaum, Previté, Lord St Cyres. But the only one he was steadily to keep up with, and who was indeed to be the greatest friend of his life, was Turner.

This was not surprising; he was exceptional. Reginald Turner, who had come to Merton two years before Max, was the illegitimate son of a rich man. He did not know who his mother was—how strange and terrible not to know one's mother, thought Max—and he had lost his father early; but an uncle had sent him to Oxford and made him a modest but adequate allowance which he later increased. Though Reggie was not the sort of man to thrust himself forward, he soon made friends. This was not due to his looks;

[1] The 'Septem contra Somnum', another college dining-club.

fantastically ugly, with a nut-shaped head, blubbery lips and a huge snout-like nose, he was continually winking and blinking. But he had intelligence and sensibility, a warm, delicate, generous nature, and an extraordinary gift of humour. Some expert judges, including Max himself and Mr Somerset Maugham, have judged him to be the most amusing man they ever met in their lives. We get an

REGINALD TURNER

occasional glimpse of his humour in his letters; as when he writes from a sick-bed in Rome, 'I am so weak from fever that I cannot write all I intend. I suppose I shall not yet be laid beside Keats and Shelley and within call of John Addington Symonds (not that I should ever call).' Or on a female friend about to join the Church of Rome:

'She said she would not become a Catholic unless she could be buried in the same grave as her husband. They told her there was no objection. I should have thought that a very pungent reason for becoming a Catholic would have been to escape that fate. And—after all—what of the Hereafter! In their graves they were not divided—but what then. However, I applaud her mightily, and I think it will do her good. . . . On Saturday she will be one with Belloc and Chesterton and Caesar Borgia.'

But it was in talk that Reggie's comic genius shone out; in mimicry, spontaneous parody, flights of fantastic comic improvisation.

Surprisingly, Reggie seldom laughed himself. In fact, in spite of his friendliness, he was not easily amused by others. Max was an exception, however. Each encouraged and stimulated the other's comic gift: to hear them together was to hear both at their best. Luckily it was possible to hear them often. They were the centre of a group of Merton undergraduates who congregated in Max's rooms of an evening. The first visitor arriving was likely to hear through the door Max humming a popular song of the day; then followed delightful hours of talking and singing accompanied by the noise of shuffling cards and the tinkle of the roulette board. Once Reggie was observed looking long at his image in the looking-glass. 'God, I *am* ugly!' said Reggie.

The pleasure the two friends took in each other's talk was soon warmed by affection. Reggie, in particular, loved Max with a romantic tenderness which expressed itself in showers of monogrammed handkerchiefs, enamelled cuff-links and beautifully wrought cigarette-holders. Max's feelings were less strong. His temperament was cooler; and anyway, never at any time in his life could he feel romantically about his men friends. But he grew very fond of Reggie, delighted in his conversation, was grateful for his presents, and basked a little in the flattering sunshine of his attentions.

(2)

Max's vacations followed with variations the same pattern as his holidays from Charterhouse. We hear rather less about the House of Commons: on the other hand, he took to attending the Law Courts to enjoy the human drama enacted there; and he went to Herbert's house in Hampstead: or Herbert would take him to supper with some friends at the Garrick Club. The conversation, beginning lightly, was likely to take a deeper turn as the night wore on. About two in the morning, Max noted, it grew theological. This was a sign for him to leave: Max was no more a theologian than he was a philosopher. Without pride, he recognized his spirit as incurably of this world. Max had the added pleasure of introducing his Oxford friends to some of these enthralling scenes. He could always get free tickets so that he could take them to the play: after it was over he took them behind the scenes to be presented to Herbert.

His brother Julius, meanwhile, had introduced him to a new form of theatrical entertainment. In his very first vacation Julius took him to dinner at the Café Royal and afterwards suggested that they should go to the Pavilion Music Hall. Feeling a trifle bewildered but emancipated and grown-up, Max found himself in what seemed to be a sort of theatre, but where the audience was made up mostly of men in day clothes and almost the only women present were barmaids: the stage was occupied by a series of singers bawling out comic or sentimental or patriotic songs. It was the first of many such visits. During the next few years and more, either alone or with some companions from Oxford, Max haunted the Tivoli, the Pavilion, the old Oxford. His pleasure, he said later, was mainly ironical. He and the sophisticated Oxonians who accompanied him enjoyed the entertainment because it was so exquisitely silly and vulgar.

'Here, in these very stalls,' he writes reminiscently about the Tivoli, 'I would often sit with some coaeval *in statu pupillari*. Lordly aloof, both of us, from the joyous vulgarity of our environment, we would talk in undertones about Hesiod and Fra Angelico, about the lyric element in Marcus Aurelius and the ethics of apostasy as illustrated by the Oxford Movement. Now and again, in the pauses of our conversation, we would rest our eyes upon the stage and listen to a verse or two of some song about a mother-in-law or an upstairs-lodger, and then one of us would turn to the other, saying, "Yes! I see your point about poor Newman, but . . ." or "I cannot admit that there is any real distinction between primitive art and . . .". Though our intellects may not have been so monstrous fine as we pretended, we were quite honest in so far as neither of us could have snatched any surreptitious pleasure in the entertainment as such. We came simply that we might bask in the glow of our own superiority—superiority not only to the guffawing clowns and jades around us, but also to the cloistral pedascules who, no more exquisite than we in erudition, were not in touch with modern life and would have been scared, like so many owls, in that garish temple of modernity, a Music Hall, wherein we, on the other hand, were able to sit without blinking. Were we, after all, so very absurd? It was one of our aims to be absurd.'

It is to be doubted if, even when he was twenty years old, Max's pleasure was quite so negative and contemptuous as he here makes out. The very fact he could mock the entertainment so cheerfully is evidence against it. For just as Max always felt an impulse to laugh at what he found lovable, so also he tended to love whatever he found laughable. Certainly within a few years his pleasure in music halls had become affectionate. And they also fed his imagination: Max, like his contemporary Walter Sickert, was to find inspiration for his art in the English music hall.

For the rest, during the vacations he relaxed in the comfort and fun of home along with his mother and sisters. Life there during the last years had been agitated by the marriage troubles of his second sister, Agnes. Before he went to Charterhouse she was already grown-up; and, as the beauty of the family, had attracted the attention of a Mr Neville, who took to visiting the house noticeably often. Agnes fell in love with him: so did her elder and plainer sister Constance. What was Constance's excitement when Mr Neville asked her to go boating with him! 'I want to ask you something,' he began ardently, as they floated on between the green banks of the river. Constance's heart leapt. 'I love your sister Agnes,' continued Mr Neville, 'will you help me to win her?' It was a cruel blow; but Constance was too unselfish to refuse. Soon after, Mr Neville married Agnes and took her to India. As things turned out, however, Constance need not have envied her. The marriage proved a failure. By the time Max went to Oxford, Agnes was back at home eking out a slender income by some amateur dress-designing. Her troubles had left their mark: at times she wore a sad and drooping air. But more often the Beerbohm spirit for life bubbled up in her. 'My sister Aggie was gay,' said Max.

With her and his other sisters he would sit round the fire talking and playing games; or he retired to his room to draw. One day in

1891 he showed one of his sisters—it is not clear which—a series of caricatures entitled 'Club Types'. She in her turn showed them to the editor of *The Strand* magazine. The drawings betrayed some ignorance of the realities of club-land: Max was amused later to note that he had pictured White's as inhabited exclusively by ageing Regency bucks and the Travellers' as full of bronzed and bearded men fresh from adventures in unexplored parts of the globe. But the drawings were deft and lively enough for the editor to accept them for *The Strand*, where they were to be published in the autumn of 1892. 'The news of their acceptance was for me a great moment,' Max relates, 'and dealt a great, an almost mortal blow to my modesty.'

Alas, his pleasure at their actual appearance was to be darkened by grief. At the end of August, Mr Beerbohm died. Max wrote to Reggie with a restraint that does not conceal his poignant sorrow.

My dear Reg,

Thank you so much for your kind letter—it seems strange that sympathy at a time like this should be of any comfort, but I do find that it is.

I was going to write to you and tell you of my Father's death last week, only I thought you had doubtless left Rouen by that time. If I had caught the train that morning, I might just have seen my Father living: but I might have been an hour too late and that would have been more painful.

He was buried last Saturday. . . .

Ever yours
Max.

He was not of an age, however, to grieve very long, especially once he got back to delightful Oxford. Encouraged by his friends and his successes his life there had begun to expand. Already in the Summer Term of 1892 he had helped Reggie to bring out a weekly paper, *The Clown*; four unsigned pages of topical jokes and skits, garnished with puns and classical allusions. It is impossible to distinguish Max's work from the rest; but as none of the paper is very good, this does not matter. This term, too, he exhibited some caricatures of an O.U.D.S. production at Shrimpton's print shop in Broad Street. Meanwhile, his social life was extending itself, and into more fashionable circles. Through Reggie and his other older friends he had begun to know people outside college: they included some of the most elegant and entertaining members of the university, the amusing Lord Basil Blackwood, the beautiful Lord Alfred Douglas. All liked him; and he was soon elected a member of the Gridiron Club where they forgathered for luncheon and dinner. By the end of 1892, though still little known in the university at large, Max was recognized by a small and fastidious circle as an outstanding personality.

Indeed, he had become so. Two years of Oxford had made a considerable change in Max. For one thing, his curious and characteristic mixture of youth and maturity had now found visible expression. Max still looked very young; boyish even, with his slight figure, delicate hands, full smooth cheeks, long curling lashes, and thick black hair parted in the middle and tapering to an odd twist in the nape of his neck. But his manner, courteous, composed, leisurely, suggested a man of thirty; so did the discreet elegance of his clothes and something detached and inscrutable in his general demeanour. He was never seen to make an abrupt or hurried movement and he did not talk much. When he did his tone was for the most part light and ironical. Now and again, and especially in the company of his friends, it would grow mischievous and effervescent: in slow and deceptively gentle accents Max would give utterance to some outrageous paradox or urbane impertinence. He had never read a book in his life, he would insist, except Thackeray's *Four Georges* and Lear's *Book of Nonsense*: or when some college athlete asked him, at the time of the boat races, if he was going down to the river—'What river?' asked Max. So spoke the heroes of Oscar Wilde's works: theirs was the tone fashionable in Max's Oxford circle and he had caught it. Along with their conscious affectations of manner and gesture—hands uplifted in surprise, eyes cast up in mock horror—he cultivated also their flippancy, their taste for the precious and artificial and nonsensical, their pose of amused self-admiration, their impish pleasure in shocking. In all this Max is, for once, as boyish as he looks. Here we can see him in full reaction against the inhibitions imposed on him at Charterhouse! Here the nonsense knocked out at school is back gaily flaunting itself, for his intimates to see and admire!

Those less intimate were less admiring. Some old schoolfellows complained that Beerbohm had changed for the worse, he made them feel themselves so depressingly commonplace; and when an elderly cleric, contemporary with him at Merton, was asked for memories of Max, 'We thought the fellow put on too much side,' he growled.

Perhaps there was something in these criticisms. Certainly Max took pride in his new-found successes. In his letters to his mother, naïvely and for once forgetting his aesthete's airs and ironies, he recounts the compliments he has received.

'I spoke last Sunday night at the Essay Society after Turner's essay on "Plays, Players and Playhouses", and really made a great success. I was told afterwards that the President (a Mr How and fellow of the College) said to St Cyres that, on light lines, it was the best speech he had ever heard.'

This is disarming. Max was clever and charming and admired and twenty years old; no wonder if his head was a little turned! And it was only a very little! Everyone who knew him at all well seems to have liked him. Nor did they think him conceited. For he never tried to dominate the conversation: rather, he listened, responded, appreciated. Besides, he did not take himself too seriously. People were welcome to laugh at his extravagances: he laughed at them himself. 'My affectations are dying for want of an audience,' he writes to Reggie, 'so come unfailingly.'

In this remark we hear the authentic voice of the mature Max; the Max whose name was to become famous. For, in the two years that had passed since he came up to Oxford, the process of his development had at last completed itself. As we have seen, his tastes and the basic features of his character were already fixed: and already he had learnt how to get on with his fellows. But there were two other important strains in his composition, not fully apparent before, which Oxford had fostered and brought to fulfilment. One was the aesthetic strain, his feeling for the beautiful. He had been born with it: and it had grown stronger during his last years at school. He had become an enthusiastic admirer of Burne-Jones's pictures and longed to paint like him: and he read *Marius the Epicurean* in bed at night. But aestheticism was suspect at Charterhouse as at most public schools. Max got little chance to cultivate it there. At Oxford, on the other hand, its home and hot-house, it burst into full flower. Max's aestheticism was of an individual brand. He was never an enthusiast for Pater himself. Besides finding him inaudible and unromantic-looking, he could not admire his style. 'I was angry,' he said, 'that he should treat English as a dead language, bored by that sedulous ritual wherewith he laid out every sentence as in a shroud—hanging, like a widower, over its marmoreal beauty.' Moreover, Max was too sensible or too mundane to respond to the mere mystical and high-flown aspects of aesthetic doctrine. He accepted some orthodox opinions of the school—would maintain, for example, that the artist should feel no obligation save to his art and that he must never use this as a means either of confessing his heart or preaching a gospel. But such views tell us more about his circle than about Max. He was no philosopher, had neither taste nor talent for abstract speculation of this kind. What Oxford and the aesthetic movement between them did was to strengthen and refine his sensibilities. He grew to recognize beauty as an essential quality in anything he admired. More humbly manifested as prettiness, it became also a necessary element in his own inspiration. Not the most necessary of all: Max was always primarily a comedian. But his aestheticism began to colour and modify his comic sense. He aspired to blend the comic with the pretty. It was an aesthete's idea of the comic, too. This is where the influence of Oscar Wilde especially shows itself. Wilde's writings influenced him far more than Pater's did. Witty, impertinent, stylish, they stood for all that young Oxford, and Max in particular, enjoyed most. Finally, aestheticism had intensified Max's preoccupation with style, his concern to achieve the right manner in everything he did, drawing, writing, and dress. For it was at Oxford that his dandyism found for the first time full scope.

This was not purely aesthetic in origin. It expressed also the second important strain in him to be first fully brought out by Oxford: the histrionic strain. Like Herbert, like Julius, Max instinctively desired to dramatize himself. This desire took a less extravagant form in him than in them, for it was tempered by his discretion and his taste. He did not want to make a fool of himself and he disliked crude showing off. But as much as his brothers he enjoyed cutting a figure, found it natural amusedly to create for himself a personality in which to appear before the world. This sprang from the childlike side of the Beerbohms. All imaginative children like make-believe and pretending; it is the mode in which their creative faculty expresses itself. Grown-up people do not pretend in this way. If they retain any creative imagination—and few do—they learn to exercise it in some more objective form, in writing or painting or composing music. Max learnt to do this too. But he also kept his childlike faculty of personal make-believe. He still liked dramatizing himself. Once again natural impulse had been checked at Charterhouse. Self-dramatization is all too like showing off to be tolerated at a public school. But the undergraduates of Oxford have always believed in personalities; they enjoy showing off and being shown off to. Aestheticism, too, told them their enjoyment was right. The cult of art included the art of living. Not only a man's writing and painting but also his clothes and manner should be deliberately cultivated in accordance with his ideal of the delightful and the beautiful. No doubt this made him artificial. All the better, said the aesthetes: they had no great opinion of the natural. At best it was useful raw material for the artist.

A few men pursued this line of thinking still further to evolve the 'doctrine of the mask'. According to this, man's crude spontaneous self was merely a bundle of impulses without value or significance: he should therefore choose and assume a mask that represents his personal ideal, his conception of what, taking account of his capacities and limitations, he should aspire to be. Thus he will endue his life with beauty and meaning: if he retains the mask and consistently acts in character with it, he may even ultimately assimilate his nature to it, become substantially the personality he presents to the outer world. It is noteworthy that the two children of the aesthetic movement whose work has best borne the test of time—Yeats and Max himself—were both exponents of the doctrine of the mask. Yeats, as befits a great poet, stated it splendidly and solemnly. Max, the light ironist, stated it ironically and lightly. But this should not lead us to dismiss it as one of his jokes. It is crucial to the understanding of his personality. It did correspond to something he deeply felt and which had crystallized into a conviction. The proof is that he put it into practice. Deliberately or instinctively, he had during his two years at Oxford created for himself an appropriate mask.

In it, the principal strains in his imagination found expression. It was a dandy's mask designed by an Oxonian of aesthetic sensibility, to give an impression of finished elegance. A restrained elegance: Max praised the male costume of his time for 'its sombre delicacy, its congruities of black and white and grey', and because it produced 'a supreme effect through means the least extravagant'. So with his own costume; and his mask too. Not that this was sombre! Like Max's other characteristic creations, it was comic as well as pretty. He meant it to amuse—others and also himself. 'Only the insane,' he said, 'take themselves quite seriously.' Max was eminently sane; and he certainly did not take his dandyism over-seriously—or his aestheticism either. He would have been less enthusiastic about them if he had. The predominant expression of his mask was ironical. A gay, demure, irony gleamed out through its eye-holes and com-pressed the corners of its finely moulded lips.

As well as fulfilling his creative impulse, it was also a piece of armour. Max needed armour. Social armour in the first place; though he enjoyed society and social successes, he had a reserved nature that disliked any violation of its privacy. A mask protected his reserve. Yet it was no social disadvantage: on the contrary, if it was an amusing mask, it should make him better company. It also helped to armour him in a wider, profounder and more important sense. Half a child and wholly an artist, he could only fulfil himself in the universe of his own imagination; only in his self-created atmosphere of laughter and fantasy could his genius flourish and bear fruit. He had therefore to protect it from any disturbing invasion by the grown-up world of action and responsibility. He liked looking at this world, but since he did not want to risk being involved in it, he avoided confronting it directly or closely. 'All delicate spirits,' he says, speaking of Brummell, 'to whatever art they turn, even if they turn to no art, assume an oblique attitude towards life. . . . Like the single-minded artist that he was, he turned full and square towards his art and looked life straight in the face out of the corners of his eyes.' This was truer of Max himself than of Brummell. He could not doubt he was a delicate spirit; so he resolutely turned full and square towards art and he did look at life out of the corners of his eyes. To safeguard himself still further, he also preferred to look at it through his mask.

So much so that he seldom took it off. Indeed, he wore it for the rest of his life. Here we come to the chief reason why he has been considered an enigma. For what was underneath the mask? It has been suggested that Max had something to hide: frustration, con-flict, melancholy, some murky, complex turmoil of doubt or terror. There is no reason at all to suppose this. It is true, that hypersensitive and of low vitality, Max was temperamentally disposed to shrink from life in its rougher, coarser aspects, and that this shrinking was to grow on him with years. But he never saw enough of these aspects for them to trouble him very much. Good luck and good sense together kept him happy. Besides, now and again he did take off the mask; and no turmoil or frustration was disclosed. Not much complexity either: on the contrary, the natural Max appears as simple and straightforward. His letters to his mother from college are an example of this. Obviously he could not suddenly begin speaking to her through a mask. So he wrote as he always had; and his letters—except for an occasional stroke of typical humour—are much like the letters of the average undergraduate to his mother, factual, affectionate and not very interesting. He also lays aside the mask on serious occasions when an aesthetic dandyism would be out of place. There is none of the mannered Max in his letter about his father's death to Reggie; it is just an unselfconscious, if restrained, expression of natural affection and sorrow. Nor was Max plagued by the doubts and questionings that afflict many clever young men. Metaphysics did not interest him; or moral problems either. But he had moral views and they, too, were straightforward and traditional. On the rare occasions that he makes a moral judgement, it is according to the honourable and scrupulous standards to which he had been brought up. His school-fellows had called him a freak. They were right. One of the freakish things about him was that under all his dandyism and irony and sophistication there turned out to be so much left of the considerate and conscientious little boy who had felt bound to own up when he broke a piece of the family china.

CHAPTER THREE

The 'Yellow Book'

(1)

LET Max begin this chapter himself.

'In the Summer Term of '93 a bolt from the blue flashed down on Oxford. It drove deep, it hurtlingly embedded itself in the soil. Dons and undergraduates stood around, rather pale, discussing nothing but it. Whence came it, this meteorite? From Paris. Its name? Will Rothenstein. Its aim? To do a series of twenty-four portraits in lithograph. These were to be published from the Bodley Head, London. The matter was urgent. Already the Warden of A, and the Master of B, and the Regius Professor of C, had meekly "sat". Dignified and doddering old men, who had never consented to sit to any one, could not withstand this dynamic little stranger. He did not sue: he invited; he did not invite: he commanded. He was twenty-one years old. He wore spectacles that flashed more than any other pair ever seen. He was a wit. He was brimful of ideas. He knew Whistler. He knew Edmond de Goncourt. He knew everyone in Paris. He knew them all by heart. He was Paris in Oxford. It was whispered that, so soon as he had polished off his selection of dons, he was going to include a few undergraduates. It was a proud day for me when I—I—was included.'

Max was right about Rothenstein. He was a phenomenon. The younger son of a Jewish cloth-merchant in Bradford and with no artistic connections to help him, he had by the age of twenty-one catapulted himself into the very centre of the artistic life of Europe. Various qualities had fitted him for this achievement. He combined a considerable talent for drawing with a passionate enthusiasm for good work in the visual arts; and—what was rarer—he had an eye to discern it. When he had done so, he did not rest till he had got to know the artist personally. For, to his other gifts, Rothenstein added a dynamic purposeful energy that no snub could daunt and no elusiveness evade. Already in Paris—while a penniless student still in his teens—he had contrived to make friends with Degas, Lautrec, Forain, as well as such English-speaking residents as Conder and Whistler. Back in England he was soon acquainted with all the live

THE YOUNG ROTHENSTEIN

artistic groups, more especially that connected with the aesthetic movement whose leading figure was Aubrey Beardsley, and whose publisher and general impresario was John Lane of the Bodley Head. Lane it was who had sent him to Oxford. Here was a new field for Rothenstein's talent-spotting faculty. After polishing off Pater, the

Professor of Greek, and other celebrities, he looked round with curiosity for some examples of young genius. Max's friend St Cyres —now a lecturer at Christ Church—mentioned Max and gave Rothenstein an introduction to him. Max invited him to breakfast. Rothenstein found him—Max was now living out of college—in a minute room in Merton Street, papered in blue and hung with reproductions of Pellegrini's caricatures and some originals by Max himself. Rothenstein's eyes, flashing through their spectacles, took these in at a glance. 'But they are brilliant!' he said, and turned the full heat of his admiring attention on his host. His host melted. For the rest of the term the two saw each other frequently. Rothenstein soon grew as enthusiastic about Max the man as Max the artist.

'Though we were the same age,' he writes, 'and in some ways I had more experience of life than he, his seemed to have crystallized into a more finished form than my own. So had his manners, which were perfect. He was delightfully appreciative of anything he was told, seizing the inner meaning of any rough observation of men and of things, which at once acquired point and polish in contact with his understanding mind. . . . While aware of everything that went on in Oxford he himself kept aloof; going nowhere, he seemed to know about everyone; his unusual wisdom and sound judgement were disguised under the harlequin cloak of his wit.'

Rothenstein told his other Oxford acquaintances, much to their surprise and a little to their displeasure, that Max was the most brilliant man he had met in the university. If Max impressed Will, Will helped Max. As a professional artist he had some good advice to give him about his cartoons. Why shouldn't he add to their charm by colouring them? It was Will who first suggested to Max how to make his caricatures decorative. The two friends did not always talk so seriously. Rothenstein soon felt easy enough with Max to tease him about his carefully cherished habits. Max might boast that he never wore academic dress: Rothenstein was going to make him do it. He sent him a faked form from the Proctors requiring him to appear suitably clothed before them: then gleefully he watched Max toiling up to the Proctors' Office attired in an unused and unbecoming commoner's gown. Max in his turn teased Rothenstein. Rothenstein had been a little worried because one of his sitters, Sir Henry Acland, disliked his portrait: his daughter, too, thought it was not nearly good enough. Max wrote a letter to Rothenstein, giving him some fictitious and alarming news.

Dear Will,

. . . By the way, I should have told you before. John Lane has consented to publish a series of caricatures of Oxford Celebrities by me: they are to appear concurrently with yours in order to make the running. In case any ill feeling should arise between us on this account, I am sending you the proofs of the first number. Very satisfactory, I think. Do not think harshly of John Lane for publishing these things without consulting you—there is a taint of treachery in the veins of every publisher in the Row and, after all, though our two styles may have something in common, and we have chosen the same subjects, I am sure there is room for both of us.

Yours,
Max.

P.S. I have sent a copy of Sir Henry's picture to Miss Acland, she has just acknowledged it; such a nice graceful note of thanks. She says it will be one of her chief treasures.

Max judged his new friend with customary detachment.

'Rothenstein is rather nice to look at,' he writes to Reggie, 'with his huge spectacles and thick raven hair combed on to his forehead. He looks like a creature of another world. I wonder if he will succeed. He ought to. Such utter self-confidence I have never seen.'

After Max's death there was found a notebook in which he had scribbled impressionistic descriptive notes of various persons. We do not know when he first started keeping it, so that we cannot tell whether these represent fresh impressions or conclusions reached after long acquaintance. But since they were intended for his own eye alone, they may be taken as his secret and unmodified judgements on their subjects. In this book he writes of Will Rothenstein: 'Full of gaiety and self-importance—a mascot inspiring and helping. Strong sense of humour; cerebrative power.' He liked Rothenstein very much. He warmed to his vitality and enthusiasm: and he was exhilarated by the whiff of the great artistic world that he brought with him. As Max said, Rothenstein knew everyone; that is to say, everyone who was doing important work in the arts. Max longed to do the same.

In fact he had by this time got to know a famous literary artist. It is now that the figure of Oscar Wilde enters this story. Spiritually he has been in it for a long time. During most of Max's time at Oxford Wilde had been a dominant figure in his imaginative life. From afar Max had watched and admired him; in the early months of 1893 he had written an article in his praise for an American journal. But he had only met him once; long ago at a supper party of Herbert's in 1889 and before Wilde had become a peculiar object of interest to him. Now, in April 1893, he got to know him properly. Once more Herbert was the intermediary. He was producing Wilde's play *A Woman of No Importance*, and Max met him at rehearsals. Wilde took to him immediately. He had seen the flattering article; anyway, he found no difficulty in liking witty young men of pleasant appearance. Several times during the vacation Max was a guest at luncheon parties given by Oscar at Willis's Rooms in King Street, St James's, where he sat listening to his host sparkling and rhapsodizing to his guests in a sumptuous setting of red plush and gilt and to the unobtrusive music of a string orchestra. Max also attended the first night of *A Woman of No Importance*. In the spirit of its author, he describes the scene to Reggie.

'... The first night was very brilliant in its audience. I could not see a single nonentity in the whole house. ... Balfour and Chamberlain and all the politicians were there. When little Oscar came on to make his bow there was a slight mingling of hoots and hisses, though he looked very sweet in a new white waistcoat and a large bunch of little lilies in his coat. The notices are better than I had expected: the piece is sure of a long, of a very very long run, despite all that the critics may say in its favour. Last night I went again: ... After the play I supped with Oscar and Alfred Douglas (who is staying with him) and my brother at the Albemarle. Oscar talked a great deal about my article—said that he knew no other undergraduate who could have written it, that I had a marvellous intuition and sense of the phrase, that I must take to literature alone, and that my style was like a silver dagger. I am becoming vainer than ever. He told us one lovely thing. A little journalist who had several times attacked him vulgarly came up to him in the street the other day and cordially accosted him. Oscar stared at him and said after a moment or two "You will pardon me: I remember your name perfectly but I can't recall your face."

After supper I walked as far as Hyde Park Corner when I saw a glare in the sky like some false dawn. A cabman told me it was a fire and drove me to it—right away past Westminster. It was quite lovely, though there was no life lost I am afraid. Still, the timber yard was quite burnt and as I walked away the dawn was making the helmets of the firemen ghastly. It was bright daylight when I reached home and the sun shone brightly into my bed. I slept very deeply.

Write to me—how I have rambled and how marvellously!

Yours

Max.'

Back at Oxford the acquaintance continued. Now Reggie was gone, Max spent less time in Merton and much more with the aesthetic and fashionable circle whose most famous member was Alfred Douglas. This meant he saw more of Oscar, who was the presiding spirit of the group, entertained them in London or came down to Oxford for luncheon and dinner. Max was often of the party. He turned his scrutinizing eye with a special interest on the ideal of his undergraduate days: and, composed and unhurried, began to form his judgement on him. It was a mixed judgement. He had been a little shocked by his first sight of him. Oscar had been drinking: hot, fat, and purple in the face, he was not an object of beauty. But he soon won Max over. There was in him a seductive and compelling magnetism beyond any Max had ever come across. If he wanted to, Max thought, Oscar could charm, for the moment at least, those who had been most repelled by him. And his conversation was irresistible. No other talker—and he had met many brilliant ones—could compare with him, Max said later. Others were witty or humorous or poetical; Oscar was all three. Others told anecdotes vividly or were brilliant at repartee: Oscar did both. He had all the conversational qualities. What was more remarkable, he did not use them to extinguish others; he drew people out, made them feel themselves agreeable as never before. Nor was there anything forced or artificial in his talk. It was always a fresh, spontaneous improvisation; and spoken in such a beautiful voice! 'Was it fruity?' someone asked Max. 'More like a flower than fruit,' he replied, 'a mezzo voice, uttering itself in a leisurely fashion with every variety of tone.' No wonder his Oxford friends worshipped Oscar. Smilingly Max fell in with the worship: along with the rest he alludes to him as 'the Divinity'.

But the smile retained its irony. Though Max delighted in Oscar, he was not, even at twenty-one, subjugated by him. Years later he was once asked to compare Wilde and Shaw. He much preferred Wilde as a companion, he said, but Shaw had the better character. This remark is the more interesting in that Max was not fond of Shaw. No doubt, in 1893, he would have been more enthusiastic about Oscar, partly because he was excited by him, and partly because Oscar's weaker side was not yet so apparent as later. It was apparent enough, however, to figure in Max's letters. Again we have to be careful how far to take what he says in them literally, for his tone is playful. But, as he said to Reggie, 'Most of my true words are spoken in jest.' His jests about Oscar are often too near the painful truth not to represent his real opinion. Gaily and ruthlessly they mingle appreciation and derision.

'Oscar was speaking the other day of old Irving's Lear and was furious that all the "wretched little donkeys of critics" had dared to attack him. "Surely," he said, "a gentleman has a right to fail, if he chooses." I am sorry to say that Oscar drinks far more than he ought. . . . He has deteriorated very much in appearance—his cheeks being quite a dark purple and fat to a fault. I think he will die of apoplexy on the first night of the play.'

Or again:

'Did I tell you about Oscar at the Restaurant in my last note to you? I think not. During the rehearsal, he went to a place with my brother to have some lunch. He ordered a watercress sandwich: which in due course was brought to him: not a thin, diaphanous green thing such as he had meant but a very stout satisfying article of food. This he ate with assumed disgust (but evident relish) and when he payed [sic] the waiter, he said, "Tell the cook of this restaurant with the compliments of Mr Oscar Wilde that these are the very worst sandwiches in the whole world and that, when I ask for a watercress sandwich, I do not mean a loaf with a field in the middle of it."

It seems that he speaks French with a shocking accent, which is rather a disillusionment—and that when he visits the Decadents he has to repeat once or twice everything he says to them and some-times even to write it down for them. They always speak of him as "Scurroveeld"—French for Oscar Wilde!'

Some notes in the private character book give a more detailed impression:

'Luxury—gold-tipped matches—hair curled—Assyrian—wax statue —huge rings—fat white hands—not soigné—feather bed—pointed fingers—ample scarf—Louis Quinze cane—vast malmaison—cat-like tread—heavy shoulders—enormous dowager—or schoolboy—way of laughing with hand over mouth—stroking chin—looking up sideways—jollity overdone—But real vitality— . . . Effeminate, but vitality of twenty men. magnetism—authority—Deeper than repute or wit—Hypnotic.'

And the caricatures themselves—for Max's pencil was more ruth-less than his pen—emphasize Oscar's flamboyant overblown gross-ness.

For in fact poor Oscar was far from being a fine flower of civiliza-tion. Though posing to himself and to others as the champion of culture and sensibility whose life was dedicated to the disinterested contemplation of beauty, he was in fact nothing of the kind, but rather a genial, brilliant, spirited Irish buccaneer, with a thirst for self-advertisement, incurably crude taste and a strong streak of senti-mental vulgarity. Max was too perceptive not to realize something of this fairly quickly. At the same time he continued to be taken in by Oscar's cultural pretensions—at least so far as his writing was concerned. Oscar Wilde's art is an accurate enough reflection of the man who created it. He was an admirable entertainer; his jokes were delightful; *The Importance of Being Earnest* is a masterpiece in its kind. But when he went in for being beautiful or moving or pro-found he succeeded only in being derivative and meretricious. Yet Max admired Wilde's work in all its phases, the essays and fairy tales as much as the comedies; called *Dorian Gray* a 'splendid sinister work', and could even find something to say in praise of the deplorable *Salome*. 'Terribly corrupt,' he wrote to Reggie, 'but there is much that is beautiful in it, much lovely writing.' Max always

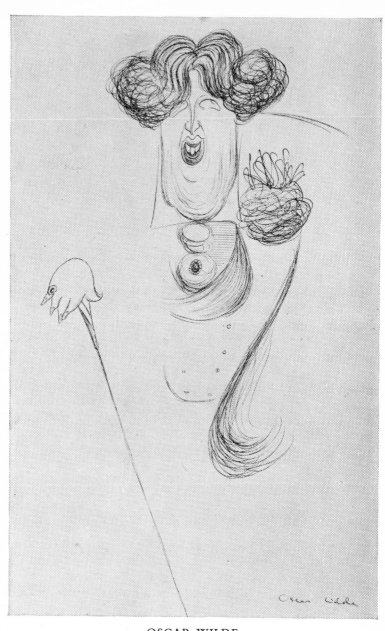

OSCAR WILDE

praised Oscar Wilde's writing. He spoke of him as the best stylist since Ruskin. This is all the stranger when we remember that Max's own style is notable for precisely the merits that Oscar Wilde's lacks: subtlety, precision, distinction. The truth is that creative writers tend to admire those other writers who are attempting to do something of the same kind as they themselves are and thus can assist them to solve their own problems. Oscar had already hit on the idea of combining aestheticism with comedy: Max was feeling his way towards the same end. Oscar's writing therefore acted as an inspiration. It sparked off something in Max that set his imagination on fire: and for ever after he saw it transfigured by the glow of the consequent conflagration. In fact the two men produced very different results. For one thing, the element of beauty in Max's work was of fine quality, whereas in Wilde's it was false and flashy. Further, Max fused the two elements into a single harmonious compound; Wilde merely alternated them so that they appear as discordant stripes. Max took Wilde's will for his deed and overrated his work in consequence.

It was Oscar the man, however, rather than Wilde the author that Max watched and analysed and judged, sitting amused and silent at Willis's Rooms or at Alfred Douglas's luncheon table. What on his side did Oscar think of Max? He was understandably upset by the figure he cut in Max's cartoons: but—and this is proof of Oscar's genuine good nature—he did not hold it against him. Otherwise, such evidence as we have shows him as finding Max entertaining but mystifying. He was so much more composed and enigmatic than his age led Oscar to expect. 'The gods have bestowed on Max the gift of perpetual old age,' he said. And again, to a common friend, 'Tell me, when you are alone with Max, does he take off his face and reveal his mask?' He enjoyed teasing Max in a friendly fashion: Max teased him in return. He noticed that Oscar sometimes plagiarized other men's jokes. Once at luncheon with Herbert, Oscar tried unsuccessfully to draw Max out. 'Max is jealous of his wit,' he said at last, 'he keeps it to himself.' 'If I didn't,' replied Max, 'it might prove unfaithful to me.'

His relation to Wilde's circle was similar to his relation to Wilde. He enjoyed their company immensely. They were the most amusing set he had ever come across and he saw a great deal of them. But he was not intimate with any of them except Reggie. Nor did he ever fully belong to them. By nature he was a freelance in life. 'I was never a member of a group even as a young man,' he once told Virginia Woolf. Moreover, there were deep differences between him and the Wilde circle. Gay, witty, daring and stylish, they were also silly, reckless and feline, while round them floated always a heavily perfumed atmosphere of homosexual flirtation. Max was not put off by any of this. Their silliness was an amusing silliness: the hint of perfumed corruption added an exotic glamour to their other fascinations. But he could not feel one of them. For ultimately Max was sensible and prudent, and at peace with the conventional world: nor was he homosexual. Reggie in London showed himself a little jealous of Max's new friendship with Alfred Douglas.

'You need not,' answered Max, 'be jealous of Alfred Douglas as he does not peculiarly fascinate me: he is for one thing obviously mad (like all his family I believe) and though he is pretty and clever and nice, I never judge my friends from an aesthetic, an intellectual, or an ethical standpoint: I simply like them or dislike—that is all. You are fortunate enough to have fallen into the former category—and even if tomorrow you become as stupid as Slender or as ugly as Caliban or as horrid as most of my friends, I should like you none the less.'

Max's new friends might be pretty and clever—and nice, in the sense that they were nice to him—but he noticed that some were mad, and more of them, judged by impartial standards, were 'horrid'.

He had nothing against their agreeability, however. Here they influenced him. His letters this year show the Wilde influence at its strongest. Rescored for Max's lighter, defter instrument we notice the characteristic Wildean paradox:

'If I were not afraid my people might keep it out of the newspapers, I should commit suicide tomorrow.'

Or again:

'Please keep my letters for the present if you can: it would interest me hereafter and perhaps throw some light on a character that I find almost unintelligible.'

There are also examples of the Wilde type of cheerful nonsense:

'How I hate being in the provinces: we are, it is true, quite near to London but Totteridge is terribly rural and the house has a large green garden full of those coloured things—(flowers, I think they are called)—that you can buy at Solomon's.'

Now and again there is a pretty patch of aesthete's purple:

'I walked all the way back from your place to my home the other night: fearfully tired too I was by the time I reached Piccadilly, and by the time I reached Park Lane I simply followed my feet at a weary and seemingly respectful distance—but oh—I saw the dawn, the lovely dawn of London: what a privilege to live in a city through whose vapours and buildings the sun rises with solemnity and fitting slowness: how different to the country where it pops up over the bare horizon like a yellow jack-in-the-box. How lovely in London is the growing of grey into blue and blue into grey and the hardening of all outlines against the sky. Why do I write all this? I suppose because I am clever. But I don't know that it isn't all thrown away.'

The literary influence of the Wilde school showed itself more significantly this summer in an article entitled 'The Incomparable Beauty of Modern Dress' contributed by Max to the June number of *The Spirit Lamp*, an Oxford periodical edited by Alfred Douglas. This is typical of its time; a mixed collection of essays, stories and poems, written in a style of extreme preciosity about Pan and Pierrot and world-weary prostitutes and beautiful youths with names like Narcissus and Hyacinthus: and, though compared with the productions of modern undergraduate journalism it is a remarkably professional affair, most of its contents look faded today. Not so Max's. Superficially it is of a piece with its companions; a satirical fantasy about foppery, written in a manner itself deliberately foppish. But Max has infused the convention with his own sense of fun, his own sharp intelligence and taut, vivid sense of language, to produce something fresh and original; and executed with a confident accomplishment astonishing in a young man of twenty-one. In it Max Beerbohm the mature artist makes his first appearance on the literary stage.

(2)

Meanwhile, his Oxford career proceeded on the same lines as it had begun. He did not do any more work than before. He had thought, indeed, of taking a Pass instead of an Honours degree, but the college objected.

'I have got off Collections!'[1] Max writes. 'Isn't it clever of me? Thus: I told How that at the beginning of the Vac I had decided to read a pass and so had not done a stroke of work. At the same time I was willing to stay up for the four years and read for Honours if *he* thought it any good. . . . However, Bowman spoke to me this morning and said that I had plenty of ability—tho' many interests; and strongly advised me to read Greats.'[2]

Accordingly, Max studied Greats, but on lines which may well have surprised his tutor. A book of his weekly essays survives: it is wonderfully unlike the weekly essay books of most undergraduates. Apart from anything else, it is primarily remarkable for its illustrations. Almost every page is ornamented with portrait sketches of Oxford dons and of Max himself; and there are several elaborately finished full-page pictures, notably one entitled 'The Long Vacation' and representing Max himself suspended between two pillars surmounted with busts of Aristotle and Plato, while beneath his dangling feet lie a pack of cards, a cigarette case and a champagne bottle labelled 'Pleasure'. The essays themselves, though always gracefully written, vary in interest. Max has nothing to say about philosophy or history. On human beings and the art of literature, however, he is odd and characteristic. His approach is uncompromisingly aesthetic: he has a good word for Plato, but only because he wrote beautifully, and he delights in Herodotus on the ground that the stories he tells are as entertaining as the *Arabian Nights*. But he disapproves of him for sometimes doubting their truth. Even if he did not believe them, he should not admit it, said Max; it destroyed the atmosphere of marvel which pervaded his book, it offended against 'the uniform spirit of faith so necessary to the treatment of fiction'. Elsewhere also Max shows an antipathy to

[1] Test paper set by the College.
[2] The colloquial name of the Honour School of Humane Letters at Oxford which is concerned with Philosophy and Ancient History.

sceptics, unexpected considering that he himself was no believer. He likens Plato's picture of Socrates to Renan's picture of Christ, and goes on to condemn Renan on the ground that his sceptical treatment of the subject weakens the dramatic force of his story. 'Better a muscular Christian than an unbeliever without a backbone,' says Max. The volume is handsomely bound in leather: illustrations and letterpress alike are executed with delicate and decorative care: altogether it is a little work of art. Alas, this was not what the college required! What it did require, and failed to get, was a thorough study of the subject-matter laid down in the syllabus. The minutes of the tutors' meeting at the end of the Summer Term of 1893 include an ominous item: 'It is resolved that Mr Beerbohm be told that he is expected to do *good* Collections in October.'

Meanwhile he went on doing the things he liked. Every day his waste-paper basket was full of discarded caricatures: he started, so he tells us, a short story in the manner of Maupassant, contributed occasionally to the undergraduate journals and attended societies. It is a measure of his increased confidence that he spoke this summer once or twice at the Union.

'I am becoming a very keen politician,' he writes to Reggie, 'you will be surprised to hear. Last night at the Union, you must not laugh at me, I spoke on a motion that the clauses of the Home Rule Bill were formed inadequately for the needs of Ireland. I spoke sixth and made really rather a success. Beauchamp, the president, has asked me to speak third next Thursday, but it is not yet fixed what the motion shall be, so I am not sure whether or not I shall do so.

. . . All this is *really* true: write and advise me whether it is worth while seriously to follow it up. I think I made really quite a success—though rather nervous at first. . . . I should not care to drift into the character of irregular Union-man but I think I may as well speak again now that I have done so once.'

For the rest he talked, dined out and took part in social life—with the Wilde circle, with Rothenstein, with aristocrats of the Gridiron Club, and with such of his old Merton friends as were still up. Many had gone or were going down. One, for instance, after a trying ordeal at the Examination Schools, was now a schoolmaster. With pity and amusement Max contemplates his fate.

'Really I cannot but smile through my tears—it seems so queer a development and after all I dare say he will like the life well enough. Can't you picture him correcting Greek verses at his desk and look-ing up suddenly and saying with forced calm to some tiny boy "Hawsbury, bring that piece of paper from under your desk to me! Come Sir, this instant!" I can picture him too at supper, with his bearded colleagues, implying that he went the pace at Merton and not being believed. And then at the end of term walking over to his home with a hand-bag. The Usher's Return! . . . Fancy a man of any culture or power of life following in the footsteps of Dr Arnold and Mr Squeers—going out into the desert to live amongst those poor little creatures, half-formed in body and half-formed in mind, that we call boys: getting up every morning at six-thirty to frighten them till night-fall: making himself the tyrant of their miseries and the sharer—if he be an athlete like our friend—of their wretched pastimes. . . .'

Max is writing to Reggie, now in London reading reluctantly for the Bar. His absence should have made a great gap in Max's Oxford existence; but they still kept in close touch, saw each other during the vacation and Reggie often came down to Oxford for a Myrmidon dinner or just to see Max. In his best mock-aesthete manner Max welcomed him.

My dear Reg,

In a certain house in the best street in Oxford there is a little room papered in blue and white. In this room between two windows, stands a soft, small bed. At this moment it is being smoothed and warmed by the hands of serving-girls. Someone is going to sleep in it when night comes tomorrow and when the day after that is wrapped in night. It is so, is it not? How nice it will be!

Yours

Max.

P.S. I have engaged you a bedroom at Adamson's. Hope you'll turn up in good time tomorrow.

This letter is one of many. During 1893 the friends wrote to each other very often, sometimes several times in a week. Reggie's letters have disappeared, for Max kept few letters. But we have Max's. They give a lively impression of him at this phase of his existence—at least as he showed himself to Reggie. He was a very sympathetic

audience and Max really let himself go to him in this early correspondence. Exuberantly he parades before Reggie the whole repertory
of his undergraduate poses; is in turn foppish and flippant, romantic
and mischievous, precious and nonsensical; exultantly he confides
his ambitions, recounts his conversational triumphs, expatiates on
the beauty of his new buff overcoat. Sometimes he lets himself go a
little too much. There is no denying that these letters are occasionally absurd. Max grew to think so himself in later years. He was
glad, he said, that his letters to other people were not so asinine as
those to Reggie had been. But the letters to Reggie have their charm;
the charm of their gaiety and their irresponsibility and their youth:
and if they are occasionally facetious, they are often very amusing.

'To what did you refer when you wrote the other day that you
heard "X" was in difficulties? Needless to say I was awfully interested
by the news. Are the difficulties financial? Or does he think of joining the Roman Catholic faith and cannot make up his mind? Or is he
very ill? Do write and put me out of suspense or I shall have to infer
that "no news is good news" and that would be dreadful.'

Or again:

'Yesterday I felt exceedingly depressed—partly, no doubt, because
of your departure in a neat grey suit and the prospect of not seeing
you for a long time: partly too because of my liver that the hot
weather had upset and partly because the vitality of a healthy young
Englishman is always at its lowest ebb on Sunday and the day that
precedes it. But today I feel very different and ready for anything—
not that I am fond of Monday as a day but there is a certain charm in
recovering from that prostration of Sunday—the charm of con-
valescence. What is your favourite day? Tuesdays make me feel very
gentlemanly, Wednesdays bring out my cleverness—do not think
this is affectation for it really is not—my moods vary always in this
way. On Saturdays I am common; have you noticed that?'

The letters are not all comic; for the friendship was not wholly un-
troubled. It was Reggie who made the difficulties. From time to time
the sense that he cared for Max more than Max for him would
sweep sadly over him; venting itself now in a pang of jealousy—
surely Max was talking too enthusiastically about Rothenstein or
Alfred Douglas—now in an accusation of unresponsiveness. The

affection was all on his side, he complained; Max was a cold-hearted egotist who only kept up their friendship because it suited him. At these moments Max soothed him with diplomatic skill. He would make a little fun of Alfred Douglas or Rothenstein just to prove there was no ground for jealousy; or carry the war into the enemy's country by telling Reggie that he took his ill humour to be a sign of waning affection: then serious and restrained, he repeats that his feelings for Reggie are unchanged.

'I wish, though, you yourself would come very soon: you amuse me so and really, though I fear that other surroundings and occupations have rather weakened your sympathy with me, yet my appreciation and liking for you have not undergone the slightest change. Usually I become quite indifferent to people behind their backs and my friendship is all at the mercy of time and space; so you really ought to try to be kind to me—and not (as on your last visit to Oxford you did somewhat) to "terrify" me.'

Too much should not be made of these moments of friction. They were few, they were not serious and they lasted a very short time. Before long Max always managed to bring Reggie round.

(3)

Max's confidences took a fresh turn as the summer wore on, and one which seemed likely to put a greater strain on Reggie's patience. Back in London after term, Max once more haunted the music halls. During his absence a new star had appeared at the Tivoli, Cissey Loftus, 'The Mimetic Marvel'. Only fifteen years old, unrouged, in a pink frock and yellow strapped shoes, and with her straight hair falling Alice-in-Wonderlandlike on her shoulders, she stepped demurely forward, made a little bow and proceeded to imitate various popular comedians of the day. She did it with a diabolical skill rendered all the more piquant by her childlike appearance.

Max saw her and was conquered. This odd, charming blend of youth and sophistication appealed exactly to his taste: was it not a blend to be found in his own art? But indeed he liked everything about Cissey Loftus; her little bow, her unrouged cheeks, her strapped shoes, and the satiric force of her mimicry: and he thought

CISSEY LOFTUS

her exquisitely pretty. Accordingly, night after night found him at the Tivoli standing at the end of a row of stalls applauding her act: after the performance he waited at the stage door to get a glimpse of her driving off in a shabby little carriage attended by her actress mother, Miss Marie Loftus. For, so he learnt, she had only just left a convent school and lived with her family, strictly chaperoned, in the respectable residential suburb of Herne Hill. Max took to haunting Herne Hill of an afternoon. Now and again after her act she and her mother would come down into the audience and hold a little court. Max plucked up courage on one such occasion to scrape acquaintance with her on the pretence that he was a journalist asking for an interview. She proved just as attractive as on the stage and graciously promised to sign a photograph of herself for him. Altogether he thought her the most delightful object he had ever beheld. He made up his mind to be in love with her.

'I am in love—in love with Cissey Loftus,' he wrote, ' . . . and though it may not seem paradoxical to say so, it is very very charming to be in love: you may not believe me—I could not have foretold it two weeks ago but now my whole being is changed: I have become good and am really happy at last: . . .

She has a small oval face and long eyes and full lips: her hair is quite straight as it falls over her shoulders and she has been in a convent for four years. As yet, in spite of her great success in art, she is utterly unspoiled. My love for her is utterly reverent: you, I know, regard woman simply as the accusative after the second auxiliary verb: do I wrong you? I could not ever wrong *her*, but I should love to marry her. I am so good and changed.'

This letter is written to Will Rothenstein. Max hastened to announce his grand passion to all who might be interested; not only Will but Herbert and his family, Robert Ross, and, of course, Reggie. To Reggie, he wrote almost daily about it. The letters are in his most full-blooded, dandy-aesthete style; dizzy flights of rococo fancy, sentimental and flippant, poetic and preposterous. Every day, almost, he came out with some new name for the object of his affections: Lady Cecilia, Mistress Mere, the White Girl, the Infanta, the Small Saint, the Blessed Damosel. Almost every day he luxuriates in some new daydream fantasy about her, happy or sad as the case may be. How delightful to be married to her and living in pastoral seclusion, or to join the family circle at Herne Hill, savouring the simple joys of domesticity and lawn tennis with the beloved one—'I am sure Mistress Mere plays tennis,' he says, 'with a strong overhand service.' Or he fancies that she has died young and that he is attending her funeral in a rural churchyard, lost in reverie and despair: or that she has renounced the world and gone back to her convent.

'Picture her moving always between the walls of some nunnery—wearing at first the veil of the Novitiate and dying long after either of us and being buried in the parcel of ground where the nuns' graves are—Sister Cecilia. It would be lovelier almost than if we married—unless she were to die in childbirth. I cannot imagine anything lovelier than that. Think of one year's happiness—always at its height: then a great sudden grief that will sanctify the rest of one's life, though it grows less day by day: a grief growing fainter, instead of a joy, as would happen if she had not died. Happy the man whose young wife dies in childbirth! His pain is not degraded by any knowledge of how good the gods have been to him. But generally "Love *is* stronger than death"—that is the great drawback of married life. I am going to buy a dear little revolver that I have long had my eye on: it is in the window of a gun-shop on the right side of Bond Street as you walk down. Not that I suppose I shall ever use it, but, as I am always saying, the feeling that you may at any moment solve the whole problem of life (simple division by death) is certainly a consolation. Life is a prison without bars—but I begin to realize that it *is* a prison. However that is talking at large—time enough for suicide later on: at present I think more of Cissey than of anything else. It may not ~~~d paradoxical to say so, but it is very very charming to feel rea~~~ love—and for the first time. . . .
    Isn't Cissey absolutely sweet to look upon? And when she comes on to the stage with her eyes down and looks up suddenly as her song begins . . . Her hair waves when she dances, have you noticed that?'

In spite of her waving hair, Max was not quite sure that he approved of Cissey being on the stage. No doubt she fulfilled herself as an artist there; but will it not corrupt her to live in such an atmosphere and in such company? Is it right for a girl like her to sing such songs? This anxiety of Max's is surprising in view of the fact that he was always saying that he looked up to Cissey morally, and felt her influence on him to be exalting and purifying.

'Much as I have loved my love of the Small Saint I cannot pretend that it leaves me as happy as I have been. She has shewn me what a small distorted career mine has been. After all what have I done since I came to Oxford with power to make myself? What have my pleasures been? To dress carefully, to lie in a canoe in the summer and read minor verse by the fire in the winter, to talk of Oscar, to sit down to dinner looking forward to rising from it drunk, to draw more or less amusing caricatures—a few friends, a few theatres and music-halls and a few cigarettes a day—and there you have my life. Accompanied by a sense of humour, an utter absence of the moral sense and an easy temper, it has been fairly happy I suppose—but now that the moral sense is suddenly, suddenly returning because of the Small Saint, disgust comes with it. I am no longer contented— and she is only the end of the old life to me I am afraid—not the beginning of a new one. I haven't the vitality for that. "As one sows so shall one reap" and the wisest are they who sow well and of those who sow ill they are wisest to avoid harvest altogether. That is what I should love to do if I had the courage.'

Reggie, we gather, read these effusions without great enthusiasm. If Max truly loved Cissey, he felt jealous; if not—and this seemed from the tone of the letters to be more likely—then Max was just putting on an act of which Reggie soon tired. However, he played up as sympathetically as he could. In order that he fully understood Max's sentiments, he even came out with the news that he was in love with a Miss Cumberlege. Max declared himself delighted to hear this news. How charming for Reggie to be in love, he says, and what fun they will have confiding the secrets of their hearts to one another! However, nothing of the kind happened. After a few letters the name of the mysterious Miss Cumberlege disappears from the correspondence. Did she ever exist, one wonders? Or, if she did, was Reggie really in love with her? For his part he continued to doubt if Max was really in love with Cissey and could not help telling him so. Max brushed the suggestion scornfully aside. 'How can you ask if my love of her is genuine?' he asked. 'I think I shall pay another visit to Herne Hill tomorrow afternoon.'

The end of August brought a temporary separation from the

loved one. The Beerbohm family shut their London house and Max accompanied them to Broadstairs. During the few instants he could spare from the thoughts of Cissey Loftus, he examined Broadstairs with disfavour. He wrote to Rothenstein:

My dear Will,

I made my entry into Broadstairs quite quietly last Sunday. I find it a most extraordinary place—a few yards in circumference and with a population of several hundred thousands. In front of our house there is a huge stretch of greenish stagnant water which makes everything damp and must, I am sure, be very bad for those who live near to it. Everybody refers to it with mysterious brevity as the C: I am rather afraid of the C. And oh, the population—you, dear Will, with your love of Vulgarity would revel in the female part of it. Such lots of pretty, common girls walking up and down—all brown with the sun and dressed like sailors—casting vulgar glances from heavenly eyes and bubbling out Cockney jargon from perfect lips. You would revel in them but I confess they do not attract me: apart from the fact that I have an ideal, I don't think the lower orders ought to be attractive—it brings Beauty into disrepute. Never have I seen such a shady looking set of men in any place at any season: most of them look like thieves and the rest like receivers of stolen goods; and altogether I do not think Broadstairs is a nice place. . . .

At Broadstairs Max met Oscar Wilde's brother Willie—nearly as amusing as Oscar but without his charm.

Quel monstre! Dark, oily, suspect yet awfully like Oscar: he has, Oscar's coy, carnal smile and fatuous giggle and not a little of Oscar's esprit. But he is awful—a veritable tragedy of family-likeness!'

This passage is almost as hard on Oscar as it is on Willie. Max's references to Oscar this summer are increasingly harsh. He minded his faults more now that he saw them in contrast with the flowerlike freshness of Cissey's charm.

'Apropos of my former self Oscar was at the last night of the Haymarket: with him Bosie[1] and Robbie[2] and Aubrey Beardsley. The

[1] A nickname for Alfred Douglas.
[2] Robert Ross, Wilde's friend, literary executor and editor.

last of these had forgotten to put vineleaves in his hair, but the other three wore rich clusters—especially poor Robbie. Nor have I ever seen Oscar so fatuous: he called Mrs Beere 'Juno-like' and Kemble 'Olympian quite' and waved his cigarette round and round his head. Of course I would rather see Oscar free than sober, but still, suddenly meeting him after my simple and lovely little ways of life since the Lady Cecilia first looked out from her convent-window, I felt quite repelled.'

All the same, Lady Cecilia's conventual fascinations were not going to maintain their power much longer. Back in London at the end of September, Max was also back in the Tivoli every evening. What was his horror after a week or two when Cissey appeared for her act heavily rouged and with a curled fringe! For a moment it seemed as if the White Girl was white no longer, that the Small Saint had lost her sanctity.

'It is all over,' he exlaims to Reggie. 'I hate Cissey Loftus or rather I can see her now with no emotion but regret—cold regret. I saw her last night and she had gone a step *too* far. She had piled a Pelion of rouge upon an Ossa of powder: . . . Anything less like that sweet creature with the grace of a fawn and the gaucherie of a young elephant—the white girl that I worshipped.'

But he remembers a true lover is not fickle, and so:

'In spite of her, I think I love Cissey Loftus more than ever: I love her for having been so beautiful and for all the good she has done me unknowingly and for the pain and happiness that I have had by reason of her. And I love her because she is still far more beautiful than anyone else in the world.

Your affectionate

Max.'

There are 25 copies of this letter of which this is copy Number 17.

Reggie, in spite of the protests, clearly thought Max was cooling off, and said so. For once it was Max's turn to be annoyed. He told Reggie that he found him most unsympathetic. Reggie apologized. Max accepted the apology; but in a tone that showed his feelings were still ruffled.

'No, my dear Reg, of course I do not think you are angry with me—

why should you be; I don't think I have done anything to make you angry. After all the whole 'incident' or whatever one would call it comes to very little: simply that I had been writing long letters to you chiefly about one subject thinking you very sympathetic about it: then, when I spoke to you about this same subject I thought you rather less sympathetic than might be and felt—not unnaturally— rather foolish and—rather unwisely—said so. You say that you were not really at all unsympathetic except in manner and I quite believe you were not and there is an end of it! I hate being the aggrieved party and it was quite refreshing to me when I came to that part of your letter where you speak of your sympathy being quite equal at least to anything I ever showed or am likely to show for things or people which interest you. Now we resume our old footing once more. I the cruel monstrous egoist with not a word except in scorn or a glance except in derision for any of the thoughts and interests of poor, silent shrinking you. I am quite myself again. Your picture of our intercourse always flatters my vanity though I am afraid the shorthand reporter might not quite bear you out. I am sure Mr Bull knows shorthand—why not station him behind the screen when- ever I am going to see you and in time perhaps I shall become less conceited than you tend to make me. Really, dear Reg, I think you are rather morbid—though I tremble for the consequences when I call you so. Let us be friends again for the present.'

Whatever Max might say, however, the romance was fading. Cissey's name occurs more and more rarely in the correspondence, till on 1 January 1894 he writes 'Dear Lady Cecilia, how I do wish I was still in love with her: for I never was so happy before nor have been since the time.' He goes on, in a spirit of world-weariness, to say that he is tired of the Life of Masks and wonders if he should give up everything and go into the Army. We need not suppose that he meant this surprising proposal to be taken literally. But it was true that a phase of his life was at an end. On 21 February he writes another letter to Reggie, unusually straightforward in tone: it may stand for Max's epilogue to the story of his love for Cissey Loftus.

'My dear Reg,
    You cannot think how pleased I was to see your familiar hand- writing (much improved by the way) upon my breakfast table today. . . . Do come but not merely for a wretched 48 hours—that

terrible old fallacy about your being the heart and soul of our friendship and my being a cold unresponsive but calculating acquaintance prevents me from saying much—but really I do want to see you and shew you and ask you and tell you very many things. Rothenstein comes to Y. Powell on Saturday and you know how exacting he is and how divided my company—though not my heart—would be—so that do not come before next Wednesday—but *do stay* then. Possibly you have important things to do in London and it would be foolish—but we are at the age when foolish things should be done. I ought to read every moment of my time now but I would far rather see you.

The White Girl figures largely upon my mantelpiece—how goes *your* love? You have not mentioned it lately. Do you remember asking me blunt-point-blank "Are you still in love or not?" and my exquisite reply "I still *reverence* the Lady Cecilia." ' '

So ended Max's first romance. If indeed we can call it a romance! For, of course, Reggie was right: Max had not been in love as the word is commonly understood. A man really in love with a real girl does not take pleasure in fancying his feelings at her funeral or when watching her take the veil. Nor does he choose to discourse on his passion for her in a sustained vein of high-spirited burlesque. So far Max is simply dramatizing himself as a lover as he has previously dramatized himself as dandy and aesthete—and, as usual, doing so in a comedy vein.

Yet the emotion that stimulated it was not wholly false or even wholly frivolous. Max's relation to Cissey Loftus was a significant event in his life-story. But it was an event in the imaginative life of Max the artist, not in the actual life of Max the man. The fantasy world in which he spent so much of his time—constructed as it was out of elements he observed in the real world—altered as his experience of the real world altered. By the age of twenty-one Max had grown up into a man easily, though not passionately, susceptible to feminine charm; with the result that his dream drama, if it was to satisfy him, now needed a love interest and a heroine. Cissey Loftus filled this role perfectly. For Max knew and loved her not as a real woman but as she appeared when impersonating a figure in the make-believe world of the stage and, as such, appropriate for incorporation into his own make-believe world. It was to be expected too that inevitably he should make fun of his feeling for her: for his make-believe world was always a comic world. If, as he said, most of his true words were spoken in jest, so now he celebrates his true ideal in jest. Possibly too his flippancy was a species of double bluff. Max wanted to talk about his love but feared people might laugh at him, and so spoke of it as if he did not mean it to be taken seriously.

In fact, however, when Reggie did not take it seriously, Max was displeased. His annoyance betrayed the fact that Cissey meant more to him than his deliberately flippant tone suggested. Indeed, along with Oscar, she was the dominating influence in Max's imaginative life during these early formative years. As Oscar's books had given him an ideal and a model for his own role in his fantasy drama, so Cissey's performance had given him an ideal and model for his leading lady's. The influence of this ideal persisted long after Max had ceased to care for her who had been its temporary incarnation. He might lose interest in the real Cissey Loftus; but he still 'reverenced the Lady Cecilia', the charming image of the White Girl still kept her place in his heart and on his mantelpiece, a sacred object of love and worship—and later a living inspiration of his art.

(4)

A second effect of his preoccupation with Cissey was to divert his attention from his home. This was just as well; for the home-life of the Beerbohms that summer had suffered a sad loss. Dora Beerbohm became a postulant of the Anglican Order of Sisters of Mercy at St Saviour's Priory, Ilford. This did not come as a surprise, she had been wanting to for years. As she began to grow up, her interest in art and letters had given place to an overwhelming desire to dedicate herself: to God and also to the service of her fellows. She had an active, pitying heart that could not see suffering without trying to relieve it. Once on a holiday in the country when she was only fourteen, Dora learnt that a little boy from a poor house in the village might be crippled for life unless he had some special and expensive treatment. She had heard people talk about the rich and charitable Baroness Burdett-Coutts; so she wrote off and told her this story. Some days later when she was walking in the garden, a gentleman appeared at the gate saying he had come from the Baroness and would like to see Miss Dora Beerbohm. 'I am Miss Dora Beerbohm,' said Dora. 'I

thought you would come.' Soon after, the compassionate spirit revealed in this story combined with her fervent piety to create in her
a vocation. At fifteen she wrote in her diary, 'I wish to be a Sister of
Mercy.' Her parents persuaded her to wait till she had some experience of life in the world. She 'came out', went to balls and
parties, and apparently enjoyed herself at them. But her determination persisted: and it was strengthened, it is thought, by her sister
Agnes's unhappy experience of marriage. If this was life in the
world, reflected Dora, better keep out of it! Accordingly, on 14
August 1893, she left home and, escorted by Max, drove off in a
hansom cab to Ilford. It was a sad journey for both of them. Max
says that at that age he imagined Sisters of Mercy to be 'a solemn
race apart', utterly unlike the Dora he knew, and that therefore he
was saying goodbye to her for ever. Dora's feelings at this moment
are not recorded; but she loved Max very much and cannot without
regret have said goodbye to her life with him. During her first
years as a Sister of Mercy, walking through the streets of East
London or in the stillness of her cell at the Priory, visions of the past
hovered before her mental eye, flooding her heart with tender
emotions that a year or two later flowed forth in song. On his
twenty-third birthday Dora wrote Max some verses:

> There was a time when you and I
> Did all we did with one another,
> My mind so often wanders back
> To those old days, my little brother.

> We ate each other's birthday cakes
> We shared our toys and nursery pleasures
> Our inmost thoughts, our little griefs,
> Canary birds—and other treasures.

> Then you got old, and went to school,
> And wore top hats and Eton collars—
> Thought less of nursery cakes and joys
> As is the way with public scholars.

> In fact Alas! for most of us
> As life grows real and we grow taller
> Its joys seem very trivial things,
> And Oh! the cakes seem so much smaller.

How I did love your holidays
And later on, the long Vacation
I wept so when the hansom came
That drove you to the railway station.

Life seemed a blank when you were gone
We'd had such fun with one another,
I liked the play and all gay things
When you were with me, little brother.

I liked our walks with Dandy too,
My mind still wanders—is it silly?
Where once we wandered slowly down
The gentle slope of Piccadilly.

You'd stop to buy an opera stall,
At Solomon's a pink carnation,
We'd have an ice at Charbonel's—
Who does not know the fascination?

The darkened room, the French coiffures
The Persian cats—a little table,
A muffled fragrance in the air
Mysterious as an Eastern fable.

'Twas sweet to breathe outside again
The freshness of the fair Spring weather,
'Twas sweet to wander slowly home
Across the sunny Park together.

And still you're there, but now I walk
Through other streets and scenes without you
Our walks lie very far apart—
And yet, I think so much about you.

Some day I think, that you and I
Will walk again with one another—
Just hand in hand, as once we did,
And never part, my little brother.

Max was the more saddened by Dora's action because he found it hard to understand her motive. He wrote to Reggie, 'My sister is quite young and is determined to cut herself off from life. Strange isn't it?' But should he have found it so strange? He lacked it is true the spiritual sense to enter into her religious motives; but he shared her hypersensitive child's shrinking from the grown-up active world and its ugly turmoil. The time was coming when he too, in his own fashion, was to turn his back on it.

(5)

Not in 1893 though! On the contrary, he was just about to take his first big plunge into the world—and to make a considerable splash in so doing. Getting to know Will Rothenstein proved to be one of the most important events in Max's whole career. Rothenstein, ambitious for his own success, was equally and generously so for that of his friends, and left no stone unturned to foster their achievements and spread their fame. When he got to London after the Summer Term, he began at once to introduce his new discovery to his literary and artistic acquaintance there, notably to the Bodley Head group—Lane himself, Beardsley, his chief artist, and his writers, among them Arthur Symons, Richard Le Gallienne, Lionel Johnson, Henry Harland. These—the Decadents as they were called by those who disapproved of them—were regarded, especially by themselves, as the most advanced and 'modern' writers of the period. Certainly they were the most discussed; so much so that, along with Oscar Wilde, they have come to be considered its representatives: to this day, when people speak of the artists and writers of the 'nineties, they mean the Decadents. This is odd: for compared with some of their distinguished contemporaries—Hardy, Shaw, Kipling, Bridges, to name no others—the Decadents were not worth much. Beardsley's was the only really original talent among them, and that, judged by fastidious standards, has something cheap and flashy about it. Most of the Decadents' work is a feeble English version of a French phenomenon; languid little poems and stories in which half a grain of Baudelaire is diluted in many gallons of London water.

As human beings, however, the Decadents are much more interesting, and marked by an intensity noticeably absent from their art. In fact, the lives of several were as picturesque and lurid as they would have liked their work to be: and they themselves—though poor, desperate and sickly—retained a tatterdemalion swagger which still invests their figures with pathos and even a kind of shabby glamour. 'I hope you don't dislike absinthe,' said Lionel Johnson, welcoming a friend to his poverty-stricken lodgings. 'It is all I have to offer you, I am afraid.' Londoners all by birth or choice, they associate themselves in the imagination with the London of those days; the murky, tawdry London round Soho and Leicester Square, with its gaudy music halls and gas-lit public houses and jangling barrel organs and hansom cabs gleaming in the rain, and street lamps glimmering through the November fog. It was in this London that the Decadents used to meet each other: at the Crown in Cranborne Street where they forgathered after the theatre, rubbing shoulders with prostitutes and confidence men, and, for later lengthier sessions, in the domino room at the Café Royal.

Rothenstein took Max to these new haunts. The domino room made a great impression on him.

'There,' he tells us, 'in that exuberant vista of gilding and crimson velvet set amidst all those opposing mirrors and upholding caryatids, with fumes of tobacco ever rising to the painted and pagan ceiling, and with the hum of presumably cynical conversation broken into so sharply now and again by the clatter of dominoes shuffled on marble tables, I drew a deep breath, and "This indeed," said I to myself, "is life!" '

He went there often after that—and to the Crown too. In those days Oxford allowed an undergraduate in his fourth year to spend one term away from the university if he chose: this autumn Max stayed in London. He got to know the Decadent circle very well; enjoyed their company, observed their idiosyncrasies and judged them with detachment. John Lane himself did not appeal to him, a bustling, pushing little man with little real taste and stingy to his authors. 'That poor fly in the amber of modernity,' Max called him: and also 'Art's middleman the publisher—for of such is the Chamber of Horrors!' And as for Arthur Symons, 'He was perfectly agreeable,' said Max, 'but perfectly uninteresting—like one of those white flannels that nurses give children to wipe their faces on.' He was not enthusiastic about Le Gallienne either, though he admired his thin

MAX BEERBOHM AND WILLIAM ROTHENSTEIN
AT OXFORD

Pre-Raphaelite countenance under its spreading cloud of hair—'like a mixture of Dante and Beatrice', Max noted in his caricature book. On the other hand, when Rothenstein took him to call on Beardsley at his home in Cambridge Street, Pimlico, Max was immediately impressed. The twenty-year-old Aubrey Beardsley was an arresting personality. Already, when no older than Max, he had created a new style of drawing which had made him famous, or, rather, notorious; for many looked on it as the essence of decadent corruption. Already too, alas, he was infected with the consumption which was to kill him within a few years. Max had never seen anyone look so frail. Frail but not languid: the thin angular body and hatchet face, over which the tortoiseshell-coloured hair hung in a heavy fringe to the eyebrows, quivered with the febrile vitality of the consumptive; so also did his restless movements and the quick, hard, staccato accents of his speech. This prevented him, Max thought, from reaching the highest rank of conversationalists; for it meant that his talk oppressed one with a sense of strain. But it was always interesting. Beardsley seemed to have read and seen everything in literature and art: and though he expressed himself with a modish aesthete's extravagance —'Really, how perfectly entrancing!' he would exclaim. 'Really, how perfectly sweet!'—his judgements were founded on what Max described as 'a stony common sense'. Altogether Beardsley was not the man his art might have led one to expect. Though Max admired Beardsley's art, yet he understood why others thought it morbid and distasteful. Beardsley the man he liked unreservedly. He discovered that, in addition to being sensible, he was also generous, affectionate, courteous, and a devoted son to the mother and sister with whom he lived. Beardsley on his side liked Max at once and admired his caricatures. They became great friends. The records of this period of Max's history are full of glimpses of Beardsley; neatly dressed with a butterfly tie, handing round the cakes at his mother's Thursday-afternoon 'at homes': or whiling away the afternoon with Max watching the fencing at Angelo's school in St James's Street: or, again, with Max driving off for an evening's pleasure in a hansom, each of them in the full dandy's uniform of top-hat, white tie and tail-coat: or—a more distressing memory—Beardsley in his own house at a party, of which he had been the life and soul, suddenly falling asleep at the dinner table from sheer exhaustion, 'with his head sunk on his breast,' says Max, 'and his thin face white as the gardenia in his coat'. They often went to the theatre together, too, in particular to patronize the new serious drama. On one such occasion Max for the first time set eyes on Yeats. It was—as he describes it—a memorable experience and not without its comic side.

'In the winter of '93 Aubrey Beardsley had done a poster for the Avenue Theatre and had received two stalls for the first night of Dr Todhunter's play *The Black Cat*; and he had asked me to go with him. Before the main play there was to be a "curtain-raiser"—*The Land of Heart's Desire*. Yeats was not more than a name to us then; nor were we sure that it beseemed us, as men of the world, to hurry over our dinner. We did so, however, and arrived in good time. The beautiful little play was acted in a very nerveless and inaudible manner, casting rather a gloom over the house. When at length the two curtains of the proscenium swept down and met in the middle of the stage, the applause was fainter than it would be nowadays. There were, however, a few sporadic and compatriotic cries for "Author". I saw a slight convulsion of the curtains where they joined each other, and then I saw a long fissure, revealing (as I for a moment supposed) unlit blackness behind the curtains. But lo! there were two streaks of white in the upper portion of this blackness—a white streak of shirt-front, and above that a white streak of face; and I was aware that what I had thought to be insubstantial murk was a dress-suit, with the Author in it. And the streak of Author's face was partly bisected by a lesser black streak, which was a lock of Author's raven hair. . . . It was all very eerie and memorable.'

Max's new friendship had a very important practical result for him. Soon after they had got to know each other, Beardsley suggested they should collaborate over a book. He shared Max's interest in masks: the book he had in mind should be called a 'Comedy of Masques'. His idea was that he himself should do a series of pictures and that Max should write verses to accompany them. This proposal came to nothing. A second project was more fruitful. Some time at the end of the year Beardsley and Henry Harland and John Lane between them conceived the idea of bringing out a new periodical, a quarterly, tastefully produced and devoted to literary and artistic subjects, its name the *Yellow Book*. Harland was to be the literary and Beardsley the artistic editor. Beardsley, supported by Lane, proposed that Max should be asked to contribute. Harland demurred; was it fit, he said, that an undergraduate's name should appear on the same list of contents with those of Henry James and Edmund Gosse? However, Harland let himself be persuaded. Many years later Max, in dramatic form, related the next stage in the story.

'Scene: Cambridge Street, Pimlico.
Persons: Aubrey Beardsley and myself.
A.B.: "How are you? Sit down! Most exciting. John Lane wants to bring out a Quarterly—Writings and Drawings—Henry Harland to be Literary Editor—Me to be Art-Editor. Great fun. . . . " '

Max also thought it would be great fun. But what was he to write about? It has been suggested that he first offered Lane a satirical fantasy about Oscar Wilde—which still survives—called 'A Peep into the Past'. Max denied this and in fact it is incredible. 'A Peep into the Past' is a surprisingly daring production for 1893; not only does it hint unmistakably at the abnormal nature of Oscar's amours, but it does so in a light-hearted tone, and with no suggestion of moral disapproval. Clearly Max's education had been progressing fast during his sojourn in Alfred Douglas's Oxford and Aubrey Beardsley's London. He appears now to be wholly emancipated from Victorian conventional opinion about sexual matters. But he must have realised that a piece like this was unprintable. In fact Max decided to write an essay in praise of cosmetics. He took this light task seriously. Back in Oxford—for by now the Easter Term of 1894 had begun—he spent long hours in the Bodleian Library studying Ovid's *Art of Love* in order to get information about cosmetics in ancient Rome: and once he had got down to writing, he polished each of his sentences till it glittered. In a high state of excitement about the *Yellow Book* and his prospects, he poured himself out to Reggie.

'Aubrey has done a marvellous picture for the *Yellow B*—"L'éducation sentimentale" he calls it. A fat elderly whore in a dressing-gown and huge hat of many feathers is reading from a book to the sweetest imaginable little young girl, who looks before her, with hands clasped behind her back, roguishly winking. Such a strange curved attitude, and she wears a long pinafore of black silk—quite-tight, with the frills of a petticoat showing at the ankles and shoulders. . . . This time tomorrow, I take it, you will be in love, cynic that you are. I am so sorry if you do not like the interest I take in your character, career, conduct, past, future etc. etc. Next time you must talk a lot about me—I shall not be angry. Will R. is going tomorrow to do a heavenly and elaborate pastel of me—sitting straddle-legged over a chair—my hat tilted back—a white carnation and trousers of a very pale gray—it will be in his exhibition. Cannot you imagine the public pausing before it and exclaiming "Is that Max Beerbohm?" and thinking of the paper on Cosmetics?'

It is likely that the public did. But not in friendly tones: the *Yellow Book*, appearing in April, made a sensation all right—a sensation of scandal. For us living in 1964 it is hard to understand why. The *Yellow Book* seems a remarkably innocuous production. It opens with a distinguished and unexceptionable story by Henry James: other contributors include Lord Leighton, President of the Royal Academy, and Arthur Benson, a well-known Eton schoolmaster, both official and recognized guardians of respectability, and others like William Watson who were on the highroad to becoming so. For the rest, except for an insipid little poem by Arthur Symons, referring in veiled terms to an encounter with a prostitute, there is nothing remotely shocking in subject. The general tone is pale, mild and refined.

However, the reviewers did not think so. 'A combination of English rowdiness with French lubricity,' thundered *The Times*: while the *Westminster Gazette* called agitatedly for 'an act of parliament to make this kind of thing illegal'. For some reason professional humorists found the *Yellow Book* especially disturbing. *Punch* attacked it week after week: Barry Pain, famous as a creator of popular Cockney characters, opined darkly that the Café Royal, where the contributors were said to meet, would be 'the better for a whiff of grapeshot'. The critics objected especially to three items in the *Yellow Book*: Symons's poem, Beardsley's drawings and Max's essay. One can just understand why they disapproved of the first two. Symons's effort did, after all, deal with a forbidden subject, however ineffectively; and Beardsley's drawings, though discreet for him—for the real subject of 'L'éducation sentimentale' is not made clear—did exhale a disquietingly 'decadent' smell. But what in the world upset them so much about Max's little piece? 'A Defence of Cosmetics' is the most frivolous of trifles; an essay in light-hearted paradox in which Max preaches the superiority of artifice to nature in a manner that, half-mocking, half-delighted, exploits the various dandyish affectations of style cultivated by the aesthetic writers of the day.

'Loveliness shall sit at the toilet,' runs a typical passage, 'watching her oval face in the oval mirror. Her smooth fingers shall flit among the paints and powder, to tip and mingle them, catch up a pencil, clasp a phial, and what not and what *not*, until the mask of vermeil tinct has been laid aptly, the enamel quite hardened. And, heavens, how she will charm us and ensorcel our eyes! Positively rouge will rob us for a time of all our reason; we shall go mad over masks.'

Punch drew the line at this kind of thing. Prose was not an adequate vehicle to express its scorn and indignation; it felt impelled to burst into verse.

ARS COSMETICA
How would the little busy bore
Improve on Nature's dower,
And praise a painted Laïs more
Than maidens in their flower!
How deftly he dabs on his grease,
How neatly spreads his wax;
And finds in dirty aids like these
The charm that Nature lacks.
In barber-born, cosmetic skill,
'Art' would be busy too;
And folly finds some business still
For popinjays to do!

Such an effusion as this shows us how very earnest the nineteenth century was. Its author—and Max's other critics too—could not conceive that he did not mean what he said: they thought he was seriously attempting to undermine man's natural reverence for God's handiwork. The fact that he did it flippantly—and with all sorts of rococo airs and graces disgusting in a young Englishman—only made his conduct worse. Did the shameless youth reverence nothing, not even the complexions of his sweethearts and sisters? If they had known it, Max entirely agreed with them so far as his own sweet-heart and sisters were concerned. Cissey had appealed to him largely because she had appeared on the stage without make-up; and, as he subsequently explained, he would have been outraged if Constance or Agnes had taken to rouge. Only the *demi-monde* wore rouge. Besides, he thought the natural complexion of the English girl particularly pretty.

'It was a delicate rose pink, don't you know,' he said, talking of the subject many years later, 'and rouge would only have blemished it. In those days, the houses were very irregularly heated; . . . The ladies moved from room to room, and their complexions had to guess the next temperature they would encounter. It was this act of guessing that kept their complexions suspended, don't you know, between the lovely pink, the lovely rose.'

All the same, he did not mind being attacked. Never at any time in his life did Max take much heed of hostile criticism. He was at once too confident and too lacking in vanity to pay attention to other people's opinion. Moreover, at twenty-two, he enjoyed battle. He was at an age that likes making a sensation, the more shocking the better. On 25 April he wrote gaily to Reggie: 'Like Meredith or Keats or any great striker of new notes, I am rejected at first. But so long as I attract notice I am happy.' In later years too he enjoyed relating this story of the '*succès de fiasco*' with which he said his literary career had opened. 'As far as anyone in literature can be lynched, I was,' he would say with reminiscent pleasure. He answered his critics in an open letter published in the July issue of the *Yellow Book*. The manner of this letter is admirable; good-humouredly ruthless and genially impudent. 'It is a pity,' he says, 'that critics should show so little sympathy with writers, and curious when we consider that most of them have tried to be writers themselves once.' His actual line of argument, it must be admitted, is disingenuous. For, while he begins by explaining that the whole thing was an ironical burlesque of the extravagances of the new writers and mocks his critics for not realizing this, he goes on to present himself as a champion of these same new writers and attacks the critics for their obscurantist inability to appreciate original types of genius like Ibsen or Zola or—by implication—himself. Both these lines of defence are tenable; but they are not consistent with each other. Max's essay cannot be at once a burlesque of the modern movement and an example of it. In truth, his own attitude was ambiguous. No doubt he was burlesquing the aesthetic style: no doubt he did not in reality admire rouged cheeks. On the other hand, in a broader sense, he was against Nature unadorned: he did stand for artifice and civilization and the conscious cultivation of style. The essay itself expresses his ambivalent attitude to his subject: and the manner in which he fuses its two strains into harmony by saturating its whole texture in a light shimmering irony, adds to its complex charm. But, as a matter of fact, he is attempting to make the best of two incompatible intellectual worlds. None of his critics pointed this out. They were, we must presume, too stupid: and the result of the controversy was wholly to Max's advantage. For it launched him. Along with his caricatures, 'A Defence of Cosmetics' made him a known name in literary London.

At a time when he needed to be, too: at the end of the summer he had left Oxford for good. His career there had petered out. For though he had gone back into residence after Christmas in preparation for his final examinations in the summer, he never got down to work for them. The *Yellow Book* had absorbed him too much. After it came out a newspaper reporter called to interview the new genius; he asked him about his studies. 'I have been too much interested in the moderns to have yet had time for the ancients,' explained Max. In the end he quitted Oxford without taking the examinations necessary to obtain his degree.

Up to the end, however, he enjoyed himself there. 'I am very happy as always,' he wrote to Reggie during his last months at the university. Too happy to be cautious; Max was in some difficulty about money at this time. More than once he apologetically asks Reggie to make him a small loan; his own money, he says, has gone in roulette debts: and when John Lane proposed putting him up for the Hogarth Club, Max refused on the ground that he could not afford it 'owing to the great sums I have had to disburse in hush money to strangers and bribes to examiners!' Max can never be said to have sowed wild oats in the full sense of the phrase; but the nearest he ever got to doing so was in 1894. His innate prudence was temporarily weakened by the company he kept.

Meanwhile, his new-won reputation encouraged him to make his career as a writer and caricaturist. Max did not fancy the idea of a

regular profession. As a young man he had toyed for a short time
with the idea of going to the Bar. It would not have suited him and
his friends told him so. One night when he was staying with Herbert
at Hampstead he brought the subject up. 'Ah . . . the Bar. You at the
Bar,' said Herbert. 'I should have thought you had better be a sort
of writer and then perhaps,' he added, 'drift into diplomacy.' Herbert mentioned diplomacy, Max thought, merely out of tact. He
did not want to give the impression that he thought Max incapable
of success in an established profession. But he genuinely believed he
should be a 'sort of writer'. It was the right phrase; for Max was not
cut out to be every sort of writer. Solely and wholly an artist, he
could fulfil himself only if he took his time; choosing exactly the
subject that suited him and then subjecting it to a long process of
polishing and rewriting. He was too fastidious and also too lazy to
set up as a thorough-going professional wage-earner either by his
pen or his pencil. Luckily he did not have to. There was enough un-
earned income in the Beerbohm home for Max to live there without having to add to it himself. He had the good luck to be able to
work at what he wanted in the way he wanted. But only if he was
strictly economical: Mr Beerbohm's death had left the family much
poorer than before.

Accordingly he settled down to a leisurely life as freelance writer
and caricaturist. He did more caricatures than writing, for he found
the work less of an effort. During 1894 and 1895 he published
drawings in *The Sketch*, the *Pall Mall Budget*, *Pick-Me-Up*, and *The
Strand* magazine. He also did some odd pieces of journalism, notably
and unexpectedly an interview with C. B. Fry, the famous cricketer.
His important literary work, however, was done for the *Yellow
Book*: an ironical rehabilitation of George IV for the autumn number
of 1894, and for the spring number of 1895 a playful re-creation of
social and literary London fifteen years earlier entitled '1880'. Both,
like 'A Defence of Cosmetics', are examples of his characteristic
type of occasional essay, at once pretty and satirical. They are also
the first of Max's works in which he reveals his imaginative sense of
the past. Max loved to turn away from the present to contemplate a
former age. Past ages were tranquil and completed; so that they
could not be a cause of worry or guilt. 'One isn't responsible for the
past,' he said; and again, 'If one could only look on the present as
an advance copy of the past!' Besides, Time, the great editor, had

been at work on past ages to give them an aesthetic charm. 'A past age has been filtered, it has style,' Max said. Not that all previous ages appealed to him. On the contrary, his sense of the past was restricted; for it did not extend further back than the eighteenth century. But he had an acute perception of the elements giving characteristic flavour to the different phases of the nineteenth century, especially the Regency and the 'seventies and 'eighties. This perception inspired the two new contributions to the *Yellow Book*: and though *Punch* again attacked them both—*Punch* was a confirmed enemy of 'Max Merebohm' and 'The Studious Beerbohmax' as it liked humorously to nickname Max—they consolidated and increased his literary reputation. By Christmas 1894 Max was as well known a figure as Aubrey Beardsley himself.

The Sketch, a fashionable magazine, devoted a special article to an interview with him. His interviewer was Mrs Leverson, the wife of a successful businessman and herself well known as a hostess, and friend of the Aesthetes and Decadents in general, and in particular of Oscar, who enjoyed her conversation and called her the Sphinx. She called on Max at his home and, after noting appreciatively his youth, his elegant frock-coat and his gentle musical voice, asked him if he intended to devote himself to literature.

'No,' said Max, 'I intend to draw as well—always caricatures. You may have seen my series in *Pick-Me-Up* and the *Pall Mall Budget*. One or two of those drawings have been thought rather cruel, I believe. I can't understand how anyone can resent a mere exaggeration of feature. The caricaturist simply passes his subject through a certain grotesque convention. That the result is not a classically beautiful figure proves nothing about the personal appearance of the subject. There is no such thing as a good or bad subject for caricature. To the true caricaturist Adonis or Punchinello is equally good game. I never pretend that my caricatures are meant for portraits. And I do not think that the men themselves whom I have drawn have ever been offended.'

'Perhaps their wives have been?' said Mrs Leverson, and went on to question him about his essays on cosmetics and George IV and the attacks that had been made upon them. Max took his accustomed line about the cosmetics essay:

'My article on "Cosmetics" was a very good joke, but—I thought when I wrote it—rather obvious. I was surprised the critics did not see it at once. It is not often a new writer has to complain of being taken too seriously. "George IV" was received in a far more reasonable manner. My point of view was more nearly understood. I meant all I said about George, but I did not choose to express myself quite seriously. To treat history as a means of showing one's own cleverness may be rather rough on history, but it has been done by the best historians, from Herodotus to Froude and myself. Some of my "George" was false, and much was flippant; but why should a writer sit down to be systematically serious, or else conscientiously comic. Style should be oscillant.'

'Oscillant?' said Mrs Leverson. 'Is that one of your queer words, of which we have heard so much? Do you intend to abandon them, as an affectation?'

'Certainly not. They are not affected. At times there is no word in the English dictionary by which I can express my shade of meaning. I try to think of a French, or Latin, or Greek one. If I can't, then I invent a word—such as "pop-limbo" or "bauble-tit"—often a compound of some well-known English word with an affix or prefix to point its significance. Sometimes I invent a word merely because the cadence of a sentence demands it.'

In conclusion, Ada Leverson asked Max what he was writing at the time. He said:

'I am doing some work for the new *Saturday Review*, and I am in treaty with a publisher to produce a little book of studies and essays. At this moment I am writing a treatise upon "The Brothers of Great Men", including a series of psychological sketches of Mr Willie Wilde, Mr Austen Chamberlain, and others.'

'You are a brother of Mr Beerbohm Tree, I believe?' interposed Mrs Leverson.

'Yes,' said Max, 'he is coming into the series!'

Ada Leverson writes as if after meeting Max for the first time. But in fact, she had been a particular friend of his ever since the summer. She was a small, soft-voiced woman, with her own odd turn of wit and a taste for the exotic and unconventional. Max and she took to one another at once. Within a few minutes of their meeting, there had sprung up between them a light, romantic flirtation, which looked to some people as if it might warm into something more. As it was, it meant a relationship with a real woman, not a fancy for a daydream figure like Cissey Loftus; and so far it was a step forward in Max's sentimental education.

He enjoyed his success and also the money it helped him to earn. He did not get much from the articles and the caricatures, but it helped to pay for his modest pleasures. For they were modest. From now till the end of his days Max tried carefully to live within his income. Soon his life had fallen into a pattern which it was to maintain for the next ten years. His family were now living in Hyde Park Place. His room was at the top of the house with a pretty view over the park. Its decoration reproduced his room in Merton Street: he had it papered in blue and hung with his own drawings and Pellegrini prints. Most of his day was spent there drawing and writing. When evening came he dressed himself with leisurely care and—unless he was invited out—sallied forth after dinner to a music hall or to meet his friends over a cup of coffee at the Café Royal. Now and again he stood himself a well-chosen but inexpensive dinner at Solferino's restaurant. Otherwise his chief expenses were telegrams —they only cost sixpence and he hated writing letters—and hansom cabs—he did not like getting his clothes wet—and the clothes themselves. He had not many of these and he ironed and pressed them himself. They were carefully chosen, however, and aspired to an individual elegance. We hear talk of his gleaming white collars, high even for the period, of a claret-coloured dress suit, a tasselled ivory-handled cane and an overcoat of his own design, very long and fastening with one minute button.

Thus beautifully attired, Max made his entry into London social life. As at Oxford, he enjoyed this: as at Oxford, he did not confine himself to one set. His name crops up in the records of diverse groups. There was a good deal of social life going on at home. Mrs Beerbohm kept open house at luncheon-time, though, as Constance was always nervously pointing out to her, she could not afford such extravagance. Max also took part in Herbert's social life at his theatre, his home, at supper parties at his club. We hear of him also at gatherings of the *Yellow Book* set; with the Decadents at the Crown and Café Royal, with Beardsley at his home in Cambridge Street and at parties given by the editor, Henry Harland, in his house in Cromwell Road. Here the lady and gentlemen contributors

'Some Persons of "the Nineties" little imagining, despite their Proper Pride and Orname
Aspect, how much they will interest Mr Holbrook Jackson and Mr Osbert Burd
(Jackson and Burdett had both recently written books on the 'Nineties.)

From left to right
Back Row Richard Le Gallienne, W. R. Sickert, George Moore, John Davidson,
Oscar Wilde, W. B. Yeats.
Front Row Arthur Symons, Henry Harland, Charles Conder, William
Rothenstein, Max Beerbohm, Aubrey Beardsley.

of the *Yellow Book* were invited to meet each other. Harland was a cosmopolitan, highly artistic American, with a small beard and an expansive manner: 'Darling of my heart, child of my editing!' he would exclaim, rushing forward with outstretched hands to greet a young female protégé. The atmosphere of his home was cultured and mildly bohemian. In the intervals of exchanging progressive opinions, the guests would crowd into the kitchen to help cook an omelet, or fall silent while Mrs Harland sang a song in French. Trained at home to make conversation and readily responsive to the pleasures of feminine society, Max made a good impression on the lady contributors of the *Yellow Book*. 'One felt more at home with him than with the other men there,' said Miss Netta Syrett; and Miss Ella Hepworth Dixon grew rapturous as she recalled 'his beautiful manners, long curling eyelashes, the most marvellous clothes and a habit of offering subtle compliments to women'.

Introduced by the indefatigable Rothenstein, Max also spent evenings among the painters of Chelsea, and made friends with Sickert, Shannon and Ricketts. He also continued to frequent the Wilde circle: Oscar himself, Robbie Ross and Alfred Douglas. 'Oscar and Bosie lunched with me today,' he writes to Reggie, soon after coming down from Oxford, 'and were very charming. Oscar was just in the mood that I like him—very 1880 and, withal, brimful of intellectual theories and anecdotes of dear Lady Dorothy Nevill and other whores. Bosie came in a Homburg hat—dove-coloured—and wearing a very sweet present from you in his shirt-cuffs.' Reggie himself he saw more regularly. The Beerbohm ladies liked him almost as much as Max did and he was often at their home. Some time in the summer of 1894 he introduced Max to a young man called Robert Hichens, a music critic and journalist and destined later to become a successful popular novelist. He was a plump, genial-looking youth, of simple straightforward manners, who enjoyed a good game of golf and a good dinner after it. He was also quick and clever and immediately appreciated Max. Max—who never minded simplicity and enjoyed being appreciated as much as most people—responded. Hichens—or 'Crotchet', as Max nicknamed him in reference to his musical activities—became, if not a close friend, a boon companion with whom he was pleased to dine from time to time and sometimes to go off with for a weekend holiday at the seaside. Crotchet found Max's idiosyncrasies delightful and surprising. Never had he seen anyone so calm, so incapable of hurrying or bustling! Max's humour, he noted, was also unhurried; the jokes exploded like a time-bomb after a leisurely, artful preparation.

One day he said to Hichens, 'Do you think, Crotchet, that a word can be beautiful, just one word?'

'Yes,' Hichens said. 'I can think of several words that seem to me beautiful.'

'Ah?'

A pause.

'Then tell me, do you think the word "ermine" is a beautiful word?'

'Yes,' Hichens said. 'I like the sound of it very much.'

'Ah?'

Another pause.

'And do you think "verm in" is a beautiful word?'

Another time Max said to him:

'My brother, Herbert, spoke of you to me the other day.' Naturally enough, Hichens asked what he had said.

'He said you were like me.'

'That's a compliment,' Hichens said. 'But in what way am I like you?'

'Herbert says because in you, as in me, there's more brain than heart, and an entire absence of passion.'

'Do you think your brother is a good judge of character?'

'I leave the decision about that to you,' Max replied.

Early in their acquaintance Hichens showed Max a book he had written called *The Green Carnation*. It was a skit on aestheticism and its chief characters were drawn from Oscar Wilde and Alfred Douglas, who he had met abroad. Max found it very entertaining and went through it carefully with the author. It appeared in September and made a sensation—also a scandal. For it touched on what had become a scandalous topic. The clouds were gathering above Oscar's head and he was rapidly acquiring an extremely sinister reputation, mainly on account of his association with Alfred Douglas. Max felt the repercussions of this. It was becoming bad for a young man's good name to be a member of the Wilde circle. In consequence Max's friends and relations were growing worried. Already, a year before, Rothenstein, who, beneath his bohemian and cosmopolitan surface, retained a foundation of solid Bradford prudence, warned Max against being seen too much in Alfred Douglas's company. Max paid little attention to all this. Though discreet, he was also basically independent. The fact that he lived so much in his own universe meant that he paid little attention to other people's opinions. 'I saw Bosie Douglas today and am dining with him to-night,' he wrote to Rothenstein. 'Aren't you, dear strait-laced timid wonderful Will, very shocked?'

Max was the more indifferent to public opinion because he realized, as Rothenstein perhaps could not, that his association with Wilde and his friends was no danger to him, though it might be bad for his reputation. Max had the confidence of his conscious innocence. It was not that he was ignorant of the sexual tastes of the Wilde circle. For they did not hide them from him. They talked of them in a jargon of their own, spoke of them as 'the love that dares not tell its name' and of heterosexuals as 'mulierasts' as distinguished from homosexuals who were paederasts. Max, it will be noted, when he is writing to members of the group, uses these terms. This is evidence they talked freely in his presence. But though he showed no moral disapproval of homosexuality, he was not disposed to it himself: on the contrary, he looked on it as a great misfortune to be avoided if possible. This appears in a letter he wrote to Ross about Reggie in the spring of 1895. Max, remembering Miss Cumberlege, was convinced that Reggie could love a woman; but he noticed that lately his affections seemed to be turning towards his own sex and he suspected this was due to the influence of Ross and Alfred Douglas. He therefore wrote to Ross asking him to refrain from exerting this influence.

'This is one page to hope you are happy and well, and to *implore* you not to look after Reggie Turner while I am away. He is very weak and you, if I remember rightly, are very wicked. Also you are a delightful person to be with and just calculated to lead poor Reg astray without intention. Do not see too much of him. I wish he could get into a good ecclesiastical set and become good again, as I am sure he very soon would. Also keep Bosie away from him (give my love to Bosie). Bosie is more fatal to Reg than you—if anything.

All this is quite serious. I really think Reg is at rather a crucial point of his career—and should hate to see him fall an entire victim to the love that dares not tell its name. You are a person of far stronger character and it doesn't affect you in the way that it would affect him.'

This is a very interesting letter; apart from what it tells us about Max's view of homosexuality, it is a remarkably assured and skilful document for a young man of twenty-three. Max writes in a light and friendly tone; he is obviously anxious not to put Ross off by appearing prudish. But neither is he hesitant. Under a surface lightness he makes clear a genuine concern. He was very fond of Reggie. When Max was fond, he felt responsible.

PART II

CHAPTER FOUR

'The Works of Max Beerbohm'

(1)

THE year 1895 was to be a landmark in Max's life. For it saw the end of its formative phase. He cannot be said to have grown up then; Max never completely grew up. But in 1895 he did stop developing; it was then that his character and personality took a lasting shape.

The process began in January. One morning in that month, young Mr Sydney Cockerell, arriving at a London railway station to see his daughter off to America, noticed a beautifully dressed young man, standing absent-mindedly on the platform, apparently bound on the same journey. It was Max. Herbert was taking his company on a six weeks' tour of America and Max was accompanying him as his private secretary. He shared a cabin with an elderly actor called Lionel Brough. He found this trying. The sea was rough; Max was sick, Brough was not.

'I only wish,' Max said, 'he had not been so perfectly, so exuberantly good a sailor as he was. He and I shared a cabin. The sea was very stormy indeed. For three days and nights I remained in my berth. I preferred the nights to the days, for then Brough was sound asleep in the berth beneath me, and even the sight of Brough's saucy little yachting-cap, swaying to and fro on its peg whenever I opened my eyes to the dim lamp-light, was preferable to the knowledge that Brough himself might at any moment come breezily in at the door with that same cap surmounting his fresh pink face and his crisp silver hair. He was the kindest of men, and was always coming down from the smoking-room, laden with the scent of that meeting-place, to cheer me up for a few minutes. He was the bluffest of Yorkshiremen, and the best of professional *raconteurs*, and he was always asking me: "Have yer heard the one about the parson's bullfinch?" or "Have yer heard the one about the coal-heaver's ticket to Blackpool?" or "Have yer heard the one about the old lady who didn't like shrimps?" Also, he wore in his scarf a large and unusual pin which I think he thought might act as a talisman for me against the sea-sickness. He had recently appeared in some "command" performance at Windsor, and "This," he would tell me, "is the pin Her Gracious Majesty gave me"; but somehow it always made me feel worse.'

By the end of the voyage Max was recovered and able to give full attention to the first impressions made on him by New York. These were not pleasant.

'At first I hated it,' he told Ross—'the dreadful passage, with the sea like a lake of glass and the vessel pitching like Hell and the disembarking at the hideous harbour with the statue of Vulgarity towering over us. It was awful.

I told a reporter that I did not like the statue and said to him "It must come down." '

And to his mother:

'The town appeared picturesque with rough-paven streets—as we drove from the dock—quite the Nuremberg of the West. As we neared Fifth Avenue, it shewed itself in its real, hideous colours. Imagine rows of streets—all numbered not named—in which the infinitely lowest house is higher than Hankey's Folly—and imagine railways running along on a level with the entresol and imagine shriekings and whistlings and clatter of horses' hoofs over the cobbles. It is a terrible, horrible place—the people are not so bad.'

This was an understatement. The people were so far from being bad that in a day or two they had succeeded in persuading him to like New York very much indeed. The party stayed at the luxurious Waldorf Hotel and were entertained splendidly every hour of the day by millionaires, opera singers, critics. When he was not being entertained Max sat in the Waldorf and amusedly watched the other guests. 'The Waldorf is an interesting place,' he told his mother, 'so you see there is a great deal to do. . . . I look very well dressed.' His only trouble was the secretarial work. It consisted mainly of answering Herbert's letters for him. Max wrote and rewrote them as carefully as if they were contributions to the *Yellow Book*, with the result that he got hopelessly behindhand. After two or three weeks Herbert engaged another secretary. However, he generously insisted on Max retaining his salary. Max now devoted his free time to his own work. With considerable success; he wrote two new essays which were bought by *Vanity Fair* and executed and sold a number of drawings. He became well enough known for an enterprising impresario to suggest that he should give some lectures. Max shrank from the thought of such an ordeal but felt it awkward to refuse. Instead he proposed conditions. He would give the lectures, he said, if they could take place in an open space called the Castle Garden and if the audience could be limited to twelve persons. The impresario withdrew his offer. Max had saved himself: but he had learnt that success brought problems with it. All the same it was delightful. Max's spirits rose.

'I have a charming time here', he told Reggie—'New York has given itself to me like a flower. Tomorrow I must throw away the petals for we start to Chicago which everyone says is quite a beastly place. . . . I have no time to write more lest I should lapse into brilliancy— I must keep my brilliancy for this beautiful town. I am certainly going to settle here for some years when we have finished the tour— you can come out and see me, if you really miss me.'

For the time being he had to put off these agreeable plans. During the six weeks of Herbert's tour in the United States he had arranged to visit not only Chicago but Philadelphia, Boston, Washington and Baltimore. Chicago did not turn out to be so dreadful as Max had feared. Both Herbert and he came in for a great deal of flattering attention and some broadening experiences as well.

'Last night Herbert gave a large supper to the critics—afterwards Herbert and I and Brough were taken to see a town-ball—a scene of vast and hideous debauchery. Also we visited certain houses where black-women danced naked to the sound of the piano—and one where French women gambolled with one another in a room cushioned with blue silk, just as the bells began ringing for early mass. I did not get to bed till six, just as the sun began his daily task of painting and gilding.'

Boston was the scene of more decorous pleasures. Max visited Harvard with Herbert, who recited some Shakespeare there. Max noted with interest that all the undergraduates parted their hair in the middle. He also gathered some impressions of American youth which were to be useful to him as an author later. It was at Harvard that he met a youth who was to be model for Abimelech Oover, the Rhodes scholar in *Zuleika Dobson*. In Baltimore he encountered another English author: Rudyard Kipling came behind the scenes to call on Herbert and was introduced to Max. 'You are Max Beerbohm!' he said in some astonishment. 'So young to have a style!' It was the only time the two met. Max was to employ his style too effectively against Kipling for either to wish to renew the experience later.

The company spent a short time in New York before sailing for England. One evening Herbert sent Max to report on a successful play called *Trilby* in case Herbert might want to buy it for England. Max said the play was nonsense and certain to fail in London. Herbert, not wholly convinced, went himself to see *Trilby* the night before he left. He disagreed with Max and bought the play. Produced later in the year in London, it was the greatest success of his lifetime. The story illustrates revealingly the difference between the two brothers. For they were very different, and now that Max was grown-up, this had begun to show. No longer the schoolboy who had hung round the Haymarket Theatre lost in undiscriminating admiration, he was now a sophisticated, fastidious, ironical young man, out of sympathy with the crude and the popular, and with 'advanced' tastes in literary and artistic matters. Not so Herbert: he found the new Max a little formidable. Max realized this and was embarrassed by it. Neither felt completely at ease in the other's company, and all the more because they had been so much at ease in the past. 'You seem to live in a state of armed neutrality with each other,' said a friend. 'No,' said Max, 'terrified love.' This was a fair enough description; for the brothers were still very fond of each other, so that their new-found sense of a gulf between them in matters of taste produced in both a feeling of frustration and tension. However, this was eased by the fact that they could still amuse each other. A common taste in humour is the strongest of bonds; and holds when others are broken. Herbert and Max relaxed to enjoy each other's jokes, especially nonsensical jokes. 'Can you think of a powerful curtain line to end a scene?' Herbert asked Max on one occasion. 'What about this,' replied Max, ' "I am leaving for the Thirty Years War!" ' Herbert was much entertained. On another occasion he said to Max, 'I can stand any amount of flattery—if it is only fulsome enough!' 'Oh,' Max returned, 'I make no conditions of any sort.'

Seeing America and travelling with a theatrical company could not but broaden Max's experience of life. At the same time it was being deepened by another kind of event. During the night journey to Chicago, Max, walking through the portion of the train reserved for Tree's company, noticed two pretty girls in their nightgowns who were looking at him from between the curtains of an upper berth. One of them—she was dark and Irish-looking—gave him an apple: this led to conversation. Max found Miss Grace Conover, for this turned out to be her name, very pleasant in a genial outspoken way: she also looked extremely attractive in her nightgown. No doubt her voice and manner were what his mother and sisters would consider 'common'. But Max was exhilarated rather than not by commonness, when it was combined with friendliness and a pretty face. This is not unusual among hyper-refined males. It gives them the sense of an earthy vitality in which they themselves are deficient.

The acquaintance, so gaily begun, quickly warmed up to full-blooded flirtation. During the rest of the tour Max and Grace Conover spent their spare time alone together; at theatres and restaurants, and driving round the town hand clasped in hand. The flirtation involved a good deal of teasing. Max professed to think Grace Conover a very bad actress. He even made her cry by assuring her that she was nicknamed 'Kill-scene Conover' on the ground that she killed every scene in which she took part. The name stuck; poor Miss Conover was 'Kilseen' to Max and his friends for the rest of his days. She on her side enjoyed rallying Max on what she considered his faults of manner.

'I am,' he told Reggie, '(not a word to dear Mrs Leverson) in love with a certain Miss Conover in my brother's company—a dark Irish girl of twenty, very blunt and rude, who hates affectation.'

He added that he thought she rather liked him. Certainly he liked her—enough to propose to her within twenty-four hours of their meeting. She refused to believe he meant it seriously; he was not sure himself.

'I see Miss Conover perpetually and have asked her to be my wife—but as we have always been upon terms of chaff—she is only just

GRACE CONOVER

beginning to realize that I am in earnest—which perhaps I am not—who knows?'

This did not stop him proposing to her again and fairly often. In the end she did take him seriously. For when the company got back to England in the spring, Max and Kilseen were—if not officially engaged—yet openly committed to each other. They were to remain so for the next six years.

What exactly they felt about each other is obscure. Here we come up against an occupational hazard of biographers—lack of information. Kilseen herself is a shadowy figure; we know so little about her—only a few brief lines of description in Max's letters to Reggie, some references in the correspondence of his friends and family, and two or three of her own letters written at a later period. These last leave a very likeable impression. The daughter of an Irish immigrant to the United States and a Danish mother, and presumably forced from early years to fend for herself in a bohemian society, she had probably had little chance to acquire refinement of voice and manner. But her feelings were far from unrefined: she shows herself modest, generous-minded and quick to sympathize with other people's point of view. Nor had her bohemian life led to low moral standards. Back in England, Max, we notice, is careful not to introduce Kilseen to people she might disapprove of. Kilseen's disapproval was a factor he had learnt to reckon with.

This indicates that the relationship was one that they both took seriously. Was it love? On her side the answer was, yes: she admitted it. Max's feelings were more obscure. That he was passionately in love is unlikely in the light of subsequent events. But he cared enough to see her very often and to feel a responsibility for her. She represented yet another step in his heart's education: his relationship with her was an advance beyond anything he had had with a woman before. Not a daydream like Cissey Loftus or an occasional social pleasure like Ada Leverson, Kilseen was an intimate friend who attracted him as a woman and in whose company he was happy to spend a great deal of time.

Meanwhile, back in London the world in which he had spent much of the last four years was collapsing in dreadful ruin. The Oscar Wilde scandal had broken and the first of his trials was about to begin. Max had read the news in the American papers.

'Poor, poor Oscar!' he wrote off to Reggie. 'How very sad it is. I cannot bear to think of all that must have happened—the whisperings and the hastenings hither and thither—before he could have been seduced into Marlborough Street. I suppose he was exasperated too much, not to take action. I am sorry he has not got George Lewis, wonder if Bosie has returned, what evidence will be brought in for the defence—and so forth. It is awful not to be upon the spot. Do let me hear *real long* details—*full accounts*. Do please not mind writing many pages—I am parched for news—the head-lines are so short here and so relentless. "Gives Oscar what-for." "The Pretty Poet and the Mocking Marquis." "Mrs Wilde sticks to him." etc. etc.—quite dreadful. Do not, I beg you, get mixed up in the scandal.'

It is characteristic of Max to warn Reggie not to involve himself more than he could help in Oscar's troubles, for fear presumably of the harm it might do his reputation. Characteristically, too, he was not concerned about his own reputation. Max's attitude to the Oscar Wilde drama is typical of himself; and also very unlike that of most people at that time. The story of Oscar's downfall, looked at in the cold light of subsequent history, is a mean and miserable tale of weakness and sordid folly on Oscar's part, of hypocrisy and sordid spite on that of his enemies. Yet everyone concerned, and the rest of England too, combined to inflate it to the proportions of a dark and tremendous tragedy. His enemies execrated him as a high priest of nameless evil; whilst his few friends set him up as a heroic martyr. Meanwhile, respectable England reacted to the whole story with a preposterous and hysterical horror. George Alexander had Oscar's name obliterated from the posters outside the theatre where *The Importance of Being Earnest* was being performed; and large numbers of unathletic males joined cricket clubs in order to safeguard their reputation for morality. Apparently they laboured under the strange and mistaken impression that cricket and homosexuality were incompatible.

Max—it was the advantage of his detachment—was impervious to these waves of feeling. There was no question of his deserting Oscar: on the contrary, since he was a friend, he never questioned that he should rally to his side. He attended his trial to give him moral support; took part in a deputation to Scotland Yard to ask that Oscar's lot should be alleviated while he was in prison—it gave him quite a shock to see one of his own caricatures of Oscar hanging on the walls of the inspector's room as if to be used in evidence against him—and in the interval between the second and third trials, dined at the Leversons' to meet Oscar, now released on bail and staying there. All his life Max was to remember Oscar coming down depressed, and then reviving under the impulse of wine and friendship to sparkle and rhapsodize in his old best form. Nor did Max's sympathy stop with the trial. We find him writing to Ross just before Oscar was released to suggest some plan by which he could get out of England as secretly and comfortably as possible. When he did come out, Max sent him a selection of books he thought he might enjoy, and also his own *Happy Hypocrite* with a friendly inscription.

All the same he kept his head. Coolly and curiously he observed the scene of the trial.

'I remember the judge,' he related years later, 'with his customary bouquet of herbs on the bench before him, the sheriff, the counsel, the spectators in the gallery and the police; and I remember thinking that here were all these people gathered together against the man in the dock.'

Nor was Max blinded by partisanship. He considered that Gill, the prosecuting counsel, let Oscar down very lightly in his cross-examination: and he realized that it was good of Leverson to receive Oscar in his house considering the harm it might do to his social position. Moreover, Max's whole tone when talking of the affair—in strong contrast to that of his countrymen in general—was normal, unshocked, even at moments amused.

'My dearest Reg,
    I am sorry I have not written before. Ever since I arrived I have been all day at the Old Bailey and dining out in the evening—and coming home very tired. Please forgive me—Oscar has been quite superb. His speech about the Love that dares not tell its name was simply wonderful—and carried the whole court right away—quite a tremendous burst of applause. Here was this man—who had been for a month in prison and loaded with insults and crushed and buffeted, perfectly self-possessed, dominating the Old Bailey with his fine presence and musical voice. He has never had so great a

triumph, I am sure, as when the gallery burst into applause—I am sure it affected the gallery. . . . Hoscar [sic] stood very upright when he was brought up to hear the verdict and looked most leonine and sphinx-like. . . . Hoscar is thinner and consequently fine to look at. Willie has been extracting fivers from Humphreys. It was horrible leaving the court day after day and having to pass through a knot of renters[1] (the younger Parker wearing Her Majesty's uniform— another form of female attire) who were allowed to hang around after giving their evidence and to wink at likely persons. Trelawny is raising money for the conduct of the case—Leverson has done a great deal. Clarke and Humphreys are going to take no fees. . . . Rothenstein is most sympathetic and goes about the minor clubs insulting everyone who does not happen to be clamouring for Hoscar's instant release.

I saw Bosie the night before his departure—he seemed to have lost his nerve. The scene that evening at the Leversons was quite absurd. An awful New Woman in a divided skirt (introduced by Bosie) writing a pamphlet at Mrs Leverson's writing-table with the aid of several whiskey-and-sodas: her brother—a gaunt man with prominent cheek-bones from Toynbee Hall who kept reiterating that "these things must be approached through first principles and through first principles alone!" two other New Women who subsequently explained to Mr Leverson that they were there to keep a strict watch upon New Woman number one, who is not responsible for her actions: Mrs Leverson making flippant remarks about messenger-boys in a faint undertone to Bosie who was ashen-pale and thought the pamphlet (which was the most awful drivel) admirable—and Mr Leverson explaining to me that he allowed his house to be used for these purposes not because he approved of "anything unnatural" but by reason of his admiration for Oscar's plays and personality. I myself exquisitely dressed and sympathizing with none.'

Of course Max was the better able to keep his head because by now he took a very detached and objective view of the chief actor in the drama. Though loyalty made him ready to support Oscar when in trouble, and though he admired his courage, he had during the last years grown steadily more conscious of his faults.

[1] Male prostitutes.

His flashier side had come to jar on Max increasingly. 'Poor, Oscar, I saw him the other day from a cab walking with Bosie,' he remarks. 'He looked like one whose soul has swooned in sin and revived vulgar.' Furthermore, in the months preceding his catastrophe Oscar had begun to display some new characteristics even more distasteful to Max.

'But you know,' Max related in later years, 'as Oscar became more and more successful, he became arrogant. He felt himself omnipotent, and he became gross not in body only—he did become that— but in his relations with people. He brushed people aside; he felt he was beyond the ordinary human courtesies that you owe people even if they are, in your opinion, beneath you.'

While the trial was on, we do not find Max criticizing Oscar in this way; he was too sorry for him. But he was well aware of the strain in Oscar of deliberate folly which had landed him in his plight. When he came out of prison, this strain showed itself leading him again and again to throw away his chances of making a new life for himself. Sensible Max was irritated by this. 'I hear that that ass Oscar is under surveillance by the French police,' he writes in 1897. 'I suppose he is playing the giddy goat. Can't someone warn him to be careful?' Yet Max never sounds really censorious of Oscar, let alone hostile to him: even these sentences are said in a tone of exasperated affection. Indeed, for the rest of Oscar's life, Max, though now moving in a very different world, affectionately remembered him. When Oscar died in 1900, Max wrote Reggie a letter.

My dear Reg,

I got your letter this morning, and read it before I read my newspaper—before I knew that poor Oscar really was dead. I am, as you may imagine, very sorry indeed; and am thinking very much about Oscar, who was such an influence and an interest in my life. Will you please lay out a little money for me in flowers for his grave? I will repay you, having (for me) quite a large sum of money in the bank. I hope to be able to write something nice about Oscar in my next article for the *Saturday*. Of course I shall have to ask Hodge, first, whether he has any objection. I think he is the kind of man who will not place any obstacles. In this morning's *Chronicle* there is a rather nice obituary and editorial note.

I suppose really it was better that Oscar should die. If he had lived to be an old man he would have become unhappy. Those whom the gods, etc. And the gods *did* love Oscar, with all his faults.

Please give my sympathy to Bobbie, and tell him how much less happily Oscar might have died.

In great haste,

Yours affectionately

Max.

This letter may stand as the considered expression of what Max had come to feel about the man whose influence had done so much to mould him. On Oscar's character and work his final objective judgement came later—in an article he wrote in 1904 after the publication of *De Profundis*. He still rated him disconcertingly high as a serious writer; he even praised his poetry. But about his character he was more penetrating and less favourable. There was—so it seemed to Max, looking back on it in the light of his mature experience—something basically false in Oscar's vision both of life and of himself.

He never was a real person in contact with realities. He created his poetry, created his philosophy: neither sprang from his own soul, or from his own experience. His ideas were for the sake of ideas, his emotions for the sake of emotions. . . . In *De Profundis* was he at length expressing something that he really and truly felt? . . .

I think no discerning reader can but regard the book as the essentially artistic essay of an artist. Nothing seemed more likely than that Oscar Wilde, smitten down from his rosy-clouded pinnacle, and dragged through the mire, and cast among the flints, would be 'diablement change en route'. Yet lo! he was unchanged. He was still precisely himself. He was still playing with ideas, playing with emotions. 'There is only one thing left for me now,' he writes, 'absolute humility.' And about humility he writes many beautiful and true things. And, doubtless, while he wrote them, he had the sensation of humility. Humble he was not.

Emotion was not seeking outlet: emotion came through its own expression. The artist spoke, and the man obeyed. The attitude was struck, and the heart pulsated to it. Perhaps a Cardinal Archbishop, when he kneels to wash the feet of the beggars, is filled with humility and revels in the experience. Such was Oscar Wilde's humility. It was the luxurious complement of pride. In *De Profundis*, for the most part, he is frankly proud—proud with the natural pride of a man so richly endowed as he, and arrogant with all his old peculiar arrogance. Even 'from the depths' he condescended. Not merely for mankind was he condescending. He enjoyed the greater luxury of condescending to himself. Sometimes the condescension was from his present self to his old self: sometimes from his old self to his present self. Referring to the death of his mother, 'I, once a lord of language,' he says, 'have no words in which to express my anguish and my shame.' Straightway, he proceeds to revel in the survival of that lordship, and refutes in a fine passage his own dramatic plea of impotence. 'She and my father had bequeathed to me a name they had made noble and honoured . . . I had disgraced that name eternally. I had made it a low byword among low people. I had given it to brutes that they might make it brutal, and to fools that they might turn it into folly. What I suffered then and still suffer, is not for pen to write or paper to record.' Yet pen wrote it, and paper recorded it, even so.

(2)

Oscar Wilde's conviction led to the break-up of his circle; and of the Decadent group too. This meant the end of Max's close association with them. It was likely to have declined anyway, for his spare time was now given largely to others and, in particular, to Kilseen. His engagement to her was never publicly announced; but he spoke of it as a fact and introduced her to his family and friends. It has been said that she warned him of the harm it did him to be associated with the Wilde circle and that he kept away from it in consequence. This seems unlikely. For he continued to be on perfectly friendly terms with Ross and the rest. Besides, if he had cared about his reputation, he would have kept away at the time of the trial. The truth was rather that his connection with Kilseen was one of several signs that he had outgrown what may be called his '*Yellow Book* phase'. This had really been the final phase of his undergraduate life. Its audacities and affectations, its friendships and fantasies, were those of an undergraduate: the time for all this was past. The change in him began to show both in the company he kept and in his manner and demeanour. He lost his boy's taste for shocking and showing off; he began to drop his Oxford poses. While retaining his mask, Max subtly altered it to make it appropriate to one no longer a youth but a grown man.

The next phase of his life was to last for many years. Its outward ordering followed in the main the pattern established before he left for America. The Beerbohms changed house once more and were now in Upper Berkeley Street, but Max's room on the top floor exactly reproduced that in his previous home, with the same pictures on the same blue wallpaper. So did the unhurried hours he spent there writing and drawing. During the rest of his day he resumed the old round of music hall, coffee at the Café Royal, dining out, evening parties. In one respect only do we find a change. To the role of artist and man-about-town Max had added that of a lover: his routine was now modified to include time for Kilseen. He dined with her *tête-à-tête* at least once a week, took her about to the theatre and the houses of his friends; and she spent a great deal of time at Upper Berkeley Street. This led to complications. The Beerbohm ladies had welcomed her at first, for they felt she was taking him away from the sinister world of Oscar Wilde. It was especially good for Max's reputation, too, that his name should be coupled with a girl's. So relieved, indeed, were they by all this that in return his mother and sisters were prepared at first to forgive Kilseen her deficiencies of voice and manner. As the noise of the Oscar Wilde scandal died down, however, they began to find it less easy, and Kilseen's voice to make itself heard louder and more grating. Moreover, the Beerbohms considered that they heard it a great deal too often. For Max, delighted to find his fiancée well received by his family, pressed her to come to Upper Berkeley Street as much as possible; with the result that by the autumn she was lunching and dining there every day. Mrs Beerbohm grew restive; she poured out her anxieties to the sympathetic Constance but refused to let her say anything to discourage Kilseen, lest Max should hear of it and take offence. It seems that Kilseen did begin to wonder if she was wanted, for she now took to absenting herself from lunch and appeared only for dinner. 'It is a comfort!' sighed Constance. Not comfort enough for Mrs Beerbohm! She now began lamenting to Constance about Kilseen's continued presence at the dinner table. Poor Constance, she had a lot to bear! Her stepmother's lamentations were not her only trouble; nor Kilseen's the only extra mouth she had to feed. The Beerbohms were much poorer than before; but Mrs Beerbohm, incurably hospitable, insisted on keeping open house at luncheon and dinner every day. 'Beef, claret and brandy fly through the house,' cried Constance, who had to try to balance the accounts and pay the bills. 'It seems such a pity to keep open house when we can't afford it.' To add to her troubles, Herbert's wife, Maud, thoroughly disapproved of Max's entanglement and told Constance that she blamed her for encouraging it, by having Kilseen so much in the house. Agitatedly Constance defended herself.

'I'm not in the least hurt—but I might be by your so totally misjudging me about Miss Conover. You have heard so much but so little about it all, that I quite understand you don't realize it. All I meant was this. Miss C. has shown extremely bad taste in dining here so often, but there have been excuses for her. Mamma has told her many confidences, called her "Kilseen" from the beginning, and has often seemed very fond of her. In the summer Miss C. wrote to ask Aggie if Mamma objected to her coming so often—Aggie wrote as from Mamma she was "always delighted". I asked Aggie if she had written this yesterday. She said *Yes* "words to that effect"— vaguely—Mamma worships Max so. She has never once been able to tell him she doesn't want Miss C. to dine. Nor shown it to him. *He* doesn't know. So when Miss C. has said "Oh, I can't bear coming so often," *he* has said "Oh Mamma likes you to come."

I, whom you think weak enough to befriend her, have been *the only one* to speak to Miss C. openly. I spoke on Saturday—and she has hardly been here since—and was too wretchedly unhappy at realizing we weren't so anxious for her as she thought. Mamma does not know I spoke. Nor Max. If Mamma did in all probability she would think that this might wreck Max's happiness. One day when I complained of her commonness as a wife for Max, Mamma said what absurd notions I had—how snobbish—thank Heaven she and Papa had never given themselves airs, etc. etc. etc.

. . . One has to be so very careful with Mamma or she gets more excited. One must say "Oh! it's a horrid bore. But Miss C. comes here so much less than before"—or "Max won't care for her long" —or something of that sort.

Miss C. is common but she has been a boon at what was a critical time for Max. He was in an unfortunate set, indeed the people he got to know were dangerous friends for him. As it was, it was a thousand pities he was seen with such people—Just at that time Miss C. diverted him from them, and had the courage to tell him that the *rumour* of his being friendly and intimate with them was misunderstood by outsiders, and harming him. As Max is *so good* a boy one didn't want him labelled with impossible people who can hardly be mentioned. . . . I won't say any more about her—I don't want her! And I should be grieved for Max to marry her—I only think there have been certain excuses for her want of delicacy in coming here.'

Maud Tree continued to dislike Kilseen enough to speak slightingly of her one evening in October, when Max was there. The result was as unusual as it was alarming. Max lost his temper.

'My dear Maud,' he wrote to his sister-in-law, 'I do not want to have any formal family-quarrel with you and so please let it be quite privately, as between you and me, when I say that your extraordinary lapse of good-feeling, good-taste and so forth this evening makes it impossible for me to have any further friendship with you.

Perhaps I ought to have expressed this at the time but I was so astounded that I was merely able to go away. However, I am under the influence of no excitement now and this letter is quite deliberate and—as far as a thing can be—final.

Yours
Max.

P.S. There is absolutely nothing more to be said, so I think it will be much better if you leave this letter unanswered. Of course you may say yes to anyone who asks if I am engaged.'

Maud wrote back protesting that a complete break with her would embarrass the family. Max agreed, but otherwise remained implacable.

My dear Maud

Thanks for your letter. I quite understand and appreciate the spirit of it—but you misunderstand me in one thing—I never meant to suggest we should 'see no more' of each other—that would be unpleasant for many people besides myself—and I don't want anyone else to be dragged into a quarrel and have been careful not to give a hint to any of my people and especially not to Miss Conover that you said or that I wrote anything at all last night.

On the other hand, I am afraid it would be absurd for me to pretend that I can—as I would wish—dismiss the whole matter from my mind. If anyone has at any time said anything horrible to me—personally—I have always been ready and anxious to forget it and forgive it as soon as possible—but what you said last night was not directed against me and I feel that if I were to forgive it I could not forgive myself. I am sorry to say this—but of course I feel rather acutely in this matter. . . .

Yours
Max.

These two letters are extremely interesting. They tell us several things about Max. About his temper and about his sensitiveness on a question of honour, for one thing: in general he hated rows and was an adept at saying an awkward thing tactfully—how adroitly, for example, had he suggested to Ross that he should refrain from corrupting Reggie!—but there is no question of adroitness and tact now. Max is too angry; partly because he is very fond of Kilseen, but also because his honour is involved. To speak ill in his presence of the girl to whom he was pledged was an insult to himself: self-respect as well as affection compelled him to burst out in protest.

Presumably the storm blew over; for soon we hear of Max dining and supping with the Trees once more. Kilseen, too, continued to frequent Upper Berkeley Street, not staying to meals quite so often but still helping to make the beef and claret fly. However, the Beerbohm ladies soon found reason to be less anxious. Max showed no signs of intending to marry in the near future. Nor, though he saw Kilseen regularly, did she absorb all his time and attention. During these years his social life steadily expanded and in many directions. We hear of him in artistic circles, theatrical circles, literary circles—it was at this time that he became a member of the Savile Club—fashionable circles, with painters and journalists, dramatists and poets, at formal receptions, at studio riotings, as the guest of Mr and Mrs Kendal, distinguished actors, Mrs Stevens, literary hostess, Walter Sickert, rising painter, and the popular dramatist Henry Arthur Jones. Jones, a vigorous-minded, warm-hearted, pugnacious man, often dressed in riding-breeches, became a real friend. Max enjoyed his society as he did that of Hichens, partly because Jones was such a contrast to his fastidious self. 'He is such an entirely *natural* little man,' he once said, 'so different from Pinero,[1] who lives in deadly fear of being seen through.' Max made several new close friends during this period. The two closest were George Street and Edward Gordon Craig. Street had the most obviously in common with Max. Indeed, he may be described as a variation on a Max theme; a dandy and wit, noted for his extreme fastidiousness, who wrote a bright little satire on the aesthetic movement called *The Autobiography of a Boy*, and also some slender elegant volumes about the eighteenth century, a period for which he felt a romantic nostalgia. Max and he met one evening at Solferino's. For the first few minutes it was noticed they vied with one another to appear gracefully aloof, as dandies should; but quickly forgot it to lay the foundations of a lifelong friendship. Max delighted in Street's conversation which he said, 'delivered in a clear, light and scholarly voice, had the flavour of the best old dry sherry'. He also for many years tried in vain to persuade people to read Street's books.

Edward Gordon Craig was a more sensational figure. In his notebook Max sought in a series of disconnected and impressionistic images to convey the startling effect of his youthful personality.

'Playing piano—leaping up—throwing back his hair—flowing cloak. German Student—Heidelberg—one expected sabre-cuts—Unearthly—the Young Bacchus—His amours, almost mythological. . . . Pure type of artist—*genius*.'

A love-child of the great Ellen Terry, Ted Craig was the heir to her effortless, radiant charm, to which he added an amorous and irresponsible temperament and a streak of white-hot creative genius that was later to enable him to revolutionize the whole conception of stage production. By the time he was twenty-three he was already married, separated from his wife, had made a success on the stage, left it, returned to it. All this was very unlike Max. Indeed, it was no wonder that at their first meting—it was one evening at the Café Royal—Craig thought Max alarming: surely it was unnatural to be so self-controlled at twenty-three! But he was also strongly

[1] Henry Arthur Jones's chief rival as popular dramatist.

attracted towards him. Max responded. Soon they were fast friends.
Each admired the other's gifts and appreciated the other's charm.
Craig delighted in Max's tranquil sweetness of disposition, so different from his own mercurial moods. Further, beneath surface
differences, and in the deeper strata of their natures there existed a
special affinity. Craig was closer than any other of Max's friends to
the child and the poet in him, and could thus enter more fully than
they into the comical dream-region where Max's creative spirit
found much of its inspiration. Craig took Max into a humbler,
more improvised, stage life than that to be found amid the social
splendours of Herbert's theatre. One evening when Craig was
acting in the suburbs, Max and James Pryde, the painter, went
down to see him, and he persuaded them to walk across the back
of the scene as supers. Craig noticed with amusement that they both
did it very badly.

Pryde, 'a pierrot', noted Max, 'with a sort of horsey make-up yet
distinguished and childlike', was one of the Beggarstaff Brothers,
the first painters in England to make a fine art of poster design.
The other Beggarstaff Brother was William Nicholson. Through
them Max entered a world of young Chelsea painters, bohemian,
exuberant and heterosexual. Max made friends with both Beggarstaff Brothers, but especially Nicholson, whom he nicknamed 'the
Kid', and who took to visiting him regularly on the last Sunday of
every month for breakfast. A dandy himself, though in a more
sporting style than Max—he affected yellow spotted bow-ties and
tight checked trousers—Nicholson observed Max's appearance with
special interest. He noted how carefully Max pressed his clothes and
ironed his silk hat, but also that he was an amateur rather than a
professional valet. The perfection of his toilet was occasionally
marred by a missing button or a split glove. Max was not naturally
tidy, his writing-table was inches deep in papers; Max neither
opened nor answered his letters. One day Nicholson arrived and
was surprised to find, on entering the room, a fireman in the act of
descending on to this table through a skylight: he had been sent
for to put out a burning chimney. Max was ignorant of the etiquette
to be followed in such emergencies. 'Should I give him a tip?' he
asked nervously. Nicholson thought there was no harm in offering
it. With elaborate courtesy Max pressed half a crown into the hand
of the fireman, who said he was not allowed to accept tips. 'Oh,

WILLIAM NICHOLSON

please treat it as a loan!' stammered Max in confusion. Another time Nicholson met Mrs Beerbohm on the stairs. She said how delighted she was that he and Max were making a success of their new venture. Nicholson was bewildered till during the course of conversation it gradually appeared that Max had amused himself by telling his mother that he and Nicholson had opened an antique shop and that it was a great success. Nicholson was much entertained. He shared Max's pleasure in hoaxes.

Charles Conder the painter, John Davidson the poet—other new friends—were representatives of a different kind of bohemian, the kind more generally associated with the 'nineties. Conder, wistful, feckless and ill-adjusted to the ordinary world, took refuge from it in drink and women; also in visions of a dream-land of romantic elegance which was the subject of his delicate art. Rothenstein— for Conder was the object of one of his special enthusiasms—took Max to call on him at his studio. Worked up by Rothenstein's excitement to expect something tremendous, Max was disconcerted to find himself in the presence of 'an ailing man, a *condamné*, incomplete, tentative, with hair luxuriant and lifeless'. But, he added, Conder's personality had a curious power. As he got to know him better he found him to be lovable too, and surprisingly naïf. Conder was worried lest his dissipations might shock someone at once so young and so immaculate as Max. Max, calling to see him at luncheon-time one day, found him in bed after a drinking bout, grey-faced and with bloodshot eyes. Conder did not dare tell him the truth. 'I was up late with some friends,' he exclaimed apologetically, 'and as young fools will, I suppose, we *over-ate*!'

John Davidson was more bitterly at odds with the world. It was surprising that he and Max should be friends; for Davidson was an uncompromising and brooding Scot, with a temper exacerbated by poverty and neglect and asserting defiantly a Nietzschean creed of splendid ruthlessness, in a style that blended thundering romantic rhetoric with rough modern colloquialism. As a matter of fact Max found Davidson's poetry hard reading although he admired it: 'His violent buffeting of clouds meant nothing to me,' he relates. 'But,' he goes on, 'he was an authentic man of genius and had all the sweetness of his tribe.' Few people found Davidson 'sweet': that Max should do so is evidence of his own power of pleasing. Indeed, Davidson responded to Max's appreciation with strong affection. On the few occasions he had some money it pleased him to forget his penury for one evening and entertain Max and some other friend to an excellent dinner, though he realized that he must pinch for weeks afterwards in order to pay for it. This distressed Max; but the generosity it disclosed made him like Davidson even more. 'Beloved John Davidson,' he wrote years after, 'there is none of my dead friends I think of more often and with more love.'

Max's social life was not confined to London. We hear of him on visits, staying with Mr and Mrs Frank Lawson at Maesllwch Castle for Easter of 1896, for instance, and spending Christmas of the same year in the country with John Lane. In the summer Max went away for longer periods. Sometimes it was abroad—there are some references to a visit with Reggie to Rouen—but more often to the seaside in England. We hear of him with a friend or with his family at Folkestone and at Bognor. He had a particularly enjoyable visit to Folkestone in 1897 with Constance—and with Dora. Dora's entry into the Sisterhood had not proved the break that Max feared it might. St Saviour's was a liberal Order; and though she took her final vows in May 1896, she was still able to see a great deal of her family. She paid them a visit in London almost every week and at least once a year took a short holiday with them. Moreover, she was unaltered. Max need not have been frightened of her growing strange and solemn. Dora was still the same Dora, laughing, throwing back her head, bubbling over with sympathy and fantasy and mischief, and—it seemed to Max—managing somehow to know as much about what was happening in the world as any of them. Delightedly they idled away the days together at Folkestone playing paper games and halma, and spinning fancies about the people they saw from their window walking by the sea. After the exertions of London social life such an existence was restful and refreshing. Refreshing to the spirit as well as the body; and the quieter it was the more he liked it. Folkestone out of season would have depressed many young men: it pleased Max.

'The place itself I find quite passable,' he tells Will Rothenstein: 'it is at present in the off-season and how charming in its contrast to London with her streets packed with faces and her pavements covered with feet! And how nice to be in a town where the season is just about to commence: charming in its expectant emptiness and

not unreminiscent of Hardy's sweet distinction between the light—
the twilight—of dawn and of sunset: "The degree of light is equal
exactly, it may be, at both times: but at dawn the bright element is
active and the shadow passive and quiescent": so here in the middle
of July there is none of the dreadful depression of spirits which falls
as one watches the boats and the trains full of departing figures and
the emptying streets and the houses as they grow blank.'

This was in the summer. But Max also enjoyed the English seaside in the winter. Stranger still, he enjoyed it particularly by himself. When he found the pressure of London too trying he would
steal off for a long weekend alone in lodgings. There, amusedly,
he sought and found a special kind of pleasure. It inspired one of his
essays.

'Around me are the usual ornaments of sea-side lodgings. Through
a little bay-window I look out over the wide sea. I have looked, so,
through many little bay-windows. But, on my heart, I do not
distinguish them one from another; they are all as one for me, all
symbolize home for me, quietude and home. . . . Yes! in whatever
sea-side town I find myself I am filled with a quiet pride, a rest-
fulness of possession. With the first breath of its wet salt, all the
stains of the town are purged, the vapours blown quite away. I
am, like Sir Willoughby Patterne, "not a poet", and so the sea does
not move me, as it moves Mr Swinburne, to superb dithyrambs,
nor send me searching, as it sends Mr William Watson searching, for
adjectives long enough to express unqualified approval. For me,
the sight of it is sacramental, not because it has any power to overwhelm my soul, but because it alone can restore that sense of self-
importance which London takes from me. . . . I look forward
to everything. As I walk Stationwards for the morning papers, I
can scarcely contain my great interest in current events; and later,
when I have learnt all that is troubling that city whose happy exile
I am, how pleasant to lean over the Parade's railing and watch
Neptune's troupe of performing waves! . . . Every pleasure is here
so generously magnified. I do even enjoy my meals—the simpler the
food, the more Gargantuan my appetite. I wonder how I can ever
have sat out the tedious comedy of dinner, when it is possible to
enjoy that variety-entertainment, high tea, in which ham and scones

and shrimps and hard-boiled eggs and honey all take their short delightful "turns". And then, when one is well satisfied, to emerge, not into the garish Strand, but upon the dark seafront, and to feel, as one notes the shimmer of the moon across the waters, that the lamp-posts are shining with a grotesquely similar radiance across the mud of every thoroughfare in London.'

Here are some more of Max's true words spoken in jest. He liked being alone at the seaside in winter because it relieved him temporarily from the rush of London life, which he found a nervous strain even when he was young. He liked it still more because in solitude he could surrender himself to the pleasure of reverie. For he still led two lives. Behind the outward life that he lived with his acquaintances and friends and Kilseen—the life of the observer, the man about town, the agreeable friend, the gentle amorist—was also the inner life of reflection and self-mocking, self-dramatizing fantasy.

His inner life was the more important to him. For it was in solitary play and musing that his creative imagination functioned. In it, therefore, was engendered his art. He gathered his fertilizing impressions from the world—at parties, in theatres, at the law courts and in the galleries of the House of Commons. But he needed to be alone and at leisure for the seed to take root and flower; only then could the shaping spirit of his imagination get to work on material provided by experience. So it was in those years. For they did produce flowers. They are primarily important in his life-story because in them appear his first important work as a writer and a caricaturist.

He caricatured more than he wrote, for he did it much more easily. He did not need so much quiet for it. Back from a party he would sit down, still in white tie and tail-coat, and dash off impressions of the people he had seen during the evening. 'I used to come home from a dinner party,' he related in later years, 'and take my brush and draw caricature after caricature. They seemed to bubble up from here,' he added, pressing his stomach, 'that was a kind of inspiration, I suppose.' The best of these drawings got published. During these years work by Max appeared in a wide variety of journals. In 1896 came his first collection in book form: *Caricatures of Twenty-five Gentlemen*, published by Leonard Smithers and dedicated to the shade of Carlo Pellegrini or 'Ape' of *Vanity Fair*, whose pictures he hung in his room and whom he looked on as his master. It was prefaced also by an enthusiastic foreword by Raven-Hill, the *Punch* cartoonist.

These early cartoons did not reveal Max's full stature as an artist. For one thing, he had yet to discover his characteristic manner: the style of these drawings still shows the influence of earlier cartoonists, notably 'Ape' and Caran d'Ache. Further, they are comic rather than pretty. Max's mature caricatures are always both. One is not surprised to learn that he was an admirer of Beardsley and Burne-Jones. In his first book all is realistic and satiric. Again, Max's later masterpieces are literary as well as pictorial. They often tell a story and are accompanied by a letterpress, both as important to the general effect as is the drawing itself. Not so in *Twenty-five Gentlemen*: it was only in 1899 that Max's gifts as combined writer and illustrator first fully discovered themselves—in the series about the Prince of Wales called *The Edwardyssey*, and in that presenting Gladstone's adventures in Heaven.

All the same, these early drawings could only be by him. The subjects show it; Max had begun to choose the main figures in his comic world while still at school, now they occupied the foreground of his first collection. He said to an interviewer who visited him before the book came out, 'There will be some of my pet personages amongst them—the Prince of Wales in a kilt and Kipling and—oh and the others!' It is also typical of him that these drawings are interpretations of their subjects, not first-hand impressions. Max never drew straight from life and in the presence of his subject. 'My caricatures,' he once said, 'are faces seen through the fog of memory, the illuminating fog of memory.' With a deceptive air of innocence he would gaze at his chosen victim, intent to observe what was comic in him. By the time he sat down to draw, these varied impressions would have fused themselves with his satiric fancy to produce an image of his model's whole personality, mental and physical. Also his judgement on it; Le Gallienne's cloudy fuzz of hair hiding his ineffective face expresses Max's view of his cloudy ineffective art; Beardsley's flippant artificiality incarnates itself in the toy poodle which Max pictures him as leading about on a ribbon. Max always denied that these psychological comments on his sitters were deliberate.

AUBREY BEARDSLEY

'When I draw a man, I am concerned simply and solely with the physical aspect of him. I don't bother for one moment about his soul. I just draw him as I see him. And (this is how I came to be a caricaturist) I see him in a peculiar way: I see all his salient points exaggerated (points of face, figure, port, gesture and vesture), and all his insignificant points proportionately diminished. *Insignificant*: literally, signifying nothing. The salient points do signify something. In the salient points a man's soul does reveal itself, more or less faintly. At any rate, if it does not always reveal itself through them, it is always latent in them. Thus if one underline these points, and let the others vanish, one is bound to lay bare the soul.'

This is what happened. 'Max gives you,' said Raven-Hill in his foreword, 'a savage epitome of man's exterior and through that the essence of the man himself.' A just account but for one word; Max's drawings are seldom 'savage', if by savage is meant done in anger and with intent to wound. Of course, he did dislike some people more than others—the Prince of Wales and Kipling, for instance—and the fun he makes of them has a sharper edge to it in consequence. But his dislike is not so fierce as to make him lose his temper; so that his portraits are not horrible. Moreover, he laughs at them partly because they were famous public figures and so stirred his impulse for irreverence. Kipling was what he called an 'idol of the market-place'; the Prince of Wales, like all royal personages, was surrounded by servility and flattery. Max had always loved impishly to pull down the mighty from their seats. His prevailing mood—and this is just as true of him in youth as in middle age—was too detached and light-hearted to be savage. Too detached and light-hearted to be kindly either: gaily and mercilessly he set out to get as much fun from his victim as he possibly could.

Max's literary productions were fewer but more varied. Much of them consisted of freelance contributions to various journals. These, though always light in tone, ranged from critical articles to what Max called 'words for pictures'—little flights of fancy inspired by works of famous painters—humorous meditations on topics like holidays, and journeys and thoughts about current events like the Boat Race or the Diamond Jubilee of Queen Victoria. These last were written for the *Daily Mail*. Between the autumn of 1897 and the spring of 1898 Max wrote a weekly commentary for the *Daily Mail* on anything he thought he could make amusing. It would be interesting to know whether these articles were a success. If so, the readers of the popular papers must have been a more cultured set than they are today. Max did not play down to them. His manner is elaborate and ironic; and he is always mocking at popular heroes and institutions. Surely, he says, it is absurd to make so much fuss about the Jubilee or the Boat Race! And what is one to think of nations where authors like Jerome K. Jerome and Hall Caine are admired!

Max makes fun of himself as well as of others. He laughs at his own poses and thinks poorly of his own manners. They were, he said, those of one who, though middle-class, is not envious; all the same the result was that the company of his superiors froze him into a reserve that inhibited conversation, while his inferiors filled him with a shyness that he strove to hide under what he described as 'a liberal urbanity which must be very irritating'. This brand of suave sophisticated self-mockery was not the kind of thing to make his duller readers feel at ease.

On one occasion he was more openly provocative. He read somewhere that some respectable citizens of Kensington, led by a Mr Crouch Bachelor, had formed themselves into a mock House of Commons, complete with Speaker and other officers, in which they conducted serious debates on important subjects of the day. Max was amused at the thought of grown men taking part in such solemn make-believe and also at the name Crouch Bachelor: he expressed his amusement in a comic article rather in the lighter manner of Matthew Arnold, an author he much admired, and who—as readers of *Culture and Anarchy* will remember—also made a great play with absurd-sounding proper names. This produced a furious reply from Mr Crouch Bachelor; Max, he said, was 'a foreign-named mounte-bank and masquerading German'. The mountebank was impeni-tent; but sought to cool the atmosphere by remarking that if the Kensington Parliament was an absurd pretence, so also were most other human institutions. Nor were they the worse for being so. 'All social life is founded on certain carefully fostered illusions,' he said. 'Let us respect them. It is through them alone that men can keep out of mischief.' Here Max is not as flippant as he sounds. He is stating what, as a believer in the doctrine of the mask, he held to be a truth. But it was not the sort of truth to appeal to Mr Crouch

Bachelor and his friends, especially when uttered in this airy tone. It is understandable that the *Daily Mail* inserted a footnote at the end of each article disclaiming responsibility for anything said in it.

Max's contributions to the *Saturday Review* were most of them unsigned: otherwise its editor might well have done the same. During this period Max published several critical articles in it; in particular, several about Clement Scott, a dramatic critic by profession, but who also fancied himself as poet and essayist. Here Max exhibits himself in the new role of Max the gadfly. A very effective gadfly too! Like his caricatures, these articles are too light-hearted to be called savage; but they are devastating. It was easy to make them so, for to judge by Max's quotations from his works, Scott was an extremely absurd writer. But few critics could have got so much fun out of him as Max did. Scott as poet was his first victim. Max never reprinted these articles: no doubt he thought them of ephemeral interest. But they deserve quotation, both for the intrinsic merits and for the light they throw on Max's life and character. This is how he starts his review:

An Unhappy Poet

'Bexhill-on-Sea is the haven for me
  Whene'er my nerves are depressed;
For there's a retreat where you golf and you eat
  And you sleep and you dream and you rest!'

'These exquisite words were written by one of the most prolific and, it may be, most popular of our modern poets, Mr Clement Scott. We quote them, not merely because their cadence has haunted us, and it is a pleasure to write them out, but also because they seem to epitomize the bitter tragedy of their writer's life.

Every great poet has had some one impulse, to which may be traced all that is finest in his work. It is a function of criticism to determine in each case what that impulse was. . . . Shelley was more particularly "the poet of the Clouds". Swinburne is the poet of the Sea. And Mr Clement Scott is the poet of the Seaside.

Circumstances, the curse of poets, compel this man to live in London, driving him in and out of glaring theatres, up and down Fleet Street. It is fearful to think of his soul being slowly crushed by so uncongenial a life. Many, many are the poems he has written about this or that seaside during a happy holiday, and are instinct with the joyous spirit of Saturday-to-Monday. But most, alas! have been wrung from him in smoky exile, and are suffused with melancholy, subdued, nostalgic. As in the lines written recently and quoted above, he writes most often, not with Horace's mild desire for the Sabine farm, but rather with Byron's terrible longing for Ravenna. Let our readers turn to his volume, *Lays and Lyrics.*

It was published eight years ago, but the spray is still salt upon its pages. When Scott (in the case of such a man we make no apology for dropping the Mr) sings the praises of this or that resort, he does it with an art so magical that we seem, ourselves, as we read, to be treading the jetty, or the sand, or the marine parade, as the case may be. Of Brighton he writes:

> 'Wandering waves on the shingle dash,
>   The Sky's too blue for a thoughtless tear;
>
> . . . .
>
> Lazily lost in a dream we sit—
>   Maidens' eyes are a waveless mere—
> There's many a vow when seagulls flit,
> And many a sigh when lamps are lit,
>   And many a kiss upon Brighton Pier.'

And of Boulogne:

> 'Old Albion's coast isn't lively, is it?
>   There are jollier places, you'll all agree;
> So cross the Channel, and come to visit
>   Our holiday life at Boulogne-on-Sea.'

Scott, you see, is not faithful to one love. . . . He describes how he once found himself "on Margate pier, in a riotous round of women and wine"; and how "the Margate air was piercing sweet to the world and him". His soft praises of Cromer are too well known to the admirers of Mr Isidore de Lara[1] and the readers of the *Daily Telegraph* to need repetition. Indeed, though he has been enamoured often, he has never written so passionately as about 'Poppyland'. The Cornish coast is the only one of his loves that would seem to have left any bitterness in his bosom. We hold that the love tragedies of a poet are as sacred as those of any other man, but we must con-

[1] The composer of *The Garden of Sleep* for which Scott had provided the words.

fess we are curious to know what prompted this poet to write so sombrely of

'The rocks and the caves
Where the sea birds find their houses, and ignorant folks their graves.'

. . . When he deals with more direct passions, with the love of a man for a woman, he is less happy perhaps. Now and again, however, the lady addressed seems to be rather an abstraction, a symbol for some seaside resort, and in these poems he is at his best. Take, for example, from the poem he calls "Violet" that stanza which runs thus:

'You meet me *with your beauty unimpaired—*
   I greet you with dull sorrow in my face;
You, with your haunting face, that souls ensnared—
   I with a past no praying can retrace!
You can remember nothing—you are fair!
   The roses all are dead that you have smelt;
You sit and laugh at men who loved your hair—
   I sigh for dear dead kisses I have felt.'

In this stanza the sentiment, the lilt, the imagery, are all the poet's own. Only the italics are ours. It is possible that a careless reader would imagine that the lines were really addressed to some lady. We prefer to think,—indeed, we are sure—that they were addressed to some seaside resort, whose identity is cunningly veiled under the pseudonym of "Violet", lest Cromer or another should wax jealous. Surely it would be rather prosaic to speak of a lady's beauty as being "unimpaired". On the other hand, if we take it that, say, Broadstairs is apostrophized, then "not built over" would be the meaning, and the phrase would be felicitous and pretty. Surely, again, no lady, worthy of the name, would sit down on a chair and guffaw at men who had loved her hair, even though their proceeding had seemed ridiculous. We are sure that the *h* in "hair" is a conversational sort of *h*, dropped in to hide a sly reference to ozone. A popular seaside resort, moreover, can afford to "laugh" at the defection of a few visitors more or less.'

The article continued for several pages more in the same relentless vein. Scott was even angrier than Mr Crouch Bachelor. Incoherent with rage, he spluttered forth confused abuse in a piece entitled 'Come out of your hole, Rat', printed in the pages of *The Era*, a journal with which he was professionally connected. This gave Max an opening to go for him again. Demurely delighted, he took it.

'Sir,' he began, 'I am sorry to disappoint Mr Clement Scott, but really I am not paralysed. "I have seldom before," says the Poet, "been bitten by a Rat who dared not show his face, and was coward enough to conceal his identity, who, when I call him out, as I do now, to fight me in the rat-pit" (a picturesque encounter!) "scrambles off to his miserable hole paralysed with fear." These prophecies in the present tense are very dangerous things. Here am I, a real, live Rat; young, it may be, but quite calm; rejoicing in a Christian name and a surname (both printed below), and in a fairly keen sense of humour; delighted to emerge from my miserable hole in the office of the *Saturday Review* and put my back to the wainscot. In a word, here I am.

I admit that Mr Scott's method of controversy makes reply difficult. In two columns of last week's *Era* he contradicts nearly as often as he repeats himself. The suddenness of his metaphors, too, confuses me, and I am simply bewildered by the menagerie of animals that he has contrived to collect—an ox, a cur, lions, tigers, an angry parrot, and a Rat "who is evidently anxious to throw explosives under a man's chair"—the intelligent little creature! A Rat with a cloven hoof, too!'

After this Scott would surely have been wise to remain silent. Possessed, however, by who knows what demon of self-destruction, he produced within a year a volume of essays, once more about seaside resorts. Max immediately reviewed them. The essays were, if possible, more ridiculous than the poems, and Max's second review more devastating if possible than his first had been. In the last paragraph he surpasses himself:

'Meanwhile I am glad that Mr Clement's attitude towards Brighton leaves nothing to be desired. Her he salutes as "the acknowledged Queen of Sussex". In courtly phrases he hymns her "three atmospheres", her splendid hostelries, her Madeira Road. One feels that his heart may be elsewhere, but he comports himself with loyallest grace in the presence of his Sovereign. "*Go up to the station*," he says, "*to meet a train or start by one; go on to the piers, or on the beach, where the children make a flower garden, paddling in their rainbow skirts with a background of grey shingle; go on to the parade among the carriages, or to the Downs and the Dyke among the hares and the rabbits, and you will see no sad or careworn or weary faces."* So let us leave him, as he paces, in "new green crocodile boots", along the Downs or the Dyke, looking wistfully this way and that, if perchance he shall see the face of a careworn hare or of a weary rabbit.'

These articles show Max to have been a much tougher customer than his subsequent reputation might suggest. They disclose the steely and intellectual hand that lay hidden beneath his frivolous and silken glove; they remind us that, to the public of 1897, Max was not the mellow, smiling sage of later legend, but a disturbing embodiment of brilliant, irreverent youth, relentlessly out to make sport of the conventional and the mediocre.

In the Christmas of 1896 the same spirit has shown itself in another form: parody. The Christmas supplement of the *Saturday Review* that year contained parodies of five writers, Meredith, Wells, Le Gallienne, Alice Meynell and Marie Corelli. Each was represented as writing on some topic associated with Christmas and the whole was entitled 'A Christmas Garland'. They were in fact a set of preliminary sketches for Max's masterpiece in this vein, the *Christmas Garland* of 1912. Indeed, the 1896 parody of Meredith is an abbreviated version of that in the later volume. These early parodies are another illustration of how early his genius found itself. Already at twenty-four he has conceived the general idea of one of his mature masterpieces. Max knew himself very well. As though to show it, he ended the first 'Christmas Garland' with a neat parody of his own work.

Max also went in for more creative forms of writing. Between 1895 and 1898 he produced a number of essays and stories. Like Lamb's, Max's are the 'pure' type of essay; that is to say, they are not written to instruct or edify but only to produce aesthetic satisfaction. As much as a poem or a piece of music, they are the expression of a creative impulse. What Max creates is a personality. Because it is a creation, it is not a self-portrait: Max the essayist is not the same as Max Beerbohm the man any more than Elia the essayist is the same as Charles Lamb the man. In each case the writer projects on to his page a personality not identical with his own, though founded on it, a figure made up of elements selected from himself and then re-arranged and displayed for his aesthetic purpose. The result is an intensely vivid impression of a living individual. But paradoxically the life comes from the fact that he is not drawn directly from nature, that he is a creation, rather than a reproduction. To effect this special purpose Max devised a special kind of style, informal enough to convey a personality intimately, but sufficiently subtle and concentrated to express each nuance of his thought and feeling.

'In essay writing,' he explained, 'style is everything. The essayist's aim is to bring himself home to his reader, to express himself in exact terms. Therefore, he must find exact words for his thoughts, and cadences which express the very tone of his emotions. Himself is the thing to be obtruded, and style the only means to this end. Wherever style is, there too is the author. . . .

Writing, like talking, is the art of expressing thoughts in words. . . . But there is, necessarily, a vast difference between the oral and the scriptural use of words. When we talk, we have for our ministers not words only, but also gesture, play of feature, modulation of the voice's tone, and regulation of its pace, whereby we may subtly temper or accentuate the words themselves, and fit them, be they never so carelessly chosen, exactly to our meaning. When we write, we have nothing but words, words, with those little summary and meagre things whose hard office is to ape the infinitely variable pauses of the human voice. . . . The writer has to balance this inequality. He has to produce through printed words the same effect as that which he would produce through spoken words. In short, he must have a style. . . . True style is essentially a personal matter, a medium through which a man expresses truth as he himself sees it, and emotions as he himself feels them; that it is, in fact, not a mere spy-hole to things in general, but a spy-hole to things as they are reflected in the soul of the writer. Thus is style in the modern sense a far more complex thing than style in the eighteenth century's sense. To express through printed words all the little side-lights of thought and fine shades of meaning that are in him is the task of the modern stylist; and the tricks and formalities which must be gone through in accomplishing that task carry him further and further away from his ordinary manner in colloquy. It is that very manner which he is trying to reproduce; but the only medium for its reproduction lies leagues away from it. Modern prose style is further removed from colloquialism than was the prose style of the eighteenth century, for this paradoxical reason: that colloquialism is its model.'

Max's essays appeared in the *Yellow Book*, the *Saturday Review* and other papers; also in a new publication, *The Savoy*. This was started in 1896 by a certain Leonard Smithers—the same who published *Twenty-five Gentlemen*—and who was described by Max as 'a north countryman known to have been engaged in the sale of disreputable books'. To celebrate the appearance of *The Savoy*'s first number, Smithers gave a supper party. There, for the second time and at closer quarters, Max saw Yeats. As before, he was more amused than impressed. Sceptically he listened to Yeats chanting portentously across the dinner table on the subject of Diabolism or 'Dy-ahbolism' as he pronounced it. He also noticed that Yeats was far too self-absorbed and in the clouds to pay proper attention to his hostess, Smithers's touchingly commonplace little wife.

'She was small, buxom, and self-possessed,' wrote Max. 'She did the honours. She dropped little remarks. It did not seem that she was nervous; one only knew that she *was* nervous. . . . The walls of the little room in which we supped were lined with bamboo instead of wallpaper. "Quite original, is it not?" she said to Yeats. But Yeats had no reply ready for that; only a courteous, lugubrious murmur.'

For all his aestheticism, Max never subscribed to the view that the artist was free from the common obligation to be good-mannered. Yeats's lofty inattention jarred on him in the same way as had Oscar's occasional outbursts of arrogance. He was even more severe when he had the luck to catch the detested Kipling being rude. This was later, in May 1898. Max got a letter from the boy editor of a little school magazine at Horsmonden, Kent, asking if he would do them a caricature of Kipling and enclosing a letter from him in which he had, apparently, offensively refused a request for a contribution. Enclosing the letter was a skilful if unintentional diplomatic stroke. Max immediately agreed to do the drawing.

'Gentlemen,' he wrote, 'Many thanks for the copy of your admirable magazine. I have read Mr Kipling's letter and agree that its tone is quite monstrous and unpardonable.

I have much pleasure in complying with your request for a caricature of Mr Kipling and, if it meets with your approval, do not forget to send me a copy of the issue in which it appears. I am an ardent collector of my own drawings.

With best wishes for your posterity, I am, Gentlemen,

Yours obediently,

Max Beerbohm.'

In August 1896 Max collected some of his essays in a single volume which he entitled *The Works of Max Beerbohm*. He expatiated on this title in his best dandy's manner to Miss Alder, an American interviewer.

'. . . Have you heard, by the way,' he asked her, 'that John Lane is going to publish those same essays of mine in book form with the awe-inspiring title, *The Works of Max Beerbohm*? He intends writing the bibliography himself. It is very gratifying to be recognized in one's lifetime. It so seldom happens! Lane has a hero-worship for me.'

'Shared, I am sure, by a goodly section of the reading public,' said Miss Alder.

'Well, of the truth of that statement I cannot judge, but I have just been informed that another devotee of mine is compiling a volume of my "Table Talk".'

' "Table Talk",' echoed Miss Alder, 'what's that?'

'Oh, mere nothings—canaries, political economy, kaleidoscopes, and so on!'

The 'Table Talk' did not materialize; we shall never know what Max thought about canaries and kaleidoscopes. But *The Works* were published and were very well received indeed. Though made up of pieces that had already appeared, the book was in a sense a new creation. The separate items had been chosen to combine into a harmonious whole; moreover, all except one, 'The Good Prince', were revised, most of them extensively, while the first piece was a compilation of various passages drawn from several earlier essays, including his old contribution to Alfred Douglas's *Spirit Lamp*. Max wrote fewer stories than essays; we know of only three: 'The Happy Hypocrite', printed in the *Yellow Book*, Volume IX; 'Yai and the Moon', and 'The Small Boy and the Barley Sugar', which appeared in *Pageant* and *Parade* respectively. All these are in the tradition of the sophisticated fairy-tale with an ironic moral attached which had been invented by Hans Andersen and copied from him by Oscar Wilde. 'The Happy Hypocrite', the longest of the stories, was so successful that John Lane reprinted it in the same year by itself in book form.

The publication of these two books, *The Works* and *The Happy Hypocrite*, inaugurated Max's literary career; and indicated what lines this career was going to follow. All Max's creative writing except parody was to take the form either of occasional essays or of story fantasies. They also commemorate the past. Max's literary work, though not directly autobiographical, always has a close relation to his own life; even his fantasies are connected with some phase of his own experience, inner or outer. These two first books are the fruit of his *Yellow Book* phase. In them we hear the voice of Max, aesthete and dandy, the Max who imitated Oscar, and sentimentalized over Cissey Loftus and shocked *Punch*. Indeed, for all that Max sets up for being so elderly, these two books are exuberantly youthful. In *The Works* he praises rouge and dandies, the artificial and the frivolous, in a style as mannered as he can make it; full of strange and invented words, 'sillypop' and 'manywhere', or ordinary words oddly used or elegant impertinences; 'To give an accurate account of that period,' he says in the essay on 1880, 'would need a far less brilliant pen than mine.' Yet his extravagancies are not ridiculous; because they are always ironic. Max's enjoyment of the dandy's affectations comes largely from the fact that he does not take them seriously. 'Affectations,' he said once, 'taken seriously become convictions, and he who so takes them is no dandy.' He takes a special pleasure in an exquisitely finished trifle, because it gives him ironical amusement to think of so much time and care being spent upon something apparently so little worth it. Now and again we do catch a glimpse of a genuine conviction lurking behind the irony. It is conviction and not affectation that leads Max in the essay on dandies to praise an indirect attitude to life and a direct attitude to art. Above all, in the last essay, called 'Diminuendo', he implies much more than meets the superficial eye. In this Max describes how, inspired by reading Pater, he came up to live the aesthetic life in romantic Oxford, only to find that Pater looked like a major in a line regiment and that Oxford was disfigured by trams. Great was his disillusionment: and by now he has, he says, outlived his time—'already I feel myself a trifle outmoded'; he proclaims, 'I belong to the Beardsley period'—and resolves to retire to a London suburb where he can stop writing and give himself up to a life of obscurity and contemplation.

'It was to thought that *my* life should be dedicated,' he said. 'Action, apart from its absorption of time, would war otherwise against the pleasures of intellect, which, for me, meant mainly the pleasures of imagination. . . . I would make myself master of some small area of physical life, a life of quiet, monotonous simplicity, exempt from all outer disturbances. . . .'

Of course, this is all Max's pleasant nonsense. Apart from anything else, he had written this particular essay in 1893 when the Beardsley period was still in full swing; and, as we know, he delighted in Oxford. Yet, implied in his words lies Max's genuine and formidable criticism of Pater's gospel. The aesthetic ideal may sound all very well as stated in the dreamy pages of *The Renaissance*, he suggests; but the world is too rushed and too prosaic a place to put it into practice. In real life, it would seem, every Oxford turns out to have its trams: aestheticism is only for those who keep out of the real world. Again, is Max merely paradoxical when he says he longs for a life of retirement? For his words were prophetic. He never, it is true, took up residence in a London suburb. But fifteen years after the publication of this his first book, he did leave the world to embrace a form of life very much like that described in the passage quoted. We are at liberty to take his words as a joke which happened by chance later to coincide with the truth; but we can also take them as utterances in which, under the guise of a joke, he expressed a profound and secret desire.

Still more are there signs of hidden depths in *The Happy Hypocrite*. This is a document of the first importance for understanding its author. On the surface it seems butterfly-light; an artificial pastoral in the Regency mode, told in delicately flippant tones and in which, if Max does indulge in a moment of romantic feeling, it is quickly to deflate it with a shaft of common sense. Yet when a friend asked him how seriously he intended the story: 'There is a certain amount of sincerity in the sentimentalism of it,' said Max. He was right; there was a piece of his own life-story in it. Here it was that his romance with Cissey Loftus bore fruit. Jenny Mere, the dancer heroine of the tale—and we recall that Mistress Mere was one of Max's names for her—is the Cissey he used to watch from the stalls of the theatre; an image of innocent childlike sweetness, whose innocence is rendered all the more piquant by contrast with the tawdry and corrupt world in which she performs. As the Lady Cecilia had represented a genuinely romantic idea to Max, for all that he made fun of it, so now in *The Happy Hypocrite* he expresses—though mocking a little at himself for doing so—a genuine impulse of romantic sentiment.

Further, its plot concerns itself with one of Max's most constant preoccupations, the function and significance of masks. It relates how the wicked Lord George Hell fell in love with Jenny, but fearing lest his countenance, ravaged by evil passions, would fill her with horror, wooed her in the mask of a saint. After he had won her, the mask was forcibly torn off, but only to reveal underneath the same saintly countenance: by assuming a virtue, Lord George had become in fact virtuous. How seriously are we to take this? We know that Max believed in masks; he wore one himself. But this was partly because it amused him to do so, and partly because he thought it helped to make social life move smoothly. In *The Happy Hypocrite*, however, he does more, he goes so far as to recommend the mask as a moral instrument. It is true that he does this in a playful tone, appropriate to the playful entertainment he was presenting. But, in fact, this particular view fits far too well with his general philosophy of life not to represent something like a real conviction. When he was an old man he admitted this. Nearly sixty years later Mr S. N. Behrman discussed the story with him. 'It would be easy,' said Behrman, 'if by just putting on a mask of goodness and a mask of beauty, you could achieve both.' 'But oh,' replied Max, 'you have to live up to the mask, you know. Lord George lived up to his mask. His love for Jenny made it possible for him to do it. . . .' And a little later, smiling, he added, 'If you live up to a good mask long enough, don't you know, perhaps it will become first nature to you instead of second or third.' This is the moral of the story. In *The Happy Hypocrite* Max states a corollary to it. 'I hold that candour is only good when it reveals good actions and good sentiments and that, when it reveals evil, it is itself evil.' Max in his own life adopted a mask and regulated his candour in accordance with the principles professed in these remarks.

The Happy Hypocrite and *The Works* confirmed and established Max's literary reputation. Before their publication he was still a 'coming' writer, though an uncommonly brilliant and promising one. Afterwards, he had arrived. He was accepted by the fastidious and recognized high priests of his profession. Already Will and Reggie had applauded him; already Ada Leverson had interviewed him for *The Sketch*. Now Edmund Gosse invited him to his house.

This meant a great deal to a young writer in 1896. Edmund Gosse had a very special position in the literary world of the day. Himself distinguished both as critic and author, he had for many years made it his business to become a close friend to most of the best authors of the period. He was also interested in making the acquaintance of such young authors as showed promise. It had to be authentic promise. Gosse had very high standards; he was, besides, a nervous prickly man, acutely sensitive to public opinion, who did not like it to be thought that he had made a mistake of judgement. To attract his favour the young writer must give solid proof of his talent. The proof led to an invitation; Gosse went in for being a host. His parties were not always agreeable. There were often too many people for the room: sometimes the entertainment provided failed to please. One young man found himself jammed against the wall by the crowd, next to Henry James, and forced to watch some tedious puppets. 'An interesting example of economy,' groaned Henry James after a time. 'Economy of means and . . .'—a glint of mischief came into his eyes—'economy of effect!' Still, it was exhilarating for a young writer to find himself at the sort of party where he might be jammed up against Henry James. An invitation from Gosse served as a sort of ticket of entry to the 'inner temple of letters'. So Max found it in the summer of 1896. Gosse asked him to an afternoon gathering at his house in Delamere Terrace.

'I think,' Max related, 'that this was the first time I was at that delightful house. My *Works* had just been published; and to Gosse, whom I had met often enough, I had sent a copy. He was not quick to patronize young men who had done nothing, nor those who had done nothing good. . . . I remember that when I received my summons to Delamere Terrace I felt that my little book really had not fallen flat. The drawing-room was very full when, carefully dressed for the part of a brilliant young dandy, and very calm, and very shy, I made my entry.'

It was natural that Max should be shy and creditable that he

EDMUND GOSSE

should be calm; for he was making his first entry into the highest literary circles, not as an admiring outsider but himself as an accepted member of them. He was treated as such; and by no one more than Gosse himself. Gosse was a faulty man in some ways; snobbish, touchy, and with a streak of governess in him. But he was possessed by a true, pure passion for the art of literature and a great power of admiration for anyone who distinguished himself in it. He enthusiastically appreciated Max's work. He also liked giving him advice about it; here the governess in him showed itself. But his advice was always intelligent: and Max, who was not touchy, took it in good part. He much enjoyed Gosse's company, for Gosse was a fascinating companion; his talk, subtle and caressing, was notable for its happy phrases, its lambent flicker of fanciful or feline humour. Max became a frequent guest at Delamere Terrace, more especially at Gosse's Sunday-afternoon 'at homes', where he often was honoured by being one of the few asked to stay on to supper. It was after supper—when Gosse felt at last able to relax among his chosen intimates—that the talk really began to sparkle. Often it went on sparkling until two or three on Monday morning.

At Gosse's and elsewhere Max got to know other important figures in the world of art and letters—Whistler, Andrew Lang, Henry James, to name only a few. He had met Henry James before, in 1895. This was during James's bearded period; Max thought he looked 'like a Russian Grand Duke of the better type' and was struck by his curious 'veiled' expression. From 1896 on, Max found himself often in James's company. As he took particular pleasure in his writing, he examined him with special attention. He was not disappointed. Henry James was all that Max liked a great man to be: majestic, benignant and slightly comical. He equally enjoyed the subtle wisdom of Henry James's remarks and the extraordinary manner—preliminary sighings, portentous pauses and anxious reassuring gestures—with which he uttered them. Now and again he noted that Henry James could be malicious. But this, though it made him more formidable, also made him more entertaining. Henry James, on his side, took to Max. He liked courteous, elegant, intelligent young men. He treated Max on flatteringly equal terms. Once, at a wedding reception, a woman friend saw the two standing together. 'How terribly distinguished you look,' she said. 'We *are* distinguished,' Henry James replied. 'But you need not look so terribly so,' said the friend. 'We are shameless, shameless!' said Henry James.

Andrew Lang made a less favourable impression. Though a forgotten name now, he was a very well-known figure in the 'nineties; a brilliant product of Scotland and Balliol College, Oxford, who had tried his hand, not unsuccessfully, at almost every kind of literary form—poetry, fiction, history, translation—and was now, at the age of fifty-two, one of London's recognized literary pundits. His judgement was especially respected by conservative-minded dons and schoolmasters. How reassuring, they thought, to find a man of letters incontestably brilliant who yet wrote ballades about cricket and announced that he had found much modern literature morbid and unintelligible! These views were unlikely to prejudice Max in his favour. Indeed, Lang was the type most abhorred by the young and intelligent; under a cultured exterior, he concealed a timid conventionality which led him to pour smooth, chilly scorn on anything likely to disturb the view of life held by respectable gentlemen like himself. Max found Lang the man as displeasing as Lang the critic. They met at Gosse's. Many years later Max recorded the scene.

'I had instantly recognized him from the photographs. He was leaning against an angle of the wall. One might almost have supposed that he had been placed there as an ornament, like a palm in a pot. From the buzzing human throng he seemed to be quite as detached as any palm in any pot. Slender and supereminent, he curved, he drooped, he was a very beautiful thing in the room. And it was even more in colour than in form that he was so admirable. To think that Nature, and not some cunning handicraft of staining and bleaching, had produced these harmonious contrasts! The long nut-brown neck was not more sharply relieved by the white of the turned-down collar than was the nut-brown forehead by the silvery hair that wavily caressed it, than were the nut-brown cheeks by the silvery vapour they had of whisker. And the moustache was jet-black, and jet-black were the eyebrows and the eyelashes. In such surroundings the whiteness of the eyeballs and the darkness of the brown eyes "told" tremendously, of course. But in a spiritual sense the eyes told nothing at all. They shone, they flashed, but with no animation to belie the general look of inanimateness. Their lustre was as lovely and as meaningless as that of jewels. Nature had in some corner of the earth produced two large brown diamonds, of which she was very proud; and it had seemed to her that Andrew Lang's face would be the best of all possible settings for them. So there they were. I wondered whether, with things of such fabulous value exposed on his person, he went about armed, or unarmed but very heavily insured. Now and again, as he stood propped against the angle of the wall, he inserted with long brown fingers a monocle through which the rays of the eye were refracted with surpassing brilliance. And his manner of doing this seemed to indicate, not that there was any one whom he particularly cared to inspect, but that he took a languid pleasure in the gesture. If to superficial observers the fixing of that monocle might have convicted him of curiosity, the marked way he had of letting it drop promptly down again to his waistcoat must have acquitted him of having found the slightest profit in the investigation. With his white waistcoat he wore a pale blue tie. That was the note he had added to Nature's colour-scheme; and it was well chosen. It was good, too, as a symbol. It suggested just that detachment from Oxford which (since your thorough Oxford man is superior to everything, not excepting Oxford) stamped Andrew Lang as one of the most inalienably Oxfordish persons of his time. . . .

Presently my host came up to me and said, "Come out on the balcony. I want you to know Andrew Lang."

There he was, gazing across the balustrade to the canal whose nymphless waters flow very near to Delamere Terrace.

"The angler aroused!" murmured Gosse. And "Yes," he said to Lang, in that tone of mock-lyric ecstasy which his friends knew so well, "that is where I always go a-fishing, the first thing in the morning. Oh, you should breakfast with us! Trout, salmon, dace—I know not what! . . . But now I want you to know Mr Max Beerbohm, whose Collected Works have recently been issued."

"Yes, I've just been hw-eading them," Lang drawled in a tenor voice to Gosse. (To me he tendered a graceful hand, and his gaze wandered away.) "Ve-wy amusing," he faintly added.'

Very different was Whistler's reaction to Max's writing. A master gadfly himself, he had enormously enjoyed Max's first article on Clement Scott; so much so that he wrote to congratulate the editor of the *Saturday Review* on his latest contributor. The approval was mutual. Max had always had an admiration for Whistler as the first of the nineteenth-century dandy-aesthetes and also a brilliant exponent of the airy, artful, colloquial style of writing which he liked best. The impressions of him jotted down in Max's notebook are picturesque and friendly.

'Tiny—Noah's Ark—flat-brimmed hat—band almost to top—coat just not touching ground—button of the Legion of Honour—black gloves—Cuban belle—magnificent eyes—exquisite hands, long and lithe—short palms.'

Max's social success was not confined to the world of writers. It extended itself to that of rank and wealth and fashion. There is always a section of this world with an interest in the arts and a taste for cultivating the acquaintance of such artists as are socially presentable. Max belonged eminently to this category. Accordingly, by the end of 1896 his name had begun to appear in the records of parties and receptions and in the visitors' books of great country houses. We find him writing to Reggie about lunch parties where he met Lady Dorothy Nevill and a weekend with the Harmsworths in Kent or with Sir William Eden in County Durham. It was his work with the *Daily Mail* that had enabled him to get to know Harmsworth, who was its owner, and later, as Lord Northcliffe, to become famous as the first great Press Baron of England. He did not look the role—at least not in 1896. On the contrary, Harmsworth, fair, thoughtful, quiet, appeared, it was said, more like a youthful man of letters. Max thought him very pleasant and also enjoyed the glories of his hospitality.

'Harmsworth is wholly delightful. I stayed with him in Kent last Saturday to Monday—Mrs Harmsworth also very nice. They have a charming house—and many, many servants. Furse the painter was there, and a man called Pollen, of the *Westminster Gazette*, very amusing, and some other people. Stephen Crane was asked but couldn't go. My toilets knocked 'em all silly. On Sunday, flannel coat, white waistcoat, purple tie with turquoise pin, duck trousers and straw hat. My scarab was a great centre of attraction. Altogether a very pleasant visit—and I got away without tipping more than one person. I hope to see much of the Harmsworths—cigarettes and a telephone by one's bed-side, and an enormous peach with one's morning-tea, and a glass of sherry-and-bitters on one's dressing-table at nightfall—and bound volumes of *Vanity Fair* in the library, and two small alligators in one of the innumerable hothouses, and generally all the things which are indispensable to a scholar and a gentleman.'

Staying with Sir William Eden was even more interesting to an amateur of the human comedy. Eden was an extraordinary character; a magnificent and eccentric patrician with a gift for delicate water-colour painting and an ungovernable temper. Also, unlike Harmsworth, he was a member of an ancient family connected by birth and breeding with what was still the ruling aristocracy of England.

'Observe this note-paper. I write from the Stately Home of a Baronet of Jacobite creation—Sir William Eden, in the County of Durham. Walter Sickert is here as my sponsor, and I have a smoking-suit of purple silk, with dark red facings—and am rather light-headed, I am afraid. W. S. has acted in *Dream Faces* with Lady Eden for a charity. He was not at all word-perfect—she was quite so. Sir W. is a delightful and surprising man. We get on very well together. I sat beside him on the bench at Petty Sessions on Monday wearing my check-suit and a fancy waistcoat—very bluff but at the same time very intellectual, and with my chin resting on a beautiful white hand. The house is very comfortable and distinguished. In the hall is a Visitors' Book over which I spend most of my leisure-moments—a Debrett in MS.'

Max, it will be noted, makes no bones about his enjoyment. Keeping such company was very agreeable; the more so because it was a sign of his own success as a writer and talker. 'I feel,' he writes to Reggie after a dinner party, 'like George Robey about the Lady Flo at the garden party "They wanted me! They wanted *me*!" ' All the same, his head was not turned. Though he had too much taste not to enjoy the elegance and the luxury, and too much good sense to be ashamed of doing so, he was not a snob. The fact that his host and fellow guests were fashionable never deceived him into thinking them more interesting than in fact they were: and, as usual, his pleasure was largely amusement. He delighted to note both what was comical about the great world and about his own reactions to it.

Further, Max always recognized—as he had with Alfred Douglas and his circle at Oxford—that the world of rank and fashion was a foreign world in which he had no thought of making his home. His old friends were not so sure of this. For the fact that Max went out so much now and in such different circles did leave him less time for them. Reggie lamented sadly that now Max was so successful he was likely to drift away from him. He was encouraged in his depression by Ross, who seems to have enjoyed making a little gentle mischief between the friends. 'Bobbie,' Reggie writes, 'half expected that you would have dropped me and your undistinguished friends, but I said you would always be the same. I hope I was right, but he gave me an uncomfortable feeling that you may be growing too large for me.' Max vigorously repudiated these suggestions.

'But why all this absurd and morbid nonsense about waning friendship? I am sure I am always coming to see you—if only at dinner because dinner is the only time I am sure to find you in. And you know how I delight in your company. Your sense of humour alone —but I suppose that is not what you want. Anyway, I am sure I am always seeking your company, and as to our respective lives, I think you are in very many ways to be envied enormously.'

Reggie professed himself reassured. Within a month Max is gaily thanking him for a Christmas present.

My dear Reg,
    I am childishly delighted with your beautiful present—the thing is such a lovely shape—so very modish and swiftly impressive. Thanks so much for it. It certainly must not establish a precedent, and I am determined to give you something vastly inferior!

Max adds that Kilseen is also very pleased with a present Reggie has given her. The relations between these two are obscure. Reggie might well have been expected to be jealous of Kilseen; and Kilseen to disapprove of Reggie. She certainly did disapprove of the company he kept, to judge by a letter of Max's written at this time. Max had accepted an invitation of Reggie's to meet a lady he refers to as H. F. Now he writes:

My dear Reg,
    I am sending you this by messenger early tomorrow. Could you ask somebody else to go in my place tomorrow? I told Kilseen on

the way home and asked her if she minded my going with H. F. Of course she told me to go and not mind what she felt and so on. But evidently she thought it in bad taste that I should be seen in a public place with H. F. and so I told her that I would not go. Probably you will think her view very absurd—and so do I—but I suppose it is a fact that if one is engaged to be married one ought to observe certain absurd conventions. And Kilseen has such lots of worries and disappointments that I should like to please her in this instance. You know how I should have looked forward to going and how I should have enjoyed myself with you there—and what a horrid thing it is to give up. But you'll understand my slight act of heroism. You can easily get somebody else to go instead of me. I suppose it is natural of Kilseen not to wish me to be seen with a lady of frayed hem—but I expect she will send me a letter tomorrow saying that she does not really mind. In any case—please forgive me for accepting with effusion and then changing my mind—it seems stupid.

Yours
Max.

On the whole, however, Reggie seems to have done his best to keep in well with Kilseen and to have succeeded. Max is always thanking him for his inquiries after her and referring to occasions on which the three had met. Possibly Reggie did like her and accepted Max's relationship to her more readily than he accepted Max's excursions into fashionable circles—where he himself would have felt shy and out of place. Max still regarded him as his closest man friend: but, inevitably, the relationship had changed—on Max's side at least—from the exciting friendship of youth into the equable friendship of maturity. His letters to Reggie show this very clearly. Gone are the nonsense and the fantasy of Oxford days. Instead we have social and literary news varied by an occasional sober confidence or request for advice.

Max saw less of the other members of the Wilde circle. They were dispersed now and, anyway, he had never been so intimate with them. Such intimacy as he had was friendly. He talked the old language with them and made the same jokes—though, affected perhaps by Kilseen's advice, he sometimes took care lightly to stress the fact that he did not share their sexual tastes. 'How is Bobbie?' he writes to Reggie, who had been seeing Ross. 'Please give him some mulierastic equivalent to my love.'

Will Rothenstein also teased Max about becoming a man of fashion. But Max did not take his words to heart. Will was himself interested in social success and could thus be expected to sympathize. Moreover, the two were often brought together by work. In 1896 Rothenstein had agreed to edit a Christmas supplement to the *Saturday Review* and asked Max for contributions. Max sent some cartoons of persons who, well known in the smart world, were not in Rothenstein's view likely to mean much to the general public. Lord Rowton, for instance—who on earth was Lord Rowton? asked Rothenstein. 'You must have heard of Rowton,' Max replied, 'Disraeli's secretary and friend and always all over the place. But even if he was not at all known outside the aristocracy—you as editor should remember that the aristocracy is a class to be catered for too. There are said to be ten thousand of them.' After this the picture of Lord Rowton duly appeared. In 1897 Will enlisted Max's help in connection with another project. He was bringing out a volume of pictures of famous men, drawn by himself this time, but with accompanying appreciations of them written by various distinguished writers. He wanted Max to write about Pinero. Max sent him a draft, but Rothenstein thought it too caustic for his purpose; he did not want to offend his sitters. Max understood this and did not resent it. Oscar Wilde proved more recalcitrant. Rothenstein had asked him to write an appreciation. To his embarrassment Oscar had written back proposing to write on W. E. Henley, a brilliant, bitter enemy of the Decadent movement and, in particular, of Oscar himself. Taken by surprise, Rothenstein accepted the proposal; but he feared the worst. He was right; Oscar took the opportunity to say what he thought of Henley. Should Rothenstein print his words? He turned to Max for advice. This was surprising in view of what Max had written about Pinero. But it turned out to be right. Max was wiser for others than for himself. Though he thought Oscar Wilde's piece entertaining, he realized that publication could do no possible good to anybody involved; and he recommended Rothenstein to refuse it. In the end Rothenstein persuaded Max to write it himself.

Max and Rothenstein also enjoyed themselves together—relaxing to spend evenings of bohemian fun along with Nicholson and

Conder and the rest of their Chelsea friends. To judge from an anecdote related by Rothenstein in later years, they did it thoroughly. The two had left a dinner so flown with alcohol and youthful spirits that they dashed up to a respectable-looking front door, pulled the bell and resoundingly rattled the knocker. Turning to escape before the outraged householder should catch them, they ran straight into the arms of a policeman who had been watching them from the other side of the street. It took ten minutes and all Max's charm and Rothenstein's forcefulness before the policeman would agree not to take them off to spend the night in the cells. Forty years later Will Rothenstein recalls with pride this episode of his madcap youth. Like Justice Shallow he was pleased to be reminded that he had heard the chimes at midnight.

Such exploits are the expression of high spirits. Max was often in very high spirits during this period of his life. The only fly in his ointment was lack of money. His success had been one of esteem only; it had not enriched him. Meanwhile, his family's financial embarrassments were increasing. Nothing could cure Mrs Beerbohm of asking people to meals. Her servants, too, were extravagant; and who could blame them, said Constance, when their mistress set them so bad an example! Constance herself was forced to borrow from Maud Tree. Unable to pay her back immediately, she offered her some of the family furniture instead. The Trees were very generous and it is unlikely that Maud took it. But the episode was painful; and especially, one would have thought, for Max. For it appears from the correspondence that Constance had needed some of the money for his use. 'Oh,' his sister sighed, 'if only dear Max could earn a little and contribute to the house.' But over this dear Max was not co-operative. He had the defects of his self-sufficiency. Though unendingly affectionate and good-tempered, he was resolved not to give up his chosen mode of living to please anyone. He offered the family two pounds a week to help housekeeping expenses: but we hear nothing of his seeking regular work. Instead, in the autumn of 1897, he took the unprecedented step of leaving home to lodge with an actor friend, Murray Carson, and his wife. Apparently he said he was going to collaborate with Carson in a play and thought that collaboration would be easier if they were both living under the same roof. His family felt his departure keenly.

'He's been away for 5 months at the Carsons,' cried Constance. 'Just when he promised to give £2 a week here to Mamma and seemed in the way of really beginning to work, to be translated to those people! And it is so cruelly dull without him here.'

She need not have worried. Within a month of her writing this letter Max was back at home again. He stayed for ten years. Nor during that time did he ever show another sign of wishing to live on his own. What made him change his mind? Did he find he missed his home when he was away from it? Had he a bad conscience at leaving his mother and sisters? Was his sojourn away a disagreeable experience? There is an entertaining account in his letters to Reggie of the horrors of a visit to a Mr and Mrs C. who were, it appears from the letters, connected with the stage.

'It rained hard all the time, and was icy cold, and they talked over old provincial tours together all the time. . . . It is an awful *ménage*. Mrs C. said to me on my arrival "We eat mostly cold here" (a most uncouth phrase!)—and so they did—and none too much of that—and there were no fires though we were all shivering.'

If C. stands for Carson one can understand why Max preferred living at home. But perhaps it did not. Many names begin with C. It is only just to the memory of Mr and Mrs Carson to give them the benefit of the doubt.

(3)

Now, in the spring of 1898, an event happened which made Max's financial situation slightly easier. He got a letter from the *Saturday Review* asking him to become their dramatic critic in succession to Bernard Shaw. Shaw was easily the most brilliant critic of the day. To be chosen to succeed him was a great honour for a young man of twenty-six. How Max came to be invited is a little obscure. Frank Harris, the editor of the paper, was away at the time, and the actual offer was made by his deputy. The original idea seems to have come from Shaw himself. When Harris heard of it, his first impulse was to try to stop Shaw from leaving. He telegraphed 'Hang on!' Shaw was not pleased. 'It makes me perfectly mad,' he replied, 'to get an idiotic wire like this in such an emergency. "Hang on" be damned! Idiots! G. B. S.' After this Harris agreed. That he should have done so and that Shaw should have urged him to, shows how high Max's reputation had risen by now. For though he had met both men often enough, he did not know them well; nor, in fact, did he care much for either. It would have been odd if he had cared for Harris, who was a phenomenon—and not an agreeable one. Stocky, red-faced, with rolling eyes and a huge curling moustache which he hoped made him look like Bismarck, he was an adventurer who had during the 'eighties burst upon the literary world of England like a tornado. He was a cad, a liar and a professional amorist, all three on a heroic scale; also a brilliant, picturesque talker, with a consider-able gift for writing—he later produced a lively and controversial book about the character of Shakespeare—and a wonderful flair as an editor. Under his auspices the *Saturday Review* had become the best literary periodical of the day. Max, who had first met him with Oscar two or three years before, much enjoyed Harris's conversa-tion; 'He had a marvellous speaking voice,' he said, 'like the organ in Westminster Abbey, and with infallible footwork.' But he had no illusions as to his character. 'Frank Harris is going about like a howling cad seeking who he may blackmail,' he remarks to Reggie in a letter about this time; and when in after-years someone asked him if Frank Harris ever spoke the truth, 'Sometimes, don't you know,' said Max, 'when his invention flagged.' Max got a great deal of fun out of Harris's weaknesses. One day in 1896 he was his guest at a large luncheon. During a moment of silence Harris's voice was heard booming out. 'Unnatural vice!' he was saying, 'I know noth-ing of the joys of unnatural vice. You must ask my friend Oscar about them. But,' he went on, with a reverential change of tone, 'had Shakespeare asked me, I should have had to submit!' Max went home and drew a cartoon of Harris, stark naked and with his moustache bristling, looking coyly over his shoulder at Shakespeare who shrinks back at the alarming prospect. Underneath was written, 'Had Shakespeare asked . . .' This was a very daring cartoon for 1896; and Max showed it to few people. It is not known if Harris was one of them. He is unlikely to have minded if he did see it; he was remarkably impervious to Max's teasing. At another luncheon he listened to Harris relating with gusto an anecdote about himself that Max recognized as taken from a book by Anatole France. At the end, 'Now Frank,' said Max demurely, 'Anatole France would have spoilt that story.' Unruffled and unabashed, Harris proceeded

FRANK HARRIS

to regale the company with some other sensational and apocryphal piece of autobiography.

Shaw was a better man than Harris; but Max did not like him much either. His first meeting with him had been in 1894 when Max was in London during an Oxford vacation. Shaw had heard him praised as a cartoonist. Suddenly he arrived at the Beerbohms' house on a bicycle: he had ridden many miles to ask Max to do a likeness of himself. Max was less gratified by this than might have been expected. He realized that he was as yet an amateur in his art and suspected that Shaw was actuated less by admiration than by a desire for the publicity the cartoon might bring him. Max also found Shaw's appearance unappetizing; his pallid pitted skin and red hair like seaweed. And he was repelled by the back of his neck. 'The back of his neck was especially bleak; very long, untenanted, and dead white,' he explained.

During succeeding years Max often had occasion to write about Shaw's work. His reaction to this was mixed. There was much in it he liked. It was vigorous, original, entertaining—in every way superior to the kind of thing that Andrew Lang and his friends wrote and admired. On the other hand there was something essentially unaesthetic about it; and something inhuman. Shaw cared more for ideas than for people; Max was the reverse. If Shaw realized Max's feelings about him he did not mind. He had the virtues of his inhumanity: he was not at all touchy. Max, he thought, would do the *Saturday Review* job better than anyone else he could think of. Harris, once he was convinced that Shaw would not stay on, agreed. The only person to hesitate was Max himself. He shrank from the effort of having to produce an article every week. Nor did he wish to be a dramatic critic. He realized that he had some qualifications for the work: he had been in touch with the theatre all his life, he had even toyed with the idea of writing for it himself. But his boyish, romantic enthusiasm for it had vanished long ago and it was no longer a form of art which ever gave him a high satisfaction. All the same, he recognized that, as jobs went, this one suited him far better than most. When he thought of his mother and sisters and the weekly bills, he did not feel he could refuse it. Anyway, he did not suppose it would be for very long. He wrote to accept; but added that he thought he should be paid more highly than Shaw. 'I have less experience of the theatre and so will find the work more difficult,' he said. What the *Saturday Review* thought of this unusual argument is not on record. All we know is that its editor settled with Max for five pounds a week. On 2 May Shaw wrote his farewell article. 'The younger generation is knocking at the door,' it ended, 'and as I open it there steps sprightly in the incomparable Max.'

The incomparable Max himself was not feeling so sprightly. 'So I have got to go on the streets of journalism this week,' he wrote to Will Rothenstein, '—an intellectual prostitute. I hope you won't pass me by.'

CHAPTER FIVE

The 'Saturday Review'

(1)

Mꜰᴀx was mistaken in thinking that his new job would not last for long. He remained dramatic critic of the *Saturday Review* for twelve years. It was to be his only experience of regular work. He did not like it. For one thing, he found the process of composition disagreeable. His standards were very high; he felt it an obligation always to write as well as he could; and he only could do this by making a painful effort. This effort had to be made on Thursday, which was the last day he could send his copy in. As a consequence, already by Wednesday he felt oppressed and anxious. Thursday itself was a day of torment. Max shut himself up in his room all day, telling his relations that on no account must he be disturbed. Mrs Beerbohm therefore gave orders that the house must be noiseless; no bell was to be rung, no door to be slammed. Once when he was interrupted, we are told, he so far forgot his customary composure as to let forth a cry like a wounded animal. But for the most part he sat silent at his desk. He found it very hard to get started. Gloomily and slowly he would, he tells us, trace an initial letter; then, uncertain how to go on, would start turning the letter into a face, then adding a figure to the face—anything to postpone composing a sentence. In the end the task did get done; and Friday, Max admitted, was always a wonderfully pleasant day by contrast with its predecessor. All too soon, however, Thursday came back again.

Nor was the suffering caused by the effort of composition made up for in the pleasure he took in his subject matter. He was right in thinking he was not a natural dramatic critic. He lacked that sheer love of being in a theatre that enabled an author like Hazlitt to write with gusto about a play he thought worthless. Moreover, Max lacked the critical temper. He knew what it was, and recognized it when he saw it; for he well defines it as 'the power to translate through one's own intellect and temperament the fine work of another man, to cast new light on its beauties, to reveal things hidden in it, to illustrate and explain its meaning'. This is true, but not of Max. Here we come up against a disadvantage of his self-sufficiency. Though broad-minded, he was too incurably detached to enter another's spirit in such a way as to penetrate its secrets. He hardly wanted to. Exquisitely he appreciates the exotic charm of the Japanese players who visited London in 1901: but he prefers, he says, not to confuse his enjoyment by trying to fathom their minds and feelings. He can be illuminating on a formal or technical issue of which he has first-hand knowledge—the reviews contain some admirable pages on the art of prose and on style in dialogue—but otherwise, though always intelligent and agreeable, they seldom add to our deeper understanding of their subject.

Finally, like other creative artists, Max wrote willingly only about those things that fulfilled his creative impulse. This was a comic impulse. Dramatic criticism only very occasionally gave scope to Max the comedian. He realized this. 'My whole position is uncomfortable,' he says in his first article, 'I have a satiric temperament: when I am laughing at anyone I am generally rather amusing, but when I am praising anyone I am always deadly dull.' This is an exaggeration; Max could not be dull. But it is true that he is more himself, and therefore more interesting, when he is making fun of Pinero's style or Mrs Humphry Ward's plots, than when he is writing seriously about Galsworthy or Ibsen. For the rest, Max's *Saturday Review* articles are most memorable when he gets away from the drama to indulge in meditation, mocking or whimsical as the mood takes him, on popular taste or Sarah Bernhardt's memoirs, or to draw a verbal cartoon of some personality like Dan Leno or Henry Irving—when, in fact, he stops being a critic and reverts to being an essayist.

Then as always he is a very good essayist indeed: and in a fashion unique in his work. The *Saturday Review* articles are different from Max's other essays. Not so creative; for they offer less scope for his fantastic vein than his pure essays do: they are more like Hazlitt's essays and less like Elia's. On the other hand, they do reveal to us what we find nowhere else: Max's serious opinions about life and about art. For he had opinions on these subjects. To avoid doing so he would have needed to be unintelligent or superficial; and he was neither. During the last five years—in Oxford, in New York and

London—he had observed, reflected, drawn conclusions. It was in his dramatic criticisms and in a few other articles written during the same years that we find them. In them we see a different and graver aspect of Max than any disclosed elsewhere. If we want a complete picture of his mind and outlook in maturity we must read them. It seems an appropriate moment to pause and examine them in greater detail. This will mean occasionally taking a step forward into the future to see what he says in pieces he wrote later than 1900. But this will not mislead us. Max, for the next ten years at least, was pretty well set in his opinions.

His journalism is also illuminating because it reveals his figure in a larger context. He often writes about topics of the day—more specifically on intellectual and artistic topics—so that we see him in relation to his own age. This age is what is generally known as Edwardian. Inaccurately, as it happens; the Muse of History is not so considerate to her servants as to arrange that the successive phases of England's development should coincide exactly with the successive reigns of her sovereigns. The so-called 'Victorian' age ended some time before the death of Queen Victoria; the so-called Edwardian period started about 1880 and went on till 1914.

It was a lively, diverse, fecund period; and at first sight it makes a cheerful impression on the imagination. The very word 'Edwardian' conjures up a vision of vigour, confidence and opulence; Sargent's portraits, Shaw's plays, Elgar's music, the first Rolls-Royce cars. It was an age of hitherto unequalled material progress and prosperity; England was still on the crest of the wave, her standard of living rising; and with new inventions—bicycles, cars, cinemas, aeroplanes —appearing every year to strengthen the Englishman's belief in himself and add to the amenity of his existence. This last was also increased by a growing relaxation of manners. Conventions were becoming less formal, morals freer, talk franker and more flippant, women more emancipated, children more indulged. Indeed, children —just because they were uninhibited—became the fashion. Peter Pan flew in at the nursery window; the wind was heard whispering in the willows. Even stern advocates of socialism like H. G. Wells, or of the military virtues like Kipling, could unbend and romp and be whimsical. For dignity counted for far less than in the Victorian age. So, in general, did refinement. Compared with his father, the typical Edwardian was vulgar. Politics were being democratized and culture along with them. It was a great age of popularizers and showmen—intellectual and material, commercial and artistic.

The fact that they found audiences was a sign that the people were looking for a creed. In fact Edwardian England, though materially so flourishing, was spiritually adrift. It was far from being so comfortable a place as it appeared on the surface. The average healthy philistine citizen, basking in the sunshine of present prosperity, might be carefree enough. But the more thoughtful, even if hopeful, felt unsettled. For that sense of solidity and permanence which characterized English society in the eighteenth century and persisted sufficiently to keep it stable throughout the changes of the nineteenth, was crumbling under the attacks of rationalism and the shock of scientific discovery. The standards—political, social, religious, sexual—on which it rested, were everywhere questioned: everywhere people were proposing new and revolutionary recipes for the good life, corporate or individual. This is why the showmen and popularizers found so many listeners. Literary England was like a market, full of sharp-witted stall-holders clamorously crying their wares. On the one hand Shaw and Wells were to be heard recommending each his own brand of salvation by socialism or science, on the other Belloc and Chesterton shouted the praises of their patent blend of democratic liberalism and medieval Christianity; elsewhere, Kipling trumpeted the sovereign virtues of discipline and imperialism; and, though early bereft of their leader, aesthetes continued to chant the gospel according to Oscar Wilde. Meanwhile a few distinguished authors separated themselves from the mêlée to contemplate independently and in solitude their private visions of experience. Thomas Hardy combined a passionate sympathy for human suffering with a sense of the incurable tragedy of the human lot: Henry James and Conrad dedicated themselves each to the pursuit of moral and aesthetic perfection as he conceived it.

Such then was the confused and heterogeneous spectacle presented by the Edwardian literary scene. How did Max relate himself to it? In one sense he refused to relate himself at all. Max had settled on his basic attitude to life long before this time; and, as at home, as at Charterhouse and at Oxford, he took up the role of an ironic onlooker on life. Both these words, however, need to be qualified. Though Max was an onlooker, he was not an outsider; though ironic, he was not hostile. The last trace of the rebellious young aesthete had left him. He no longer had any wish to shock people. It was true that he himself did not want to participate in the activities of the great world. But he did not disapprove of them and he was amused to watch them. In fact he was himself a citizen of that great world; and, so far from despising it, found it an endlessly entertaining spectacle. He found himself exhilarated by the sight of those who kept it going: statesmen, lawyers, publicists, journalists, courtiers, men of fashion. No doubt they were often absurd; but so was everyone else, and on the whole he liked them the better for it.

Nor was his irony the sign of an uncertain mind; it implied no lack of standards. On the contrary, it was a proof he had them. Max's satiric vision of the world acquired its perspective and significance from the fact that it was related to a consistent scheme of values. This was very much his own alike in conception and application. As he belonged to no one social set, so he belonged to no one intellectual or aesthetic party: he formed his intelligent judgement on his independent impressions. We note this in his dramatic criticisms. Conventional society admired Pinero; Max did not. The unconventional intelligentsia agreed to praise the acting of Eleonora Duse; Max found her performances singularly monotonous. 'Age cannot wither her,' he said. 'Nor custom stale her endless uniformity.'

All this might suggest a captious pleasure in disagreement: but Max was too indifferent to other people's opinion to be captious. As a matter of fact, he often took the orthodox view. He shared the fashionable admiration for Sarah Bernhardt; Maeterlinck, an idol of the intelligentsia, was Max's idol too; and he loved Dan Leno every bit as much as the great British public did. Nor was he frightened of being considered philistine. Was it philistine to be bored by Greek tragedy acted in English? Max did not mind if it was. But he was sure he was bored; and he suspected that other people were too. What surprised him was that they should be afraid to say so.

'So few people have the courage of their opinions,' he writes. 'Not that I am proud of having the courage of mine. Indeed, I do not see where "courage" comes in. I do not understand why a man should hesitate to say, as best he can, just whatever he thinks and feels. He has nothing to fear, nowadays. No one will suggest the erection of a stake for him to be burned at. No one will be at all angry with him. Euripides, if I remember rightly, had finally to leave Athens, so hotly were his opinions resented. He, then, had been courageous in insisting on these opinions, despite all Athens, throughout his career. But nowadays, especially in England, there is no obstruction to sincerity. Are there not, on the contrary, great inducements to it? So far from being angry, people admire and respect you for your "courage". You gain a cheap reputation for a quality to which, as likely as not, you have no real claim. It is as though a soldier in battle were accounted a hero for charging up to the muzzles of guns which he knew to be unloaded. Oddly enough, the quality which enables a soldier to advance in a hail of bullets is far more common than the quality which enables him, in civilian life, to tell the truth. I should think twice before advancing under a hail of bullets. I should be eager in so far as I knew that I should be admired. I should be reluctant in so far as I expected to be dead. You, reader, think that I show moral courage in this very confession of my lack of physical courage. Yet you are not despising me for the lack: you are but honouring me for the confession. So what in the world was there to prevent me from confessing? Clear your mind of this cant of moral courage, I beg you; and, knowing that you have nothing to fear, go in for sincerity on your own account.'

Here Max shows his common sense. Indeed common sense is one of the two elements of which is compounded that scheme of values by which he makes his judgements. The other element is aesthetic sensibility. Sensibility came first. Max approved of a thing primarily because it was beautiful or delightful; he disapproved of it because it was ugly or unpleasant. His conception of beauty was a highly civilized one. Too intelligent not to recognize that there were such things as artless or savage beauty, himself he preferred a beauty orderly, refined, delicate. Not cloudy, though: it is here that his common sense comes in. Max had a shrewd rational grasp of the realities of human existence and the movements of his imagination and heart were vigilantly checked by reference to it. The irony which pervades his work was the irony of common sense: his flights of fancy are always seen in comic relation to rational reality. However extravagant his high spirits, he is never silly. Again, though he liked a play to be well made, he cared more that it should be true to human experience. Nor was he able to accept theatrical convention obviously inconsistent with the illusion of reality: an old man played by a young actor, a suburban housewife dressed in the height of Parisian fashion, Sarah Bernhardt in the role of Hamlet. 'Hamlet, Princess of Denmark'—so he entitled his article about her.

Max's incorruptible good sense made him especially impatient of newspaper nonsense: headline hyperbole, clichés that had no basis in fact. Why must journalists, for instance, go on saying, in face of all the evidence of history, that the militant movement was likely to delay the passing of women's suffrage?

'For fifty years or so, many quiet, thoughtful, irreproachable, elderly ladies, wrote and published in the monthly reviews very able and closely-reasoned expositions of the injustice involved in depriving women of the right to vote. And the sole result of all the trouble taken by these quiet, thoughtful, irreproachable, elderly, perfect ladies was that they were called "the shrieking sisterhood". Two or three years ago, other ladies, anxious to vote, came forward and have gone around literally shrieking; and the result is that already their desire is treated as a matter of practical politics, and a quite urgent one at that. What a pretty light all this throws—does it not?—on a world governed by the animals which distinguish themselves from the other animals by taking "reasonable animals" as their label! And yet the light does not seem to have enlightened the brilliantly reasonable animals which write for the press. Invariably, solemnly, at every fresh "raid" or other escapade of the suffragist ladies, those newspapers which are friendly to the cause itself announce that "this has put back the clock of female suffrage by at least twenty years". Bless their hearts! The clock must now, by their computation, have been put back "at least" twelve centuries. And when a Bill giving the vote to woman is passed through Parliament, as will happen in the very near future, it will be hailed as yet another triumph for Reason, mistress of us all.'

Here Max is attacking moral sloth and moral insincerity as much as a journalistic cliché. Indeed the three were inseparable: cliché was the consequence of insincerity and sloth. Max applied the same standards to moral as to aesthetic phenomena. He demanded that conduct as well as art should be beautiful. Beautiful in the same way too; Max was a moral aristocrat, an amateur of fine feelings, of the delicate point of honour, the chivalrous or magnanimous impulse.

174

For these exemplified beauty in the moral sphere. Morally ugly were treachery, vulgarity of sentiment; and, as such, detestable. His feeling for style in art found its counterpart in a feeling for style in morals. No amount of intelligence or earnestness absolved a man from the obligation to behave sensitively and considerately to others. Max also thought that people should try to live up to the highest standards they knew of, whether or not these had a popular appeal. So far as he saw it, they seldom had. Max had a horror of what he called the 'idols of the market-place': Kipling, Hall Caine and Jerome K. Jerome.

Max's moral judgements were also modified by his belief in good sense. It gave him an especial dislike of humbug. Amusedly he contemplated English audiences gazing with faces of foolish wonder at performances by foreign actors in languages of which they did not understand a word; amusedly he listened to them rhapsodizing afterwards on the subtleties of these performances. Truly the vanity of human beings was something to marvel at! And what was he to think of the nonsense talked by the newspapers when Edward VII's coronation was deferred on account of his illness.

'By their coarse piling-up of the agony, the newspapers have made even our genuine emotion seem suspect. "From the highest pinnacle of joy," writes a popular and influential causeur. "We have been hurled to the deepest abyss of gloom." That is a fair sample of the cant with which we have been deluged. What was really the sensation of the average Englishman when he heard the bad news? Firstly, and chiefly, personal disappointment that there was to be no show, and (in many cases) annoyance at the loss of money laid out. Secondly, a loyal hope that the King would recover. Thirdly, an aesthetic realization of the whole tragedy, hardly more painful to him than the realization of a vivid tragedy in fiction or in past history. This may not be an agreeable analysis. But it is a true one. And it is more wholesome, and less really offensive, than all the others which have been made for us. National tragedies cannot affect us as do our own personal tragedies, as do the tragedies of those who are near and dear to us. What use is there in pretending that they can?'

Max judges the moral worth of an action by quality rather than by effect. He dislikes humbug, for example, not because it makes people unhappy—as he well knew, it often does nothing of the kind

—but because it is morally ugly. He admires a scrupulous sense of honour because it is morally beautiful. Now to judge an action primarily by its quality implies surely a belief in some absolute and eternal standard beyond human life, to which it is man's duty to adhere even if the sum of human happiness is not thereby increased. Max's view, that is to say, if pursued to its logical conclusion, should surely have led him to hold some sort of transcendental faith. But Max had not the intellectual interest nor the kind of intellectual power that leads people to pursue thoughts to their logical conclusion; and, so far as we know, he had never had any experience to suggest the existence of spiritual realities outside the limits of mortality. On the one or two occasions when he gets near to discussing ultimate questions, he reveals himself as a calm and complete sceptic, equally unconvinced by religious or by rationalist attempts to solve the mystery of life. Maeterlinck's shadowy enigmatic little dramas moved him deeply because he felt Maeterlinck's view of life so true.

'Of all living thinkers whose names are known to me,' Max says of him, 'he has the firmest and widest grasp of the truth. He more clearly than any other thinker is conscious of the absurdity of attempting to fashion out of the vast and impenetrable mysteries of life any adequate little explanation—any philosophy. He sees further than any other into the darkness, has a keener insight into his own ignorance, a deeper modesty, a higher wisdom. In his youth, the mystery of life obsessed him. He beheld our planet reeling in infinity, having on its surface certain infinitesimal creatures all astray at the mercy of unknown laws. And he shuddered. And he wrote certain plays which, as mere expressions of the pathos of man's lot, and the awfulness of the mystery of life, will not be surpassed. Little by little, the shudders in him abated. The more a man thinks about infinity, the better does he realize that what he can grasp of infinity is but a speck, signifying nothing; and, accordingly, the more important will become to him the visible and tangible creatures and things around him. Maeterlinck began to look around him, to "take notice" with babyish pleasure, with the fresh vision of a true seer. The world seemed to him a very-well-worth-while place. Who was he to say that we had no free-will? How could he possibly know that, or anything else? If we are but the puppets of destiny, and if destiny is, on the whole, rather unkind, still there seems to be quite enough of joy and beauty for us to go on with.'

Whether or not this is an accurate analysis of Maeterlinck's outlook, it well describes Max's own. He thought that the riddle of life was of its nature insoluble; so much so that it was a waste of time to worry about it. But he was not unduly depressed by this reflection. His own experience had kept him cheerful. Good luck, good sense and good spirits disposed him to think that human existence, however baffling and faulty, was unquestionably worth living.

Certainly he found it so in Edwardian London, especially in the first years of the twentieth century. In some respects Max was very much the child of his age and suited by it. His aesthetic and literary tastes were in the vanguard of his time not only in books but in plays and in the visual arts. He admired Beardsley, Sickert, Conder, and the early pictures of Augustus John; he was one of the first to praise Gordon Craig's revolutionary ideas about stage design. In the quarrel between the old and the new theatre, Max—though always independent—unhesitatingly ranged himself on the side of the new. He was also wholly in sympathy with the Edwardian reaction against Victorian solemnity and sobriety. Himself he was an outstanding manifestation of this reaction. Max's elegant impudence was typically Edwardian. So also was the way he dramatized himself for the entertainment and mystification of the public. In his own graceful well-bred way he was one of the Edwardian showmen; as much a public personality as Shaw or Oscar Wilde. The difference between him and them was that they had platforms, stood for socialism or for aestheticism. Max stood only for Max, for his uncommitted, idiosyncratic self.

Up to a point, then, Max was in tune with the Edwardian age. But no further! There was much about it that he did not like at all. It was too unsettled, for one thing. Max liked things tranquil, orderly, unchanging. The art of life as he conceived of it required, if it was to be effectively practised, a setting of calm and custom. The Edwardian age was far from providing such a setting. Nor did its scientific and mechanical innovations appeal to him. So far as he could see their only effect would be to make life more hectic and less safe. He prophesied the future with what has since turned out to be an alarming accuracy.

'When penny-stamps and steam-engines were vouchsafed to the world,' he writes in 1909, 'it was honestly thought that thereby a great deal of time and trouble would be saved for us. When, furthermore, motor-cars and telephones and "tubes" were shaken out of the cornucopia, you scrambled for them eagerly, not having learned your lesson. You have learned it now. There is not one thinking person among you that would not, for sake of the happiness of the human race, be glad to have these "tyrannous toys" smashed up and swept away and forgotten. That cannot be, of course. The world is not governed by sense. What you think good for you, what you really want, counts for little. Nobody—except perhaps a fourth-form boy here and there—wants to possess an airship. But every nation will have to possess as many of them as it can —until air-ships be superseded by some subtler and swifter vehicle, for use in the very-soon-by-some-inspired-idiot-to-be-discovered fourth dimension of space. In course of time, thanks to science, the human race will collapse and cease.'

He was against the spirit of the age in other ways too. The new cult of the child did not appeal to him. He doubted if children enjoyed *Peter Pan* as much as their elders did. As for himself, 'We may be allowed to laugh,' he said, 'this century, for which science promised a mature perfection, is vanishing in a cloud of pinafores.' More strongly did he feel a distaste for Edwardian vulgarity. Vulgarity was the quality he disliked most; and he found the Edwardian brand especially unattractive. There was something aggressive and ungenial about it, as it manifested itself in Kipling's bullying militarism, in Wells's guttersnipe hostility to ancient culture, in the expensive grossness of Edward VII, in the new bustling commercialism that was defacing the country with advertisements, tearing down the buildings that gave London its august and reticent beauty. Surely there was something deeply wrong with a nation that tolerated these things. Was England deteriorating—growing coarse and corrupt? There were moments when Max did see life more darkly, when his spirit, forgetting its usual urbanity, suddenly boiled over in a ferment of uncharacteristic bitterness against his nation and his age. This appears most signally in a series of cartoons called *The Second Childhood of John Bull* which he exhibited in 1901. In these John Bull is shown as a degenerate fallen figure without courage or self-control or proper pride; servile to foreigners he fears, contemptuous of those who do not threaten him, lethargic on the conduct of the Boer War but drunkenly boastful if for a moment he is victorious in it; and certain, through his own fault, to come to a bad end before long.

They are not very good cartoons. For one thing, Max's gift was for satirizing individuals not nations. For another, Max the cartoonist, like Max the writer, is not good when he is angry. His line lacks the strength to convey savagery. But, whatever their defects as works of art, these cartoons do express his opinions. They reveal that, underneath the smooth surface he presented to the world, he was in many ways at odds with his age. He did not like the way it was going and at times it could disgust him.

Nor had he any belief that it could save itself. Max got little comfort from the thought of the various remedies for the present discontents proposed by his vociferous contemporaries. They promised too much, for they promised salvation. Max disbelieved in schemes of salvation.

'If you hear a voice from afar, do not take the message seriously. Wisdom is a thing that can be expressed only in an under-tone. Life —even such part of it as our limited human brains can conceive— is a very weird, august, complex, and elusive affair. To have any positive theory of it, any single dogmatic point of view, any coherent "message", is an act of impertinence. To be an optimist or a pessimist, a realist or an idealist, a Thingumyite or a Somebodyan, to belong to any "school of thought" whatsoever, is to write oneself down an ass—for anyone who can read. The true sage, he who penetrates the furthest, and raises the most of the fringe that surrounds the darkness, dares not enunciate any "truth" without a hundred-and-one reservations and qualifications. It is the awe-struck whisper, then, the tremulous murmur; not the cheery or angry megaphonic shout or screech that "carries" across frontiers. He may be heard by a few in his own land. He most assuredly will not have a European reputation. That sort of thing is reserved for inspired asses like Tolstoi or Nietzsche—for men who have gone off at a tangent, men precipitated along one sharp narrow line which they mistake for the whole dim universe. It is natural that they, in their joy or their wrath, should shout or screech very resonantly;

and let us not grudge them their lungs; and let us, by all means, listen to them; they are great fun. Take them seriously?—ah no! If they happen to be artists, expressing themselves through some art-form, through poems or plays or novels, let us delight in their concentration, the narrowness that enables them to express just what they can feel, just what they can understand, so much more forcibly than if they had a sense of proportion and a little of the modesty that comes of wisdom. Our Ibsens and D'Annunzios and Bernard Shaws and Gorkis—let us harken to them and revel in them. But let us mix up all their "messages" together, and strike an average, and not suppose even then that we are appreciably one whit nearer to the truth of things.'

Further, the particular blue-prints to salvation offered by his fellow Edwardians were most of them so unappetizing: Shaw's salvation by socialism, Wells's salvation by science, Kipling's salvation by order of the drill serjeant. The religious schemes proposed by Chesterton and Belloc, Max found less offensive. But they were not for him. Nor did the statesmen of his time give him any more hope for the future than did the sages. Max kept out of active politics as he kept out of most things: he even refused to be registered as a voter. But he never lost his old onlooker's interest in the subject: and he had his opinions. He called himself a Tory Anarchist. It was as good a name as any other. Certainly he was not an orthodox Tory. He was too independent and too irreverent: Max the man was still the son of the schoolboy who had disliked the fagging system. He was also still the son of the schoolboy who felt an irresistible desire to make fun of any institution which others wanted to treat with respect. As for the new middle-class imperialist Toryism associated with Joseph Chamberlain and Kipling—aggressive, hustling, un-gentlemanlike—it was all that Max detested most. The Boer War was its typical manifestation. Max was opposed to the Boer War.

But if he was not an orthodox Tory, still less was he a Radical. Radicalism meant change and disturbance and iconoclasm. It was wholly out of sympathy with leisure and elegance and a taste for the charms of antiquity, with all indeed that made life worth living to Max. Besides, he was too clear-headed not to realize that the aesthetic mode of life in which his particular genius flowered could exist comfortably only within a framework of privilege and tradition, and this framework it was the avowed object of Liberals and Radicals to destroy. Further, they proposed to do it in the name of democracy. Max felt no enthusiasm at all for democracy. His personal experience had not encouraged him to do so. As a humorist and an aesthete, he judged others by their taste in jokes and in art. Popular taste in both was deplorable. On the evidence of music halls and comic papers Max once made up a list of the subjects that the populace thought mirth-provoking.

'*Mothers-in-law—Hen-pecked husbands—Twins—Old Maids—Jews —Frenchmen, Germans, Italians, Negroes (not Russians, or other foreigners of any denomination)—Fatness—Thinness—Long hair (worn by a man)—Baldness—Sea-sickness—Stuttering—Bad Cheese— "Shooting the moon" (slang expression for leaving a lodging-house without paying the bill).*'

Pondering on this list Max sought to discover the common qualities in these diverse subjects that made the public find them mirth-provoking. He came to a depressing conclusion.

'Take the first item—*Mothers-in-law*. Why should the public roar, as roar it does, at the mere mention of that relationship? There is nothing intrinsically absurd in the notion of a woman with a married daughter. It is probable that she will sympathize with her daughter in any quarrel that may rise between husband and wife. It is probable, also, that she will, as a mother, demand for her daughter more unselfish devotion than the daughter herself expects. But this does not make her ridiculous. The public laughs not at her, surely. It always respects a tyrant. It laughs at the implied concept of the oppressed son-in-law, who has to wage unequal warfare against two women. It is amused by suffering. This explanation covers, of course, the second item on my list—*Hen-pecked husbands*. It covers, also, the third and fourth items. The public is amused by the notion of a needy man put to double expense, and of a woman who has had no chance of fulfilling her destiny. The laughter at Jews, too, may be a survival of the old Jew-baiting spirit. Or this laughter may be explained by the fact which alone can explain why the public laughs at *Frenchmen, Germans, Italians, Negroes*. Jews, after all, are foreigners, strangers, and the public has never got used to them. The only apparent reason why it laughs at the notion of *Frenchmen, etc.*, is that they are unlike itself. (At the mention of *Russians and other foreigners* it does not laugh, because it has no idea what they are like: it has seen too few samples of them.)

So far, then, we have found two elements in the public's humour: delight in suffering, contempt for the unfamiliar.'

Popular taste in art was no better than popular taste in humour. Max's experience as a dramatic critic had taught him that.

'Wafted down to me from the gallery are shouts of laughter at the wrong moment; uproarious cheers for the cheapest and falsest sentiments; howls and groans, sometimes, for an author who has done fine work; salvoes for the charlatan. Speaking with the authority of an intelligent person somewhat expert in the art of the theatre, I say that the gallery is almost always wrong.'

He made this sufficiently clear for Chesterton publicly to reprove him for not sympathizing with the democratic ideal. Max replied:

'Mr Chesterton once chid me, in a brilliant essay, for not cherishing in my heart the ideal of democracy. It is quite true that I don't believe at all firmly in (what has always been to Mr Chesterton a dark and mystical reality) the wisdom of the people. I would not stake sixpence on the people's capacity for governing itself, and not a penny on its capacity for governing me. Democracy, wherever it has been tried, has failed as a means of increasing the sum of human happiness. Autocracy, aristocracy, bureaucracy, and all the other modes of government have similarly failed. In theory they are all of them admirable, but they won't work in practice. They would, doubtless, if man were a rational and an unselfish animal. But man is not built that way, and cannot be trusted either to wield power wisely or to obey wise ordinances. He means well; but original sin and muddle-headedness, between them, make havoc of his good intentions. Political history is the term by which we dignify the record of his ludicrous flounderings. And the political history of the future will be just as amusing or depressing, you may be sure. And let us smile rather than be indignant, since we cannot hope to remedy the nature of things, and since, after all, there will be, as there has ever been, a general impression that life is worth living. The vitality of man will always rise superior to the circumstances of existence.'

Here he ends on the same note of temperate cheerfulness as he sounded in his piece on Maeterlinck. Life, he implies, had enough to recommend it to make it enjoyable in spite of man's faults and follies. Whether it would continue to do so was more doubtful. Thus, cool, amused, unhopeful, Max surveyed the Edwardian scene.

(2)

Max's work for the *Saturday Review* modified the order of his life a little. It sent him to the theatre several nights a week, cut him off from the world on Thursdays, and kept him in London for the greater part of the year. Otherwise his days continued to follow the same easy established round of leisurely work, leisurely social life and leisurely flirtation with Kilseen. Occasionally the round was broken into by holidays; short holidays spent staying with friends or at the English seaside and a long one in summer. This he took to spending at Dieppe. From 1895 Dieppe had been a favourite holiday resort for the *Yellow Book* set: Conder, Beardsley, Sickert, Will Rothenstein and his brother Albert. They chose Dieppe partly because it was cheap, partly because it was picturesque and unspoilt. The streets, churches and harbour, relieved against the grey or sunlit ocean, still retained something of their stately eighteenth-century style. Moreover, though so close to England. Dieppe was indisputably and delightfully foreign, with gambling at the casino and celebrated cocottes like Cléo de Mérode shamelessly disporting themselves on the beach surrounded by admirers. Cléo de Mérode, as a matter of fact, was too famous and fashionable a figure to be a typical Dieppe visitor. She came in the race-week. Max and his friends were not sure if they liked the race-week.

'We used rather to resent the race-week,' he says—'the third week of the month—as an intrusion on our privacy. We sneered as we read in the Paris edition of the *New York Herald* the names of the intruders. We disliked the nightly crush in the baccarat room of the Casino, and the croupiers' obvious excitement at the high play.'

Generally the play was lower. But it was gambling and, as such, forbidden in England, and it contributed to the easy-going, hedonist, Latin atmosphere which made visits to France so exhilarating a change to the English subjects of Queen Victoria. The *Yellow Book* friends vied with one another to extol the charms of Dieppe: 'Dieppe is quite sweet,' said Beardsley, '. . . *petits chevaux* and everything most pretty and amusing!'; and, writes Conder to a friend: 'I might tell all about the place here but the sea air leaves me rather idle; one likes to believe oneself hand in glove with all sorts of poignant emotions, but this sea air is like some drug which makes one satisfied with the desire. Life is so beautiful that one thinks it must end soon.' This was a flight too romantic for Max: but he enjoyed Dieppe very much in his own way. Our earliest definite record of his presence there is in 1900, staying with Sickert at a little hotel called the Maison Lefèvre opposite the old Hôtel de Ville. Here Max became an annual visitor: for it was inexpensive, nine francs a day for everything except wine, and the wine was cheap too. Max always drank a bottle at lunch and a bottle at dinner, sitting at the same round table with Sickert and Reggie. The food too was excellent, and Madame Lefèvre, nicknamed Titine, and the soul of the Maison Lefèvre, cooked it herself. If she liked one of her guests she saw to it that they got something especially good to eat. Max and his friends who enjoyed their food took trouble to court Titine's favour. It was noted that Max was especially skilful at doing this. Between meals the painters went out sketching, and the rest of the party sallied forth—Max dressed carefully in a boater, light suit and buttonhole—to saunter up and down the quays. In the evening they went to the casino to indulge in some mild gambling, to listen to the little orchestra, and to meet some of the French artists like Pissarro and Blanche who frequented Dieppe: while day and night the friends joked and laughed at one another's jokes and talked endlessly about art and letters and the charms and foibles of their friends. Max grew romantic about France—so carefree it seemed and civilized to his holiday-maker's eye—and could hardly bear it when the time came for him to go back to England and the treadmill of first nights.

(3)

One wonders if it was quite such a treadmill as he makes out. Though he still disliked writing the article as much as ever, he seems as the years passed to become more interested in the art of drama and had evolved his own standards by which to judge it. Very exacting standards they were! Inevitably they were primarily aesthetic. 'It

MAX ON A HOLIDAY, SELF-CARICATURE

is at the production of aesthetic pleasure that plays should aim,' he writes. A good play was before all things beautiful, orderly, harmonious. But Max's conception of the theatrical art was such as to require the artist to satisfy other standards too. Art reflects life; a play could not be good if it was false to life. Again, only the intelligent could fully enjoy art. A play must have a strong intellectual content if it was to appeal to an intelligent audience. It is by these three standards of beauty, reality and intelligence that Max judged the plays he went to see. His judgement was seldom favourable. Most plays failed to come up to one or other of his three standards. The ordinary commercial Edwardian play failed to come up to any of them. A conventional entertainment, designed to provide wish-fulfilment daydreams for tired philistines when digesting large dinners, it had nothing to offer to the intellect, the sense of beauty or the sense of reality. But Max was rarely enthusiastic even about more reputable types of play. The classics of the theatre, for instance, were interesting to read and often beautifully written, but for him they generally ceased to communicate a sense of life on the stage. The works of Euripides—at least as translated by Professor Gilbert Murray—were lifeless; Milton's *Samson Agonistes* was even worse.

'For good downright boredom,' he said, 'mingled with acute irritation, commend me to the evening I spent last Tuesday in the theatre of Burlington House. The Milton Tercentenary has produced a fine crop of dullness and silliness, but nothing quite so silly and dull as this performance of *Samson Agonistes*.'

Shakespeare had much more stage sense; *A Midsummer Night's Dream* was still delightful. But, thought Max, it might be quite a good thing for actors to give Shakespeare a rest. How refreshing if *Hamlet* was forbidden the stage for a number of years! As for the lesser English dramatists like Goldsmith, Max found them merely obvious and amateurish.

This was a lapse on Max's part. It is more evidence that his sense of the past, so acute at short range, failed to operate a hundred or more years before his time. He cannot enter the conventions of these old plays sufficiently to sympathize with the feelings and thoughts of the characters in them. There was no trouble about this in his own period. As we have seen, he strongly espoused the cause of the new drama, warmly appreciated his contemporaries even when they were unlike himself. One does not associate Max with Galsworthy's lugubrious essays in social realism. But he writes with enthusiasm about *Justice* and *Strife*. They satisfied two of his standards: they dealt with ideas and showed direct observation of reality. Shaw's plays too—though in some ways Max found them unsympathetic—were incontestably the brilliant expression of a brilliant mind and as such had aesthetic value.

All the same, he seldom gives unqualified praise even to his contemporaries. Generally they failed to fulfil one or other of his three requirements, were either unreal or intellectually empty, or aesthetically displeasing. Gorki—and this was why Max was so down on him—failed on two counts. *The Lower Depths* might be true to life in a Russian doss-house—Max could believe anything of Russian doss-houses—but it contained no ideas and was unpardonably ugly from start to finish.

'There must be some kind of artistic unity—unity either of story or of idea. There must be a story, though it need not be stuck to like grim death; or there must be, with similar reservation, an idea. Gorki has neither asset. At any rate he does nothing with either asset. Enough that he gives us, honestly and fearlessly, "a slice of life"? Enough, certainly, if he did anything of the kind. But he doesn't. *The Lower Depths* is no "slice". It is chunks, hunks, shreds and gobbets, clawed off anyhow, chucked at us anyhow. "No thank you" is the only possible reception for such work.'

Shaw, too, often failed to make the aesthetic grade. He had little sense of beauty and the characters were too unlike life to gain much sympathy. Max says of *Mrs Warren's Profession* that the conflict in it between mother and daughter is 'not of that kind that makes plays effective, but is rather such a shindy as might be waged between a phantom pot and an imaginary kettle'. Even Henry James, so superb as a writer of fiction, failed to please Max as a dramatist. His plays were, he thought, beautiful works of art and infinitely intelligent; but he made all his characters talk the same language, and that so removed from the language employed in real life as to destroy any illusion of reality.

Max, then, is very hard to please where plays were concerned. Scarcely any will satisfy all three of his standards. Those that do are a little surprising. He has nothing but praise for Maeterlinck's dim little dramas. For Max they were beautiful, thoughtful and a true image of the human predicament. He also considered Barrie's *The Admirable Crichton* 'the best thing that had happened to the theatre in his time': for it was both an entertaining flight of imagination and an acute comment on the English class system. Barrie and Maeterlinck were gifted writers and deserving of more attention than they get nowadays. But it was odd to pick them out for unqualified praise from among all the writers of the age. Like that of most creative artists, Max's taste was highly idiosyncratic.

A growing interest in the theatre led to his dabbling a little in playwriting himself. His visit to Murray Carson had in the end resulted in collaboration in a comedy called *The Fly on the Wheel*, and he had also worked with Frank Harris on an adaptation from the French called *Caesar's Wife*. Both plays were successful enough to reach the London stage. *Caesar's Wife* was produced at Wyndham's Theatre in March 1902, and *The Fly on the Wheel* at the Coronet Theatre in 1904. Neither play added to Max's fame, nor indeed do they show much sign of his authorship. A short dramatic effort made earlier deserves more attention. This was a one-act dramatization of *The Happy Hypocrite*, produced by Mrs Patrick Campbell as a curtain-raiser at the Royalty Theatre in December 1900. It is cruder and more farcical than the story; there is nothing in the play to show Max is toying with a real conviction or that there was something sincere in its sentiment. But it is lively, it shows a sense of the stage, and was well received by the first-night audience. Max was too prudent to be there himself, so he went for the night to Brighton. There, after the performance was over, his friends rang him up to tell him of its success. He ordered a bottle of champagne and sat down to write the good news to Reggie.

'Here am I, all alone, "remote, unfriended" etc., in order to avoid the temptation of going before the curtain—a practice for which I have so often condemned those whom I may now call my fellow-dramatists. If I had been in London, I should have been horribly frightened, and I could not have kept away from the theatre, and I should have been dragged on, pallid and deprecating, by Mrs P. C. This lady, by the way, really is a rather wonderful creature. As stage-manageress she has been absolutely intelligent and sweet and charming all through. I do wish you had been here (or there, rather) to see the production. I wonder what the papers will say. Rendle, I am sure, will say it was "very thin", and will ask why we should go back to the drama of bib-and-tucker. But I fancy the *Daily Mail* will praise it as being "pure". Archer, too, may possibly call it a humanity-poem, and will urge me to greater solidity. Meanwhile, I find myself very happy, and slightly tipsy, having finished a bottle of "the boy" "on my own".

I don't care a damn if the papers slate the affair. There were five "curtains" after the show. The public, after all, is the *final court of appeal*. The public is on my side.'

The critics were as friendly as the audience had been, except for William Archer, the pioneer translator of Ibsen, who took Max seriously to task for his bad taste in depicting an innocent young girl in the arms of a middle-aged debauchee! This came strangely from the translator of *Ghosts*. Max felt sufficiently stung by Archer's words to take counter-measures.

'Archer has turned traitor,' he tells Reggie, 'however, I wonder if you saw his notice? A terribly flat-footed, stodgy, stupid, thoughtful, able, idiotic two-columns-full. I sent him a caricature of himself in a kilt, his eyes bandaged with a tartan handkerchief, holding in one large raw hand a large cartwheel, in the other a butterfly-net with which he was making wild lunges in the air. Far above him was flying a very graceful and exquisitely-coloured butterfly. On the drawing I wrote "My dear W. A. Breaking a butterfly on a wheel is all very well, but—you must 'first catch your butterfly' "—He wrote back very nicely, but I think he was rather frightened.'

Meanwhile his reputation grew. It was enhanced by periodical publications and exhibitions. He held two one-man shows during these next years at the little Carfax Gallery run by Robert Ross in Ryder Street. The first, in November 1901, consisted of a hundred caricatures of individuals and the satirical series described in a previous page and called *The Second Childhood of John Bull*. The second exhibition, held in April 1904, was more important, for it contained the set of cartoon fantasies about famous writers, dead and alive, which was published in the same year in book form under the title of *The Poets' Corner*. In this, for the first time, Max fully explores the vein which is his unique and peculiar contribution to the art of caricature. Here he first blends Burne-Jones and 'Spy' to create something which is equally pretty and comical. Indeed, one quality enhances the other. The crimson and yellow and turquoise carpet and wallpaper, amid which Tennyson is represented as reading aloud to Queen Victoria, please the eye and are also a sharp piece of visual satire on mid-Victorian fashions in interior decoration. In this series, too, Max develops the literary strain in his cartoonist's inspiration. The captions are as important and as amusing as the drawings.

Three years earlier in an essay on 'The Spirit of Caricature', Max had set forth his credo regarding this branch of his art. It is a militantly aesthetic credo. Max believed in caricature for caricature's sake. The caricaturist should not work with a moral purpose or a personal; neither to mock at what he disapproves of nor to bring someone he dislikes into contempt. Apart from anything else he will fail in both objects.

'Such laughter as may be caused by a caricature is merely aesthetic. It corresponds with such tears as are shed at sight of a very beautiful statue. I do not pity Venus when I see her statue in its chamber at the Louvre; yet there are tears in my eyes. I do not despise Disraeli when I look at Pellegrini's picture of him; yet I laugh. It is even so with any one else who is affected by beauty and by absurdity. If caricature affected us at all towards its subject, it would affect us favourably towards it. Tragedy, said Aristotle, purges us of superfluous awe, by evocation, and comedy likewise purges us of superfluous contempt. Even so might idealism of a subject purge us of superfluous awe for it, and caricature purge us of superfluous contempt. If the sight of Pheidias' masterpiece ministered to our reverence for Venus, she would pass out of our minds as we passed from the gallery. If the sight of Pellegrini's Disraeli satisfied our hostility towards Disraeli himself, we should forgive him all. Indeed, does nothing of the kind happen? This theory of purgation has a dangerous charm for me. I have often been tempted to attribute the Romans' decline in faith to the fair statues of gods and goddesses imported from Greece by victorious generals. The extraordinary preponderance of ugly men among those who have shaped the world's history—may it not be due to the chance they gave to the contemporary caricaturists? No, no; let me be sensible. Caricature never has had moral influence of any kind.'

Further, the caricaturist's aim, like that of all artists, should be beauty; beauty to be achieved, Max thought, by the perfect adaptation of means to ends, the use of style whose qualities are those particularly fitted to its purpose. For caricature, said Max, these qualities should be economy, spontaneity, and the ability to work on a small scale. A caricature is a joke; and a joke on a big scale is seldom amusing. Max ends with a definition:

'The most perfect caricature is that which, on a small surface, with the simplest means, most accurately exaggerates, to the highest point, the peculiarities of a human being, at his most characteristic moment, in the most beautiful manner.'

Max's only prose book of these years came out in April 1899. It was a second collection of essays, entitled *More*. Fastidiously selected from his published writings of the previous year or two, the book reveals how Max has modified his mask and literary personality since the appearance of *The Works of Max Beerbohm*. He is not so flamboyantly dandyish and paradoxical; and he has dropped his 'old man's' pose—since he was no longer very young this had ceased to be amusing—to take up that role of ironical onlooker on the world which he was to retain for the rest of his writing life. His tone too is not so uniformly light-hearted as in the earlier volume. There are one or two passages in the book—notably those in which he praises Ouida and dispraises Mrs Meynell—where Max actually seems to be treating himself and his own opinions a little too respectfully. Now and again, too, an astringency, wholly absent from *The Works*, steals into his voice: as when he proclaims his contempt for the vulgarity of popular taste, or—ironically for us who know that he will one day be Sir Max Beerbohm—for the author knighted for his services to literature.

'Poor fellow! Why should he not receive his heart's desire? What shoulders are more appropriate . . . to the touch of the royal sword? Disappointment may embitter him, and, if he were to be bitter, what would become of his books? If, on the other hand, his Sovereign summon him, I shall be at Paddington when, with elastic tread and boundless smile, he passes down the platform to the Windsor train. It will do my heart good to see him. For my own part, I should like him to have a life-peerage. We have our Law-Lords—why not our

Novel-Lords? It matters not what title he receive, so it be one which will perish, like his twaddle, with him.'

Even here, the astringency is slight. Max's conception of the essay as an agreeable entertainment made him vigilantly careful to avoid any harshness that might jar against the prevailing and agreeable tone he wishes to produce. For he was always keenly aware of the limitations alike of his own talent and of the form which he was employing. Firmly he grasped the first law of literary composition, namely, that no author writes well on subject-matter that does not fire his especial talent, that he must keep to the creative range with which he was born. Max's own range—confined as it was to light fantasy and light irony—was narrow, and his critical articles show that he could have thoughts outside it. But he realized that these thoughts did not inspire the artist in him. So he strictly excluded them from his specifically creative works. How mistaken, he thought, were those critics who urged an artist to attempt a work beyond his scope! Disaster overtook the artists who took their advice.

'The critic's aim,' he says, in a review, 'should be to encourage every writer to do what he can do best, what is most natural to him; not to implore him to persist in tasks which (be they never so superior) he will never accomplish. To every artist that form of art to which his own talent is best suited should seem the highest form of art. It is curious how often the artist is ignorant of his own true bent. . . . How many charming talents have been spoiled by the instilled desire to do "important" work! Some people are born to lift heavy weights. Some are born to juggle with golden balls. The lifters are far more numerous in England than are the jugglers.'

He knew himself to be a juggler. If he ever felt any temptation to try weight-lifting he did not yield to it; but concentrated on learning to juggle as well as he could. Max understood his own talent very well. Henry Arthur Jones wrote to congratulate him on *More*, remarking incidentally that he found Max's writings surprisingly mellow and more urbane in spirit than his caricatures. Max replied:

'I was very much honoured by what you told me about your pleasure in my new book of essays. As to the difference between my writings and my drawings, I myself have often been puzzled by it. But I think that in the past few years the two dissimilar "sisters" of whom you speak have really been growing a little more like to each other. My drawing has been growing a little more delicate and artful, and losing something of its pristine boldness and savagery; whilst my writing, though it never will be savage or bold, is easier in style, less ornate, than it used to be. At least I think so.'

This is a very just comment; and a prophecy of the course of Max's development. By the time *The Poets' Corner* was published five years later, the gulf between the spirit of his writing and that of his drawing had completely vanished. Nor even at the time did Max seem to have resented Jones's words. More than most artists, he preserved detachment in the face of criticism. Gosse had constituted himself as literary mentor: sometimes he was a severe one. Max's *Saturday Review* articles struck him sometimes as culpably below standard. He doubted if Max took his duties seriously enough. What, for example, did he mean by shirking a special performance of Swinburne's poetical tragedy *Locrine*? Subsequent generations may find it easy to sympathize with Max about this. Not so Gosse; he felt it his duty to rebuke him for his slackness, and, judging by Max's reply, did so very sharply indeed.

My dear Mr Gosse,

Many thanks for your letter. I need hardly say that I appreciate the kindly feeling which prompted you to write it, and that I value your good opinion far too highly not to take your bad opinion to heart.

I meant no 'insolence' when I wrote the little note for this week's *Saturday*. Still less have I the dreadful joy of being concerned in any 'ignoble commercial intrigue' against Swinburne, or the Elizabethan Stage Society, or, indeed, anyone, or anything. To 'carelessness' I must, however, plead guilty. The Elizabethan Stage Society never sends a seat to the *Saturday*; but I had been particularly anxious to see *Locrine* and had intended to apply for a seat. On Saturday night I caught a chill, which developed into a kind of influenza, and so I did not, as I had intended, send a messenger to St George's Hall on Monday morning. In saying that I had 'nothing to write about', I ought to have inserted that I had not seen *Locrine*. I forgot; and I am sorry.

In the more general part of your letter, you complain that every week I write 'so badly' and 'so insincerely'. As I am never *conscious* of insincerity, I cannot admit the second half of the indictment. But the very fact that I am not conscious of writing badly does but make me the more uncomfortable about the second half. It makes me feel that such literary talent as I had must have been gradually debased and blunted by my indulgence in the hebdomadal habit. This much I can say with perfect truth: I have acquired no journalistic *fluency* in writing—I still take as much trouble as I ever took. If I scamped my work, then your letter would only be a sharp prick to my conscience —I could 'pull myself together', as you urge, and forthwith write something that would please you. As I do *not* scamp my work, your letter comes as a rather forcible suggestion that my talent has been diminishing, deteriorating, and that I am no longer capable of writing well. You hint that while I take less trouble with my writing I take more trouble with my humour. You say that I 'force the giggle'. Well, in point of fact, such jests as I make come as easily to me as they ever did. If, in print, they seem 'forced', that simply shows that they are less good than they used to be, and that my sense of humour is on the wane. Altogether, I seem to be in a rather bad way. And since I cannot, on the one hand, take less trouble with my jokes, nor, on the other hand, more with my actual writing, and since my bad opinions are the result of bad judgement, not of dishonesty, I cannot hold out much of my immediate improvement. Some day, perhaps, I shall be cured of the hebdomadal habit—the 'gold-cure' is the only cure I know for it!—and then I may re-emerge as I was in the beginning—possibly as something even better. Meanwhile, it is some consolation to know that among the first to congratulate me on my redemption will be Edmund Gosse, to whom no young writer owes more gratitude than the young writer signing himself 'Max'.

This letter shows considerable poise. Max refrains from arguing; but he does not give in either.

Though he published no other book during these years, he was meditating several literary projects, and one more ambitious than he had attempted before. By June 1898 he had already conceived a fantasy on a more extended scale; its setting Oxford, its theme the incursion into that monastic community of a woman so fascinating that all the undergraduates were driven to drown themselves for love of her. A letter to Will Rothenstein at the end of 1899 reveals that he had already chosen his heroine's name, Zuleika Dobson, and had even written a description of her which he showed to his friends. Twelve years, however, were to elapse before the finished work was published. Not long afterwards came the publication of *A Christmas Garland*, another book already sketched in its first form before 1900. Max continued to be an early developer. The works of his maturity were most of them conceived in his youth.

He had decided too, for the time being at any rate, the pattern of his social and personal life. Time and circumstances did make some changes in its composition. Though Max still considered Reggie and Will Rothenstein among his closest friends, he saw less of them than in the past. After trying journalism and law, Reggie gave up the idea of a regular profession—his love-life, too, was of a kind more easily lived out of England—and now spent most of his time on the Continent leading a leisurely existence; now and again he whiled away his idle hours by writing a novel. These novels were not very good; and few read them. 'Other people's first editions are rare,' said Reggie. 'With me it's the second editions that are rare; in fact they don't exist.' He sent his books to Max who wrote back letters professing to have enjoyed them. He also declared himself envious of Reggie's life, abroad and at ease, far from the rush and philistinism of London. 'What a beautiful life yours is! Geneva, Nice, Paris. For me Dieppe, London, London, London.' These remarks are evidence less of Max's true opinions than of his anxiety to please Reggie. He was still deeply fond of him and in a crisis would still, before anybody else, go to him for sympathy. But circumstances made it harder than ever for him to keep in touch with the old regularity. Besides, Max had begun to find frequent letter-writing almost impossible. When he did write, a sense of guilt made him lay stress on his undying affection.

Will Rothenstein did not live abroad. But domesticity can be as effective a cause of separation between old friends as foreign travel: and in the spring of 1899 Rothenstein had married. Not that his bride—a beautiful actress, Alice Knewstub—wished to come between the friends. On the contrary, Max was one of the two persons invited to the wedding at the Kensington Registry Office; and after the marriage Mr and Mrs Rothenstein often asked him to dinner. But Will was no longer free to spend gay bachelor evenings with his men friends. Moreover, Max moved much in different circles to that of the Rothensteins. As a result, from now on his correspondence with them consisted largely of notes apologizing for not being able to accept invitations or excusing himself for failing to keep engagements with them that he had accepted. He telegraphed often to the same effect. In a letter he explains why:

'I *will* cure myself of the telegram-fever, if I can. It is a deadly disease, to which all are liable who live in this fetid city. You must guard your son against it. Have his arm injected with the glue off the back of a postage-stamp. I am going to have mine done.'

Max was a faithful friend and did not like the idea that Will should fancy him to be fickle. To salve his conscience and make up for his defections, he asked the Rothensteins to come to theatres and concerts with him. 'Would you care to come to the Albert Hall,' runs a typical note, 'tomorrow night to Box 10—Patti will *screech* for your pleasure.' As time passed Will's personality began to change slightly. The adventurous bohemian artist in him was giving place to the temperate, Bradford-bred citizen. This made his hospitality less attractive, Max thought; he was pleased to notice that Mrs Rothenstein seemed disposed to agree with him about this. 'I saw a lot of the Rothensteins,' he told Reggie in 1904, 'very plain living and very high thinking, and Will very happy therein; but Alice and I hankering after richer food and poorer cerebration.'

The ranks of Max's close friends had been more fatally thinned by the death of Aubrey Beardsley. At the beginning of 1898 his illness had taken a sharp turn for the worse: after some months of extreme suffering he died. In the previous year he had been received into the Roman Catholic Church. This had profoundly changed his outlook. He was filled with a horrified revulsion against luxury, sensuality and flippancy. Since his eye offended him, it must be plucked out. He read a great deal of Pascal, and 'Pascal', he wrote to a friend, 'is a great example to all artists and thinkers. He understood that to become a Christian a man of letters must sacrifice his gifts just as the Magdalene must sacrifice her beauty.' Beardsley's new-found faith enabled him to bear his sufferings with uncomplaining courage. But his last hours were darkened by pangs of conscience for what he now felt to be the sinful drawings of his unconverted days. After his death a poignant letter to his friends was found among his papers. 'I implore you to destroy all copies of "Lysistrata" and bawdy drawings,' he wrote. 'By all that is holy all obscene drawings.' The letter was signed 'Aubrey Beardsley—in my death agony.'

Beardsley's sin and repentance alike reveal a spirit far remote from that of Max. Yet his death did make a profound impression on Max. Apart from the fact that he had been very fond of him, he was moved because of the likeness between Aubrey's position and his own; both at first associated with the same movement in the arts and both famous so young. This sense of kinship expresses itself in a memorial article Max wrote about Beardsley, published in *The Idler* soon after his death.

'Thus ended this brief, tragic, brilliant life,' so ran its peroration. 'It has been filled with a larger measure of sweet and bitter experience than is given to most men who die in their old age. Aubrey Beardsley was famous in his youth, and to be famous in one's youth has been called the most gracious gift that the gods can bestow. And, unless I am mistaken, he enjoyed his fame, and was proud of it, though, as a great artist who had a sense of humour, he was perhaps a little ashamed of it too, now and then. For the rest, was he happy in his life? I do not know. In a fashion, I think he was. He knew that his life must be short, and so he lived and loved every hour of it with a kind of jealous intensity. He had that absolute power of "living in the moment" which is given only to the doomed man—that kind of self-conscious happiness, the delight in still clinging to the thing whose worth you have only realized through the knowledge that it will soon be taken from you. For him, as for the schoolboy whose holidays are near their close, every hour—every minute even—had its value. . . . Yet, though he took such a keen delight in all the manifestations of life, he himself, despite his energy and his high spirits, his frankness and thoughtfulness, seemed always rather remote, rather detached from ordinary conditions, a kind of independent spectator. He enjoyed life, but he was never wholly of it.

This kind of aloofness has been noted in all great artists. Their power isolates them. It is because they stand at a little distance that they can see so much. No man ever *saw* more than Beardsley. He was infinitely sensitive to the aspect of all things around him. And that, I think, was the basis of his genius. All the greatest fantastic art postulates the power to see things, unerringly, as they are.'

The artist with a sense of humour at once proud and ashamed of his fame, the artist as spectator enjoying life but yet never wholly of it, the practitioner of a fantastic art which yet postulates the power to see things, unerringly, as they are—these phrases apply more aptly to Max even than to Beardsley. Pondering the fate of this other youthful artist, Max involuntarily began to identify him with himself.

Though Aubrey was dead, Max continued to keep in touch with his actress sister, the exotic Mabel Beardsley. He used to spend afternoons playing cards with her: and one summer holiday she came to Dieppe where, to his amusement, she attracted a lot of attention by walking about the quays in the afternoon, dressed apparently for the evening, with neck and bosom bare and with a long train that she was forced to carry slung over her arm. Another link with Beardsley was Ross, who was one of the few people who had managed to be on friendly terms both with Aubrey and with Oscar Wilde. At the end of 1898 he sent Max an appreciation he had written of Beardsley's work. Max replied:

'I have read your essay with much admiration, and with much irritation that you don't write often. Why don't you? . . .

I don't really think that the misprints in the essay matter much. When one has written a thing it is horrible to find a misprint—but my experience is that no one else ever finds them at all. On page 24 of my *Works* there is a misplaced comma, which has darkened much of my life and has often made me appear more bitter than I really am. It and the death of Lucien de Rubempré[1] are the only things I have never been quite able to dismiss. And yet no one has ever called my attention to it. So be comforted. I admit that I am still, even with the grave between us, a little jealous of Aubrey—but I feel all your admiration for him, and I love your essay because it is so charmingly written and erudite. . . .'

Max's attitude to Ross is at all times a little mysterious. This letter and several others are friendly, even intimate; and he was sufficiently on easy terms with Ross to ask him for help. Max felt it embarrassing to criticize his brother Herbert's productions and sometimes he asked Ross to act as his substitute. On the other hand, writing to Reggie he often refers to Ross in a critical tone. The most likely explanation for this discrepancy is that Reggie did not like Ross—Oscar Wilde's friends were apt to dislike each other—and Max,

[1] The hero of Balzac's *Lost Illusions*.

anxious as he had now become not to say anything that might suggest the presence of a gulf between Reggie and himself, may have altered his tone in consequence. For the rest, Max saw little of the *Yellow Book* circle. Lionel Johnson was dead, Harland often away, Le Gallienne was in the United States. His fame had been somewhat eclipsed by the sudden popularity of another poetaster, Stephen Phillips. 'Richard Le Gallienne is staying in America to wait until Stephen Phillips blows over,' said Max mischievously.

But if some old friends were dead or distant, many were available as ever: notably Nicholson, Conder, Gordon Craig and George Street; Craig still beautifully exuberant, Street still curiously fastidious.

'I dined the other night with George Street,' Max writes to Ada Leverson, 'who was very much upset because Chesterton, in some article, had referred to him as "that brilliant and delightful writer, Mr G. S. Street".

This, according to Street, was a sort of impertinence and breach of good taste. *How* I cannot exactly recall: indeed, I couldn't even at the moment quite understand: of so coarse a fibre am I. But there is no doubt that Street himself will take a long time to get over it.'

The name of a new friend of Max's is mentioned in this letter. At the turn of the century there rocketed up into the English literary empyrean a coruscating new luminary of wit and fancy, G. K. Chesterton. His success was immediate. Max said in later days that Chesterton cut him out completely as a representative of brilliant youth. This is to be doubted: Max's followers were a faithful band. What is true is that Max himself was dazzled by Chesterton's brilliance. He thought him a genius. This made him anxious to know him; partly because he was curious to see what Chesterton was like, and partly because he felt it would be prudent to get on to friendly terms with so powerful a figure. In 1902, therefore, he wrote Chesterton a letter.

Dear Mr Chesterton,

I have seldom wished to meet anyone in particular: but you I should very much like to meet.

I need not explain who I am, for the name at the end of this note is one which you have more than once admitted, rather sternly, into your writings.

By way of personal and private introduction, I may say that my mother was a friend of your grandmother, Mrs Grosjean, and also of your mother.

As I have said, I should like to meet you. On the other hand, it is quite possible that *you* have no reciprocal anxiety to meet *me*. In this case, nothing could be easier than for you to say that you are very busy, or unwell, or going out of town, and so are not able—much as you would have liked—to lunch with me here either next Wednesday or next Saturday at 1.30.

I am, whether your come or not, yours admiringly,

Max Beerbohm.

P.S. I am quite different from my writings (and so, I daresay, are you from yours). So that we should not necessarily fail to hit it off.

I, in the flesh, am modest, full of common sense, very genial, and rather dull.

What you are remains to be seen—or not to be seen by me, according to your decision.

Here was an invitation hard to resist. Anyway, Chesterton had no inclination to try. He was a genial, sociable figure, who welcomed friendly overtures; also he was an enthusiastic admirer of Max's drawing and writing. The meeting fulfilled the hopes of both guest and host. The two got on at once. Chesterton was impressed by Max's wisdom. He told him that a publisher had suggested that he should write a book on Browning. 'A man ought to write a book on Browning when he is young,' said Max pensively. Chesterton found this remark extremely thought-provoking. Max meanwhile was amused by Chesterton.

'Enormous apparition,' he noted down. 'Head big for body—way of sinking head on chest. Like a mountain and a volcanic one—constant streams of talk flowing down—paradoxes flung up into the air—very magnificent.'

He was attracted too by a strain of sensitiveness and shyness that he detected in Chesterton, and by his generous-minded disposition to like people. 'He thought everybody very jolly,' Max notes; and he was amused by the contrast between Chesterton's agile mind and physical bulk. This first luncheon was the start of a friendship which grew stronger in the next few years. Chesterton took Max as part model for Auberon Quin, the humorist hero of his romance *The Napoleon of Notting Hill.* Soon after its publication Max met Chesterton and his wife at a dinner given by John Lane, its publisher. Mrs Chesterton describes the scene:

'A delightful dinner party at the Lanes. . . . The talk was mostly about *Napoleon.* Max took me in to dinner and was really nice. He is a good fellow. His costume was extraordinary. Why should an evening waistcoat have four large white pearl buttons and why should he look that peculiar shape? He seems only pleased at the way he has been identified with King Auberon. "All right, my dear chap," he said to G. who was trying to apologize. "Mr Lane and I settled it all at lunch." I think he was a little put out at finding no red carpet put down for his royal feet.'

Mrs Chesterton clearly did not accept Max's view of himself as modest. But Chesterton did; it was one of the things he liked best about him.

'Max,' he wrote, 'was and is a remarkably humble man for a man of his gifts and his period. I have never known him, by a single phrase or intonation, claim to know more or judge better than he does; or indeed half so much or so well as he does. Most men spread themselves a little in conversation, and have their unreal victories and vanities; but he seems to me more moderate and realistic about himself than about anything else. He is more sceptical about everything than I am, by temper; but certainly he does not indulge in the base idolatry of believing in himself.'

Max made other new friends besides Chesterton. He saw a great many people during these years and got to know some of them very well. The records of his life are thronged with names, many of them often repeated. The trouble is that our knowledge is so often confined to names. We do not know where Max met their owners, whether he knew them well, what he thought of them or what they thought of him. Nor can we be sure that there were not others, he knew well or better, whose names do not happen to have been mentioned. Sometimes he may say something about them in his notebook. But not always: there are no references in it to several people who, we know, he saw much of at this time, notably Belloc and Shaw. For the most part we have to pick up such information as we can from anecdotes of his talk and chance sentences in his correspondence. All this means that it is very hard to give a definitive picture of Max's relations with friends and acquaintances at this time; or, indeed, at any time during the next ten years. The effect of such knowledge as we have is that of a shifting crowd moving confusedly past us in a light so dim as to make it often impossible to discern their faces. Occasionally a vagrant gleam flits across them to give us a clearer glimpse. More rarely it pauses to allow us a longer look.

We get a fairly long look at George Moore, for instance. Max says that he met him for the first time in the early 'nineties; but it seems to have been after 1900 that he began to see much of him. He found him odd and interesting enough to collect and note down some impressions which many years after he elaborated into a finished portrait. It opens very vividly:

'I am sure there never was in heaven or on earth any one at all like him. It is conceivable that in the waters that are under the earth there *may*, vaguely luminous, be similar forms, and—stay, it isn't odd, after all, this lapse of memory. It is explained by that quality of luminous vagueness which Moore's presence always had. . . . He never seemed to enter or leave a room. Rather did he appear there, and in due time fade thence. It was always difficult to say at what moment he appeared: one had but become aware of his presence, which was always delightful, and later one found oneself missing him: he had gone. . . . He sat rather on the edge of his chair, his knees together, his hands hanging limp on either side of him. Limply there hung over his brow a copious wisp of blond hair, which wavered as he turned the long white oval of his face from one speaker to another. He sat wide-eyed, gaping, listening—no, one would not have said "listening" but hearing: it did not seem that his ears were sending in any reports to his brain. It would be an understatement to say that his face was as a mask which revealed nothing. His face was as a mask of gauze through which Nothing was quite clearly visible. And then, all of a sudden, there would appear—Something. There came a gleam from within the pale-blue eyes, and a sort of ripple passed up over the modelling of the flaccid cheeks; the chin suddenly receded a little further, and—*Voilà Moore qui parle! Silence, la compagnie, Moore parle.*'

GEORGE MOORE

The tone of this passage is benevolent. Max did not wish to appear censorious; he admired Moore's work too much and found him too entertaining. In fact, however, Moore did sometimes gravely offend his moral taste. Elsewhere in this account, in fact, Max says he averted his attention when Moore talked of the ladies who he claimed had loved him. In private Max spoke more sharply. 'Judas betrayed Jesus Christ for thirty pieces of silver,' he said, 'but George Moore would betray his best friend for nothing.' It is not the only occasion that we find Max's private opinion startlingly more severe than that which he allows himself to express publicly. This is not to accuse him of being double-faced. His public and private opinions never actually contradict each other; and it was both sensible and mannerly of him to refrain from abusing someone in public with whom he was officially on friendly terms. All the same, it is a little disturbing to find so merciless a judgement hidden beneath an exterior so charmingly bland. Now and again the perfection of Max's mask inspires fear.

Moore, it will be remembered, was a keen amateur of painting. Max used often to meet him among his Chelsea studio acquaintance, with Sickert and Steer and Tonks and Augustus John and Sargent. Of all these men he has left us brief impressions. Here are some of them.

'*Steer*: Walking carefully—like a large seal—eyes—head from side to side—big neck—sloping shoulders—Thinks with his eyes. Devoted. *Sickert*: His charm—for *all* women—Duchess or model—kind, shrewd, then domineering . . . two sides—like Shaw. Cruel mouth —kind eyes. Hair beautiful—Peg-tops. Extreme of refinement— love of squalor: Lodged in Jack the Ripper house. *Tonks*: Monk—thoughtful . . . look of being resigned to muddle of life—determined to leave off worrying.'

The youthful Augustus John was a more sensational figure:

'man of great personality—wholly unaffected—face—*voice*—silver bell—. . . Pale—sitting in window seat—Sense of something power-ful—slightly sinister—Lucifer—*Chelsea*—pedlar's pack— . . . His singing of a song of the Daumier period—all there—craque-craque —walking to and fro—wild—enigmatic smile—Upper Berkeley Street in the small hours— . . . would stay any length of time— drink anything you gave him—well-read.'

It is not clear how often John came to Upper Berkeley Street. Himself he remembered with gratitude a visit while still a penniless student at the Slade. He had called on impulse; and the interview was an awkward one, as John was too silent to keep up the conversation and too shy to go away. At last, very late, he rose and said he must walk back to his Chelsea lodgings. Max, horrified at the thought of anyone taking so much exercise, especially late at night, summoned a hansom cab; and, pressing the fare into John's hand, ushered him into it.

He never felt any need to pay Sargent's cab fare; for Sargent was the most successful of living portrait painters. He was also very sociable and Max met him often. He observed that Sargent was curiously hesitant in manner, uttering his remarks with as many preparatory grunts and gaspings as Henry James himself. Max took notes of his demeanour at a dinner party.

'Sat high—glaring—minatory and prosperous—eating—. . . But nervous—drawing in breath—finding word—as if outside him—slight groan—. . . Could be witty—But talking not his game. True painter.'

Max met Sargent more often in the world of fashion than among the artists. His own excursions into this were growingly frequent; he was becoming more and more of a social success. Not only did he get more invitations than before, but his invitations were also of a more glorious kind. We read of him lunching and dining with the musical Lady Maud Warrender, the gorgeous Lady Féo Sturt, with Mrs George Keppel, racy friend of King Edward VII himself, and with Lady Elcho and Mrs Grenfell, afterwards Lady Desborough. These last two were conspicuous and fascinating representatives of the set called 'The Souls' which, more than any other, was considered to combine the attractions of elegance, charm and intellect. Among its male members were Arthur Balfour, George Wyndham, Lord Curzon and Maurice Baring. Lady Desborough was also the most celebrated hostess of the age. On Monday morning the names of the guests staying with her for the previous weekend would appear in *The Times*; the long list of statesmen, proconsuls, diplomats English and foreign, reigning beauties, terminated generally with a few men of learning or letters. Among these the name of Mr Max Beerbohm began to appear.

Max made no secret of enjoying his success.

'I lunched last week *chez* Lady Elcho—sat between her and Arthur Balfour—George Wyndham on her other side. Altogether I felt quite the gentleman. It is funny that with really distinguished people I do not feel at all shy, though I feel shy with everyone else. My one difficulty is to keep myself in check. As it was, I distinctly patronized Balfour, drawing him out about the ventilating arrangements in The House, and so forth. . . . '

And again:

'I dined with Lady Maud Warrender the other night, and am dining with Lady Féo Sturt on Monday. I pretend to myself that such people are useful to me in my career. As a matter of fact they don't seem to be; and my pleasure in them is mere disinterested flunkeyism, I am afraid.'

Reggie's reply to this is lost. But Max's other friends made their comments on his spectacular social progress. 'Max is happy enough, with a large balance at the bank, and great success with Mrs Keppel and other smart reprehensible folk of the kind,' writes Rothenstein to Ross in February 1901; while he rallied Max a trifle ponderously on his success in surmounting the risks he ran amid the glittering corruption of the Babylon of fashion. Though the tone of his comments is ostensibly light, we can hear in them a note of censoriousness. It is hard to see a friend rise socially without envy; and envy tends to disguise itself as moral disapproval. In this instance the disapproval is confined to the circles Max frequented; it did not extend to Max himself. There was no reason it should. Max had nothing to be ashamed of. He was no more tempted to be faithless to his old friends than he had been earlier. Indeed, his excursions into the great world—though fairly frequent during the London season—were still only excursions. Nor, in spite of what he says about his flunkeyism, had Max learnt to be a snob. He could enjoy the company of aristocrats—'those tall cool ornate people' as he called them—but he did not romanticize them. He was further preserved from snobbishness by self-confidence. Snobbishness when it is not romantic comes from a sense of inferiority: to know himself on friendly terms with the great fortifies the snob's shaky self-esteem. But Max suffered from no sense of inferiority. Whatever he might say, it was no trouble to him to feel easy at the great houses to which he was invited.

Nor did he need to be a snob to enjoy himself there. At its best, Edwardian high society would have appealed to any man of civilized taste. 'The Souls' in particular, and above all the female souls, were exquisitely agreeable, combining an eighteenth-century wit and stylishness with a refinement of feeling, a dash of imaginative sensibility, that proclaimed them the contemporaries of Henry James. The charming spontaneous Lady Elcho, the subtle brilliant Lady Desborough, was each in her own way supremely accomplished in the art of pleasing. Max savoured their agreeability to the full. It was also an aid to his own art. He may have been right in saying that frequenting London society did not help his career in any practical sense. But it was an inspiration to his talent. His imagination had always been stimulated by the spectacle of the great world: all the more because of its association with politics: the English aristocracy were still an active ruling class, and as such an absorbing spectacle to one who had been interested in his rulers ever since, as a child, he had haunted Parliament Square for glimpses of Gladstone and Randolph Churchill. Now in these great houses he was able to meet and talk to men as eminent as Gladstone had been in his boyhood: Rosebery and Balfour, Curzon and Haldane, Wyndham, and Randolph Churchill's sensational young son, Winston. Others besides statesmen engaged Max's attention: financial magnates like Mr Benjamin Cohen, men about town like Lord Grimthorpe, *bon viveurs* like Harry Chaplin, sportsmen like Lord de Grey. And there was an exotic little group of distinguished foreign diplomats that appealed strongly to his sense of the picturesque: the Austrian Count Mensdorff, the Russian Count Benckendorff, the Portuguese Marquis de Soveral. All these habitués of the Edwardian social scene came as fresh grist to Max's mill. Here was a new lot of persons for him to sit down and sketch in his room at Upper Berkeley Street, late at night and back from a party.

Max's interest in statesmen and city magnates and men of fashion, however, was never so deep as that he felt for his fellow writers. His most memorable and fruitful encounters were still with distinguished men of letters, more especially those of an older generation. These last had what was for Max the added attraction of being a link with the past. During these years he took pains to get to know several of them, notably Meredith and Swinburne. Since he was courteous, composed and a good listener, Max made a very good impression on both of them. He had been an enthusiastic admirer of Swinburne since his schooldays; for he was of the generation whose heart beat instinctively in response to the tumultuous rhapsodizings of Swinburne's Muse. The fact that the meaning of her words did not amount to much bothered Max no more in Swinburne's verse than it did in Oscar Wilde's prose. For him Swinburne was the modern Catullus: he knew by heart the chiming, tolling stanzas of *The Garden of Proserpine*.

> From too much love of living,
> From hope and fear set free;
> We thank with brief thanksgiving
> Whatever gods may be
> That no life lives for ever;
> That dead men rise up never;
> That even the weariest river
>   Winds somewhere safe to sea.

Swinburne for Max had the added attraction of being a survival from the age of the Pre-Raphaelites; he had caroused with Rossetti himself. Now his life was changed. Cured alike of alcoholism and of inspiration, he resided quietly in Putney under the care of the vigilant Watts-Dunton. Max, meeting Watts-Dunton at a literary gathering in London, scraped acquaintance with him. The result was an invitation in June 1899 to lunch at Putney with 'Catullus'. It was the first of many such luncheons. Max has described them in one of his most memorable pieces, 'No. 2 The Pines', in words too well known to repeat and too concentrated to summarize. There may be some interest, however, in printing a few of the first rough notes on which Max's delicate structure is founded.

'The romance of seeing him—Luncheon on table—door opened—Little gray figure—huge dome of head—pale—revolving eye—stomach—pink nose—slippers—But "And did you once see Shelley plain? And did you speak with him again?" Old-fashioned—aristocratic—bow from the waist—Deafness cutting him away—Tremulous hand—painful Longing look at a pint of Bass— . . . . Always same procedure—(boiled mutton and caper sauce—apple tart—cheese—Both at dinner and luncheon) Theodore not so deaf—Monopolizing—Then a shout—Give him his head—Lyric outpour—Rhapsodies—sing-song—effeminate—babyish. . . . . Intoxication—saturation—fusty, musty—Go out into street—sunshine, or gas-lamps—Vulgarity—Certain horror—yet relief.'

Max's punctuation, or the lack of it, makes these last phrases obscure. But it would seem that he is suggesting the mixed relief and flatness he felt on descending to the humdrum comfortable vulgarity of the ordinary Victorian world from the ethereal heights of Swinburne's conversation. In later years he was once asked what Swinburne's talk was like.

'Ecstatic beautiful arabesques,' said Max, 'which, especially since he was deaf, had little connection with anything real—though occasionally he would rhapsodize about something unexpected to which his attention had been called, as for example Tenniel's political cartoons in *Punch*. In general, however, it was beautiful but confined within the limits of his interest; babies, Mazzini and that sort of thing. His voice was beautiful and strange like the sound of someone singing in the distance.'

The same interlocutor went on to ask him about George Meredith's conversation. 'Florid and splendid like his books,' replied Max, 'because of deafness also a monologue.' It is not certain what year he first met Meredith. But it was at Meredith's house where, deaf and paralysed, he now lived in retirement, Max went down with an introduction to see him; and the visit led to at least one other. Max's admiration for Meredith was extravagant and unbounded. This is surprising; but the admirations of their forefathers are often surprising to subsequent generations. Gerard Hopkins considered Canon Dixon of the first order of poets; Henry James preferred Stevenson to Dostoievsky; Max thought Meredith the greatest author alive and possibly the greatest English author since Shakespeare. He bent all his faculties to the task of observing such a phoenix; and though he never worked up his scattered observations into a full and finished portrait, such as he had painted of Swinburne, they are vivid and perceptive enough.

'Little prosaic box of a house—Grey dressing-gown. Olympian—

GEORGE MEREDITH

Battered statue of Jupiter. Blurred outlines—eyes dim, but magnificent—Same with mind. *Beaux restes*—But extraordinarily agile—not echoes—Not thought out before—mind still working—image chasing image Larger—spacious—Just like writings. . . . Usually you don't think of gentleman—You did with Meredith—English gentleman—squirearchic—The drawl of the swell of the 'sixties—Leis*ah*! (for leisure) Talked of *laughter*—Said *I* had it—Quoted an article of mine at great length— . . . . . . Splendid old age—Serene—And yet sad—lonely—Self-conscious. His talking to the dog, as we went out—This loveable being's modesty. His look up and down at me as I stood up—slim and agile. Appealing—jest—sly look—saw you laughing—then roared—body thrown back—bringing down hands on arms of chair—then resuming—upper part of body seemed to be all the more vital by reason of atrophy of the lower. . . . rugged Northern nature—Take a joke as a wave takes a boat—just shoulder it away—with a fine rolling gesture of arm. . . .'

Henry James was a far more important figure in Max's life. The nature and significance of this importance is unique and complex. Since it lights up and defines Max's moral and aesthetic attitude throughout his mature life, we may as well take this opportunity to try to analyse it. It was partly personal. The two men were still often in each other's company. As Max said, they were always dining at the same houses. When they met, Henry James continued to be kind to Max and Max to be impressed and amused by Henry James. Gradually Max accumulated his impressions. They are recorded both in his notebook and his talk. Here are a few from his notebook.

'Delightful company—you had to wait—worth it—very literary—enormous vocabulary—great manner, as in books—never smiles—rather appalled by life—cloistral . . . priest—fine eyes—magnificent head— . . . strong voice—holding table.'

In his conversation he expanded some of these hints.

'Henry James took a tragic view of everyone,' he once said, 'throwing up his hands and closing his eyes to shut out the awful vision. Rocking his chair and talking with tremendous emphasis. . . . His talk had great *authority* . . . there was a great deal of hesitation and gurgitation before he came out with anything: but it was all the more impressive, for the preparatory rumble.'

James's talk too, with its curious felicity of phrase, delighted Max; as when he said, after a conversation with George Moore, 'for one and a half hours he was *unimportantly* foolish'.

Yet the two men never became intimate; and Henry James's importance in Max's history was not primarily personal. This is most clearly apparent in an incident which took place some years later, in March 1909.

'Such an odd thing happened to me today,' he wrote to a friend, 'I had lunched with Maugham at the Carlton. As I made my way towards Piccadilly, I wondered which thing I would do: go to the "Fair Women" at the New Gallery—a good exhibition which I haven't seen—*or* go to the Savile to read the *English Review* for March, in which is a story by Henry James. I decided on the Savile. Half way down Piccadilly I met H. J. himself, and we stood talking. He asked if the McCulloch show at Burlington House was still open. I thought *not*, and advised him to go to the New Gallery. He placed a fatherly Jacobean hand on my shoulder, and said "What a pity you are going in the other direction. Now, if only you were coming in *this* direction, and if we two, together, could visit the collection you recommend." . . . Without an instant's hesitation I replied "Ah, if only I could! But I have to be in Kensington at four!" Wasn't it odd, the double coincidence? And odder still that instead of going with *him* to the place I had been almost going to alone, I should choose to go and read his story, which I could have read at any time later on! I can't explain my choice, and much regret it. It would take *him* to elucidate the subconscious subtleties that led to that choice. It is a theme after his own heart.'

The episode stuck in Max's mind, and forty years later he made a broadcast about it. At its close he described settling down at his club to read James's story.

'It was, of course, a very good story, and yet, from time to time, I found my mind wandering away from it. It was not so characteristic, not so intensely Jamesian a story as James would have founded on the theme of what had just been happening between us—the theme of the disciple loyally—or unloyally?—preferring the Master's work to the Master.'

The last sentence indicates the nature of Max's relation to Henry

James. It was less that of two friends than of master and disciple. Though he found Henry James the man fascinating, Henry James the artist mattered more to him. Henry James the artist mattered very much indeed. Max spoke of no one else as his 'master', nor of himself as the 'disciple' of any other man. This is not to say his admiration for James's work was unqualified. He recognized blemishes and limitations in it. 'His characters are ghostly,' he notes, 'nobody is capable of eating or drinking.' And though he thought James's genius as an interpreter of life shone out most impressively in his later books, he did not think these well written.

'That terrible grey eye of Henry James,' he wrote in 1908, 'that misses nothing, and that great brain that understands everything—but he can no longer *write*. He did write so well—with such elegance and clarity and insight! Now all these crawling broken-backed inarticulate sentences that have to be helped along by the reader!'

As for the prefaces that Henry James composed for the standard edition of his works, Max thought them disastrous: intended to explain, they succeeded only in confusing. Sometimes, too, he wondered if Henry James was less a novelist than an 'evocative' writer with an extraordinary power of suggesting and conveying the especial feel and flavour of a situation, a personality, a place. All the same, Max's admiration for James was more intimate and heart-felt than that he felt for any other contemporary writer. Moreover, it grew with the passing of the years. To begin with he had regarded James as an exquisite rather than a great author—'The perfect master of a small method,' he calls him in 1901. By 1907 he is praising him as an original genius of the highest quality, who, better than anyone before him, had succeeded in reproducing in words the very texture of human experience.

'You need search heart and brain for epithets to describe the later James—the James who has patiently evolved a method of fiction entirely new, entirely his own, a method that will probably perish with him, since none but he, one thinks, could handle it; that amazing method by which a novel competes not with other novels, but with life itself; making people known to us as we grow to know them in real life. . . .'

Indeed, for Max all Henry James's blemishes grew to seem trivial, measured by the strength of his genius. James's books gave him a steadily increasing pleasure; till at the end of his life he used to say that he turned to other writers only to come back in the end to Henry James.

The truth was that, more than anyone else, Henry James stood for art and literature as Max conceived of them. He wrote in the way Max liked best about the things that he best liked reading about.

'Mr James,' Max wrote, 'does not deal with raw humanity, primitive emotions and so on. Civilization, and a high state of it at that, is the indispensable milieu for him; and just when the primitive emotions surge up in the complex bosom of his creatures, to cause an explosion, Mr James escapes with us under his wing, and does not lead us back until the crisis is over—until the results, the to him so much more interesting results, may be quietly examined.'

Quietly examined; but also beautifully! Intensely did Max appreciate the way that Henry James invested his every page and sentence with aesthetic quality. 'Meredith is first in Poetry and Philosophy', so runs a sentence casually scribbled in one of Max's notebooks, 'but Henry James is first for Beauty.' This shows how high Max put him; for to Max, child of the aesthetic movement, beauty was the supreme virtue. Equally with his achievement did Max praise Henry James's attitude to art; his belief in its absolute value, his complete dedication of himself to its service, his determination, in his own work, to adhere to the highest standards, regardless whether or not this made him popular. Max himself, either because he was too lazy or less often inspired, did not dedicate himself to his art with the same industry. But when he did set to work, he was equally concerned to let nothing pass that did not satisfy his highest standards, equally indifferent to popular approval, equally convinced of the absolute value of art. Henry James was the high priest of Max's chosen and professed faith.

Nor was it simply an aesthetic faith. It was also moral. Indeed the two could not be separated. Max and Henry James were both moral aesthetes; admirers of beauty as manifested in things of the soul as well as in the things of sense. It hardly needs to be said that Henry James, though so careful to make no open moral judgement in his books, was profoundly a moralist. His vision of reality was a moral vision, its elements organized in relation to moral standards. Max recognized all this. He also recognized that Henry James's moral standards were extremely high. Too high perhaps always to be applicable to humdrum human life; here Max's good sense modified his unqualified reverence for the Master. 'Henry James,' he said, 'loves a sense of honour so punctilious that its effects are apt to be rather exasperating to readers who are only averagely good.' Yet such punctiliousness for Max was an error on the right side: he thought Henry James completely and outstandingly on the right side. He is the only author whom he praises specifically for his moral views.

'When I think of Mr James' books,' he writes, 'and try to evaluate the immense delight I have had in that immense array of volumes, it seems to me that in my glow of gratitude the thing I am most of all grateful for is not the quality of the work itself, but the quality of the man revealed through that work. Greater than all my aesthetic delight in the books is my moral regard for the author. . . . Despite his resolute self-suppression for his "form's" sake, Mr Henry James, through his books, stands out as clearly to me as any preacher I have seen perched up in a pulpit. And I do not happen to have heard any preacher in whom was a moral fervour, or one whose outlook on the world seemed to me so fine and touching and inspiring, so full of reverence for noble things and horror of things ignoble—a horror and a reverence that are never obscured for me by the irony that is so often Mr James' way of writing.'

Henry James touched a string that set the depths of Max's nature vibrating in harmony. They went on vibrating all his life. Nearly sixty years later, in extreme old age, sitting in the Italian sunshine with his friend Behrman, Max suddenly said, 'Do you know my favourite line of Henry James? . . . It is "be generous and delicate and pursue the prize". He didn't live up to it, of course, who can? But in his work he did live up to it.' Max sought to live up to it too. This was why the phrase meant so much to him. He, too, believed in delicacy and generosity and in the pursuit in art of the highest, the winning perfection. Henry James is thus a key figure for the understanding of Max. We cannot say for sure that Henry James influenced him: for there is no actual evidence to prove that Max would not have followed the same ideals, had he never met Henry James or read his books. But he looked up to James as the man of his

HENRY JAMES

time who best embodied these ideals. Max's spiritual history may be described as a journey from the crude aestheticism preached by Oscar Wilde to the finer aestheticism—moral as well as literary—manifested in Henry James.

CHAPTER SIX

Love

(1)

ALL the names in Max's notebook with the exception of one or two actresses are male. The reason is that Max took only notes about people who were possible subjects for his art; which—since he was a comedian—meant people he could make fun of. It offended alike against his taste and his tradition to laugh publicly at living women. He did very few caricatures of them; and those that he allowed to be published he was careful not to make grotesque.

This did not mean that he never thought women laughable. Max could laugh at anything or anyone. Still less did it mean that women—because they were not a subject for his art—played an unimportant part in his life. On the contrary, his personal history after 1895 is primarily a history of his relationships with women: it is the story of Max the lover. Unluckily our information about him in this important role is peculiarly scanty. Max was not the sort of man to talk about his love-life: if the women he knew ever did so, their words have not survived. What we do know about the subject is in harmony with the rest of Max's character. His romances were not passionate affairs: physical languor and a dislike of drama combined to keep them on the light, cool side. But they were romances all right, not sexless friendships. Max had learnt from his mother and sisters that there was a special sweetness in feminine sympathy and intimacy: now he was grown-up he also found himself stirred by feminine beauty and charm. The two strains together provided him with a pleasure which gradually grew to be a necessity. Life for him was insipid without the interest given by some gently amorous entanglement. Nor were these entanglements strictly platonic in their manifestations. His flirtations went well beyond mere words. Young women were surprised to find how soon after a first meeting Max offered to kiss them. And Will Rothenstein used to reflect with amusement that the outside world little realized how enterprising the aloof and fastidious Max could be when alone with a girl who attracted him. His idea of attractiveness was normal and straightforward. Those who charmed him, though different in other respects, were all of them young, pretty, pleasant and feminine. And they attracted him in a normal way—if by normal is meant in the same way as they would have attracted the average young man. Their charm, that is to say, was physical and romantic and not at all intellectual. Max did not actually require women to be stupid. But he did think that a strenuous, trained, masculine-style brain was incompatible with feminine charm. He liked women partly because he could relax with them. It was impossible, he found, to relax with a woman of powerful intellect.

His first entanglement had been with Kilseen. Their connection continued to drift along for several years, obscurely and indeterminately. There is no doubt that during this period Max did look upon himself as engaged to her. In the summer of 1897, when she was on a theatrical tour and he was on his holiday, he wrote her a letter every day: and during the next four years he was always referring to her in letters to his friends in the tone of an engaged man; quoting her opinions, explaining that he cannot accept an invitation because of an appointment with her, and evincing a proprietary interest in her health, her plans and her clothes. He also shows himself anxious that his friends should not look on her as a mere appendage to himself but should appreciate her as a person in her own right. We find him writing, for example, to Alice Rothenstein, who had asked them both to dinner, to explain that, though he can come, Kilseen cannot. Do they really want him without her? Max asks. He must have known perfectly well that it was only on his account that the Rothensteins asked Kilseen at all. But he felt that he owed it both to her and to himself as her future husband to take the line that she was as attractive socially as he was.

On the other hand, the engagement was never properly announced; nor does he ever speak in his letters as if marriage was in prospect. The two continued to dine with one another regularly at least once a week. But these dinners do not seem very lively, to judge by such accounts of them as have been left to us. One spectator, watching the couple from the other side of a restaurant, noticed that Max talked vivaciously when choosing the meal from the menu, but afterwards lapsed into silence; Kilseen never spoke at all. Another reporter claims to have overheard a fragment of dialogue: 'When shall we be married?' asked Kilseen. 'Whenever you like, my dear, whenever you like,' Max replied. 'But *you* must make all the arrangements.' Not thus speaks an ardent lover; nor a prospective husband either. Certainly Max's friends did not take his engagement very seriously. 'I trust Max's engagement continues to be a success,' writes Ross to Will Rothenstein in the autumn of 1899. 'You might paint a cassone or an engagement chest in the Italian manner with the Beerbohm betrothals . . . it would form an admirable museum piece for future generations and should contain poor Kilseen's trousseau intact.' Ross's amusement here is mixed with sympathy. In fact he was sympathetic enough with Kilseen to become a close friend in whom she confided. In 1901 she wrote him a letter, one of the few by her that survives, and also one of the only documents which sheds any light on the mystery of her relations with Max. It appears that people had been criticizing him strongly for procrastinating about the marriage.

Dear Robbie,

Don't think I didn't enjoy my lunch. It was awfully nice of you to ask me and I am not stupid enough to not understand your reasons for speaking on such a difficult subject and I do appreciate the kindness in it. I won't say any more about it. I feel mean discussing it even. Mean to Max, for either I should not discuss it, or I should break it off. But all the argument on the earth cannot undo the last six years. All I ask Max's friends is not to judge him too unkindly, and they can go on thinking me 'a fool'. It's a case of 'the heart knoweth its own bitterness', and I am paying for going by my heart's instincts. I don't mean this for anything heroic, and don't think I look upon myself as a martyr! But I have not passed the last six years without thinking and observing and feeling!

I was a more hopeful person when I said in 1900 that it would be settled soon. Since 1900, many things such as my mother's illness and mine and other business matters one can't explain, have made it difficult for Max and me. Don't misjudge him though. You *might* be wrong and I don't want the added unhappiness of thinking that Max has lost any of his friends through me. I have changed since 1900 and I *know* that either things will be settled by the end of this month or I shall pass out of the whole thing and go away. But if I can care for Max and believe in him, don't make me unhappier by being unkind about him. Dear Robbie,

Kilseen.

It would be interesting to know what Max had to say about this matter. Alas, no word of his remains to us. But certainly he was worried. His later references to Kilseen show him to have been troubled by guilt; and a year or two after this letter of hers he says to Reggie, referring to his private life, 'I have had a harassing and unhappy time.' It could hardly be otherwise. He had found himself in a situation from which he must have felt it impossible to emerge without embarrassment, if not discredit. The fact was that as a very young man he had fallen in love with Kilseen and committed himself to her. Now he was out of love with her; and, once out, he realized that, though he liked her very much, they had nothing basic in common. Yet his virtues and his weakness alike combined to make him hesitate before breaking with her. He felt to do so would be dishonourable and he shrank from the unpleasantness the breach would involve. His discomfort was increased by the fact that he was far too sensitive to other people's feelings to be unconcerned at the thought of Kilseen's possible disappointment and also at the mortification she might feel at being jilted. The effect of all this was to make him put off deciding and—while saying nothing to Kilseen about getting married—to let the affair drag on.

In the summer of 1903, however, a new factor entered the situation which forced him to come to a decision. The new factor was called Constance Collier. She was also an actress; but a more successful one than poor Kilseen. Very handsome in the stately, showy style admired by the Edwardians, with flashing dark eyes, magnificent shoulders, and a classical profile, she had made her first success as a beauty of musical comedy. But she was ambitious for higher things: and since, in addition to her looks, she was endowed with a shrewd intelligence, a purposeful will and the luck to attract the attention of Herbert Tree, she achieved her aims remarkably quickly. By the age of twenty-three, Constance Collier was a leading member of Tree's regular company and also a fully fledged public personality, complete with a histrionic manner, a rich-toned languid mode of speaking and any amount of warm flamboyant temperament. Max and she must often have met at Herbert's theatre. In fact, she describes watching him at supper parties there 'smiling insidiously, bowing gently to his partner while his great eyes stared dreamily ahead'. They do not seem to have known each other well, however, till 1902. By the following summer Max was talking of

CONSTANCE COLLIER

her by her Christian name—this was a significant sign of intimacy in those days—and making arrangements for her to join him and his friends in their August holiday at Dieppe. It was natural that they should be drawn to each other. Max responded to the glamour of the star actress, Constance to that of the star wit and dandy. For Max, friendship with a member of the opposite sex meant flirtation: Constance was of the same mind. Flirtation led insensibly to something warmer. A second visit to Dieppe found the two in love with each other. It was a gay, light-hearted, summer-holiday kind of love, unmarked alike by strong animal passion or by a deep affinity of spirit. But it was none the less agreeable for that. And Dieppe that year was the ideal setting for it. The weather was lovely and the company delightful: Sickert, the Nicholsons, Reggie Turner, Herbert Tree for a day or two, while the background was made ornamental by famous and picturesque figures from the world of art and the theatre—Maeterlinck, Jacques-Émile Blanche, John Barrymore, Marie Tempest. From the records left to us, these days rise before the mind's eye like a series of sketches by Boudin or Bonnard; Max and Sickert sipping their *bocks* outside a café on the *plage*—the long-hair bohemian Sickert in baggy corduroy trousers and a beret, the immaculate Max in a high collar and boater tilted jauntily on one side, and with his delicate hand clasped on the ivory knob of his walking-stick, as he gazes idly at the sea glittering in the August sunshine; parties for *déjeuner* in a little woodland restaurant inland, with the light flickering through the leaves on to the coloured table-cloth, on which Max, Nicholson and Sickert are scrawling sketches and caricatures, while by the banks of a neighbouring stream someone sings French songs to the tinkle of a guitar. Back in Dieppe, Max and Constance pose for their photographs, he in a smart white flannel suit and button-hole, she in a light summer dress and floppy hat, her parasol open on her shoulders—'Isn't she beautiful?' Max would say, showing the photograph in after-years—Max and Constance, dressed for the evening, strolling up in the warm summer dusk for a little mild gambling at the casino or to watch the play at the local theatre. Constance knew no French. This led the mischievous Max to play one of his jokes on her.

'Well, you know, there used to be visiting theatrical companies who came there from Paris and played,' he recounted. 'I took

Constance to a matinée of one of these performances—a comedy. . . . The audience started to laugh, and as Constance hadn't the faintest idea of what was going on and as I imagined she felt stupid at not seeing anything to laugh at, I began to improvise the play for her. I converted it into a drama, so there would be nothing to laugh at. My drama was so heart-breaking, you know, that Constance began to cry. But the audience kept laughing, and this laughter seemed callous and incomprehensible to Constance. She asked me what the others were laughing at. I explained to her that this was a provincial audience, very crude and insensitive to pathos. By the time the curtain fell, Constance was so *émotionnée* that I confessed what I had done. It took me some time before she forgave me.'

It was not very long really. They enjoyed each other's company too much. Before they left Dieppe they had begun to talk of marrying. The wedding must be at Dieppe, they agreed: they inspected the English church there and decided it would do.

Such talk was only half-serious. Apart from anything else, Max felt it impossible to make a firm offer to Constance till he had broken with Kilseen. When he got back to England he went to her and told her the truth. She took it well and understandingly. Max went off to Constance to make a formal proposal and was accepted. But throughout the autumn he felt awkward enough about the matter to want to keep the engagement private.

My dearest Reg,

By the way: please don't breathe to Bobbie or anyone about my engagement to Constance—I want it to be a dead secret. The position of fiancée to Max Beerbohm is rather a ridiculous position, after poor Miss Conover's experience, and I don't want Constance to be placed in it publicly. So we mean to be married quite suddenly (so far as the public is concerned). If anyone asks about Miss Conover and me, then you can say that we have agreed to dissolve our engagement: and if anyone asks whether Miss Collier had anything to do with it, of course say 'no'. But don't volunteer the information. . . .

Your affectionate
Max.

Fifty years later, when he was eighty-two, he gave the woman who was to be his second wife a brief summary of the story.

'I was engaged to Grace Conover,' he said, 'but we didn't suit each other at all. I felt relieved when we broke off the engagement after I had fallen in love with Constance Collier; but of course I didn't get engaged to Constance till Grace and I had agreed to part. But we remained great friends.'

No doubt they did in the sense that each felt well disposed to the other. But, in fact, after this Kilseen ceased to play a part in Max's life.

Meanwhile Max had begun to follow his customary practice of bringing his family and his fiancée together. Constance became a regular attendant at Mrs Beerbohm's Sunday luncheon parties. She enjoyed them immensely. The house, she noticed, was shabby and the food simple—it was always roast beef, Yorkshire pudding and apple dumpling with cream—and the other guests were generally rather poor. But they were all interesting; she was struck particularly by Rothenstein, Conder, and the youthful Somerset Maugham. The Beerbohm family she found charming—not only Max but also Constance, Agnes, elegant Julius, and Mrs Beerbohm herself, sitting keen-eyed in black silk at the top of the table. It is unlikely that the Beerbohms were equally pleased with her. Though intelligent and more a woman of the world than Kilseen, she did not attain to their standards of refinement. Further, Herbert's wife and daughters did not like her and said so: possibly they were biased against her by the fact that Herbert liked her very much. But this, too, was not a fact to recommend her to Mrs Beerbohm and her daughters as a suitable wife for Max. In fact she was just as unfitted for that role as Kilseen had been. More so in one respect: Max, for all his flirtatiousness, was a man of cool sexual temperament. The full-blooded Constance was very much the reverse. Such a discrepancy was not likely to lead to a happy marriage. Max's friends, amused at the ups and downs of his love-life, commented on this. 'Max has jilted Scylla in order to get engaged to Charybdis,' said Ross: and Rothenstein remarked that the marriage was bound to end disastrously since Constance could hardly be expected not to take a lover and Max would never be content to accept the role of a complacent husband. Anyway, he was never to be faced with such a prospect. Constance's amorous proclivities showed themselves long before she got near the altar. In March 1904 she went off on a theatrical tour. Max found himself missing her dreadfully and all the more because her letters after the first week grew rare and chilly. The reason for this was that the leading man of her company turned out to be handsome and attentive. 'You know what it is on tour!' she explained, relating the story afterwards. The experience also made it clear to her that Max was from her point of view inadequate as a lover; 'Something more exciting turned up,' was the way she put it to a friend. Accordingly, she wrote to Max breaking off the engagement, giving as her reason that, though she was still fond of him, she did not think, on reflection, that either of them were fit for the responsibilities of life. Max took this very well, and refused to admit that Constance was in any way in the wrong: he may have felt that he had no right to do so after the way he had treated Kilseen. But for the time being he was extremely unhappy. He turned for sympathy to Reggie.

'Now for a bad sad and beastly piece of news; Constance and I are not going to be married after all. I had thought before she went on tour that she seemed rather different, but I put it down to her rehearsals and hard work. Then when she went away, her letters were different from what they used to be—colder and fewer. And last Saturday I had a letter from her saying she had been so wretched and had not known how to tell me that she felt it would never do, after all, for us to marry—neither of us being the sort of people for the serious responsibilities of life. It was a very sweet letter indeed, and of course I don't blame her the very least. Indeed, long ago I had always been telling her that it would be madness from the common-sense point of view for her to marry me. I thought I was right then; and I think she is right now. But of course it is sad— being without her—breaking off so many ties of love. She says she cares for me as much as ever; and so do I for her; but that of course only makes it worse. It *is* a pity I was not born either rich or the sort of solid man who could be trusted and who could trust himself to make his way solidly in the world. . . .

. . . Don't mention *a word* of this news to a soul. And I know you and your sense of proportion and character and things too well to imagine that you will feel the slightest inclination to blame Constance. I never shall feel anything but gladness for all the happiness I have had since I met her that year in Dieppe.'

Next day Reggie got yet another letter:

'I have heard again from Constance—another very sweet letter. I hated yesterday to take up, in writing to you, a sort of apologetic attitude for her. She really needs no apology at all from me to anyone. Circumstances and I myself are such an ample explanation, and I am sure you agree with me about that.'

He goes on to say that he hopes to come and visit Reggie in Paris some time soon:

'I might come by the Dieppe route, because it is cheapest; but I think that is all I shall see of Dieppe this year, much as I love the place. For it means to me Constance, more than anything else. And I don't think I could stay in it this summer. I couldn't quite bear that little place on the terrace where they make the electric light, and where we used to sit together at night, and the English Church where she wanted to marry me "next Tuesday", and the dining-room of Lefèvre's, of which the abiding and most distinct of all memories is that birthday dinner at which she sat between you and me, and had from you a laurel-crown, like mine, and a cake with ROMA on it. All this sounds very "literary" and sentimentalistic. But it is real enough to me. I shan't take my holiday on "our sunny south-coast": somewhere in France; but not Dieppe.'

Max's unhappiness was not simply due to the loss of Constance. He was also deeply disturbed because the whole episode forced him to confront a hitherto unrecognized and painful truth about himself; it made him realize for the first time the sharp limitations imposed on him by his nature and his mode of living. For Max had to pay a price for being a detached spectator of the human comedy. The price was solitude. Such a role could only be performed in a life of leisure; Max had enough money to afford a leisured life for one person only. He had not realized this before because he had not before wished to share his life with anyone else. But now his love for Constance—stronger than he had felt for Kilseen—had turned his thoughts to marriage; only to be brought up short by the realization that marriage was an impossibility unless he gave up his present mode of life and settled down to work hard regularly for his living. There was never any question in his mind of doing this. He knew it would mean the frustration of his deepest creative instincts. His imagination could not breathe except in that fantasy world which was the creation of his leisure hours. He therefore had for the first time to face the fact that, so far as he could see, marriage was not for him; also that he was in a sense an incomplete human being. A complete human life, as most men conceive it, was incompatible with the full use of his specific gifts. He might please himself by falling in love: but the fulfilment of that love in marriage turned out to be just another of his daydreams; an iridescent frail bubble that burst at its first contact with the exigencies of practical reality. With relentless, rueful insight, he summed up his situation.

'Of course I am a success in a way, and may continue to be so for some time; but that is in virtue of a sort of humble fantastic irresponsibility; for solid worldly success this is no good at all. And I now, for the first time clearly, see myself as on the whole a failure —I have never coveted the *solid* quality till now, when I find that without it I cannot get, and don't deserve, Constance.'

These sobering reflections sank into his mind lastingly to modify his view of himself: and with important results in the future. But in 1904 he was too young to allow them to depress him for very long. Nor the loss of Constance either; indeed, his love for her had been too brief and holiday an affair to have inflicted a lasting wound on him. On the other hand, the pleasure he had got out of it had confirmed him in his taste for light romance. Some sort of flirtation had become necessary to him. By May he was sufficiently recovered to be ready to welcome a successor to Constance and to Kilseen. He had not long to wait.

At the beginning of June he got a letter from an American acquaintance asking him to be friendly to a young actress called Florence Kahn over in London for the first time, alone and knowing nobody. Accordingly Max called on her at her hotel. He was ushered into the public sitting-room to wait. After a few minutes there stole in a fragile, girlish, Pre-Raphaelite-looking figure, in a copper-coloured dress, with pale skin and red-gold hair, a soft expressive voice and a manner that oddly and charmingly mingled youthful ardour and an old-fashioned deferential politeness. The short talk which followed revealed Miss Kahn as shy and timid but quivering with sympathy and sensibility. Max was immediately attracted; he left the hotel resolved to cultivate her acquaintance.

He was by now an expert at doing this. Within a fortnight he had taken Miss Kahn out several times to plays, luncheons, dinners, had introduced her to his family in Upper Berkeley Street, and was beginning his letters to her—he wrote several times a week—with the words 'Very dear little friend'. He had also tried more than once, but unsuccessfully, to persuade her to let him kiss her.

It is interesting that he should have been so strongly attracted to her. For, except that she too was on the stage, she was strikingly unlike his previous loves. Born in 1876, Florence Kahn was the only daughter of a Jewish family living in modest but respectable circumstances at the town of Memphis, Tennessee. The Kahns were a devoted family; but its other members—Florence had four brothers—were, to judge from their letters, a simple, homely lot of people, addicted to small-town gossip and small-town amusements, and without cultural pretensions. Florence herself, however, though not intellectual, was artistic and imaginative; and early showed a remarkable talent for acting. She went on the stage and did so well that at the age of twenty-four she became for a time leading lady to Richard Mansfield, the most distinguished Shakespearean actor in America. Indeed Mansfield, it was thought, was too jealous of her success to keep her with him. She left him to make a considerable name for herself in the *avant-garde* theatre of the time, notably in the plays of Ibsen. Fastidious critics praised her for her emotional sincerity and the expressive beauty of her voice. In spite of these assets, however, Florence Kahn was never a popular success on the stage. This was partly due to the fact that the plays she liked to appear in were seldom popular plays, and partly due to something in herself. She took her art so very seriously that she was liable to leave a play after three months' run on the ground that, if she stayed longer, she would be unable to induce the emotion required to make her performance sincere. In consequence managers, who had a natural liking for long runs, became reluctant to employ her. In other ways, too, Florence Kahn was unfitted for the profession of her choice; nervous and retiring, during her first visit to London she liked to walk about heavily veiled in order that no one should see her face. She was also so easily shocked that she was known to rush from the room in tears at the mere mention of the word 'adultery'. In fact she was a strange mixture; half an artist, with an artist's imaginative sensibility and an artist's high-strung self-dramatizing temperament,

FLORENCE KAHN

and half an old-fashioned American lady, scrupulous, tender-hearted, idealistic, frightened of the animal side of human nature and with very little sense of humour.

She was certainly a great contrast to Kilseen and Constance Collier. This, however, was in her favour so far as Max was concerned. Kilseen had turned out to be wholly unsuited to him: and he was now coming to the conclusion that Constance was altogether too exciting a personality to be a comfortable lifelong companion. Florence, on the other hand, was sympathetic and gentle; and as such a tranquillizing influence. In certain important respects, too, she had affinities with him which her predecessors had lacked. For Max too was refined and aesthetic and easily tired; Max too sympathized with her dislike of rush and push. Otherwise he was very different. There was nothing moralistic and idealistic about Max; and humour, after all, was his ruling characteristic. These differences, for the time being at any rate, did not bother him. On the contrary, they even added to Florence's charm in his eyes. Sceptical and sophisticated, he was at once amused and touched by her ardour and puritanism—accompanied as they were with a trustful innocence and a fresh Pre-Raphaelite prettiness. Florence appealed to the strain in Max that had imagined Jenny Mere in *The Happy Hypocrite*. Even her lack of humour contributed to her charm. Max's mirth had always been self-sufficient, a pleasure which he felt no need to share with others. That Florence often did not understand what made him laugh gave him a chance to tease her; and Max delighted to tease.

Though he teased very gently, it did sometimes cause trouble. From the first the flirtation was ruffled by an occasional breeze. It did not matter if the teasing took the form of a mild practical joke. Once Max—in a new version of the hoax he had played on Constance—took Florence to a play he had already seen, and whispered to her a misleading version of the plot, explaining that an Indian servant who had just entered was really the hero's father, and so on. This, when she realized the truth, appealed to Florence's simple sense of fun. But if Max teased her about more serious and sacred subjects, about her loyalty to American Republican institutions, for example, or her disapproval of blood-sports, she became flustered and a little frightened. She was also mystified and shocked when he declared he could not appreciate Shakespeare. As for his attempts to kiss her, they made her seriously upset. By her code, they must mean that he did not respect her; and, if he did not respect her, she began to wonder if it were not her duty, reluctantly, to break off the acquaintance. Max apologized deeply; but next day he tried to kiss her again. Florence found herself reduced to tears. These were April showers, though; brief and followed by sunshine. Max was always adroit at apologizing and Florence ready to forgive. She delighted far too much in his company to be displeased with him for more than a moment. Knowing him had transfigured her time in England; and his family was as congenial to her as himself. Thus for the two of them June and July passed in a shimmer of romantic gaiety and playful sentiment.

We can follow its passing in Max's letters to her. These are not completely revealing. Except when he felt very seriously indeed, Max kept his mask on. And, for all that he found Florence so winning, he did as yet not feel very serious. In these first letters to her he enacts playfully the role of lover, as he had, in his Oxford letters to Reggie, enacted playfully the role of dandy-aesthete. He does it according to the ideal of his time. His manner of approach, arch and gallant, full of elegant little flourishes and grace, notes of banter and compliment and sentimental suggestion, is as much an Edwardian period piece as the music of *The Merry Widow*. But it is better to give examples, so that they speak for themselves. Here are a few to suggest their flavour and indicate the way the relationship developed. Max seldom dates his letters. But the first was written very soon after the two had met.

'I did have such a very happy yesterday evening, though I am afraid it left you rather appalled by the combined dulness and levity (of *imponderability*, as *you* would call it, I fancy) of Europeans. You mustn't take me as a type. But, imponderable though I be, I have one quite solid conviction; and this is that you are absolutely delightful to be with—(if I may be allowed to say so).

I much disliked saying goodbye to you, and the thought that I might not see you again for a long time. I wonder whether I might come and say goodbye to you *again*, some time on Monday afternoon? I would not stay more than five minutes, and I would not mention dead pheasants or monarchy or any other such subject. Please let me know whether you could stand me on these conditions.'

Very dear little friend,

I wonder what you are thinking of me, when you happen to think of me at all. Probably I seem to you a very dreadful person—mildly dreadful, but still dreadful. And perhaps I *am*. Only it is rather difficult to be always quite on one's best behaviour in the presence of a pretty person with a pretty voice and pretty ideas and pretty hats. Anyhow, I find it rather difficult. And for my crude soul the difficulty is rather intensified by your Tolstoiesque doctrine of non-resistance. Of course it is a very beautiful doctrine, and makes the attacker feel very much ashamed of himself after the attack. But— at the moment . . . I believe that the best mode of procedure, for practical purposes, is that which is recommended by the etiquette-books: Draw yourself up to your full height; let your eyes flash; pause; then say 'Sir!'—But I suppose you could not descend to these coarse expedients. On the other hand, how can I raise myself to your level? Let us discuss the difficulty tomorrow afternoon. That is, if I find you at home. If you have something else to do, don't scruple to be out.

Good night.

Yours very sincerely

~~Mr~~ Max.

I have scratched out the *Mr*, because it is so ridiculous that you should be the only one of my friends who does not call me by my Christian name.'

Very dear little friend,

It did make me so unhappy to see you being unhappy this after-noon—And now, I daresay, you are blaming your little self for that: you 'never do anything of that kind in America', etc. etc.—But you ought not to blame yourself at all. It is so silly to be always re-pressing one's feelings and never confiding in any one. And also it would have made me much unhappier to *guess* that you were being unhappy than it made me to be *told* so. But I don't think you *ought* to be unhappy, dear. However much sadness there may be in things that have happened for you, it is obvious that you have very many things to console yourself with—things to congratulate yourself on. There are such lots of people with sad things to remember and with nothing to gladden them at all. But *you* aren't one of those people, dear little friend. Good night, and God bless you. . . .

This last letter was written in the second half of July. By this time everyone in Max's world was beginning to leave London for a summer holiday. Florence went to stay in Berlin with some German friends called Bernhardt. Max saw her off at Victoria. Within three days of her leaving, he had written her three letters. Here is the first of them:

Dearest little friend,

It is one o'clock, and I suppose you are on the water—nice calm water, I hope. You looked such a very little schoolgirl, going away all by yourself. I think you ought to have had several chaperons—myself among them. It was dreary for me, going back all alone, without the excitement of travelling and being on my way to old friends . . . being in the same town with the Grand Hotel, where I had had so many happy times . . . and with the little restaurant in Jermyn Street . . . I can hardly believe they are standing now that you are gone, dear. But I shall see you again soon, shan't I? I wonder if you will be in Berlin for a month, or for how long? I usually stay at Dieppe till the end of August. You ought to come there, if you aren't staying very long in Germany. Anyhow, we shall meet in London, shan't we? It was quite true, what I said about the likelihood of everyone else seeming to me very horrible after the dear little friend. Mind you have a happy time in Berlin—and don't live up to *too* many dear little self-made standards of what must and what must *not* be done. There is no need for you to make rules for yourself—still less to keep them. For you couldn't do anything that wasn't sweet and dear, however hard you tried. . . .

A week later he was abroad too; back at Madame Lefèvre's hotel at Dieppe. He did not find it such fun there as in previous years. He missed a feminine companion. The result was that a steady stream of letters began to flow from Dieppe to Berlin. Here once more are some examples.

Very dear little friend,

How glad I was to have your letter—and your poem about the Mayor, which is delightful. I am sure you are right about the paintings of Böecklin. I never heard of him, and don't know at all what sort of painter he is; but I am sure he is bad, since you—infallible in the arts—think so. Also, I am sure that even the most obtuse of Germans must have known that you thought so. I remember so well the demure eloquence that comes into your eyes when you say nothing, on these occasions. There is a thunder-storm punctuating this letter as I write it—quite tropical and tremendous. All day long there has been blazing heat, wherein I and three other men drove and had lunch at a restaurant at Martin Église—a place not far from here. Not a restaurant in the ordinary sense:—an apple-orchard, with a trout-stream passing through it, and with ducks and geese and a cat and a dog wandering from table to table with a view to crumbs or anything else that one may offer them, as one sits eating in the shade of one of the apple trees. It was rather sad, in a way, going there. For I remember how, last year, my 'second fiancée' cried when we arrived there, simply because the place is so beautiful, and because she had remembered it so much from the year before, when we had also been there. However . . . it doesn't do to be sentimental about sentimentality, *does* it? The thunder goes rumbling on, and I shall be soaked through before I have posted this letter. Dear little thing, goodbye till tomorrow, and may all your days be as happy as the one of which you wrote to me.

Max.

Very dear little friend,

No—I never heard of horse-psychology. It sounds *very* German— and I suspect you of having invented it. In France animals are not supposed to have any souls: that is the one thing I don't like about the French people. Horses, dogs, cats, and the rest, are pariahs here except in so far as they can be made useful—a piteous, nervous, rib-showing race of creatures. The best horses here are the 'little horses' which spin round at the Casino: they are kept brightly varnished— but only to make one lose one's francs in backing them. Not bad, too, are the horses in the merry-go-round at the Fair which is an annual institution here. Have you such things in America? I am very fond of them. I have had many nice rides this year—renewing my youth. It is quite sad how young I can feel, at a pinch. I, who might be the father of a large family, am always quite capable of behaving like a schoolboy, and only afterwards do I detect the impropriety. One midnight last week found me, in company with one or two men as old as myself, depositing an array of empty champagne bottles, noiselessly, in the bedroom of a chauffeur who lay sleeping innocently on his bed—also putting his watch back by two hours, and performing similar tricks which, lamentable as they seem in narration, thrilled me through and through with happiness at the moment of performance. Other practical jokes, too—writing letters in disguised hand-writing with a view to ridiculous complications— what *would* you think of me—poor old me? You really ought to go to some Berlin library and read up Professor Penfulsdruck or another on 'Praktikaljokismus'—and try to explain me to myself . . . what a lot of writing about myself! But it isn't egoism in the ordinary sense of the word. I am not thinking that 'I am I' and must be interesting to everyone else. I am something more than I—a detached and puzzled spectator—detached, yet knowing more about myself than about any other subject, and offering myself humbly for the inspection of others. I think there is a difference between this and egoism. I don't know whether I have expressed it. But I think it is there. Poor little friend, I simply mustn't bore you any more. I talk of myself, but I think much more about you—and I do so very much look forward to the time when I shall see you again—whenever that may be. How about your going to Paris? You really and truly ought to. Duties are not the less duties for not being painful—are they, dear?

Max.

Very dear little friend,

You can't think how glad I was to have your letter yesterday. I had thought perhaps you were ill, when you wrote telling me not to expect any letters for two or three days. Afterwards, it struck me that perhaps you had met some man who had fallen in love with you—and you with him—and you wondered whether you ought to continue a correspondence with a man who kissed you in London. . . . And perhaps there *has* been such a meeting, and such a result— and you have come (rightly) to the conclusion that it would be silly to break off the friendship with me? All this, of course, is vague guess-work on my part; but it seems not unlikely . . . and if it is the fact, then, you dear little thing, let me . . . but I had better delay anything in the shape of good wishes till I know whether I am right or wrong. What you say about youthful high-spirits being a safety-valve, is no excuse really for my habit of playing practical jokes. I am *not* young, and my spirits are *not* high. And when you ask how

I can stand the routine of gadding about in London, I can only say that I detest it, and think it lamentable. Dear, goodbye till to-morrow. Have a very happy time.

Max.

Very dear little friend,

Thank you very much for your nice little letter today. I am glad you have broken your 'silence'. It is so much better *not* to be silent, generally. I myself (always?) am rather too silent—keep things too much to myself. I hate being sympathized with. But I wish I weren't like that. The expansive people are the happiest,—though, of course, one can't be expansive 'to order' or 'by taking thought'. Yesterday I went to Offranville, to dine with Jacques Blanche, the painter. Oh, how glad I was to get away! Dieppe demoralizes one. One does just as one likes—sauntering around talking for a moment to this person or that—all the day and all the evening. And then to find oneself in a large, cold salon, with a large, stiff family—all so formal, so insipid—'Aimez-vous vous monter à automobile, Monsieur?' etc. etc. French family life is quite awful. My time here is drawing to an end: I go to London on Sunday. Dear little thing, when shall *you* be in London? I wish very much you would go to Paris; but if you won't, you won't. Good night, dear.

Max.

These are only a few of the letters he wrote to her from Dieppe. It will be noticed that they are a little different from those he had written to her in London. He still teases—but his tone is less uniformly flippant. He will stop joking to discuss the French character or to paint a pretty vignette of the French landscape. Moreover, there are two new strains in his discourse. Now and again he speaks of himself, seriously and intimately—more intimately than in any previous correspondence that we know of. Not even to Reggie had he stated so openly that teasing with him was a sign of love, or admitted his fundamental lack of animal high spirits and that compulsive reserve in himself that makes him shrink from sympathy. Not even to Reggie had he so frankly analysed his sense of his own immaturity, 'It is quite sad how young I can feel!' Most men only give themselves away to women. In this respect Max was typically male. Though he may say he shrank from open sympathy, he had been accustomed to tacit tactful feminine sympathy from a child. From a woman sensitive enough not to jar on him, he responded to it still. Florence was such a woman; and for her he does now and again for a moment let slip his mask to reveal his real face.

At the same time, in these Dieppe letters, he declares his affection for her in a new tone, graver and more tender than that he had used in London. 'How I wish I could see you act. But not even that could give me nearly so much pleasure, dear, as seeing you yourself, with no foot-lights between us—you yourself with all your dear little graces and virtues, and moods of happiness and sadness—so utterly unlike all the other people I have known.' There is nothing like these in the earlier letters of the summer.

September found them both back in London; Max first, Florence a few days later. She was as polite and responsive and idealistic as ever; and as nervous. Max at the foot of her hotel staircase watched with affectionate amusement as she crept down the stairs with hands behind her back and then looked anxiously through the stained-glass window in the lounge to see if she would have to face a crowd of strangers on her way out. Going up the stairs at Upper Berkeley Street too she would suddenly stop in order to get the strength of mind necessary to steel her to enter the drawing-room. She still visited Upper Berkeley Street very often. In every respect their life resumed its old course—of dinners and luncheons together and plays and expeditions to famous sights and letters written almost daily. The tone of Max's letters reverted to that of the summer; less tender and self-analytic, more gallant and flippant and teasing. He is going to take her to the new musical comedy at the Gaiety Theatre, he tells her; she may not like it, he fears, but he will. Under his influence Florence was learning herself to be a little frivolous. When Max took her down to Oxford—she must see a place, he said, that had been so important in his life—it was she who hid behind the buttress of a college chapel and watched him with amusement, as he hurried about anxiously searching for her. She was not so apt a pupil, however, if he tried to persuade her to do anything that threatened her sense of propriety. She was even upset if he tried to hold her hand.

'I am not such a *very* dreadful person,' he writes soothingly. 'I did hold your hand, I admit. But, dear, why shouldn't you let me hold your hand? Surely mutual sympathy may be allowed to have its outward manifestation. Surely that is very right and natural. But of course I *will try* not to do it, if you feel afraid of it. Only do come with me to the play tomorrow. I will call for you ten minutes before the time of the performance, unless I hear from you that you really can't stand the prospect.'

For good or ill, Florence was not going to be troubled in this way much longer. She and Max were to be forced apart. Florence had her art to think of; partly because she was deeply interested in it, and partly because she was too poor to go on living in London without earning anything. It seems she had come to England largely with the idea of getting work. For American managers—partly because of her habit of leaving a play after a three-months run—had lately shown themselves reluctant to employ her. Alas, nothing had come of her efforts to get work in England. She had no choice but to go home. Max and she agreed to keep in touch with each other by frequent letters. Early in November, he took her down to Liverpool and saw her off; and came back to a London where nothing remained of her but a photograph on Mrs Beerbohm's mantelpiece. He sat down and wrote her a letter.

Very dear little friend,

I hope you are having a good voyage and will have a very happy homecoming. Of the second I have no doubt at all, but of the first I *am* rather doubtful. I am afraid there may be a bad fog for you at this moment, with clanging bells and shrieking syrens—no sirens, I mean. My sense of spelling is gone because I am permeated and suffocated with the fog that there is in London—the fog that makes me think there may be one also at sea. I hope that London has the monopoly of it, and that you are ploughing through nice clear starlit and moonlit waters—and that you are comfortably asleep in that nice cabin—the *lower* berth, so that if you do ever tumble out you won't hurt yourself, dear—and that you will wake up and eat a nice breakfast on deck, in your yachting-cap—and in your bag—and all correct and happy and comfortable. But it is a dreary thing for me to know that every moment is taking you further away from me—every few minutes while I wake or sleep adding another mile—*knot*, isn't it?—to the distance between me and the dear little friend who made such a happy summer for me—such an unforgettable summer. I didn't realize *how* much I was going to miss you till I got back into familiar London last night. Everything was blurred till I got back into the place where I had known you. I keep five pennies, for remembrance. Two were in the envelope you gave me from the gangway —and the other three were in the envelope you threw over the water, with such good aim. How remote all this must seem to you now—now that you are home again (I project myself)—home in that country of which I always so cordially acknowledge the size— and more especially home with your mother and brothers, whom, though I have never seen them, I seem to know and to love because they love you.

I post this letter tonight, on the chance of there being a boat tomorrow. I will always write on Tuesdays and Fridays. Good night, and God bless you.

Max.

My mother misses you so very much and she sends her love.

This letter may stand as the end of the first chapter in the story of Max and Florence. It was an indeterminate and ambiguous end; for it was the expression of an indeterminate and ambiguous state of mind. The language Max uses in it is loverlike: and it expressed his true feeling. He was aware in Florence of an affinity of taste and spirit that he had not felt with Kilseen or Constance Collier. Yet to both of these he had proposed marriage. There is no hint of anything of the kind in this farewell letter to Florence—or in any others to her that he wrote in these earlier years. It is possible that Florence indicated she did not want it. Nervously virginal, she may have flinched from a proposal as much as from a kiss. Besides, we know from other sources that she thought a woman should leave the stage if she married; and at this time she still cared too much for her art to contemplate leaving the stage. Yet, if Max had wished to propose, he would surely have done so in spite of her objections. Far more it looks as if the disillusioning end of his engagement to Constance Collier had put him off matrimony. He realized that in his present circumstances he was unable to marry; and that he did not feel enough in love—he had never felt enough in love with anyone—to be willing to make the sacrifices needed to change these circumstances. To do so would threaten the existence of that inner life of his, which he cared for more than he cared for any human being.

All the same, when he was with Florence he could not help talking to her like a lover; stirring in her, it might well be, all sorts of unsettling thoughts and emotions and conjectures. Perhaps it was just as well for both of them that Florence had gone back to America.

CHAPTER SEVEN

'Yet Again'

(1)

WITH Florence gone, Max resumed his old mode of living. It was to continue unchanged for six years more. He went on working in his usual leisurely fashion; contributed caricatures to various periodicals, notably *Vanity Fair*: and held two exhibitions at the Carfax Gallery, one in April 1907, the second in May 1908—this last was his most successful up to date—as well as joining with some other artists in a group show at the Baillie Gallery in February 1907. Exhibitions involved Max in what was for him an unusual amount of correspondence. He cared passionately about the way his work was presented: it was one of the few things that could make him openly agitated, for it stirred his concern to present himself and his products to the world as works of art finished and perfected to the smallest detail. Before an exhibition he was always writing to the director of the gallery about mounting and framing, just as before one of his books came out he was always writing to his publisher about type and binding and margins.

He brought out two books during these years. The first was *A Book of Caricatures*, published in 1907. This consisted mainly of single figures and was the fruit of the wider social life he had been living. In addition to what may be called his regular subjects— Shaw, Henry James, etc.—there are drawings of statesmen and men of fashion and artists most of whom he had not tackled before. The book is one of his less important collections. It does not represent his full range: there is little of his fantasy in it or of that literary strain which had enriched *The Poets' Corner*. Only the pictures of Henry James are accompanied by long captions. But Max by now is in full command of his art and *A Book of Caricatures* contains some very entertaining work. It has a special interest, too, in that it illustrates the detached and independent attitude he took to public affairs. Like a true classical satirist, Max is against extremes. The fact that he was by taste and temperament Conservative does not stop

MAX BEERBOHM

him laughing equally at men of the Right and men of the Left. He draws an unappetizing picture of the future as imagined by the progressive Wells: but he also mocks Charles Whibley's romantic belief in hereditary aristocracy. Indeed Max himself paints many of his aristocrat models—Lord Spencer, for instance, and Lord Grimthorpe—with an unsparing mischief. It was even rumoured that two very Conservative newspapers refused to employ him on the ground that his drawings were calculated to bring the peerage into contempt.

As always, Max wrote less than he drew. The only book he produced during these years is *Yet Again*, a collection of essays published in 1909. This was good enough, however, to maintain and even advance his reputation. His characteristic qualities—observation, humour, intelligence, sense of beauty—show themselves more richly here than in any previous volume. So also does his mastery of his craft. His style, though still unashamedly artful—Max never aimed at the art that conceals art—has by now dropped all its more flagrant affectations to be characterized by a restrained and classical grace. If he still uses an odd word—'what did he mean by "irrepleviably" ', wrote a bewildered reader—it is rarely and only to give his own individual turn of humour to a sentence. For his style is more intimately individual than before; he knew it was. He hoped it was.

'Your letter about *Yet Again* was so kind and friendshipful,' he wrote to Ross, 'and puffed me up very much, especially what you said about my having "shed" my influencers and achieved a style of my own. That is just what I wanted to get said to me. *Style* I always had; but, in reading the proofs of the book, I dimly discerned that I had achieved my style; and am glad this wasn't a delusion.'

The general tone and type of subject in *Yet Again* is much the same as in *More*. Max has not changed his mask. But the effect, within the limits imposed by the light key he has chosen to write in, is more poetic and more thoughtful. Now and again we get even more of a glimpse at his serious views and sentiments; his hatred of coarseness and vulgarity, for instance, as displayed in comic papers or at a prize-fight. But he never lets the tone get too grave to suit the general mood of the book; and he is vigilant to avoid sentimentality. This, he realized, was the occupational disease of the occasional essayist: all too often one of them came to grief through trying too obviously to touch the heart. Never must he let this be said of him! Meditating on the wax effigies of the mighty dead in the Islip Chapel of Westminster Abbey, he seems about to indulge in a flight of pathetic eloquence about the transience of all things mortal, when adroitly he modulates into another and more flippant key.

'I feel that I ought to be more deeply moved than I am by this sad state of things. But—well, I seem to have exhausted my capacity for sentiment, and cannot rise to the level of my opportunity. Would that I were Thackeray! Dear gentlemen, how promptly and copiously he would have wept and moralized here, in his grandest manner, with that perfect technical mastery which makes even now his tritest and shallowest sermons sound remarkable, his hollowest sentiment ring true! What a pity he never came to beat the muffled drum, on which he was so supreme a performer, around the Islip Chapel!'

In 1906 Max's especial brand of aestheticism got a chance to show itself in a new form. Some time in the summer of that year Max met an old friend at William Rothenstein's studio, Harmsworth of the *Daily Mail*. Max said he had never been to Italy. 'You ought to go,' remarked Harmsworth breezily, 'Italy is up to sample. So,' he added, rather disconcertingly, 'is the Hudson river!' A day or two later he wrote asking Max to go to Italy for a few weeks at his expense in order to write some impressions of it for the *Daily Mail*. In October Max set out. Venice, his first stop, surpassed all his expectations. With his imagination already set stirring by memories of *The Wings of the Dove* and *The Aspern Papers*, he wandered entranced through *calle* and *campo*, lingered in dark, incense-scented churches, sat over his cup of coffee in the Piazza, staring with delight and wonder at St Mark's—less like a church, he thought, than a garden, 'an Eastern garden that had been, by some Christian miracle, petrified just when its flowers were fading so that its beauty should last for ever to the glory of Christ and St Mark'. His pleasure in Venice was so acute that he prudently left after a week. 'I don't want to get *used* to Venice,' he said. He expected Padua to be an anticlimax after Venice. It was. After a few hours there, he took the train back to Venice to spend a day or two more there. Verona was a little better than Padua; 'The old part really beautiful,' he commented, 'the modern dreadful but comic.' Then came Florence.

At first he did not like it anything like so much as Venice. But Max's talent for pleasure had taught him how he personally could best enjoy foreign travel; and he set to work to enjoy Florence after his own fashion. This meant not bothering about important sights; Max knew himself to be less a sightseer than a sentimental traveller, unenthusiastic about museums, and who liked to come upon beauties casually at street corners. Florence, approached like this, yielded pleasure and interest. As he looked round the stern stonework of the Piazza della Signoria, Max wove fancies about it. Surely this was an alarming place, fit setting for riots and executions! The very statues seemed to feel it to be so: Michelangelo's David frowned in fury, the Tritons seemed to be bursting from the great fountain to join in the fray. Max the realist also found food for satisfaction in Florence. He noted that the inhabitants were modernists, pleased to improve the amenities of their ancient city by introducing trams and electric light. The English tourists Max met were displeased about this. Max was not. What right had the English to complain, anyway? They had done far worse things in their own ancient cities. Soon Florence began to exert a sombre charm on him. So he wrote to Florence Kahn.

This charm was enhanced by the presence of Botticelli's pictures. To see them was for Max a unique experience. He took the not unreasonable view that they were the most beautiful pictures ever painted. It outraged him to find an English acquaintance standing unresponsive in front of the 'Primavera'. 'Have you no sense of beauty?' Max burst out with uncharacteristic vehemence. 'No,' answered the acquaintance simply. Max observed with interest that the English were not ashamed to be thought unaesthetic. Not quite all the English, however; in Florence, Max made friends with Herbert Horne, the art critic, who showed him the surrounding country and finally drove him over to Siena. Max liked Siena almost as much as Venice. He found its atmosphere was such a delightful mixture of the medieval and the cosy, though he himself was better equipped to appreciate the cosy than the medieval. At Siena he was faced with a choice. He had a few days left to spend abroad. Should he go on to Rome or go back to England? Uncomfortably he hesitated. His inclination was to return to England: he felt he would be unable to digest any more impressions. No doubt people would blame him for missing Rome. But this very fact roused a spirit of contradiction in him which made him more unwilling to go than ever. Should he toss up? No. The only good that ever came of tossing up was that it made the mind clear as to what it really wanted. It was already clear to Max that he wanted to go back to the November fogs of London. By the end of the month he was installed once more in Upper Berkeley Street. He had brought back with him some important and influential memories. Italy at its best seemed to him the nearest he had yet been to an earthly paradise. After this, when oppressed by the pressure of life he indulged in daydreams of retirement, he always pictured his place of retirement as in Italy.

At the moment he had the task of writing his articles for the *Daily Mail*. It was not a congenial task. Primarily, it meant describing Venice; and Max, aware as he was of the limitations of his talent, feared that the exalted rapture which Venice had inspired in him was outside his creative range.

'For the first time in my life,' he said, 'I wish I were a poet, so as to do some sort of justice to Venice. I feel it so impossible to *describe* beautiful things. Not even such a poet as Ruskin can really describe them (I have been reading *Stones of Venice* with much delight and surprised reverence for Ruskin); but he can give *something* of them; and I shall only be able to give pretty little personal-fantastic irrelevancies. However . . . I shall take a melancholy pleasure in giving these as best I can.'

Max's best was not at all bad. He took pains to counteract his natural bias; he puts in fewer personal or fantastic digressions than are usual in his work. But not too few: the articles are humorous and pretty enough to be recognizably by Max. And they do convey his discriminating sense of the beauty, at once exquisite and shabby, that, in these twentieth-century and latter days, distinguishes the Bride of the Adriatic.

'These mouldering old palaces, gazing so ruefully down at their reflections, wondering whether they really look like *that*, not knowing that they are more beautiful, so, than they ever were; these wan reaches of ghost-enclosing palaces, with the plaster peeling off them and showing their bricks in patches, and with the clear green water lapping and sapping their foundations. See how time has thinned with rust the iron bars of the windows, and with dust has thickened the cobwebs! Soon it will be hard to know which are the bars, which the cobwebs . . . there can only be ghosts behind those shutters.'

Such a passage is not in the style ordinarily employed by writers for the *Daily Mail*. What did its ordinary readers think of it, one wonders. Harmsworth, perhaps in order to compel their interest, published the articles under huge headlines of the type generally used when reporting a sensational murder case. Max—concerned as he always was that his work should be properly presented—saw these and was horrified.

Such excursions into freelance journalism were rare. In general Max's literary energies were sufficiently exercised by his weekly theatre articles for the *Saturday Review*. He was to go on with these till 1910; and in much the same way. Alike in style and point of view, Max's later reviews were much like his earlier. He still judged plays by the same three standards. They had to be lifelike, intelligent and aesthetically pleasing; and he still found most of them wanting in one of these three respects. As before, the new drama fared better at his hands than the old. He remained, officially as it were, a modern, who praised Shaw and Galsworthy, declared himself against censorship, and took Somerset Maugham sharply to task for saying that serious ideas were out of place in the theatre. As a matter of fact, Max at heart was not very enthusiastic about the new drama. He never had been. Much of it was too drab and too cerebral for his taste. With the passage of time, his enthusiasm waned still further. In 1898, when the new drama was just starting, aesthetes and preachers of revolutionary ideas united in its defence against their common enemy, reactionary philistinism. But by 1906 the philistines, if not routed, had been forced to accept the existence of the new drama: with the result that a split began to show itself in the ranks of their opponents. The aesthetes in particular became growingly critical: they thought the work of the preachers joyless and ugly. Max the aesthete found himself again and again disliking characters held up by the new drama for admiration. The new type of erring daughter, for example, dogmatizing complacently about the moral duty of practising free love—better Olivia Primrose, he said, better Little Em'ly, than her! And the conventional polite young man of fashion was surely a more civilized and agreeable object than the priggish ill-mannered rebel against convention who so many new dramatists made their hero. Nor was Max so sure as once he had been that cleverness was the beginning of wisdom. The young 'intellectuals', who were responsible for the morals of the new drama, were often the reverse of wise.

'Mental ability is not safely gauged by height or depth of topic. The value of the thing said depends not on the value of the thing it is said about. We are compelled to rank higher the mind of the average young man of fashion than the mind of the average "intellectual" at those literary tea-parties. . . . Good sense about trivialities is better than nonsense about things that matter.'

At moments Max began to wonder if the theatre of ideas might not lead to something even further from true art than the theatre of pure entertainment. In a late article reviewing a drama of social realism, he says so openly.

'There! ought I not to have spent a happy afternoon? Here was just the sort of play that I am always reviling people for not writing, or managers for not producing, or critics for not praising. Here was a sincere presentment of actual life, with plenty of food for reflection —special reflection on the evil of the tally system, the betting system, the money-lending system; general reflection on the wrongness of the whole social system by which such lives as we see here are possible, and on the unlikelihood that we shall ever, with the best intentions, evolve a preferable substitute. And yet, and yet, all the while, I was but longing to be amused, excited, uplifted; longing for the workman's cottage to be suddenly transformed into a palace, with ornamental and delightful people doing the most preposterous "theatrical" things in it; longing for fantasy and joy; wondering whether, after all, the theatre is a place in which . . . ah, I won't set forth in shameless print the doubts which, even in my breast, I tried to stifle.'

This growing conservatism was increased by the fact that what had been the new art of Max's youth was by now new no longer; and that the movements that succeeded it were not the kind of thing that Max liked. What was he, the apostle of taste and good sense, to think of Futurism and its leader Marinetti who advocated the destruction of all the monuments of past culture in order to make room for a new and glorious world of violence, irrationality and machines!

'With the best will in the world,' Max wrote, 'I fail to be frightened by Marinetti and his doctrines. When he glorifies "the beautiful Ideas that kill", I ask what are they?—knowing very well he couldn't tell me. When he says that "Art can only be violence, cruelty and in-justice", I murmur, with a smile, that those are three of the few things that art just *can't* be. When he asks why we "poison ourselves" by "a daily walk through the museums", I assure him that his meta-phor has no relation to fact. There are a few pedants who walk daily in museums; but even they don't poison themselves; on the contrary, they find there the food that best agrees with them. There is a vast mass of humanity which never sets foot in a museum. There are the artists who go now and again, and profit by the inspiration. It must be a very feeble talent that dares not, for fear of being over-whelmed and atrophied, contemplate the achievements of the past. No talent, however strong, can dispense with that inspiration. But how on earth is anyone going to draw any inspiration from the Future? Let us spell it with a capital letter, by all means. But don't let us expect it to give us anything in return. It can't, poor thing; for the very good reason that it doesn't yet exist, save as a dry abstract term.

The past and the present—there are two useful and delightful things. I am sorry, Marinetti, but I am afraid there is no future for the Future.'

The tone of this passage, though merciless, is yet amused. This is true in general of his later *Saturday Review* articles. For our delight and his own, he sets to work to make devastating fun of Pinero's literary style or the vagaries of the tragedian's temperament as ex-hibited in the memoirs of Sarah Bernhardt. But once or twice as in former days his mood grows darker and more disturbed. It is during these years that he makes his bitter attack on Jerome K. Jerome's 'religious' play, *The Passing of the Third Floor Back*. With a similar cold scornful anger he exposes the ignoble arts of self-advancement as practised in Max's view by an actor-manager called Arthur Bourchier or sums up his feelings about a distasteful farce by Mr Carton purporting to satirize the vices of high society.

'We cannot, then, accept his play as true to life. But the play is a mere farce? I am breaking a butterfly on the wheel? That is what I intended to do. Ugly butterflies deserve to be broken. If a butterfly is not beautiful, it has no right to exist. If a farce is unpleasantly invented, it has no right to exist.'

Once again we note that beneath his frivolity Max was a moralist. It was the moralist in him that made him dislike Wells' and Kipling's writings. He disliked them for other reasons as well. They both stood for things that depressed and disgusted him; Wells for science and socialism, Kipling for machinery and the Boer War: neither set much value on the things Max did care about, on irony or aestheticism or the private life. As artists, too, they aroused Max's disapproval. He thought they were both men of genius who had misused their precious gift. Wells had prostituted his to the service of propaganda; and he was a slapdash, careless craftsman. How well his books began! How seldom they fulfilled the promise of their beginning! 'Heaven forbid that there should be a definitive edition of all his novels,' said Max, 'but the first hundred pages of some might be well worth having: after that they slip over into nonsense.' Kipling's art suffered from a different defect. He was an expert, dependable craftsman; but, Max thought, he used his craft in the service of a crude, in-the-know effectiveness that jarred horribly on a sensitive taste. All his work—even what might be thought less characteristic—was spoilt by this fault. 'I read *They*,' Max once remarked, 'I was told it was a good ghost story. But it is metallic. The house and garden and children all seem made of zinc. A ghost deserves better!'

However, these ideological and aesthetic defects would not have made him dislike these authors so much had he not also found them distasteful morally. There was to him something hysterical, perverse and even feminine in Kipling's strident admiration for mere maleness. Could his name be a pseudonym for a female author, Max asked wickedly; for surely real men take masculinity more for granted. He hated Kipling's apparent approval of the brute and the bully, 'the smell of blood, beer and "baccy" ', which, he said, exhaled from Kipling's pages.

Wells offended in a different way. His books also showed a vulgar heart; how cheap and unlovely were the Utopias he painted as ideals for men to work for! Max also found him morally insensitive in his conduct; he was shockingly unappreciative of the finer feelings or of the obligations of honour. What excuse was there for his putting people to whom he was bound by the ties of friendship and affection into his novels recognizably and, as often as not, in an unpleasant and ridiculous light? Max could not forgive Wells for this.

He was the more severe because he himself had grown with the passing of the years extremely scrupulous about making professional copy out of his friends. To do so is a strong temptation to the caricaturist; and he felt it his first duty to resist it. At the time of his 1907 exhibition, an interviewer from a newspaper asked him if he had ever felt guilty about a caricature. Yes, Max told him; once in the 'nineties he had written to Wilson Barrett, a popular actor of romantic heroes, asking him for a ticket to his theatre as he wished to do a drawing of him. Barrett had been extremely kind, had given him a box and received him hospitably after the performance in his dressing-room. 'Well, I suppose you are going to make fun of me,' he said. 'Well—it is the sort of thing I do,' stammered Max. It was. Barrett was on the short side and running to fat: Max represented him in high-heeled shoes with plump shoulders bulging out of a *décolleté* toga. Remembering Barrett's kindness, Max, ten years later, felt a stab of conscience.

(2)

Side by side with his professional, Max's personal life pursued its own course. He still lived at home, and home was unaltered. Perhaps it was a little shabbier—for money was shorter than ever and there was even talk of letting a room on the ground floor—but the house looked much the same, with the same crowd of mementoes on the walls and tables, the same gilt mirror over the mantelpiece. The atmosphere of the Beerbohm family life too was still refined and dishevelled, agitated and amused, and Mrs Beerbohm still kept open house, especially on Sundays. Herbert Tree's daughters were often there, Viola, Felicity and Iris. They noted that the house revolved round their uncle Max; Mrs Beerbohm saw to it that his convenience was the first thing to be considered by everybody. Uncle Max himself seemed very young—the Tree sisters thought of him less as an uncle than as an elder brother—exquisitely dressed in pale grey tweed, his manner a little detached and remote. But he was polite to his nieces and amused them. 'Oh Yorkshire ham, how tired I am!' he would sigh as he carved the ham for the guests. He also made them laugh by making up nonsense rhymes, on the subject of his sister Constance's dog, a small Pomeranian, which lurked in her lap and peeped yapping from the folds of her fichu. It is to be hoped that Constance enjoyed the rhymes; for she alone of the family seems to have been occasionally critical of Max. As the house-keeper she lived in a growing state of anxiety about expenses. Some-times this exploded in a fit of nervous agitation in which the frantic and the inconsequent were curiously blended:

'. . . can't you stop at *Canterbury?*' so runs a characteristic letter written to a friend travelling to Kent. 'The *Cathedral* is *very* very grand. En route too is *Rye*, so like Siena—so *preserved*, where Henry James lives.

I am much over-worked and thinking of taking poison, the hourly anguish is too awful. If I suggest a thing to help Mamma becomes fearfully excited. I give all I can—and so does Aggie and Herbert sent money today, though he has *none* to send.

Oh! It's awful, not one tiny thing will she let us decide. Cheques, money, all goes astray; and waste, waste, waste, for absolutely *poor* people.'

More than ever, Constance felt that Max ought to contribute more to the family funds. Certainly he ought not to add to the family expenses by asking his friends in to meals. Yet Sunday after Sunday saw Street and Reggie and others at the luncheon table in Upper Berkeley Street, consuming Yorkshire ham and apple pie. 'If only Max would help a little!' Constance lamented. Yet she was very fond of him, they all were. And she took pleasure in his idiosyn-crasies. Once when he was unwell, Dora suggested that he was a nervous patient. 'No,' said Constance, 'he takes suffering bravely but *seriously.*' During this year two events occurred to cast a shadow over the family circle. In 1908 Dora Beerbohm was taken very ill. The doctors told her that if she was to recover she must leave the Priory, at least for the present. Luckily some friends called Curtis—Dora, like Max, had a gift for collecting devoted friends—took her to the Mediterranean. There she was gradually cured, partly by the gentler climate, and still more, people thought, by her own faith and prayers. Max much admired Dora's talents. She ran a little magazine for the Priory and wrote stories for it. For some years past Max had tried to get these published in book form. As early as 1902 we find him writing to John Lane about them.

'Please, when you have time, consider whether something could be done with them,' he pleaded. 'They seem to me to have a charm of their own.'

In April 1906 the darker shadow of death fell over the Beerbohms. Julius Beerbohm, exhausted by a life of adventure and failure, died at the age of fifty-three. Even on his death-bed he managed to maintain the strict standards of his dandyism. His brother Herbert came to see him dressed in a reddish-brown suit that offended against Julius's taste. 'Ginger!' he said disgustedly, and turned his face to the wall. Max also visited him several times; when he died, he mourned him sincerely. Meanwhile, his other youthful hero, Herbert, went on from success to success. The mature Max found the atmosphere of his home a little too hectic to suit his own leisurely temperament; and, from the days of Kilseen on, he never seems to have felt wholly at ease with Herbert's wife. Herbert's own company he still found exhilarating. One way and another he still saw a good deal of him. In 1909 Herbert was knighted. A lady acquaintance asked Max if she should address a letter to Maud Tree by her new title before Herbert had actually received his accolade from the King. 'Oh, well,' said Max, 'there is no harm in writing Lady. I am sure in the eyes of Heaven my brother is already a Knight.'

In London and on his holidays Max kept up with his old friends. Reggie and Will Rothenstein seem still to have been the closest, though his relations with them were not always unclouded. Reggie had always had a mercurial disposition that oscillated between rollicking spirits and fits of black gloom. As the years passed, either the gloom grew more frequent or Max minded it more. 'I lunched at the Arts,' he writes to Florence in September 1908. 'Reggie Turner was there in a state of considerable gloom. He has begun to be a real bore.' These words sound more ominous than in fact they proved. Reggie cheered up as readily as he grew melancholy: when he cheered up he was as entertaining as ever. Moreover, he remained generous and affectionate. Three months after this letter was written,

MAX BEERBOHM AND HERBERT BEERBOHM TREE

hearing that Max was hard up, he sent him a cheque and some beautiful handkerchiefs.

'My dearest Reg,' Max replied to him, 'What *can* I say? It is very wrong of you; *much* too generous and sweet of you. And my first (and better) instinct was to send the cheque back defaced and to ask you to knock off £15 and write another. However (I began to think) if you *will* do that sort of thing—after all—you are not "a minor"—I am not my brother's keeper, etc. etc.

And so I am going to pay the lovely £20 into my bank—under protest—and shall devote it to some definite purpose that will (I am not sure *what* it is) give me true solid pleasure. I don't feel I can devote the money to personal adornment: I am, for the moment, excessively "broke"; and it would be a mockery to hang myself with jewels. In due time I shall be able to come to some decision what to do with the money. Meanwhile I am not telling anyone about it, except my banker! And then the handkerchiefs—how very beautiful *they* are! You are much too good—so are they.'

When all was said and done Reggie Turner was still the man friend Max loved best.

His feelings for Will Rothenstein were more fluctuating. With the passage of years Rothenstein was losing more and more of his youthful light-heartedness. With it went his self-confidence. He felt himself a failure, especially in contrast to the brilliant Max. Max on his side found it harder than ever, with all his other engagements, to see as much of Rothenstein as he had in the past. This produced a tension between them. One evening in March 1909 it exploded in a row.

'I have been having a correspondence with Will Rothenstein,' wrote Max to Florence, 'of a kind quite fresh to me. On Friday night, at Mrs Chadburne's, he said I was a very "corruptible" critic—and of course, in deference to the hostess and guests, I laughed pleasantly. But early next morning I wrote him a long and deadly letter, packed with rankling home-truths. And he, poor friend, seems to have been horribly upset. And my rejoinder (to which I suppose there will be a reply today) was of a gentler and friendlier kind. It is such a rare feeling for me—anger; and I didn't like it at all, and was so glad when I had got rid of it by venting it!'

Max's letter to Rothenstein has not survived. But Rothenstein's answer to it has; and it suggests that Max's words were as formidable as those in which he had rebuked Maud Tree for her treatment of Kilseen. On the rare occasions when he did lose his temper, Max lost it properly. In this instance he seems also to have lost it unreasonably. Max was so conspicuously disinterested a critic that no one, let alone an old friend, can have really thought him corruptible. To have reacted as he did, Max must have suspected some hidden hostility in Rothenstein's tone. Rothenstein was appalled by Max's letter. He wrote pouring out apologetic explanations for any weakness Max might have detected in him. Of course his words had only been meant as a joke. He feared that his jokes were not very good; he knew, he said, that he did not amuse Max as much as other people did; but he dearly loved him. Mollified, Max replied:

My dear Will,

You can't think how I rejoiced to have your letter today, and to know that all is well between us now and hereafter,—not only *well*, indeed, but *better*, so far as I am concerned; just as one realizes more clearly the value of a treasure after one has been scared by chance of losing it. We have disabused our minds of much. But it still remains for you, apparently, to get rid of a notion that 'other people amuse' me more than you do. On the contrary, there is no one whose presence delights me more than yours; in a small degree because your strenuousness gives my sense of humour a chance; and in a far greater degree because your brain is so very cogent and brilliant. Also; what is all this about your work being 'dull and unpopular', and about yourself being 'not very successful'? I daresay you haven't all the success you deserve. But what good artist has, in his lifetime? Meanwhile, the Universities and the Colonies and a decent number of private persons are yours to command—and your position in art is firmly established, and acknowledged. You are one of the very few outstanding persons. Evidently you hanker after the dignity and picturesqueness and pathos which go with failure and which are so lamentably lacking to success. But you can't, dear Will, have it both ways. And personally (gross though you will think me) I am glad that you have it in the way that is vouchsafed to you!

Yours affectionately,
Max.

The row was over. The friendship revived to continue for the rest of their lives without friction.

Max kept up his other established friendships too. The pages of his correspondence are sprinkled with familiar names—Street, Craig, Nicholson, Ross, Chesterton, Ada Leverson, Edmund Gosse. Gosse and he kept in touch with each other by pen as well as by word: Gosse wrote Max letters of praise and criticism. Max sent him back parodies and light verse. They played a game, too, with one another; composing sonnets in which each wrote an alternate line. One or two new names added themselves to the list of close friends during these years, notably Desmond MacCarthy and Katie Lewis. MacCarthy was a young man lately down from Cambridge. Himself a fascinating talker with a gift for the happy phrase and a subtle responsive sensibility, he also delighted in the conversation of others. He seems to have had unlimited time to spare for cultivating an intimacy. Calling casually at Upper Berkeley Street, he would stay for hours up in Max's room, talking, or listening in fits of laughter to Max's latest parody of Henry James or Kipling. He was an amateur of human nature who appreciated, as few did, the strain of imaginative poetry in Max's personality. 'Max,' he said once, 'has a reverence for life itself, like most of the poets I know.' Moreover, he shared Max's taste for small private pleasures, his sense of their importance.

Katie Lewis was the child of a rich man, the quiet, soft-voiced Sir George Lewis. He and his wife Elizabeth had made their home a centre for artists of all kinds; Henry James and Burne-Jones, Meredith and Sargent were among its habitués. Max liked the whole family but was most intimate with his contemporary Katie. Sensitive, intelligent, and susceptible to the gentler type of charm, she responded warmly to him; and would even have been willing, some people thought, to have married him. But Max's heart, if it was given to anyone, was given to Florence Kahn. Besides, he felt that dependent as he would have been on Katie Lewis's money, he must inevitably have been swept into the whirling orbit of the Lewises' home-life. This would have been fatal to the spiritual independence he prized so supremely. So long as they lived, however, he liked going to the Lewises'; and especially was he fond of Katie.

Another friend was Arnold Bennett. Max met him first in 1905.

He still bore traces of the raw boy from the Five Towns, stuttering and sensitive, and Max was touched by him. 'Arnold Bennett has been lunching here with me,' he writes to Reggie, 'I find him very sympathetic—all the more so because of the crust that encases him at a first meeting!' In later life Max became more critical. He said that Bennett was all too liable to make a fool of himself.

'It's the same thing of having to know *everything*, of being omniscient, of being unable to say the simple words "I don't know".'

Bennett's talent he admired enormously. At his best, in *The Old Wives' Tale* for example, he was, Max thought, as good as any writer of his time.

'Such a fine book,' he wrote to Florence. 'I didn't send it to you before, because I thought there were things in it that you might disapprove of. . . . But I think you would be bound to enjoy *this* novel. Barring Meredith and our dear H. J., I have never read anything to approach it in point of largeness—(not that H. J. is *large*, or sets out to be so;) he is only deep and exquisite.'

Deep and exquisite though Henry James might be, he was wrong about *The Old Wives' Tale*. For once Max found himself out of sympathy with the Master. Henry James told him he did not think much of it; 'What's it about?' he asked, and repeated testily, 'What *is* it about?' 'Why,' said Max, relating the incident in later years, with reminiscent indignation, 'why, I told him, it's about the passing of time, about the stealthy merging of youth into age, the invisibility of the traps in our own characters into which we walk unwary, unknowing.' Max's admiration of *The Old Wives' Tale* throws light on Max himself. For, though it is in its way a consummate work of art, this way is not what the superficial observer might judge to be Max's way. There is nothing stylish about *The Old Wives' Tale*, nor is it in the obvious sense 'beautiful'. Its strength lies in its vision, at once penetrating and heartfelt, of the basic human situation as it presents itself to the average human being. Max's words to Henry James show that he understood this. His sympathies were wider and more normal than his mask led strangers to suppose.

Max lost friends as well as making them during this period of his existence; but only by death. Conder died in 1909, and in the same year John Davidson gave up his long struggle against despair and killed himself. 'It is a tragic end to a tragic life,' wrote Max to Florence, 'I wish I could banish it from my mind.' The year 1909 also saw the death of the two grand old men whose society Max had cultivated with so amused a reverence. Swinburne went first, in April, Meredith in the month following. Max had been to see the latter only a week or two before.

'Meredith was charming again,' he told Florence. 'He seemed a little older than last year, but was just as full of talk and laughter. He seemed to have felt the death of Swinburne deeply, and there were tears in his eyes when he began to speak about him. He said he himself would soon be "under the grass with the Prussians walking over him". Also, that three years Prussianizing would do England a lot of good. He also had a scheme for a raid on France, to capture five hundred or so of French women, to brighten the breed of the future. He said he didn't like old people, and read me a sonnet on old age—a sonnet attacking the old—with great gusto and élan.'

Max was indignant that the Dean of Westminster refused to let Meredith be buried in the Abbey on the ground that he had advocated five-year contracts of marriage. 'What a nation, or at any rate what a Dean!' exclaimed Max scornfully. The Dean does seem to have been a muddle-headed person, for he saw no reason not to allow this notorious subverter of Christian morals to be given a huge ceremonial memorial service in the Abbey. Max attended it, gazing with the sharp eye of a caricaturist at the distinguished representatives of the arts gathered together to do honour to their dead confrère: Holman Hunt and Ellen Terry, Hardy, J. M. Barrie and Henry James. Henry James eclipsed them all, Max said afterwards; 'his forehead was more than a dome, it was a whole street!' With his caricaturist's eye Max kept also his spirit of mischief. Even his respect for the mighty dead could not subdue it into inactivity. As he came out of the Abbey a girl approached him, 'Oh, Mr Barrie,' she said, 'can I have your autograph?' 'I felt a devil rising in me that I could not resist,' related Max. 'I took her book and wrote in it "Aye lassie, it's a sad day the noo, J. M. B." '

The thought of Barrie easily aroused the devil in Max. Not a savage devil; he was on friendly terms with Barrie and had admired some of his work. Indeed, we have seen that he praised *The Admirable Crichton* with extravagant enthusiasm. All the same, there was something in Barrie's personality that antagonized him. Though not averse to the sentimental if it was administered discreetly and with a grain of irony to save it from sickliness, Max found Barrie's brand altogether too lush and sticky. Further, he doubted if it expressed a genuine emotion. In later years he used to relate with relish a fable he had composed about the author of *Peter Pan*. 'Barrie the great sentimentalist died,' he said, 'and consented after death to be buried in Westminster Abbey: but he ordered his heart to be buried elsewhere. The doctors, on investigation, found that there was no heart.'

Max, we note, was always writing to friends apologizing for not having seen them or for being unable to accept an invitation. It was no wonder: his social life grew fuller every year. In the season he was often out for every meal except breakfast. By 1907 he must have been one of the most popular guests in London: and, as always, in many different circles, bohemian, theatrical, fashionable. He spent a great deal of time in the houses of the *haute bourgeoisie* like the Lewises and the Leversons, at luncheons, dinners, concerts, receptions, even fancy-dress parties. We have a glimpse of him at one dressed as a cardinal, and at another, more characteristically, as himself, wearing a specially designed mask caricaturing his own face. In these houses he often met fellow writers and artists. He also saw them at men's dinners, at the Savile Club and on visits to Oxford and Cambridge. In this way Max got to know a very large number of the distinguished literary and artistic figures of the day—Hardy, Gissing, Galsworthy, A. E. Housman, Belloc, Sturge Moore, Rodin, Caruso—while it enabled him to amplify his knowledge of those he had already met, like Shaw or Yeats or Augustus John. Always they made a vivid impression on him; so that his letters and notebooks and the reports of his talk are illustrated at every turn by verbal sketches; footnotes, as it were, to his cartoons. They are not always favourable footnotes. Nothing could make Max like Yeats, for instance.

'Me he drives to excesses of grossest philistinism,' he writes to Florence, 'sympathetic though I generally am to men of genius. A genius he is of course; and geniuses are generally asinine: but his particular asinineness bores me and antagonizes me, especially since he has put on flesh.'

Housman was another admired poet who made a poor impression.

'He was like an absconding cashier. We certainly wished he would abscond—sitting silent and then saying only "there is a bit of a nip in the air, don't you think?" '

Max's feelings about Shaw were more qualified. Shaw was brilliant, of course; and he could, Max recognized, be both disinterested and kind. But Max still felt there was something inhuman about him; and inconsiderate too. In 1906 Max lunched with him to meet Mark Twain, on a visit to England. Lunch was scarcely over when Shaw looked at his watch, jumped up and left, saying that he had an appointment with his dentist. Was this the way, Max exclaimed to Florence, to treat an aged and distinguished author from hospitable America! Nor could he reconcile himself to Shaw's appearance. 'He has a temperance beverage face,' he said. Altogether Shaw was too much of a good thing.

'Bernard Shaw is back in London,' Max tells Florence in 1906. '. . . It had been quite a welcome rest from him, during the past month or so: he has been in Paris. Rodin has been doing a bust of him, for Mrs Shaw and posterity. It is difficult to imagine that tremulous beard in marble—rigidly fluttering its way down the ages.'

On the other hand, Max liked both Belloc and Galsworthy—in spite of the fact that he differed from both of them about almost everything. Galsworthy he described as 'a dry man but sympathetic and looks very like his manner of writing': while he thought Belloc a magnificent talker though a wild one. 'When you really get talking, Hilary,' he once said to him, 'you are like a great Bellocking ram, or like a Roman river full of baskets and dead cats.' For Thomas Hardy, Max felt not just liking but enthusiastic veneration. 'He was wonderful,' he said, 'so modest, with his plain irregular face that had such beauty.' Gissing's countenance had also stirred his admiration. Max in earlier years met him at luncheon one day at Will Rothenstein's in Chelsea. 'He had a very beautiful but frightfully sad face—' he related, 'and seemed as if everything but virtue had gone out of him.' As for the poet Sturge Moore, a gentle figure with rough hair and dressed in shaggy tweeds, 'a sheep in sheep's clothing!' Max called him. There are fewer glimpses of artists and actors. But these few are vivid. Max saw Rodin when he was over for the Whistler Memorial Exhibition and found him touching; 'He has a hairdresser twice a day to curl the grey lock on his forehead so that he may do full justice to the fuss that is being made of him by the smart people.' Irving he described as 'a dandy with perfect face, hands and wrists . . . an ecclesiastical diplomat'; and Ellen Terry, 'a Christmas tree decked out by a Pre-Raphaelite . . . never an actress, in the strict sense of the word, but a delightful sort of creature, symbolizing what we imagine to have been Merry England in the days of Elizabeth': Augustus John, met suddenly at the Café Royal, came to the Nicholsons' house 'looking more than ever picturesque and sang old French songs without accompaniment, quite remarkably; and seemed like all the twelve disciples of Christ, and especially like Judas.'

Along with his impressions of writers and artists, Max also recorded his impressions of statesmen. Lord Curzon, he said, looked like 'Britannia's butler'; his notebook includes some phrases about Arthur Balfour:

'gentle dignity—benign, girlish—not superior, Cambridge . . . Rising late—"seemed dazed" . . . Charming manners—eyes like a gazelle's. "I never kept a tame gazelle"—way of entering room . . . remote, never helping . . . strength—real politician—unlike Rosebery, he *poses* as dilettante.'

On Haldane, Max writes:

'Big cat—purring—benign—mediator—impossible to bicker in presence—spreads like treacle:'

and of the youthful Winston Churchill:

'Clumsy edition of father—very like—stoop—eyes . . . like a waxwork—dry hair—no wrinkles . . . pallor of one who has lived in limelight . . . frock-coat—rubbing his hands . . . Also hereditary bad manners . . . courteous and brutal alternately.'

These men he met on his periodic excursions into the world of politics and fashion. Such excursions continued to be frequent; in summer, especially, Max was always setting off in a hansom cab to dine in Mayfair or St James's, or packing his bag to go down for a weekend party in a large country house. We hear of him staying with Lord Elcho and Sir Bache Cunard and General Sir Ian Hamilton and Lord Desborough. Or rather, with their wives; for it was the hostesses who controlled social life and gave each party its especial flavour. Lady Desborough was the hostess, Max thought, whose invitations reflected most glory on him. He was amused at how proud he felt when she asked him to dinner.

'Yesterday I had a note from Lady Desborough asking me to dine on Friday week: "the de Greys, Soveral, Mr Balfour, Lord Rosebery, the Edgar Vincents, Evan, and a few others"—I think I shall try and go. . . . I do hope they'll have a list of the guests in the *Morning Post* on the following morning . . . "and Mr Max Beerbohm" would look so nice, and would make Barry Pain and Charles Goetz very angry. Why I enjoy my periodical plunges into Society is that Society is a sort of substitute for an Academy of Letters . . . "Mr Max Beerbohm's recent articles in the *Saturday Review* have been 'crowned' by Lord and Lady Desborough": that and my gray hairs would be gladdened by the recognition of my integrity and purity of taste.'

He also stayed with her at her country house, Taplow Court, a large mansion in French château style, set high amid green lawns overlooking the shining reaches of the Thames. He writes from there in 1908 at a party 'with Balfour and Milner and Curzon and other carvers of national destiny'; or in July 1909, 'There are nice people staying here as always: the Benckendorffs and Lord Milner standing for politics and Lady Helen Vincent for beauty.' These visits were proved later to inspire his art. Meanwhile he found them delightful. Staying at Taplow was to be remembered as the high spot of life in the great world.

Some similar memories were not so pleasant. To someone like Max this kind of social life could bring its anxieties.

' . . . My thoughts,' he writes to Reggie from the house of General Sir Ian Hamilton at Tidworth, 'turn towards you, my old friend, as I sit in this large and unfriendly bedroom, to which I have retired early accompanied to the threshold by my host (Sir I. Hamilton) who is sleepy after his military duties. The whole country round, as

I saw it from the window of my railway carriage, is an armed camp; and this house (a much larger one, I feel, than the H's can afford) is full of majors, captains, subalterns, etc., who talk deferentially to me about Bernard Shaw. And the General has asked me whether I have my "riding kit" with me, as he would like to show me some manœuvres which are taking place near here tomorrow. In the flurry of the moment, I merely murmured something about *not* having my riding kit with me. Heaven help me if, tomorrow, he offers to lend me his boots and spurs!

My position in regard to Lady Hamilton is scarcely less false. For she talks to me all the time about modern French literature—I occasionally, for a change, saying "No! *That* I *haven't* read . . . though I have been *meaning* to . . . I can imagine it's just the sort of thing I should like."

At my time of life, I really ought to be able to rely on myself: to say "I don't read French· and I have never ridden a horse." I suppose my duplicity is a sign of preserved youth—"some late lark singing"—and therefore not wholly lamentable?

Your affectionate
Max.'

Nor did he feel altogether at home staying with the Cunards at Nevill Holt, near Market Harborough. Max did not take to Lady Cunard, an exotic American whose conversation was full of embarrassing audacities: George Moore might call her 'dear lady of dreams' but they were not the kind of dreams that Max enjoyed. He looked forward to a weekend at her house with apprehension. However, it was not so bad when he got there. Moreover, it brought its compensations in the shape of an afternoon visit to a relic of the past, of fascinating interest to any amateur of the human comedy.

'Sir Bache, Mrs Beckett and I and Cambon (French Ambassador),' he wrote to Florence, 'went over to visit Lady Cardigan—who is 88 (and says she is 84!) and has just published a book of memoirs. Had you heard of her? She is a well-known character. She eloped with the Crimean Lord Cardigan—and the house is full of souvenirs of him. But she herself has the manners of an early-Victorian girl; and dresses in white, and wears a wig of pale gold ringlets. She sang us three songs—two in French, and "Love me all in all, or love me not at all" (by Julian Fane), and sang with much romantic brio;

kissing her finger-tips to us at the close of the performance. I should like you to see her—though she would shock you! One feels that she won't go to Heaven—but one also feels that she will never die.'

Indeed, one of the attractions to Max of his visits into the great world was that they brought him into touch with unusual types of human being. One day it was Lady Cardigan, another a member of the Royal Family. Max had often caricatured Royalty; now for the first time he got a chance to meet it in the flesh:

'. . . such an odd lunch,' he is writing to Florence again, '—quite an experience in its way. Two young Princesses and their brother, and everyone curtseying to the ground, and waiting for them to start the various topics of conversation: and they so shy, poor things, and seeming to feel the anomaly of it so acutely (so far as they could feel anything—they seemed like three beautifully-groomed and very young cows; their beautiful eyes adding to the illusion). I suppose royal people get used to the anomaly later on; but when they are young and near to the natural state of humanity, it must be rather awful for them. I felt really sorry, and puzzled—just like an American!'

Hardly more lively was an encounter with the Princess of Wales, afterwards Queen Mary.

'I met the Princess of Wales the other night, and had a longish talk with her—or rather *to* her; for the system is that *she* starts a topic, and then expects *you* to dilate till you are out of breath; and then after a pause she starts another topic for you. She began on caricature. I went on as long as I could. Then, after a pause, she started me on the weather. And so on. That sort of thing is more amusing afterwards than at the time of actual performance!'

If Max's performance was not more amusing than he makes out, the Princess of Wales may well have been disappointed. For his social reputation was due his conversational gifts. Deservedly; his talk was as much an accomplished art as were his writings and his drawings. It was the same kind of art too. Max was not a voluble, still less a dominating, conversationalist. On the contrary, he was easily put to silence. Even when he had the field to himself, he never took an undue advantage of it. Always he was ready to listen, deftly he followed the lead suggested by another person's remark: and he was careful to keep his own contributions short. But he also kept them intelligent, surprising, delightful. 'There is no excellent beauty,' said Bacon, 'that hath not some strangeness in the proportion.' The strangeness that made Max's conversation beautiful came from the contrast between his leisurely manner and his lightning-swift mind. Hesitant and self-deprecating, he would come out with an observation: it was a split second before his hearer recognized the unexpected or witty turn it had given to the topic under discussion, and had appreciated the picked felicity with which it was phrased. Max's talk too was embellished by those actor's talents and arts which proclaimed him to be Herbert's brother; the rich, soft, dense tones of his voice, saved from lushness by his crisp old-fashioned diction; his expressive and economical gestures; his delicate power of mimicry and, above all, that essential gift of the comedian, his perfect sense of timing that operated so that a joke of his, made apparently in a tentative, casual manner, was calculated unfailingly to create its maximum effect. 'X,' said a friend to him about some well-known philanthropist, 'is the kind of man who is needed.' Max paused; then shyly, 'Needed—but not wanted,' he commented.

Talk loses its quality in fragmentary quotation, Max's talk particularly. For though witty, it was far from being a string of *bons mots*. On the contrary, it was varied and relaxed, ranging easily from discussion to anecdote, from anecdote to flights of fancy, with jokes and witticisms only occurring as they happened to rise spontaneous and unforced from the subject. Yet because they are more easily related, it is mostly his *mots*, his formal jokes, that have been remembered and recorded. Even these lose their finer edge when removed from their original context. Still, it is worth recalling some of them[1] since it was they that went the round of clubs and drawing-rooms to give Max his conversational fame. Of Galsworthy's writings, for instance, he said, 'He has sold his literary birthright for a pot of message.' One day in 1909 he went to the Savile Club wearing a newly grown moustache. Man after man entering the room where he was said, 'I shouldn't have recognized you, Max, now you have grown a moustache.' Max found this tedious. As the next man came

[1] Remarks of this kind are seldom fully authenticated; and sometimes they sound too uncharacteristic to be true. In selecting them I have had to trust my own judgement as to what is probable.

in, he forestalled him; 'I should hardly have recognized you,' he said, 'now I have grown a moustache.' Some anecdotes show him dealing adroitly with importunate female admirers. Once he was asked if one might come and see the room where he worked, bringing another lady with her. 'Yes, yes,' replied Max, 'she may as well kill one bird with two stones': and to another, an American who remarked, 'You are thought a lot of in England, Mr Beerbohm,' Max answered, 'Oh yes, but I am in no immediate danger of being buried alive in Westminster Abbey.' To yet another, who wished to read his horoscope, Max's reply was more comical than consciously humorous. 'What date and hour were you born, Mr Beerbohm?' she asked. Bored, not knowing the answer, yet unwilling to be rude, Max said desperately, 'Oh, the usual hour!' Mr Clive Bell remembers him in a more relaxed and characteristic mood remarking, 'Why do Englishmen, when offered a glass of port, always say "Yes, I would like a *little* port"—never "I would like a lot of port", or even "I would like some port"—though one of the two is generally what they mean.' Mr Hesketh Pearson, then a young actor in Tree's company, describes his first meeting with Max behind the scenes at His Majesty's Theatre. Max seems to have been infected by the atmosphere of the place in such a way as to make him talk for once in Herbert's crazy comedy style. Herbert had sent Mr Pearson to fetch Max, whom he found gazing dubiously at himself in a looking-glass 'as if apologizing at his reflection for being too familiar with it'. 'Are you Mr Beerbohm?' Pearson asked him. Max did not reply: with nervous loudness Pearson repeated the question. Max turned round, 'Have you a warrant for my arrest?' he asked. No,' stammered Pearson. 'Then I will go quietly,' Max said; Pearson delivered his message. 'It sounds like an ultimatum,' murmured Max, as if to himself, walking towards the door. As he reached it, 'Thank you, constable,' he said.

Some of the stories told about him refer to written jokes; as when he contributed to a shilling fund got up to pay for a presentation to W. G. Grace. 'I send you this shilling,' he wrote, 'not because I am a great admirer of cricket, but as an earnest protest against golf.' A facetious friend once sent him a postcard addressed to 'Max Beerbohm, God knows where'. It reached him in the end, and Max sent a return postcard. On it was written, 'He did.'

CHAPTER EIGHT

Marriage

(1)

T HE more some people succeed, the more success they want. This
was not so with Max. On the contrary, as time went on, his
social and professional triumphs were a diminishing pleasure to him.
By now he detested his work for the *Saturday Review*. Going to the
theatre so often was boring. Any fame he acquired by it was not
worth it. Social success was more agreeable: Max continued to enjoy
parties at Taplow and elsewhere; and he liked people laughing at his
jokes. Yet the satisfaction he took in both had lost its first fine careless rapture. The very fact that he had so high a reputation for agreeability made his life more of an effort: for it meant he felt bound to
try to live up to it. He had created his personality as a conscious
work of art: and now it seemed to be permanently on exhibition.
Besides, social life brought its accompanying worries. Max's naturally low vitality grew no higher with the years. More and more he
liked life to move in an idle, tranquil fashion that allowed plenty of
time for rest and pleasant wool-gathering. Moreover, he found that
many new impressions ruffled the quiet pool of his thoughts.
London social life was always thrusting new impressions on him;
thus it took away much of the mental energy needed for the cultivating of his inner life. Further, social life involved him in a throng
of agitating telephone-calls and note-writings—of acceptance and
refusal and apology and excuse.

Even those social engagements that he did enjoy had their tiresome
aspects.

'If I were naturally a brilliant and copious talker, I suppose that to
stay in another's house would be no strain on me. I should be able to
impose myself on my host and hostess and their guests without any
effort, and at the end of the day retire quite unfatigued, pleasantly
flushed with the effect of my own magnetism. Alas, there is no
question of my imposing myself. I can repay hospitality only by

strict attention to the humble, arduous process of making myself agreeable. When I go up to dress for dinner, I have always a strong impulse to go to bed and sleep off my fatigue; and it is only by exerting all my will-power that I can array myself for the final labours: to wit, making myself agreeable to some man or woman for a minute or two before dinner, to two women during dinner, to men after dinner, then again to women in the drawing-room, and then once more to men in the smoking-room. It is a dog's life.'

Dinner and luncheon engagements were no better: yet somehow when in London he could not avoid them. The longer he lived, the more people he knew, and the more invitations there were to accept or refuse. He found the last especially difficult; Max was so anxious to please that he flinched uncontrollably from saying no. There were moments when he actively hated his London life. He had some less personal reasons for doing so. As we have seen, there was a great deal about Edwardian London deeply distasteful to him. More so every year; every year London seemed to him to grow vulgarer and noisier and more democratic and commercialized; every year saw the destruction of yet another relic of the graceful and dignified past; every year London became more like the capital of Kipling's England, Shaw's England, Wells's England, and less like the capital of his own England: John Bull every year sank deeper into that ignoble second childhood which Max had already portrayed so scathingly at the turn of the century.

When he was feeling like this the old daydream flooded back into his imagination. Why not leave it all and settle in some far-away beautiful hermitage of the spirit, preferably on the shores of the unchanging sea? Not English shores, England was not far enough away. Besides, the climate was too bad.

'Oh how awful the weather is here,' he writes to Florence in 1907, 'cold—grey—rainy, all the time—I long for the time when I shall turn my back on it all and live in Italy.'

In the same year an odd incident occurred which suggested that this would in fact be his fate. Prompted by who knows what motive of curiosity, Max visited a fortune-teller who told him, first, that his fame would be undiminished during his lifetime, and, secondly, that he would either travel extensively or live abroad. These words made a strong impression on him. It might be thought strange that one of his sceptical temper should be impressed by the words of a fortune-teller. But he was no more consistent than are most human beings; and mingled with his scepticism ran a strand of superstition. He was disturbed by the sight of crossed knives on a dinner table; he did not like peacock feathers indoors; and, if a guest returned to his house to fetch something after saying goodbye, Max would ask him to sit down for a moment as an antidote to the ill luck that his return might bring. Superstitious or not, Max's faith in the fortune-teller might seem to have been justified. Both her prophecies were fulfilled.

Meanwhile, another trend in his life was working all unconsciously towards his departure from England. After 1904 Max's love-life had for some years marked time. No other woman appeared to displace Florence from the first place in his affections. But his relations with her remained ambiguous. They seem especially so to us because, once again, we do not know enough about them—only what we can gather from their letters to each other, or rather from his letters to her. For though Florence kept Max's letters, Max did not keep Florence's. There are a great many of Max's, though—he seldom wrote to her less than twice a week—and from them we learn, however imperfectly, much that is interesting. Max confided in Florence as in no other correspondent. We are struck, for instance, how naturally and freely he mentions his former flames to her. He saw both Constance Collier and Kilseen during this period, and tells Florence about it in a way that indicates that he had talked to her of them before. Constance he met at Dieppe in the August of 1907.

'Miss Collier is here, but returns to England tomorrow. It seems rather odd to us both to be here, because it was here that we fell in love with each other, just three years ago. And now that is all over—and each of us is the one person in the world that the other could not possibly fall in love with, now.'

His reference to Kilseen is more significant.

'Tonight I have been dining with Miss Conover (to whom I was engaged to be married, some years ago); and was so pleased to find her seeming happy and well—so much happier and better than in the old days—and also prospering now in her dress-making business—

and thus lightening my conscience; for I did not treat her well—though I remember you had a theory that I was not really to be blamed.'

His words here confirm the fact that he felt guilty about Kilseen. Apart from the fact that he hated the idea that he might have caused her pain, he feared that his conduct had been a breach of that scrupulous code of honour in personal relationships which was a central article of his faith. Florence was most likely right in saying that he had not been very much to blame about Kilseen. None the less, the subject preyed on his mind. That he told Florence about it shows how peculiarly sympathetic and understanding he found her. He confessed smaller weaknesses to her too; how apprehensive he was before a journey and when he was driven fast in a motor-car, the lack of will that led him to accept unnecessary engagements and the deceits he then had to practise in order to get out of them. He alludes to these last in a tone of light irony which, it is to be feared, was wasted on the serious Florence. But the irony concealed a genuine disturbance of spirit. Now and again he comes out with flashes of a deeper self-revelation. Sometimes they are about his work.

'My bout of caricature still is on me,' he tells her, 'I am glad to say; and I do revel in the obsession, and hope not to lose it yet awhile. What an odd thing the human body is! (and how trite *I* am!)—that this mania for drawing should suddenly descend on me after months in which I had no desire to draw a single stroke, and then should pass away, and absent itself from me for some mysterious interval.'

Sometimes he lets fall revealing remarks about his own character.

'My letters to you always seem to me so very egoistic; and yet you say you don't know enough. Am I well? Am I happy? Quite well, thank you, dear. And nothing to complain of on the score of happiness. I don't think I ever am or shall be happy in the full sense, as some people are. As I think I told you. I can only stand life when it is made pleasant for me. Usually it *is* made pleasant for me. I have really been rather pampered than otherwise. So I have been all right, on the whole. But I do not like life when it does not offer me something nice every day. And if it ever offered me something *not* nice I should feel myself very much aggrieved. A *happy* person, it seems to me, is the sort of person who requires no aids to happiness—who can grapple with life on any terms. And I shall never be that sort of person. That is all I have to complain of. And it is little enough in comparison with average grounds of complaint.—So *there*, dear. I have told you as fully as I could—at tedious length, I am afraid. But you did ask me to tell you.'

Here Max shows his usual self-knowledge. He was quite right in saying he lacked the high spirits to be happy in any circumstances, but that in favourable ones he could always enjoy himself. His success in the art of living came from the fact that he realized this and knew how to contrive the right circumstances for himself. He is frank to Florence too about his feelings.

'Why do I burden you with this querulousness? Somehow, I always seem to be complaining to you. I never complain to other people. Cheerfulness is one of my good points, in the eyes of the world. And, as things go, I have really no reason to complain—— There! I am becoming brighter!'

Though he may start plaintively, Max contrives in this passage to end on a cheerful note. Indeed, for all his grumblings about London life and in spite of the fact that he enjoyed it less than formerly, the general tone of Max's discourses was growingly benign. He had lost the gay intolerance of youth, he was coming to view human beings—individually if not in mass—with a more indulgent eye. He was aware of this change in himself.

'So glad to have your letter,' he wrote to Florence in October 1908. 'Did I ever show you my fable (written many years ago) "The Liberator"? I think I can quote it correctly: "A very good little boy was given sixpence. This he took to the fowler, and bought a caged wild bird. And this, with a sweet smile, he took to the middle of a meadow. There he opened the door of the cage, and waited. Presently the bird hopped out, and, with an adroit motion of its beak, pecked out one of the little boy's eyes. Then it hopped in again." I used to be a great cynic!'

The reader will note that Max is careful to use the past tense here. No longer was he any kind of cynic, especially when he was talking to Florence.

However, too much should not be made of Max's self-revelations. Even to Florence, these are momentary and rare. His letters are short and consist largely of news; still more of inquiries about Florence and comments on the news she has told him. He shows himself very interested in her health: here he was the true blood-relation of his mother and sisters. Is Florence feeling tired, he asks, has she been resting enough? Since she has not written for a week or two, he fears she may be ill: will she promise faithfully never to conceal ill health from him? There is something comic about all this solicitude, considering he had no reason to suppose Florence was not in good health. Moreover, she was the other side of the Atlantic, so that Max could not possibly expect an answer to his anxious inquiries till at least a month after they were made, when presumably she must have recovered from any fatigue she might have been suffering from when he wrote to her.

He takes a more intelligible interest in her career. This was not going well. When she got back to America no parts came her way; so that she even thought of giving up the stage and devoting herself to alleviating human suffering by becoming a hospital nurse. Max expressed horror at this high-minded suggestion; he also urged her not to despair, since failure was probably a sign that her talent was too original easily to be appreciated. Most distinguished artists, he said, had to wait for recognition.

'And, dear, I am sure your happiness won't long be of the negative kind that you describe. I can well imagine your feeling that it is a foolish thing that you should not be doing the thing which you can do pre-eminently well—the thing that you have a genius for. (*You* didn't say exactly this. But I know that my paraphrase is right enough—know it by instinct, as well as by hearsay.) But so many people are not always doing the thing that they can do best. And so few people, with one especial bent, have other little bents to go on with. So few born actresses have any real humanity or any intellectual interests outside their art. You *are* rather an exception, aren't you? And I am sure you are grateful for that—for that "something to go on with". Nor do you need more than this something to go on with. For a power in art like yours makes its way surely in the long run. I imagine—and it seems to me so very natural—that it is a certain fastidious idealism in you—a shrinking from contact with

274

dull false people—a disinclination to meet them half-way—an incapacity for those little compromises and amenities and that "push" which is so horribly necessary in this world and most especially necessary in the theatrical part of this world—which has (? have—I am losing the thread of this interminable sentence) prevented you from being at this moment on the little pinnacle that is being reserved for you. "Reserved", I am sure. As I say, a power like yours makes its own terms in the end; just as, conversely, all that "pushful" diplomacy of coarser natures is no use for long. It is the power to *act* that tells, in the long run, on the stage.'

Encouraged by Max and her own ambitions, Florence stuck to the stage; but only to be disappointed. Again and again she seems to have been on the point of obtaining a part. Almost always it came to nothing. As a matter of fact some of these roles do seem to have been strangely unsuited to her. Remembering how upset she had been by Max's discreet caresses, it is hard to believe that she would have been a convincing impersonator of Cleopatra, still less of Oscar Wilde's Salome. But apparently she was considered for both these characters: and Max himself wrote to say he thought she would play them splendidly. It was not so odd that he should think she could play Cleopatra; for, as he admitted, he had never read Shakespeare's play about her—though he hastens to tell Florence that he will certainly do so now. *Salome*, on the other hand, he knew well; yet he was sure that Florence should attempt it. She herself had doubts; not because she thought she might fail in it, but because she feared lest the public might confuse the role with the actress and imagine that she—Florence Kahn—behaved like Salome in real life. Here Max was ready to reassure her. There was no possible danger, he said, that anyone should ever suspect her of behaving like Salome! We have every reason to suppose he was right about this: anyway, the issue was never put to the test. Subsequent letters do not mention Salome, or Cleopatra either; and Max was spared the painful ordeal of having to read *Antony and Cleopatra*. Meanwhile, poor Florence continued to be out of work. All Max could do was to express his sympathy and continue to urge her to have faith in her genius. At last, in 1907, she did get an engagement, as Mrs Elvsted in Ibsen's *Hedda Gabler*. This seems a sad comedown after Cleopatra: for Mrs Elvsted was an insipid personage whose function was chiefly to set off by contrast the baleful magnetism of the heroine Hedda. However, Max, touchingly anxious to keep up Florence's spirits, congratulates her on playing so interesting a character and one so much more likeable than Hedda's.

'Mrs Elvsted,' he said comfortingly, 'surely is the normal and well-grounded *human* person: definitely a foil to the hysterical and in-human Hedda.'

All this sympathy and interest show Max to have been very fond of Florence. He wrote to her often and regularly over a long period of years. Yet the nature of his affection at this time remains doubtful. Did he consider himself in love with her? He still begins his letters 'Very dear little friend', he still goes on teasing her affectionately—about her shyness and her culture and so on. But his general tone is noticeably less flirtatious than in the letters written during the first summer of their friendship. It also oscillates uncertainly between the sentimental-romantic and the unsentimental-friendly—as if at one moment he wished her to realize how much he liked her, but at the next has been seized with fear lest she should begin to imagine that he liked her even more than he did. He began to waver in this way early in the correspondence. In the spring of 1905 she had written wondering sadly if they would ever meet again. Max wrote back:

'Dear, of *course* we shall see each other again—somehow at some time. I am quite sure of that. I should be *very* much depressed if I thought we were never going to meet again. Such absurd things as that never happen.'

What Florence thought of this we do not know. Possibly she was wounded and showed it: for within a month or two Max speaks far more tenderly:

'Dear, I am glad you felt I was with you when last you wrote. And indeed I constantly am with you, so far as thinking about you goes, and *wanting* to be with you. And I sometimes think you are thinking about me—instead of about something more profitable and worthy.'

His tone remains fairly affectionate throughout the first part of the following year. Then in the autumn of 1906 it cools perceptibly. Florence had managed to pay a short visit to Europe, stopping in London and Paris. Max saw her in both places—it was the year he went to Italy for the *Daily Mail*—and perhaps he fancied he saw signs indicating that she was more interested in him than he thought desirable. Certainly in October his letters are markedly unlover-like. A month or two later, however, he has resumed his former tender tone. Any woman might have found him bewildering. Florence did; and told him so. He replied:

'What do you mean when you say that I sometimes speak to you as if I had known you all my life, and sometimes as if I had only just met you? You say I am like that in my letters—at least in the last letter you had received—and also when you see me. Am I really like that, dear? It seems a very uncomfortable effect to produce, and I must try to find some means of not producing it! Certainly I am never conscious of the sensation of not having always known you. I seem to myself to have known you always; and this illusion in some wise compensates me for all the years that passed before I actually did meet you.'

Here Max is doing his best to reassure her. But the general impression left by these letters is that absence had not made Max's heart grow fonder: and that, by 1907, he felt less romantic about Florence than he had in the summer of 1904.

Moreover—though he was careful to keep this from Florence—he was now beginning to feel a little romantic about other women. In a letter to her written in the summer of 1907, he says:

'One of my present activities is sitting for a statuette by a Miss Bruce, rather a talented sculptress. Here, I feel, is my genuine métier; to sit for *rather* talented sculptresses.'

The tone of this remark is misleading in view of the fact that he was on sufficiently intimate terms with the sculptress in question to be writing to her during the very same month, 'Dear Kathleen, you can't think how much I delighted in seeing you yesterday. And you were so sweet and charming all the time.' Max was not the only man who took pleasure in Kathleen Bruce's company. The daughter of a Canon, handsome, gifted and bursting with vitality, she had early emancipated herself from the rigid conventions of her home to embark on a life designed to satisfy her taste for art and adventure. She studied in London and Paris, where her work was favour-ably noticed by Rodin himself; unchaperoned she explored the forests and mountains of Italy; she took part in a famine relief expedition in the wilds of Madagascar. Now, at twenty-eight years old, established in London as a well-known personality in the world of art and letters, she occupied herself in modelling the figures and cultivating the friendship of distinguished men. Max was one of them. They had known each other since 1905, but not well. Then in June 1907 Kathleen Bruce asked him to sit for his portrait; she also won his good will by getting an eyelash out of his eye. Soon they were engaged in a high-spirited flirtation. It was not at all a serious one on either side. Max was careful to avoid anything of the kind, and Kathleen Bruce was only seriously attracted by heroic adventurous men. Moreover, it was rumoured that she had resolved not to mate except with one likely to make her the mother of a hero. Both she and Max must have realized that he was not a suitable candidate for this Wagnerian role. All the same, the two found each other's company pleasantly exhilarating. In June, Kathleen had suddenly to be operated on for an appendicitis. Max visited her sickbed and wrote her letters. They are among the liveliest in his whole correspondence.

Dear ~~Miss~~ Kathleen,

(I scratch out the middle word because, after all, it is about two years since I first met you.) Also because you are lying down and can't spring up and say 'Sir'! But *why* are you lying down? Do please be more explicit. What exactly has happened? Are you in pain? I am so sorry that anything should have happened to you of that kind—but, again, *what* kind? I suppose you, as a rationalistic open-air person, will think it very absurd of me; but do burn those peacock feathers. There are heaps of other kinds of feathers, just as pretty. Have some of them instead. I can't, of course, justify my distrust of peacock feathers. But, if it comes to that, what *can* one justify? There is no such thing as pure reason. At least we mortal creatures have never hit on it. We have to depend on superstitions, some of which *seem* reasonable, whilst others . . . but here I am arguing about what can't be argued about, instead of merely begging you to destroy those beastly feathers. I shan't feel happy about you till you have done that. Really and truly. Do be afraid, malgrez vous. Also, do please get well quickly, and tell me meanwhile what happened and how you are. And forgive me for bothering you.

Max.

My dear Kathleen,

A very delightful letter from you. But I do think you are as mad as a hatter, and stark staring mad, not to destroy the feathers once and for all. I am sure you won't get well, so long as you hang on to them, you foolish creature. Or at any rate, I am sure other unpleasant things will happen to you as soon as you do get well. Possibly shipwreck on your way to the Rocky Mountains. If you do get safely there, you won't catch any horses. Very likely they will catch *you*, and make an example of you. A furious breed. *I* know them. You wouldn't be ill now, but for the feathers. Your diagnosis about dancing and sculpting is all nonsense. But for the feathers, you might have danced all night and sculpted all day, you might have danced sculpting, and sculpted dancing, without being a penny the worse. All the fault of the feathers. Into the fire with them, this instant! Otherwise you are simply flying in the face of providence. This must be a very alarming sensation for providence. But . . . oh well, I suppose there is no use in adjuring you to be a little sensible. How are you feeling? (Physically, I mean. Mentally I despair of you.) Much better, I hope? Nearly well? I do so look forward to the time when I shall have the privilege of seeing Miss K. Bruce again. Is there anything I can do for her, meanwhile? If so, let her 'command' me.

One thing I can do for her: the 'patern' on her bedroom wallpaper is really spelt with two t's! Goodnight, and good morning, Kathleen.

Max.

My dear Kathleen,

I was so *very* glad to see you; and I only wished you were as well as you looked. I did not stay long—tore myself away—partly because I supposed you ought to be 'kept quiet'; and partly because I assumed that the American was in love with you; and partly because you may, for aught I know, be in love with *him*. The possible gooseberry, therefore, rolled down the stairs as soon as it could, well-pleased, however, to be clasping to its rotund surface those feathers. As soon as I reached a place where the water flowed right up to the embankment, over went the feathers—gorgeously protruding from their envelope, and exciting utmost curiosity in the breast of a costermonger who was leaning over the parapet, and who, I do trust, didn't presently dive in to clutch them and present them to his doner. *Such* a good day's work, I feel,—taking those feathers away from you. Lord Cromer had been for thirty years in Egypt; but who knows that his work will really benefit Egypt in the long run? Whereas I know quite well that you are going to be completely well very soon, now that the feathers aren't there to bedevil you.

I suppose the American thought me *quite* mad; and perhaps Kathleen is rather of that opinion too.

Good night. Please let me know where it is you choose to go.

Goodnight again

Max.

Max also sent her books: *The Aspern Papers*, which he said that he admired intensely, *The Way of All Flesh* because Shaw had recommended it, but which he himself could not get through—and his own *Happy Hypocrite*.

'I am much pleased that you like the *Hap. Hyp.* . . . . It is the only popular thing I have written; I might be quite rich now if I had continued in that vein. But the vein left me; and I have to make the best of myself as a more or less earnest critic of things. . . . Really it is too awful, to be solemnly dilating on one's own self to a lady who might have died a few days ago. And the *most* awful part of it is that it is so like me! No, perhaps I am hardly fair to myself . . . Myself again! *What* a man! But all this is on the surface. I am thinking much more about you, really, than about me— . . .'

After this, each left for the Continent to take a holiday, Max to Dieppe, Kathleen Bruce to less civilized regions. He wrote to her:

My dear Kathleen,

Here am I, mildly enjoying myself. Petits Chevaux have been abolished, and their place is taken by a game called 'La Boule', on which I expend most of my time and most of my money. What a lamentable sort of holiday this must seem to your wild adventurous soul! I wish I were like you, going boot-less about distant parts of Europe, and frightening shepherds on hills, and sleeping on sand or shingle till the tide wakes you up. All these joys have been denied me. I don't know even how to dance in the Casino: I sit rooted at 'La Boule'. And bathing makes me liver-ish always: I sit watching other people bathing; and I hope you are getting *quite* well, and are now sitting up, dear Kathleen—and are gradually recovering from your inevitable infatuation for the doctor 'of the soft hands'. You say good-bye to me 'till December'. But I do hope I shall have the pleasure of renewing your acquaintance before then. You won't be away from London *all* that time, surely? Or is it that you don't feel you could tolerate me without a four or five months' interval? I feel that I could tolerate *you* quite continuously; but no doubt I shall be able to fight that sentiment down.

Goodnight Kathleen
Max.

Max might say he was anxious to keep up the friendship. But in fact they did not see each other very often after the summer. For the flirtation was coming to an end, each found other distractions. There is only one letter from Max in September and after that no more until the following July. Then he wrote to congratulate her on becoming engaged to be married. For Kathleen Bruce had found her hero; and a real hero too, Robert Scott, afterwards world-famous as Scott of the Antarctic.

Kathleen Bruce was not the only attractive woman to stir Max's interest during 1907. In November of that year William Nicholson and his wife took him to stay at the little fishing village of Portofino on the Italian Riviera at the Castel San Giorgio, a villa which had been taken by some patrons of Nicholson's, the Baron and Baroness von Hutten; Nicholson had been commissioned to paint the Baroness's portrait. Max arrived late at night after twenty-four hours' journey and went straight to bed. He woke at ten o'clock next morning to find himself in a room bathed in southern sunshine, from whose window he gazed through olive and cypress trees down on to a picturesque harbour far beneath, from which rose the sound of Italian voices singing to the twang of guitars. Further investigation revealed the villa to be set on a narrow rocky promontory between the harbour on the one hand and on the other the shimmering Mediterranean. 'It's a lovely place,' Max told Florence, 'full of loggias and gardens and grottoes and all sorts of nice things.' The other inhabitants of this earthly Paradise turned out to consist of the Baron and Baroness, the Baron's seventy-seven-year-old mother and his eight-year-old son Ulrich. Of these the Baroness was easily the most noticeable. Bettina von Hutten was a cosmopolitan young

American married to a blue-blooded German nobleman. She had lately spent much time in England where she had created a considerable impression in artistic and bohemian circles, partly by her writing—she was the author of some entertaining society novels—and still more by her personality, exotic and alluring with Titian-red hair, milk-white skin, and all on fire for a life of gaiety and romance. Too much so to settle down as a wife; in fact, just before going to Portofino, the Baron and Baroness had secretly agreed to separate. However, they were parting on friendly terms and saw no reason why they should not, before doing so, try to give themselves and their family and friends an enjoyable holiday in Italy. They succeeded: the days at the Castel San Giorgio passed in a delightful dream of carefree pleasure.

We are enjoying ourselves very much here,' writes Max to Reggie. 'It is a really beautiful life here—very free and sunshiny and sea-airy, with a great deal of nonsense talked, and nap and poker played, and pictures and books discussed, and going to bed in the small hours and getting up in the big ones. The Baroness turns out to be a charming creature, and so does the Baron, whose mother, aged seventy-seven, and brought up exclusively in Court circles of the dullest and smallest kind in Germany, is enjoying immensely her sudden immersion into English Bohemian society. She is very anxious to go down with us into the village of Portofino and share our daily vermouth; but this rapture will have to be postponed, I fear, as she is suffering from a bilious attack brought on by over-excitement.'

It is unlikely that the old Baroness took part in another amusement especially enjoyed by Max, the Nicholsons and their hostess; namely, the writing of communal sonnets which competitors vied with one another to make as shocking and scandalous as possible. Max professed to be alarmed at discovering how good he was at this kind of thing. 'Really,' he said, 'I have to tear them up and watch them well on their way to the sea before I can regard myself as fit to mix in decent society!' He was certainly a success in the free and easy society gathered at the villa. 'That young man has uncommonly good manners,' said the Baron; and little Ulrich von Hutten gazed with curiosity at the sad-faced young gentleman with the hesitant manner who, it seemed, had only to speak for the rest of the grown-ups to burst out laughing. One evening the spirits of the party rose to carnival height and they dressed up; the von Huttens, jewelled and splendid, as an Indian rajah and ranee, Mrs Nicholson in Max's dinner jacket, William Nicholson as a clown, while Max himself appeared as a baby, with round face and round eyes looking out calm and enigmatic from the folds of a gigantic *Steckkissen*, a sort of embroidered pillow in which German babies used to be carried about. Thus attired they all descended to the village where they improvised an entertainment on the moonlit little piazza. The villagers joined enthusiastically in the fun; William Nicholson swarmed up a post to deliver a comic harangue; at a neighbouring café table Max dashed off caricature after caricature of the company.

It is to be noted that Max said nothing about these revellings when writing to Florence. More significant still, in none of his letters to her does he talk about his hostess. This did not mean that she did not interest him. On the contrary, his fellow guests at the villa had the impression that he was very interested in her indeed. The Baroness herself thought so: in later years she went so far as to say that she could have married Max at this time, had she felt so inclined. Everything else we know about him at this stage in his career makes this last idea unlikely. Besides, Baroness von Hutten is known to have been a colourful and imaginative talker, especially when inspired by the subject of her admirers. But there is no doubt that Max did behave at Portofino like a man in love. Both the Baron and William Nicholson noticed it: Max himself, after the episode was over, admitted to having been fascinated. William Nicholson—rightly or wrongly—thought that the Baroness responded to Max's attentions; enough at any rate to leave him with some agreeably romantic memories of his visit.

Meanwhile he was in trouble with Florence. She had been in England again this summer looking for work and Max had inevitably seen a good deal of her. He left her in England when he went to Italy. She was at times very depressed; and we gather from his letters to her, she had indicated that he was in some ways the cause of her depression. She found his feelings for her increasingly difficult to understand and asked him for an explanation. He replied:

'I wonder what it is that in my "explanations" I have either left out or do not know? So far as I *do* know, dear, I haven't left out anything of actual relevance. Ask me any question, and I'll answer it, dear. I do wish you were happy in the abstract, general sense; and I am sure you will be.'

Three days later he follows this up with a fuller communication.

Very dear little friend,

Your letter of this morning, saying that you expect to sail on the 30th, makes me very sad. I had so hoped you were going to act.

Perhaps the chance which you say is too remote to wait for will yet come off. If you *do* sail, they might yet in due time want you to sail back? I hate the probability, meanwhile, of not seeing you when I come back. I had so thought you would still be there. However, I mustn't be selfish. And indeed in our great friendship I do think more of you than of myself. And I constantly reproach myself with what has so often seemed evident: that I tend to make you unhappy. It rather seems that making people unhappy is my *métier*. I like you better than any person in the world. But the other sort of caring is beyond me. I realize quite surely now that I shall never be able to care in that way for any one. It is a defect in my nature. It can't be remedied. Dear, you have brought *so much* happiness to me. I can't bear to think of being the cause of unhappiness to you.

It is difficult to express myself. Whether or not you will have sailed on the thirtieth, nothing can alter our friendship, dear, can it?

Max.

These letters do not tell us much, but they are unusually unreserved for Max; and, viewed in the context of his previous relations with women, they become more intelligible. It looks as if he had begun to suspect that Florence was unhappy because she had grown to care for him seriously—with a seriousness in fact that must end in wanting to marry him. His experience with Constance Collier had convinced him that marriage was not for him unless he was more deeply in love than he was with Florence. His experience with Kilseen, on the other hand, had taught him that if he let matters drift he was likely to be entangled in a situation painful to Florence and discreditable to himself. He decided to make the position clear to her before it was too late. One cannot help wondering if his determination to do this was not reinforced by his experiences at Portofino. Surely it would have come home to him that if he had cared for Florence with what in his letter he called 'the other sort of caring' he would not have been so susceptible to the very different charms of the Baroness von Hutten. Here, however, we enter dangerous realms of conjecture. What is certain is that his conscience had begun to worry him about Florence, and that he was resolved not to let himself slip weakly into a situation in which he would treat her as badly as he feared he had treated Kilseen.

A week or two later he returned to England. Before leaving, he spent a few days in Florence with the Nicholsons and the Baroness. According to the Baroness's account, the parting between Max and herself was very affecting; though they were travelling in different directions, he leapt impulsively into her train so as to go at least part of her journey with her; and when the time came for a final good-bye, he broke down entirely. 'The darling wept,' she related with reminiscent satisfaction. We are at liberty to believe this or not as we feel disposed. But there is no doubt that Max much regretted leaving Italy. He took back with him enchanted memories of the Italian Riviera in particular; that first awakening in the sunlit room had made a deep impression on him. 'If I can ever get away from England,' he said to himself, 'it will be to settle near Portofino.'

Alas, there was no question for the time being of anything of the kind. December found him at his old round of first nights, Thursday articles, dinner parties, evening receptions, Sunday lunch at Upper Berkeley Street—and many hours every week spent writing or talking to Florence. For his letters from Portofino had made no apparent change in their relations. Max himself had not wanted a change. He was delighted the friendship should go on as before, if Florence was willing. As if to indicate this, he had followed up his letter of 22 November with three others in the same week; cheerful and friendly and containing no allusion in them to the fact that there had been any difference between himself and her. Whatever she may have secretly felt, Florence followed his lead; stayed on in London and saw as much of the Beerbohms as ever. She had another reason for remaining in England. Early in 1908 an impresario engaged her to play Rebecca West in a production of *Rosmersholm* that he was putting on in February for a week of matinées at Terry's Theatre. Florence's spirits rose; and all the more because the engagement had the effect of bringing Max and herself closer together. He also was excited and pleased about *Rosmersholm* and threw himself into the task of helping her in every way he could. He discussed her role with her, attended rehearsals and went round urging his influential friends in the world of fashion, of the theatre and among dramatic critics, to go and see the performance. Those who did so were not disappointed: on the critics in particular Florence made a very good impression. On Max she made more. Everything he admired in her —her grace, her imagination, her sensibility—shone forth on the stage, concentrated and intensified by her finished art. Max was afraid he had not done justice to her in his article.

'I have just been correcting my proof. It seems to me that my criticism of your performance is rather like a bad copy of the performance itself: suppressed emotion. But I think a certain amount of enthusiasm exudes through my difficulty in doing justice to a friend. I have managed to credit you with force and emotion, intellect, sense of beauty, and so on. It is a long, rather well-written notice that your brothers will like; but it would have been more aggressively flaring if I had never met you. And you will like it, because you will see I have done my best, such as it is.'

Florence would have been hard to please had she not liked it. Max's review is the most enthusiastic piece he ever wrote for the *Saturday Review*.

The emotions roused by the performance extended to the actress. Max wrote her a letter that week:

Very dear little friend

I hope you had an evening that satisfied you. It always seems to me so odd, your being able to differentiate between your performances at one time and another. You must be right; but I expect that the *effect* must always be much the same. I have thought of you often throughout the evening, hoping all was well at the theatre.

It is late, and I am only just home. I hope you are sleeping. Dear, all my thoughts and hopes are for you and for your happiness. There is little else that I care about. . . .

Good night, dear.

Max.

This is nearer to a declaration of love than anything he has said to her before. Florence might well have felt that Max's feelings for her were growing stronger. Perhaps they were; it looks like it in the light of subsequent events. But it was not a steady strengthening. His letters to her during the next month show him relapsed into his old ambiguous, oscillating condition of mind. Mostly they are light and lively letters in which jokes and inquiries after her health are interspersed with scraps of news about the books he has been reading and the people he has met.

In late summer he went to Dieppe where, in company with Reggie and Ada Leverson, he idled and played *boule* at the casino. In the autumn Florence was engaged by Mrs Patrick Campbell to act with her, first in London and then on tour in Scotland and Dublin. Max, who liked the Irish because they seemed so out of date, wrote to Florence urging her to like them too.

Very dear little friend,
    So glad to have your letter, and to know that you are all right—and that you feel the *restfulness* of Dublin. Restful, because it is so behind the times. The very violence of the newspapers is but an echo of the century before last.
    Don't you love the *voices* of the people. Do talk to them, and listen to them. They really are 'dears'. I mean the shop-people, and the crossing-sweepers, and so on: all of them gentlefolk. How awful that they should all be driven to emigrate as fast as they can to America—there to lose their own souls by gaining the whole world —there to become the most blatant and successful type that America has. What a pity there isn't any scope for their genius in their own place, so that they could be prosperous *and* sweet. . . .
                Good night dear. Please write to me.
                                                    Max.

All these letters are in the same tone as that in which he had been writing to her for the last three years. But now and again a shadow falls across the page; Max's voice alters to disclose the presence in the relationship of some hidden tension. We gather that Florence has announced she thinks she had better go back to America for good. Still striving to talk lightly but with an undertone of serious anxiety, Max asks her not to: 'I do think the idea of going to America for good would be a really not good idea,' he says. At intervals during the year, too, he breaks out in agitated apologies for making her unhappy.

'I hope you are in bed *and* asleep, and not feeling unhappy, dear. I do wish I made you happy, instead of making you on the whole *un*happy, as it seems. I wish I were different, or—but no, I couldn't wish *you* different from what you are—except in the respect of not being happy through me.'

So he speaks in March. He says the same kind of thing in July and again at the beginning of November. And then suddenly, all un- prepared, comes a change. Within a fortnight we find a letter disclosing the fact that Max has just asked Florence to marry him and go to live in Italy.

Very dear little friend,

Good night. I hope you are asleep and well. Did my idea seem to you very preposterous? It does seem rather so to me—from your point of view. It would seem so to me if I were you—I suppose. But if it doesn't seem so to you, as being yourself,—why then, dear, all is well. I am perfectly certain about my own feelings. I know *I* should be happy, if you were. You are very much more to me than anyone else in the world, and always will be—and I know I should be happy with you, dear sweet, if you were happy with me. 'Here I am,' as I have so often said. 'No catch'—But all yours—what there is of me—if you would care to take it.

I shall pack my things early tomorrow, and be quite calm and collected—no fusses! Won't you come and see me have a sandwich at half-past twelve?

Goodnight again dear.

Max.

Florence seems to have hesitated, for a day or two later he wrote again.

Darling little friend,

It was thoughtful and sweet of you to send that note. I wired from Chelsea on my way home to ask how you were (and in the hurry forgot to prepay reply) and was grateful, when I got home, to find you had forestalled me. Are you asleep, dear? I hope you are— though it is only midnight or so. What a grotesque thing life is!

Three very young men singing with enormous animation the score of a comic opera composed by one of them—bawling and screeching it out for my benefit. And then dinner at the Colefax's—

with a lady-novelist on one side of me, and the débutante daughter of an eminent lawyer on the other. And all the while my thoughts so very far away—all with you.

Darling, don't try to decide quickly. Think it over, *and think only for yourself*. That is also the only way of thinking for *me*. For if you were happy I should be happy in exact proportion. And if you were unhappy, I should be unhappy also in exact proportion. It would be no good at all to marry me just in kindness—for my sake, as it were. For I should very soon find *that* out, and should be miserable at your unhappiness. So take time to think, dear. . . .

Max's tone in this is tentative for a suitor. He seems curiously anxious to explain to Florence that she must not think of marrying him if she does not want to. However, a third letter of Max's indicates that she has accepted him; but still not so enthusiastically as to make him certain of her feelings.

Very dear little friend,

I hope you are well and happy and got home safely yesterday: it was so nice of you to come stationwards with me, and I felt much honoured. I shall be home tomorrow morning; so do come and lunch at U.B.S., please, if you will. I wonder if you will change your mind about our plan. I know *I* shan't. But it seems to me so *very* much more attractive for me than it can be for you. Meanwhile, I am 'glad'.

Till tomorrow, sweet.
Max.

Her demeanour when they met reassured him. His next letter shows him at last confident.

Dear sweet, I feel so much happier than I have felt for a long time. A sort of feeling of peace—of being able to look into the future, hand in hand with you.

Goodnight, sweet.
Max.

Thus ends the long-drawn-out story of Max's courtship. To the last it is a mysterious story. We have no first-hand knowledge of Florence's feelings during 1908, and only intermittent knowledge of Max's. In particular, we do not know what made him suddenly decide to marry her between 2 November and 23 November. However, in the light of his previous history, it may be permitted to his biographer once more to hazard an interpretation. Max had been held back from marriage for the same reasons which held him back before: marriage meant giving up his chosen mode of life, and he did not feel he cared enough for Florence to make the sacrifice. But during 1908 three new factors had entered into the situation to alter his mind. The first was a change in Florence. After Portofino, Florence may have intended to accept her uncertain situation, but, in fact, as time passed she found she could not. All the more because *Rosmersholm* had not, after all, led to any other important engagements: no longer quite young, Florence was losing heart about her theatrical future. This in its turn led her to think more about Max; and in such a way as to make his ambiguous attitude harder than ever to bear. If there was to be no firm future with him either, she felt inclined to break with England altogether. This surely was her reason for suddenly saying she might go to America for good. However, she cared too much for him to do this willingly and burst out that he made her unhappy. Inevitably, Max was very much distressed; and his conscience was disturbed as well. Was it going to be the Kilseen story all over again? He flinched from the thought; and began to wonder if he was not already bound to Florence by a sacred obligation of honour. But not honour alone; also by his heart. Here we come to the second new factor in the drama. The stronger protestations of affection which Max had made to Florence after *Rosmersholm* were not meaningless. When she suggested going back to America, he was horrified: he had grown to know her and care for her as never before. By the autumn he had become sufficiently devoted to contemplate making the sacrifice marriage would involve.

But need it involve such a sacrifice? the third factor operating to make Max change his mind about marriage was his growing desire to leave England. More and more during 1908 he disliked the strain of social life, the grind of his weekly article. This grind put him off doing any other writing.

'I have absolutely nothing left to say about the theatre,' he wrote to Florence in October, '—and it is such an effort to go on pumping up with an air of liveliness what I have said before. On the other hand, I feel it would be just as much, or probably more, of an effort to write about anything else. Possibly, if I were quit of any necessity to write about anything, and if I had a long rest, I might feel a certain recrudescence of the impulse which I once had for writing. Otherwise I shall continue to detest the sight of a pen!'

The result of all this was that the notion of leaving his country turned from a daydream into a determination. This removed the main practical objection to marriage. For it was married life in London that was likely to be so expensive. Life abroad in those days was far cheaper. Max began to think that it would be possible even on his small income to combine marriage and a life of leisure in Italy, so long as he was prepared to live simply. Max did not mind living simply. On the other hand, he disliked living alone. Though independent, he was not solitary: sociable and affectionate, he depended on some company, especially feminine company. Also he needed a woman to look after him. If he was to live abroad, he ought to have a wife.

Florence was surely the right wife for the purpose. Many women —Constance Collier, for example—would have objected to being shipped off to live a life of economical retirement on the Italian coast. But Florence—now that she was losing her theatrical ambitions—might well like it. She was shy, she was fragile, she liked simple living, she shrank nervously from the social round. Indeed, this very shrinking was likely to lead to difficulties should she and Max settle in England. For one thing, they would have been expected as a married couple to return some of the hospitality they received. Florence would have been far too nervous to have done this willingly, quite apart from the fact they could not possibly have afforded it. Further, Max's social success was a bachelor's success. The world of fashion, in particular, had invited him as an agreeable single man; it would never have invited his wife too. This should not have mattered. Max would not have minded giving up the world of fashion. But—and he must have realized it—his closest friends would also have preferred to see him alone. Besides, Florence herself was far too nervous to want to live a very social life. Some husbands met such difficulties by continuing their bachelor habits after marriage, and going into society without their wives. Max was too considerate, and too affectionate, ever to do such a thing. And he realized that not to go to parties by himself must have led to difficulties too. Florence would have been embarrassed by the sacrifice he was making and the result must have been to create a strained, uncomfortable situation between husband and wife. Max made it his first principle to avoid uncomfortable situations. Here was another reason for living abroad.

Max was so popular and sociable that his decision to leave England mystified people at the time and has continued to do so ever since. On two recorded occasions he was asked why he had so decided. To one questioner he replied with another question: 'How many people are there in London?' asked Max. 'About five million,' said the other. 'I knew them all!' said Max. Another, who made the same inquiry, received a graver answer. To him Max replied, 'I wanted to be alone with Florence.' Both these answers were true. On the one hand he was sure, alike for personal and for economical reasons, that married life with Florence would be happier abroad. On the other, he had come to think London life such a social strain that he thought the only thing to do was to break with it altogether and seek a tranquil refuge in another country. It was the most crucial decision of his whole life: and not till November did he finally make up his mind.

(2)

This did not mean that they got married at once. On the contrary, they waited nearly a year and a half. Money seems to have been the obstacle. To set up house Max needed in addition to his small income a small capital sum. There seemed little prospect of collecting this sum for the time being. At the beginning of December, therefore, Florence went back to America: she had no offer of work in England and she wanted to see her brothers to tell them about her engagement. In England, however, it was kept a secret. Florence liked keeping things a secret; and Max had painful memories of the embarrassments attendant on engagements prematurely made public. Florence sailed in December. She was away six months.

This time there was no question of absence weakening Max's love for Florence. It was by now far too strong. His engagement had served to release his emotions. It was as if his love had been inhibited by uncertainty; so that now, when the future was secure, it flowed forth with an ever-growing warmth and intensity.

'Darling love,' he wrote to her just after she sailed, ' . . . Today, on the red sofa in my room—on the bolster of it—I found Baedeker's *Italy* just where you had left it one day when you had been reading it lying down; and it did so remind me of you—not that any reminder is needed!—reminded me of all the times you had spent there, protesting that the time was wasted if you were not reading; and reminded me of all the times we shall spend together in the place named on the book's cover. Dear darling, how lovely it will be, won't it? I feel so happy in the thought of it, in the thought of you. I love you so much dear, and think of you all the time, and wish I could project myself through space on to the upper deck of the *Campania*, at the risk of startling you.

Tonight I go to the performance of *Samson Agonistes*—I have been reading part of it, and find it *very* dull. I think I shall be able to write something amusing about it, especially if the performance is bad—and poor William Poel's honoured name is a guarantee of badness.

The Tube was another reminder of you. It seemed so strange not to be going up Heath Street, and sad, and yet not altogether sad, because things are so much happier now than they were then; though there was a very great deal of happiness then too, wasn't there, dear sweet? Let me know how long you will be in Brooklyn, because of the address I am to put on the envelopes. And write to me, dearest, and don't tear the letters up: there is no need to do that now, surely—and try to read into my letters all the things I cannot express in letter-writing. And take all my love, because it is all yours. And take care of yourself in the different climate, and wrap yourself up well whenever you go out, and think of

your own
Max.'

And again:

'Darling sweet, I think of you always, as I am always telling you, and long to see you. And life for me exists only so far as *you* exist—and the centre of gravity is also in the *future* for me.'

And again:

'I miss you all day. How lovely it will be when I shan't have to miss you ever! When I shall always have you by me—to look at and talk to and kiss.'

Now that she had the positive proofs of his love, Florence might have been expected to have been as happy as he was. But very soon after she got to America she began to suffer from moods of depression. The sense that he was far more popular and famous than herself began to nibble away at the foundations of her confidence in their future together. Would Max really be content to spend his life alone with so undistinguished a person as herself? Would he not regret the brilliant society in which he had been himself so shining a light? Perhaps, she said to him, she should spend three months away every year so that he could spend the time with his old friends. Max gaily dismissed this proposal. 'I think you won't ever want to leave me,' he said, 'because I should so hate it'; and he threw himself into the task of reassuring her.

'You say "I often wonder how it will be when you do not see many people." And I can tell you. It will be very nice. In fact, it will be quite lovely. I shan't want to see many—or *any*—people. You will be the whole population of the globe, so far as I am concerned. Though, in the past few years, I have "gone out" such a lot, I don't think I have a really gregarious nature at all: wherever I am, I am always detached, however genial my surface—never really mingling in the thing. So there won't be any act of *detaching* myself when I leave it all behind. . . .'

The more to convince her, he carried the war into her country and pointed out that it was she rather than he who was making the great sacrifice; for it was she who was giving up her art in order to marry him.

'Darling, it seems to me such a huge thing for you to be giving up because of me—your acting—and I hope you won't be sorry later on? Even if I hadn't *seen* you act, the sacrifice would be known to me as a great one. But no acting of yours could make me "prouder" of you than I am. I should be almost as proud of you as I am if you couldn't act at all!'

As if to indicate how little his social life meant to him, he says relatively little about it in his letters to her. Instead he writes about plans and practical matters—George Alexander has asked him to write a comedy, he tells her, and he has an idea for one with a hero modelled on the young Winston Churchill—and a great deal about his own work. He is giving a lecture, he says, discussing the curious fact that all fashionable plays seem to be about the upper classes: and he tells her about the cartoons he is drawing, and the progress of his new book, *Zuleika Dobson*.

In July she came back and they saw each other constantly. This was easy, because during previous visits Florence had come to be on intimate terms with the Beerbohms. Mrs Beerbohm saw much less of Max than she liked, now that he had become such a social success, so that she encouraged him to bring his friends home. Moreover, she thought Florence was so much more presentable and likeable than Kilseen or Constance Collier that she was glad at first to further Max's friendship with her. She wrote often and affectionately to her and treated her as a sort of honorary member of the family. The result was Florence was a great deal at Upper Berkeley Street. She came to see Mrs Beerbohm even when Max was not at home. When he was, she spent long hours up in his room reading or sewing while he drew and wrote. He was well into *Zuleika Dobson* by now, showed her each passage as he finished it in order to get her views on it. She had, Max noticed, an artist's insight into the nature of his talent and its requirements. 'I have had the good fortune,' he said in later years, 'to have a wife who has always inspired me to do only what I could do best and in my own way.'

When he was not at Upper Berkeley Street Max often spent time at Florence's lodgings in Hampstead, where she sometimes cooked a meal for him: she was an admirable cook. At other times they dined or lunched quietly near Jack Straw's Castle. Of an afternoon they would take a stroll on Hampstead Heath. When the August holiday came, they separated; she stayed in London, he revisited Dieppe. He found himself more critical of it than formerly. The English visitors were such a seedy, shady lot: 'There is no one here,' he said, 'but the unfrocked, the drummed-out, and the struck-off-the-rolls.' He was joined there by Reggie, the Nicholsons and Baroness von Hutten. Florence must have heard something of Max's pleasures at Portofino in 1907, for his letters to her show him anxious to assure her she has no need to be jealous.

'I am not "fascinated" by the B.v.H. and shall not be! I am in the position of *having* been somewhat fascinated two years ago: the safest of all positions! Dear darling love, how unnecessary for me to say these things. You know how I feel.

Your own own
Max.'

Meanwhile he sought to raise her spirits and stiffen her confidence by painting rosy pictures of their life together. She might even, he suggested, do something to educate him!

My own dearest and darling,

You shall teach me to enjoy, as well as respect and bow to, Shakespeare. I can imagine myself, at any rate, feeling quite happy while we read *Cymbeline* or some other play together—even without a James, or some other person of one's own time, in the offing. I daresay that our detached life together, for which I long, will give me a detachment in my sense of the art of fiction—a power of appreciating the *essential* things. But even otherwise we shall have great fun out of my *not* being able to appreciate.

He got back to England to find Florence at Bognor where she had joined Mrs Beerbohm and Constance. After they had gone she stayed on for her health; she was not well this autumn. Max was kept in London by his work for the *Saturday Review*. He went down to Bognor when he could. His letters show him fussing about her health.

'I wired "don't bathe"—because I am sure the water is not warm enough. Also because you were not well after bathing at Margate last year. People ought never to bathe (even in decently warm water) till they have been by the sea for some days, and have got acclimatized. However if you *must* bathe, don't stay in the water longer than *five* minutes. Also don't swim out far from the shore: swim *along* it. Anybody is always liable to "cramp". I expect you think me an awful fusser, darling? But I don't mind that a bit! Good night, and have a nice breakfast, and a happy day, and don't forget all about your own

Max.'

Gaily he announced an approaching visit:

Darling,

Bognor tomorrow! How lovely the idea of that is! I long to be on

296

the platform of Victoria, and anon to be at Barnham Junction, knowing that only Arundel and one or two other little negligible stations intervene between me and my darling. I am so glad to hear of you sleeping for *two hours* after luncheon. Brava! and many encores. It is simply a question of habit. You shall sleep in my arms after luncheon, quite soundly. . . . Tomorrow, or rather today, I see you, my own love.

Max.

The latter part of the year was diversified by the arrival of Florence's brother Morris, the first of her family to meet Max; 'I think him very delightful,' Max informed Florence, 'simpatico—no angles—all curves—a mind and nature unspoiled by knowledge—a charming brother-in-law.' With the new year, events began to move. Max's financial prospects at last grew brighter. Alexander gave him an advance of a hundred pounds for his comedy; and he opened negotiations for an exhibition with Brown and Phillips of the Leicester Galleries. He began to make plans to get married in the spring and informed the *Saturday Review* that he would soon be giving up his work with them.

Faced with the fact that she was soon actually going to be married, Florence was once more swept with moods of despondency. She could not help it, she said, but in spite of his comforting words, she felt sure that Max was not looking forward to marriage as much as she was. It struck her as ominous that he should tell her how much he enjoyed Lady Desborough's parties at Taplow. To these old doubts Max replied with his old reassurances. Of course he was looking forward to marriage; and as for Taplow and the parties:

'I don't want tea or dinner with any one but you. And I shall be glad when there are *no* interruptions. Darling, *I* shall never "miss" anything. What I meant about the Taplow parties was merely that I should look back on them with pleasure, as being the outstandingly pleasant feature of the life I have led—the social life, I mean, for which I have no innate aptitude or desire.'

Anyway, he reiterates in letter after letter, she must not give way to depression.

Sweet darling love,

I had a nice evening—but, darling did *you* have a nice evening? Don't have been dull or unhappy, sweet love. I hate to think of that.

Let us be *happy*—and let me be forgiven for the defects of my qualities. Nobody is perfect, except (I do believe) *you*. I expect I shall be more or less perfect by communion with you, dear love. I count myself very lucky in having met in you both the person I love best and the best person that is to be conceived.

Your own loving

Max.

Alas, it was of no use. In spite of all Max could say or do, Florence doubted and desponded. She continued to do so up to the very eve of the wedding. It is not surprising that some time before this happened Max began to think that the sooner they were married the better, even if it meant starting life together very poor. In fact, what with Alexander's money and a generous cheque from the Leicester Galleries, Max turned out not to be doing so badly. At the beginning of April he started to make arrangements for his wedding. These were simple. For one thing, it was to be in a registry office, presumably because Florence had been brought up as a Jewess and, though she no longer followed the faith of her fathers, had scruples about being married in a Christian church. Secondly, they wanted as little fuss as possible. Max told no one about it till afterwards except his immediate family and Reggie. He told his relations at Upper Berkeley Street by word of mouth and wrote to Dora.

'I send you news that I know will please you: that I am going to be married to Florence—some day next week. We are very happy about it. You had guessed that this thing would be. There were various financial reasons why it could not be sooner than now; and I did not want to "announce" it to any one before it was just to be. Mamma and Con and Aggie are very glad. I expect Florence and I will be going to Portofino; but nothing is quite settled—except that we shall be married next week. I think I am very fortunate in having met the one person with whom I could be *always* perfectly happy—don't you?'

Dora may have entered fully into Max's feelings, she generally did. But it is questionable whether the rest of his family were as pleased as Max made out. Mrs Beerbohm professed to be fond of Florence but was distressed to hear that Max was going to live abroad; and the other Beerbohms took only moderate pleasure in Florence's company. Formal, shy and intense, she did not harmonize with the Beerbohm family spirit. The Trees thought her downright tiresome: and Constance—though she recognized that Florence might well make Max an excellent and devoted wife—sometimes found her irritating. When she was irritated she burst out in exasperated exclamations. Florence was deeply offended. Seized with remorse, Constance poured forth a torrent of apologies and endearments: 'I am sorry you helpful darling old Florence. I was *hateful*.' Florence remained offended; and bewildered too. Such ebullitions of violent and contradictory emotions were not to her taste. Gradually she came to the conclusion she did not like Constance. Once she was engaged to Max, she told him so; need they, she asked, ask Constance to stay with them when they were married. Max vehemently expressed his sympathy. 'I had already quite made up my mind,' he wrote, 'that she shall not come on even the briefest visit to us. I don't want her or her sort. I don't judge or blame her: I simply won't be bothered with her.' These are surprisingly hard words for Max, especially as in general he was disposed to be fond of his relations. We must suppose that his temper flared up in defence of Florence as it had flared up in the past in defence of Kilseen. We remember also that there had been friction between him and Constance about the number of people he brought home to meals. However, any resentment he felt seems to have been passing; for the rest of his life Max was on affectionate terms with Constance. She was certainly fond of him. But this very fondness made her regret his marriage to a woman who got on her nerves. After the wedding she poured out her feelings in a letter to Ross. To this she added a remorseful postscript: 'I will *try* and be pleased he married her!' wrote Constance.

Max had also told Reggie about his engagement in a letter. 'Dearest Reg, dearest of all my friends, I am sure you will be glad of my happiness,' he ended. Reggie was accustomed to being the confidant of Max's love-life. It had been his role ever since the days of Cissey Loftus. And now, whatever his secret feelings may have been, he rose characteristically to the occasion; wrote warm letters of congratulation to both Max and Florence and—though not a rich man —presented them with a large cheque as a wedding present.

On 16 April Max's farewell article appeared in the *Saturday Review*. He was now free to make the last preparations for his wedding. They were simple. He made a present to his own dandyism by ordering himself some shirts and suits to wear on the shores of the Mediterranean—'frugal but tasteful', thus he described them—and he bought a wedding ring.

They were married on 4 May at the Paddington Registry Office in the presence of his mother and Reggie. The next day he and Florence went off for a long honeymoon in a cottage lent to them by a friend at Hythe. From it, six weeks later, Max wrote gaily to Reggie.

My dearest Reg,

It is delightful here—basking in the garden, with what we fondly pretend is a good view of the sea—though we don't really look much at anything but each other, and are as happy as the day is long (and this though June 21st is almost come).

Florence cooked a beautiful luncheon, and I ate so much that she thinks me greedy. Do write to us, please. We send you our fondest love, and all our thanks for all that you have been to us at the time of our marrying.

Your affectionate and loving
Max.

Narrowly though I watch Florence, I detect in her no touch of Anne Hathaway.

PART III

CHAPTER NINE

The Villino

(1)

Max's marriage is the most important event in his life and the turning-point in this story. There had always been two strains within him, the contemplative which got its satisfaction from his inner life of thought and fancy, and the social which led him to enjoy conversing with his friends and cutting a figure in the eyes of the world. Up till 1910 he had lived a life designed as far as possible to satisfy both these strains: and the characteristic mask which he had assumed was a means by which he could at once express his social and protect his contemplative self. The year 1910 saw the end of this dual existence. Max no longer cared so much about cutting a figure; and Florence and fatigue between them had made him out of love with social life! He decided to give it up in favour of tranquillity and contemplation—which in fact had always meant more to him. At thirty-eight years old, he made his bow and retired from the London stage. Nor in the forty-five years of life that remained to him did he ever willingly go back to it. Now and again he made a brief return for some practical reason, and twice world events forced him home for more extended periods. But he always went back to his retirement as soon as he could, and each time with satisfaction.

This is all the more remarkable because his new life did not provide him with new interests. He settled, as he had always intended to, in Italy. But he never learnt Italian nor went into Italian society. He was equally careful to avoid such English people as lived near him. Meanwhile, though he did not forget his friends in England, neither did he exert himself to keep up with them. If they chanced to be passing by, he was delighted to see them, but he wrote very rarely. Max had never liked writing letters since Oxford days: now he yielded to his dislike. Nor could Florence keep up his friendships for him. She did not much want to. She wrote regularly to Mrs Beerbohm, but, as we know, she was not at ease with most of the family. It is doubtful too if she much enjoyed the society of

Max's men friends. Certainly when he mentions Reggie or Gordon Craig or Will Rothenstein in a letter to her, it is generally in a propitiatory and explanatory tone, as of one mediating between her and them. The result of this was that, though Max remained fond of his old friends, they ceased to occupy much of his time and attention. He did not mind; he was quite content to be alone with Florence and his inner life. This inner life flourished. But it also did not develop. His daydreams and fantasies were always about England and largely about the past.

In a sense one can say then that after forty Max deliberately brought his life to a standstill. He was not wrong to do this; a man has no obligation to be on the move if he can be happy immobile. Max was happy all right. But his decision does put his biographer into a difficulty; for he is expected to tell a story, and Max's story from now on must be described as intermittent. Long periods of time passed without anything particular happening to him. The reader must pardon me therefore if I tell my tale, as it were, in fits and starts; dwelling on those short portions of time when something did occur and then passing over whole months and years in a few paragraphs.

(2)

The scene of his retirement was, as designed, the Italian Riviera. He and Florence went there in July 1910: after some weeks of relaxation in a hotel at Santa Margherita they found a house to let about twenty minutes' walk up the coast road south of Rapallo. It was to be Max's home for the rest of his life. From the first he was enthusiastic about it. Nowadays it is hard to understand why. The Villino Chiaro—for that was its name—is a poky little white cube of a building, backing on to the cliff and in front giving directly on to the dust and ceaseless roar of the main road from Genoa to Rome. But it was different in 1910 when the road was sandy and there was not much traffic on it to distract Max and Florence from the magnificent view over the cerulean glitter of the Mediterranean three hundred feet below, and across to where the mountainous outline of the bay swept round to end in the promontory of Portofino, ethereal in the distance. The Villino was a convenient house too. The ground floor was given up to a garage, and a path wound up to the second storey where a side door opened on to a narrow passage with four small rectangular rooms looking over the sea on one side, and on the other a kitchen, a bathroom and a minute dressing-room. Above came the main attraction, the roof, flat, paved and balustraded to form a terrace with a small white plastered summerhouse on it, which Max made into his study, and also an assortment of old Etruscan oil-jars in which grew camellias and his favourite gardenias. Behind the Villino a rough little garden, planted with lemons and almonds and oranges, wandered steeply up the cliff to an outhouse which the Beerbohms later acquired and converted into visitors' rooms.

So far as their exiguous income allowed they decorated the Villino according to their taste, which was of the Whistler period; white-painted woodwork and walls of pale grey and fawn—Max disliked brightly coloured rooms—furnished sparely but elegantly and with an occasional picture by Conder, Nicholson and others on the walls, while over the fireplace hung the convex gold-framed looking-glass from the drawing-room at Upper Berkeley Street. Max's study on the roof-terrace, like his previous rooms, had blue walls hung with cartoons. Round them at waist height ran a single shelf for books; in the middle of the floor stood a chair and a desk of plain unstained wood. The general effect of the Beerbohm interior was one of simplicity and quiet refinement. Also of cleanness and neatness: Florence was a born housewife, and, now that she had no acting to do, gave herself wholly up to the domestic arts. Though they had a servant—Italian servants were very cheap in those days— she did a great deal of work herself, cooked, cleaned, tidied, and industriously studied the art of living gracefully on a small income. The meals at the Villino—so visitors reported—were exquisite, and there was just enough, though only just enough, to go round. The guest's bedroom too was perfectly appointed with bath salts, cigarettes, stamps and every kind of writing gadget. But Max's comfort was Florence's chief aim. His clothes lay brushed and faultlessly folded on the shelves of the little dressing-room, his writing-desk was kept provided with everything he wanted. Viola Tree, his niece, called on them that autumn:

'Uncle Max leads an ideal life,' she wrote, 'among the orange trees and olives and can now pick his own gardenia for his buttonhole.

Florence, his wife, is an amazing woman and manages everything perfectly. His little study on the terrace is more like a captain's look-out house on a ship and his working materials are always ship-shape, always six pencils perfectly sharpened and the cream-laid foolscap he always uses.'

Max would have agreed that his was an ideal life. All his daydreams had come true. Never a Thursday passed, he said, without his waking up to remember with pleasure that he had no *Saturday Review* article to write. Italy too was as beautiful as he had remembered and was made more delightful by Florence's company. Max could not write a letter without telling his correspondent how much he loved her and how happy she made him.

'She is even more an angel than I had ever guessed,' he told Will Rothenstein, 'absolutely perfect in everything, and adorable. And I am as happy as the day is long. And I think *she* is, too. And it is a great joy for us to be together in a very beautiful place, quite alone.'

These sentences are a touch more solemn than his usual strain. For the most part Max the lover was Max the comedian too. He invented a number of comic nicknames for Florence—the Gazy-Bo Girl, the Houri-Housewife, Graminivorous Gertie, the Pittsburg Virago—and spent much of his time making affectionate fun of her seriousness and stern moral views. The newspapers at this time were full of the Crippen murder case and accounts of how Crippen and his mistress, Miss Le Neve, were behaving during their attempted flight from justice. Max was enthralled by it.

'I have, of course, been much immersed in the Crippen case,' he wrote to Reggie. 'The Paris *Daily Mail* was a great daily excitement throughout the week of Crippen's flight. Florence at first disapproved of my great enjoyment of the whole matter; but was gradually drawn in to the vortex; and surprised me somewhat, one day, by starting the subject of the *Dickman* case, quite of her own accord! I always insisted to her that the people staying in this hotel had strong suspicions that I was Dr Crippen and that she was Miss Le Neve. And whatever we did seemed to lend colour to the suspicion. "They seemed animated and cheerful at meals"—"they kept themselves to themselves"—"they used to go out daily to buy the Paris edition of the *Daily Mail*"—etc. etc.'

For the rest the Beerbohms bathed and sat outside cafés and wandered hand in hand through olive groves, Florence artistically attired in flowing white, Max correct and elegant in one of his new pale suits. With the coming of winter he read a certain amount, notably *The Finer Grain* of Henry James, which delighted him, and Chesterton's *What's Wrong with the World?*, which disappointed: 'Very cheap and sloppy,' Max commented, 'though with gleams—gleams of gas-lamps in Fleet Street, mud and slush.' As well as reading, he wrote and drew. Indeed, once they were settled at the Villino, Max found that he worked more easily than he had for some years. Caricature after caricature came from his pencil and he went steadily ahead with *Zuleika Dobson*.

March saw a break in the rhythm of his days. He was under contract to the Leicester Galleries for an exhibition of cartoons to be held in the spring; he also wanted to arrange for the publication of *Zuleika Dobson*. It was therefore necessary for him to go to London. Since they could not afford the fare for both, he went alone. Professionally the visit was a success. The Leicester Galleries found Max wonderfully easy to work with: the ideal artist, said one of the directors, from their point of view; he was sensible, unmercenary and good-tempered. This did not mean that Max was not as concerned as ever about the presentation of his work, with definite ideas about every detail of mounting, framing and hanging, and taking endless pains to see that these ideas were carried out exactly. It was worth it. The exhibition was the most successful he had ever held. The Press was enthusiastic and he sold most of the drawings. He also put himself in the way of increasing his income by agreeing to the publication of the series of drawings and cartoons called *The Second Childhood of John Bull*, which he had exhibited at Carfax ten years earlier. It is significant that he took trouble to insist that these, the bitterest of his satirical efforts, should not be taken as representing his present views. Indeed, he said, he would agree to the publication only if it was made quite clear that they were old drawings; 'historical curiosities which had nothing to do with the present moment'. Max felt better disposed to England now that he lived abroad. During his years in London, he was always tilting against English puritanism and philistinism and contrasting it with the civilized gaiety of the Latin nations. But from the time he was settled in Italy this stopped and Max grew steadily more patriotic.

Like many Englishmen, Max enjoyed finding fault with his country: but, also like many Englishmen, he did not like doing it when he was among foreigners.

Meanwhile, he saw a lot of his friends and family, stayed at Upper Berkeley Street, went to Herbert's new production of *Henry VIII*, lunched or dined with Reggie and Will, Sickert and Nicholson, Street and Gosse. In order to get models for more caricatures he attended a debate in the House of Commons where he listened to Winston Churchill.

'He speaks with plenty of *authority*,' he told Florence, 'but halts and stammers and repeats himself to an extraordinary degree. This sounds incompatible with authority, but it somehow isn't.'

He wrote to Florence several times a week telling her whom he had seen and what he had been doing, how impossible he found it to get on with *Zuleika Dobson* in the rush of life in London and of the difficulties of living economically there. This was a matter of concern to Florence. From a natural timidity in money matters, perhaps increased by an unacknowledged feeling of jealousy, she showed herself especially nervous of his spending too much money entertaining his friends. Anxiously Max assured her he had not done so. George Street had not after all expected him to pay for his dinner, he was relieved to tell her; and though Max had asked Ada Leverson to supper after the play, it was she, he said, who provided dinner before it. It would be unjust to Florence to suggest that her letters were mainly occupied with considerations of this mean and mundane kind. In the few that survive she writes mostly about such episodes of her life as she hoped might interest him—the village priest has offered to come and bless the Villino, some German street musicians had been playing odd little tunes under her balcony—or she rhapsodizes in lyrical strain about the beauties of nature and the intensity of her love.

My Beloved—
I wish I could tell you of the deep beauty of this day. One feels as if there had never been such a day before—but yesterday was beautiful and the day before and you know we have had wonderful days—but today the air is so soft and so gentle and all sounds—the voices of children—the intermittent sounds of the carriage bells—the

stir of the leaves are lovely in it. I wish the day of your return may be such a day. In my heart it will be and all things will be as they are in the light of this day if you are well my beloved. How great is my happiness. If only to know it had something of merit in it. I love you—and oh—blessed thought—you love me. I want to weep in your arms. And now, smile at this conclusion. . ..

    The love and the yearning of your own

Florence.

Indeed, Max might well be expected to smile at such a conclusion. But if he did, it was affectionately: and though himself he could not rise to such romantic flights, his words are equally and uninhibitedly loving.

'Perfect darling, it is so lovely to think of being with you again. When I say perfect darling I mean to imply perfection in the literal sense, not the slang sense; because you *are* perfect. And I send you all my love and all my thoughts, and I am your own own

Max.'

With Max away, Florence's old fears revived. Was he not likely to find it boring in Italy after the brilliant social life of London? On the contrary, he told her, social life in London had lost much of its charm for him.

'The more I see of people here in London, the more sure I am that they are not at all necessary to me, and the more I long to be back with you, dear perfect darling. I only wonder how I was able to keep going all that time when my lot was cast among them. Of course I don't mean that it isn't *pleasant* to meet old friends, as I am here. But oh to be home!'

He grew more impatient as the weeks passed: and a wave of delight rose in him when on the afternoon of 25 April he got out of the train at Genoa and caught sight of Florence's blue-clad figure waiting shyly for him in the afternoon sunshine. Back at home he showed his pleasure in her characteristically by drawing, for her eyes alone, a series of affectionate caricatures of her in which her grace and prettiness were apparent but which make friendly fun of her romantic gestures and dreamy vagueness. His home too delighted him afresh, with the sun and the sea surpassing themselves and the garden sweet with the scent of lemon blossom.

309

Soothed and stimulated, he sat down to his writing-desk and finished *Zuleika Dobson*. Then came a short holiday in Venice; a honeymoon kind of holiday, for they spoke to no one but each other; 'Some of the pigeons look vaguely familiar to me,' said Max, 'otherwise we have had our usual and delightful independence.' This independence was to continue for the next nine months save when it was interrupted in June by Dora on her annual holiday. Pleasantly interrupted, however; for Dora, unlike Constance, got on easily with Florence. Serene and whimsical, her personality harmonized perfectly with the prevailing mood of the Villino *ménage*. No one else came to stay till the following March. Max luxuriated in the leisured, tranquil days. One day he got a telegram from Will Rothenstein inviting him to attend a dinner organized by Yeats in honour of Gordon Craig. With pleasure, he refused it.

My dearest Will,

Many thanks for your wire. In one of Maeterlinck's plays an old servitor says 'Everything around this castle is so quiet that the dropping of a ripe fruit in the park draws faces to the windows.' *Here* life is so peaceful that the arrival of a telegram is as the dropping of a bomb that blows us straight up through the roof. We are both of us still somewhat shaken and jarred; but I have managed to write a note to Yeats; and I send it to you, because I am not sure of his address. Would you send it on to him?

Love from us both to you all.

Your affectionate
Max.

P.S. Please send Yeats a line to explain why I am writing. Otherwise he might be rather bewildered and fancy it was a spell cast by the fairies or by Shoon-na-Braugh or even by Krim-na-Hoo.

(3)

In October *Zuleika Dobson* was published by Heinemann. It was the great event of Max's year: and a great event in his life too. The most ambitious of all his literary works, the most elaborate and highly wrought in style and his only full-length story, it also represents his art at its most quintessential: in it his distinguishing characteristics appear in their most extreme form. First of all it is a

FLORENCE IN ITALY

fantasy, but a fantasy on observed reality and inspired by a bit of his own experience. In *Zuleika Dobson* the inspiration comes from his Oxford experience. The scene is Oxford as he remembered it in his undergraduate days, and the hero, the Duke of Dorset, stands for that ideal of dandyism which was his undergraduate ideal. In one aspect the book is sedulously realistic. The buildings and the climate, dons and undergraduates, Rhodes scholars and college servants, dining-clubs, Eights Week and the college concert—all these pass before our eyes brought to life with a detailed fidelity that makes all other fictions about Oxford seem ill informed. Yet, as always with Max, fact is there in order to inspire fancy. All this information is put to the service of a plot so openly and preposterously fantastic that there is no question of our taking it seriously. For it tells of the most beautiful woman in the world who is also a professional conjurer, who descends on the university in Eights Week, with the result that every single undergraduate falls in love with her and all, finding their love unrequited, drown themselves for her sake at the end of the races. Max tells the story in such a way as to emphasize its preposterousness. The tone is consistently and impishly frivolous; and the characters, though individualized by countless little strokes of observation, are drawn in a humorous convention which is designed to make it impossible for the reader to take their fates to heart or, in any serious sense, to believe in their existence. They have the same relation to the characters in a serious novel as the figures in Max's cartoons have to serious portraits.

Again, *Zuleika Dobson* exhibits in the most extreme form his characteristic blend of the pretty and the comic. A delicate rococo, frolicsome prettiness, flaunts itself through every paragraph, informing image and description, making itself heard in every dancing or lingering cadence of Max's prose. But so also is every page saturated with his comic sense; sometimes rollicking and farcical, sometimes sharply satiric, sometimes taking wing in a flight of whimsical nonsense. But it is always present; never for an instant is he serious. His tone is sustainedly ironical: his prettiness never softens into sentiment, even the half-ironic kind of sentiment that we find in *The Happy Hypocrite*. Neither is his satire ever serious. He is not out to castigate or correct human folly. Apart from anything else, human folly in this instance was Oxford folly; and Max delighted too much in Oxford to wish to correct her. Most of his jokes are directed against dandyism and university institutions, two of the things that pleased him most in life. The more absurdities he discovered in the Eights Week Boat Race celebrations or in the Duke of Dorset, the less he wished them different. *Zuleika Dobson* is an outstanding example of his characteristic propensity to laugh at what he loved and to love what he laughed at. In this, his natural disposition was reinforced by principle. An author, he thought, had no business to go in for correcting or castigating. As a convinced aesthete, Max held it as a basic article of faith that the artist should work with no ulterior aim, but only to delight by the beauty of his creation. *Zuleika Dobson* is an extreme if light-hearted expression of the aesthetic point of view.

The result in his view was pretty good. Reggie wrote him a letter of enthusiastic congratulation, but added that his pleasure was qualified by the fact that he found the characters almost painfully real; he believed in Katie the serving maid too much, he said, to take her sufferings in the required spirit of comedy. Max replied:

'. . . now for the almost impossible task of thanking you *enough* for your splendid letter, and telling you what a joy it was to Florence and me. What you say is so much more worth having, so much more interesting, than if you had said "delightful from beginning to end" or "essence of Max" or anything of that sort. For it throws a (for me) new light on the book—a light in which I, however, find myself blinking and doubtful. I certainly had not realized that Katie and those others were at all real; and it won't be until a year or so has elapsed, to let me look at them with a fresh eye, that I shall be able to agree that they *are* real and that you haven't merely injected some of your own overflowing humanity into them. Certainly I wanted them to *behave like* real people, within the limits of the absurdity conditioned. I wanted to forge the links of logic correctly *from my premises*; because it seemed to me that thereby—that is, by taking the characters solemnly—the fun of the absurdity would be by contrast the greater. But it never occurred to me that while I was trying to do this I was giving to the characters anything in the nature of a *real*, as opposed to a fantastical-humorous, reality. And if I have done this without knowing it—well, I have overshot the mark; but I am rather pleased at having done so; for assuredly the achievement, though it must mar the "form" of the book, makes the book more curious and interesting, and gives it the more chance of abiding in people's minds, as something to be worried about, something rather baffling.

When I say "people's" I mean of course only a few people's. I don't see how the book—whether it be what you think it, or be nearly what I set myself to make it—can be anything like a popular success. But I do think it has a good chance of surviving, in either case, as a treasure for experts in fine literature, and especially for such of those experts as are or have been or shall have been Oxford men.

I can well imagine two literary undergraduates, fifty or more years hence, standing under the Emperors, looking across the road, discussing with some heat which house was Mrs Batch's.

Yes, I think the book will survive by reason of the very beautiful writing of it, even if you aren't right about the discordant human note which would make its survival more sure.

Meanwhile, I have had press-notices good, bad, and indifferent, and am indifferent to the indifferent ones and the bad ones, because the book has its quality, invulnerable. And as for the good ones, they have none of them given me nearly as much pleasure as your good and stirring letter.

Your singling-out of that phrase about the "streak of lightning" [1] is a proof that Rothenstein and Ruskin are right about the reverence for nature. For the phrase was written after seeing a thunderstorm from our terrace, and was an attempted accurate notation! The word "slid" was in the first draft "slithered" which, though more accurate really, looked rather *cherché*, and so was jettisoned. I am afraid that from a strictly meteorological point of view the weather *preceding* the storm may leave something to be desired: I don't think the thunder-clouds would have "ponderously massed themselves" at 8 a.m. and sat tight till 6 p.m. I must keep a weather-eye from the terrace, with a view to alterations in some possible new edition. . . .

Love from Florence and from your affectionate

Max.

P.S. As to what you say about "dramatic power"—yes, I *was* conscious that there were really dramatic scenes; for one *can* get dramatic effect without humanity (though I never would have admitted this in the *Saturday*)!'

[1] 'A sudden white vertical streak slid down the sky', *Zuleika Dobson*, p. 275.

Though confident about its merits, Max was keenly interested to see how his book would be received; so much so, that he altered his habits to make what was for him the unusual effort of a frequent walk into Rapallo in order to look for reviews in such English papers as might be on sale there. He was repaid for his trouble, most of the reviews were very favourable. His friends were enthusiastic. Max got a great many letters of congratulation, including a rapturous one from Will Rothenstein and a touching tongue-tied note from Kilseen, recalling how he had read her the first chapters twelve years before. Only one thing spoilt Max's complete satisfaction. There were a few misprints in the volume and some examples of careless typography. Such things upset him far more than did hostile reviews. He wrote several letters to Ballantyne, the printer, protesting about the matter with all the sarcastic eloquence he could muster.

'As to the general typography,' ended one of them, 'I am quite ready and glad to believe that all those swaying lines, those letters bobbing up, those letters slipping down, and other defects over which I had to expend so much time in correcting the proofs, and which have not wholly been purged away from the published edition, were due merely to "a slight inequality in the alignment of this particular fount". In all friendliness, then, I implore Messrs Ballantyne to seal up this particular fount (which is evidently our old friend the *fons et origo malorum*) for ever and ever, or to set it playing only on very special occasions—as when they are called on to print "The Confessions of a Dancing Dervish", for example, or "The Random Memories of a Palsied Hottentot". And then if they do that, I will do a drawing that shall represent them as not less beautiful than the figures on the Parthenon Frieze.'

Max carried his fussiness about the small matters of presentation to unreasonable lengths: but it had a rational basis. His work he judged was of too slight a kind to succeed in spite of blemishes.

'Excuse all this to-do,' he said. 'If one is writing a history of civilization or propounding some great new gospel printers' errors do not matter—they even brighten a thing up. But a trifle must be perfect.'

The stir raised by *Zuleika Dobson* died away; and Max and Florence relapsed for another twelve months into an idyllic tranquillity. In the summer they hardly went to Rapallo at all but spent their time down at the sea bathing, or on the Villino terrace where Max, attired in a white pyjama suit, wrote and drew and idled. In the winter they still sat on the terrace if it was warm enough; if not, he read and drew and idled in the little sitting-room. Sometimes he read aloud to Florence, notably, Trollope's *The Three Clerks* and *Dr Thorne*, both of which he much enjoyed. This indicates a change in his attitude to literature. Trollope's books would have been too loose in form and too undistinguished in style for Max the aesthete of the nineties. But middle age had made him less fastidious in these matters. On the other hand, he responded far more than in youth to that genial and rational sense of reality which is Trollope's outstanding merit. And, of course, fascinated as he was by the Victorian age, he appreciated intensely Trollope's power convincingly to evoke it.

The next twelve months of Max's life were more eventful. First of all, in the autumn of 1912 he brought out another book entitled *A Christmas Garland*, a collection of parodies of contemporary authors modelled on the original 'Christmas Garland' of 1896. It was as important an achievement as *Zuleika Dobson*; for parody was a chief branch of his art, and all his longest and best parodies are in this volume. In a prefatory note he gives an account of his motives in taking up this particular form of writing.

'Stevenson, in one of his essays, tells us how he "played the sedulous ape" to Hazlitt, Sir Thomas Browne, Montaigne, and other writers of the past. And the compositors of all our higher-toned newspapers keep the foregoing sentence set up in type always, so constantly does it come tripping off the pens of all higher-toned reviewers. Nor ever do I read it without a fresh thrill of respect for the young Stevenson. I, in my own very inferior boyhood, found it hard to revel in so much as a single page of any writer earlier than Thackeray. This disability I did not shake off, alas, after I left school. There seemed to be so many live authors worth reading. I gave precedence to them, and, not being much of a reader, never had time to grapple with the old masters. Meanwhile, I was already writing a little on my own account. I had had some sort of aptitude for Latin prose and Latin verse. I wondered often whether those two things, essential though they were (and are) to the making of a decent style in English prose, sufficed for the making of a style more than decent. I felt that I must have other models. And thus I acquired the habit of aping, now and again, quite sedulously, this or that live writer—sometimes, it must be admitted, in the hope of learning rather what to avoid.'

It is to be doubted if Max is speaking seriously when he says that he wrote parodies as a method of teaching himself to write. However, he certainly both conceived and executed them with a Flaubertian care. 'I regard the book as a good example of what can be achieved by dogged industry,' he remarked. *A Christmas Garland* was received with the same acclamation as *Zuleika Dobson* had been; even by some of its distinguished victims: Max had been a little nervous as to how Henry James would react to being made fun of in this manner. He need not have worried. Just after Christmas he received a letter from Edmund Gosse:

My dear Max,
    Henry James has been eating his Christmas dinner here with us, and I am anxious to let you know that he started the subject of your *Christmas Garland*, and discussed it with the most extraordinary vivacity and appreciation. He was full of admiration. I told him that you had a certain nervousness about his acceptance of your parody of him, and he desired me to let you know at once that no one can have read it with more wonder and delight than he. He expressed himself in superlatives. He called the book 'the most intelligent that has been produced in England for many a long day'.

At a party that winter an admirer asked Henry James his opinion on some question. 'Ask that young man,' he said, pointing to Max who was a guest at the same gathering, 'he is in full possession of my innermost thoughts.'
    As is apparent from this anecdote, Max was in London for a month or two in the winter of 1912. This time Florence was with him. He came to arrange for another exhibition of cartoons to be held in the spring, and possibly to advise George Alexander who was proposing to produce a one-act play of his. This play, *A Social Success*, eventually came on at the Palace Theatre in February 1913. It is a farcical comedy in the Wilde manner about fashionable life. As usual, the underlying theme is inspired by Max's own experience:

the young hero is, as he himself had been, distracted by the pressure of life induced by too much success in society. Though not a memorable work, *A Social Success* is the best of Max's dramatic efforts and it met with a friendly, if not enthusiastic, reception. Meanwhile, Max, in order to find some new subjects for his caricatures, attended a debate in the House of Commons. The sight of politicians exercised the same fascination on him now as it had in boyhood, and he gazed with especial interest at Bonar Law, who had just supplanted Balfour as Leader of the Conservative Party.

'Bonar Law *is* common,' he told Reggie,' but has a strong antiseptic William-Archerish charm—seems so very *good* and *guid*; and the way in which his Kino frock-coat rides up over his Hope Bros. collar is a perfect dream. Also he has no back to his head—or practically none —which I suppose accounts for his many tactical errors.'

For the rest, Max's time in England was mostly taken up with social life. He had not appeared in it before as a married man; and for many of his friends it was their first sight of Florence. Arnold Bennett, for instance, first met her this year. She made a curious impression on him:

'Reddish hair, divided into two mops of unequal size, hanging loosely down in a shock on either side. Over this a black hat with a feather sticking out backwards from the left side. Very fair. Very thin. Very unassumingly dressed in black. Gloves ditto. Refined and rather worn features. About 35. Refined voice. Seriously interested in, and proud of, Max. Wondered whether his recent parodies of me and others were not *too* good for a creative artist to do. On the whole, a shade too serious, and fairly precious. Deferential. Constantly stopping, with a grave air, when we began a sentence simultaneously, and making way for me—and then going on. But agreeable, intelligent (perhaps too!) and with a fundamental decency. She thought London the most beautiful city in the world etc. But she preferred to live among Italian peasants. Impossible that a woman presenting such an odd appearance could be balanced in the normal sense.'

If this was the kind of effect Florence made on strangers, it is hardly surprising that she felt awkward in society and willing to spend most of her time in Italy.

Max took her back there early in 1913, returning alone at the end of March for the arrangement and opening of his exhibition. He wrote to Florence every day: letters in which his usual words of endearment and reassurance were interspersed with others advising her to take special care of herself—she must be sure to eat enough and to rest enough—and with pieces of news about his life in London. He had been twice photographed, he told her, for publicity purposes, he hoped she would not think this vulgar of him. He does not refer to the matter again, so apparently she did not. Instead, she encouraged him to buy himself some new clothes, to avoid getting overtired, and to wrap up if it was cold.

Once again, the exhibition was a success. Most of the cartoons were sold, the critics were warm in their praise; Max himself admitted that he was very pleased with some of his work. He spoke his judgement of it to Reggie with the same detached candour he had used when speaking of *Zuleika Dobson*. It was in reference to an article on the exhibition by Ross.

'Bobbie's "selections" are not bad from the *literary* standpoint. The drawings he likes best are the most amusing in meaning, certainly. But from the artistic standpoint, I should say that 33 is merely a bit of laborious cartoon-mongering, and 13 likewise (though it is a pretty thing in its way), and 29 rather feeble. Whereas the "very poor" Burnham and the "silly" Teixeira happen unfortunately to be just the two gems of the whole collection (two of the *three*, rather—the other one being the Balfour frieze).

These are caricature in its finest purity—caricature brought to a pitch of such simplicity and of beauty as you won't find except in very good Japanese prints. What a terrible thing to be an art critic and not an artist! But don't, for heaven's sake, repeat to him what I have written. If he wants to know what I said, say that I thought his selections very good (as I *have* said) *from the literary standpoint*. . . . What awful egoism this letter is isn't it?'

Max realized, however, that popular success was no indication of merit. Deserved or not, Max's popular success was such that his publishers wished to bring out another book of cartoons. Accordingly, a volume entitled *Fifty Caricatures* appeared at the beginning of October.

It is interesting as showing how he still kept up with the events in England; the Marconi scandal, the Ulster crisis and the changes in the habits of the English Court consequent upon the succession of George V. Though many of his old models—Balfour, Gosse, Shaw —figure in its pages, they are joined by several new ones, among them Bonar Law, John Masefield and the Duke of Devonshire. In one drawing Max turns his eye from the present to peer into the future: and depicts the urbane eighteenth century looking with amusement, and the solemn nineteenth century with shocked horror, at the twentieth century represented as a young man dressed in flying kit rushing by them with haggard, desperate countenance towards some unknown destination. Middle age had mellowed the mood in which Max surveyed mankind. But he remained just as pessimistic as ever about its future.

Himself he felt he belonged neither to the future nor the present but to the past. He was a survival from the age of Wilde and Beardsley; and as such an historical figure. For this age was literally passing into history. In the autumn of the same year an author called Holbrook Jackson brought out a book in which he told its story. He dedicated it to Max and sent him a copy. Max wrote him back a long letter of thanks. In it he sums up his attitude to the past in general, and in particular to the period of his youthful triumphs; incidentally, also to two of its most conspicuous figures, Kipling and William Morris.

My dear Mr Holbrook Jackson,

I told you with what gratification I was filled by your intention of dedicating your new book to me. Now that here the book itself is, my gratification is all the greater. It is a fine book indeed—fresh and keen from first to last, full of understanding and of the generosity that comes of understanding. To me, of course, as a survivor from the thick of that by-gone period, it is of special interest. I don't say that it plucks any particular chords of sentiment in me. Somehow one doesn't feel sentimental about a period in which oneself has footed it. It is the period that one *didn't* quite know, the period just before oneself, the period of which in earliest days one knew the actual survivors, that lays a really strong hold on one's heart. The magic of the past begins for me at the 'eighties and stretches as far as the 'sixties. Thus the interest with which I have read

every word of your book has been unblurred with tears. I daresay
the undergraduates of today will cry over your pages. *My* withers
(whatever they may be—I have never known—I really must look
them up in the dictionary) are unwrung. Write a book about
Trollope and the Pre-Raphaelites and John Stuart Mill and Martin
Tupper and Carlyle, and then my heart as well as my head will be
stirred profoundly. . . . This time it is only my head. This part of me
I hold higher since reading your book: I had no idea, before, that the
'nineties I lived through were so interesting and altogether remarkable. I wonder whether, twenty or thirty years hence, the 'noughts
and the 'teens will be as fine material for the literary historian.
Probably that will just depend on the literary historian. Probably it
is just you, and not the 'nineties after all, that make this book of
yours a thing of such high value. I am glad you have as a frontispiece that drawing of John Bull—quite the very best drawing, I
think, Beardsley ever did, and the most exquisitely simple (*and
ornate and witty*) of all his designs (though perhaps 'The Barber' is as
beautiful a thing). It is amusing to see again the cover-designs for the
Yellow Books and the *Savoy*. I remember meeting Oscar one afternoon in the domino room of the Café Royal and being told by him
that Aubrey had just been showing him the drawing for the cover of
the *Yellow Book*. I asked what it was like. 'Oh' said Oscar, 'you can
imagine the sort of thing. A terrible naked harlot smiling through a
mask—and with ELKIN MATHEWS written on one breast
and JOHN LANE on the other.' A perfect description of 'the sort
of thing' isn't it? By the way, that photograph of Oscar, dated 1895,
ought to be dated some years earlier. It was done at about the time
when *Lady Windermere's Fan* was produced. This emendation sounds
like the end of a dull review in a newspaper. As a matter of fact it
isn't even the end of a dull letter. For I want to tell you, but no,
what is the good of saying how thoroughly I agree with you about
this, or how glad I am you said that, or how illuminating is what you
say about the other? *Disagreement* is all that might interest you. But
is there any judgement of yours that I *do* disagree with? . . . Kipling,
yes, I think you much over-rate him. Of course I leave a very wide
margin for my own injustice to him. To me, who gets the finest of
all literary joy out of Henry James (his middle and later manners),
the sort of person that Kipling is, and the sort of thing that Kipling
does, cannot strongly appeal—quite the contrary. I carefully guard

myself by granting you that Kipling is a genius. Indeed, even *I* can't help *knowing* him to be that. The *schoolboy*, the *bounder*, and the *brute* —these three types have surely never found a more brilliant expression of themselves than in R. K. (Nor, will I further grant, has the *nursery*-maid.) But as a poet and a seer R. K. seems to me not to exist, except for the purpose of contempt. All the ye-ing and the Lord-God-ing and the Law-ing side of him seems to me a very thin and trumpery assumption; and I have always thought it was a sound impulse by which he was driven to put his 'Recessional' into the waste-paper basket, and a great pity that Mrs Kipling fished it out and made him send it to *The Times*. I think (absurd tho' it is to prophesy) that futurity will give him among poets a place corresponding exactly with the place reserved for Theodore Roosevelt among statesmen. Morris, again—I think you greatly over-rate *him*. He is splendid, certainly, by reason of the bulk and variety of his work. But when it comes to the quality of any part of that work ——; I think that the Coleridge title-page which you reproduce is a rather destructive sample and symbol. Here again I leave a wide margin★ for my necessary injustice. I like in visual objects a lightness and severity, blitheness and simplicity. A gloomy complexity is no doubt equally a noble thing to strive for. Morris achieved it in his wall-papers. He achieved it too in this Coleridge page. But how poorly. Compare the gloomy complexity of Aubrey Beardsley's border for the *Morte d'Arthur*, facing page 110 of your book. There (tho' of course it wasn't Beardsley's *own* work, but merely work done to order in immaturity) you have strength and rhythm. Then look back to the muddled and fuddled, tame, weak, aimless, invertebrate and stodgy page done by Morris. The only 'sense of inevitability' it gives *me* is that I shall be sick if I look at it again. To me the format of your bookling *Town* is worth all the Kelmscott books heaped together—unless indeed there were a lit bonfire underneath them. They seem to me a monument of barren and lumbering affectation: not *books* at all; for books, to be alive and to deserve their title, must be printed in such wise that the contemporary reader can forget the printing and be in direct touch with the author's meaning. Morris' pseudo-mediaevalism utterly prevents—but there, there. I am boring your head off, and my letter is so long that you will be sorry you ever dedicated your book to me.

★ I am glad Morris isn't alive to fill in the margin with decorations.

So no more. I will merely thank you again most heartily for that dedication, and for your praises of me—praises which in their now amplified form give me even more pleasure than they did before.

Yours sincerely,

Max Beerbohm.

CHAPTER TEN

London Revisited

THE Beerbohms had gone back to the Villino in April: November found them on their travels again. Florence was devoted to
her brothers, and it was four years since she had seen them. Even if
Max had wished to accompany her to the United States, which is
unlikely, he had not the money to do so. The two therefore went on
a visit to England. They spent Christmas there: then, after imploring
Max to look after himself and leaving him instructions as to how to
clean his own clothes, Florence sailed for America. They proposed
to rejoin each other in the spring in Italy. After she left, Max's life in
London followed the same pattern as on previous solitary visits. He
had a certain amount of work to do. During the last years he had
begun to write several of the essays afterwards printed in *And Even
Now*; in particular 'Kolniyatsch', 'Mobled King' and 'Books Within
Books'. This last included some literary references which Max had
been unable to check in Italy. He now occupied himself with finish-
ing the essays and checking the references in the British Museum.
He was also asked for a contribution by Bruce Richmond, then
editor of *The Times Literary Supplement*. Articles for the *Literary
Supplement* were unsigned and couched in a consciously impersonal
tone. Max was aware that his own work owed its flavour and vitality
to the fact that it was openly personal, a deliberate expression of the
literary *persona* he had created for himself. He refused Richmond's
offer unless he should be allowed to sign his articles.

Though against appearing anonymously, he was also conscious
of the dangers of over-advertising himself. This appeared in a
comical episode which occurred in February 1914. Frank Harris
had gone down in the literary world and was now reduced to
editing *Modern Society*, a shady periodical which eked out a pre-
carious existence under the threat of bankruptcy on the one side
and the libel courts on the other. It was, in fact, involved at this
very time in a libel action. At the trial Harris insulted the judge so
grossly and in such a loud voice that he found himself summarily

committed to Brixton prison for contempt of court. Max, who cherished a lurking weakness for Harris, wrote him a letter of sympathy.

My dear Frank,

This isn't to 'condole' with you on your adventure; for you have always enjoyed adventures of all kinds and come out of them smiling, and will very soon come out of this one, smiling more than ever perhaps, because this one will have had for you a special element of comedy; and meanwhile the Café Royal[1] will have been allowed to minister to you as it has ministered to you for so many years; and as for the brief confinement of your actual body—you, with your intellect and imagination, will have been much more free and at large, really, than the rest of the population of Great Britain.

I fancy that all you are worrying about is Mrs Harris, who naturally cannot be expected to take the broad philosophic view of the matter taken by you and me. For her I am truly sorry. I am afraid she must be very unhappy, in being parted from you, as are you in being parted from her; and I am afraid she must be worrying about you all the time—whether the air of Brixton is really good, whether the food from the Café Royal is really well-served, and 1001 other things that a devoted wife would worry about. Will you please offer her my sincerest sympathy. I wonder if it would at all please her at any time to see an old friend who would talk about nothing except that ever-rich topic: Frank. If so, I should very much like to go and see her, at any time before I go back to Italy. I go back in about a fortnight. My wife is on a flying visit to America, and is on the eve of return. I am afraid she will have had an unpleasant shock in reading out there the cabled news of your imprisonment. She won't have understood that the hardship is a purely technical one; and I shall hasten to re-assure her that the brilliant man whose talk so delighted her last year at the Savoy is not really to be grieved over at all, and that he has but a topic the more for his incomparable conversation.

Alas, kindness to Frank Harris only led to trouble, as Max was soon to discover. Harris's imprisonment produced a crisis for *Modern Society*. For who was to run it or write for it in his absence? Harris

[1] Harris was allowed to have meals sent in to him from the Café Royal.

was lucky enough to have working for him at this time a young woman called Enid Bagnold, pretty, spirited and extremely intelligent. She shall tell the rest of the story herself, she does it very well.

'. . . some message was sent to me from Frank Harris to say that the paper must somehow be kept on the bookstalls, or it would lose its . . . Stationer's Licence, I think. Fired by my editor I determined to be great too, to rally his friends round the martyred leader. I sat down and wrote to Bernard Shaw, to Pryde, to Max Beerbohm, Haldane MacFall, and Joseph Simpson, asking them to fill the paper instead of the usual contributors "and we will leave the other pages blank", I added. Shaw replied on a handwritten postcard in which was the sentence "You can't put an elephant to hatch hens' eggs", and refused, but said something handsome about Frank Harris. Harris took the postcard from me afterwards. Perhaps he sold it. I don't know what Pryde did, but Joseph Simpson sent a drawing. And, best of all, Max Beerbohm did a drawing of himself and Frank Harris sitting at a restaurant table, and underneath wrote "The best talker in London—with one of his best listeners". This was drawn and given on a solemn promise from me that it should neither be used as a cover to the paper nor exhibited as a poster. By special arrangements with the solicitors I went down by bus to Brixton to carry to my editor my personal triumph. It was my first visit to a prison and I haven't since known anyone who went to gaol. Frank Harris was brought at a smart pace across the prison yard by a warder, and entering the glass room (I remember a glass room) spoke to me across a wide wooden table, sitting at the farther side. He promised me that Max's stipulation should be faithfully kept, but he did not seem pleased with either Max or me, only gratified on his own account. On leaving the prison I was fascinated by the way in which the inner prison gates were shut before the outer were opened and you were left in a tunnel watching the pale faces of other visitors.

The slim advertisement girl evidently paid a similar visit: for she received contrary instructions. She was told to go out strong on publicity and never mind the promises. Arriving a day or two later at nine at the office, I found Odham's single horse-cart drawn up and the man delivering a heavy roll of posters with Max Beerbohm's drawing. I think I did not know all at once where Max lived, for I remember ruffling the telephone book with a hand that shook with

The 'Best Talker' in London, with one of his best listeners.

For my old friend Frank Harris, this scribble in record of a scene which, happily for me, has been so frequent in the past twenty years.

Max, February 15. 1914

MAX BEERBOHM AND FRANK HARRIS

rage; but soon I was in a cab, had rung his door-bell, and sent up a message as urgent as I could make it by the maid. He was not dressed, but came down in a wonderful dressing-gown, and as he listened his two very blue eyes were serious with anger, though his eyebrows, his mouth, and the rest of his charming face would not go any great lengths. He was angry enough to dress very quickly, and came with me, carrying his cane (which had a loop or bobble at the handle) in the cab I had kept. What followed was his own plan, and the pleasure he took in it banished his indignation. Driving to the office to examine for himself the iniquity of the printed posters, he dragged the roll into the cab, then drove on to the printers. There he collected the block, no one gainsaying him, and we went on to the river at the point where the Savoy Steps go down. We threw the whole burden into the river. The plate disappeared, but the posters unrolled and floated for a time down the tide.'

This anecdote throws light on Max, on Harris and on Shaw. For Max it was not a new light on Shaw: on the contrary, it confirmed his impression of Shaw's vanity. So also did a conversation he had with him this year in London.

'I saw,' he wrote to Reggie, 'the waxen effigy of G.B.S. when I was in London. I thought it might form a good basis for a caricature. Some days later I was lunching at his place, and mentioned the effigy to him; at which he flushed slightly, and waved his hands, and said he had *had* to give Tussaud a sitting, as "it would have seemed so *snobbish* to refuse"! Considering that it had been the proudest day in his life, I was rather touched by this account of the matter. I am afraid he is afraid of me.'

When Max was not working he spent much of his time with his friends and his family. He saw a great deal of his family; for he was living at Upper Berkeley Street. It was a sadder place than it used to be. The Beerbohm ladies were all growing older; and Mrs Beerbohm, the presiding and animated genius of the household, had begun to fail. For several years her memory had been gradually going; so much so that she often forgot that Max had left home. 'Is Max in to dinner?' she would ask. 'No, he has to be out tonight,' Constance would reply reassuringly. Max's absence was another chief cause of the family's sadness. Mrs Beerbohm missed him dreadfully. They all did. The house was so dull without him. Besides being amusing himself, he had been a magnet for he attracted other amusing people: Reggie and George Street, William Nicholson and Ted Craig, all came to Upper Berkeley Street to see Max. When he went, they stopped coming. Moreover, when Max did come home, things were not the same. For, though delightful and affectionate as ever, he was no longer an integral part of the house. He belonged to Florence and to the life he and Florence had built together. After Max had gone back to Italy, Constance wrote to Ada Leverson:

'Max seems 20 (twenty) to you, like at Broadstairs, but to us he seems 43 or 44, and he is *very* much married and we take him for granted. We love him just as much, but he has a home of his own and doesn't seem little Max any more; and we have the young people coming on and to think of, and whose lives are not yet settled as his is, so completely. . . .

You know what you feel about Violet.[1] Her fate not settled. When she's 45 you'll feel as *I* do about Max! She's sweet; and so was and *is* he. Florence is all right, a nice clever little woman, and suits him so well, but we've got used to her, and she's always the same.

My mother has slept since you left and is now awake, terrified, and may be so for hours.

Oh Ada! Life is simply crushing and awful. Thank Heaven you have what happiness you have.'

Max managed to see a great many people outside the family while he was in London. A procession of names, famous and less famous, streams across the pages of his letters to Florence; old friends and new acquaintances, writers and actors, hostesses and politicians, Rothenstein, Street, Gosse, Tonks, Ellen Terry, Mrs Patrick Campbell, young Ezra Pound—'A good subject for caricature,' noted Max —Oscar Wilde's son Vyvyan Holland, who made a very pleasant impression, Lady Lewis and Asquith 'Cosy and rubicund', Henry James and George Moore. Max had a mischievous interchange with Moore one evening. Moore had recently brought out a book in which he had been very scathing about his old friends Yeats and Lady Gregory. One night at dinner with Tonks, Moore talked about Carlyle. 'I have been reading some memoirs of Carlyle,' said he. 'I think he was a nasty old man. He was not nice about any of the men of his time. He was not nice about Emerson. He was not nice about Samuel Taylor Coleridge, whom he once saw. He was not nice about Mill or Tennyson or——' 'Was he "not nice" about Yeats and Lady Gregory?' asked Max mildly. The rest of the company were much amused. Max was himself amused enough to write and tell both Reggie and Florence about the incident. He also wrote to them about Henry James.

'I met old Henry himself several times,' he said to Reggie: 'he has become one of the stock ornaments of dinner-tables, uniform with Sargent, Claude Phillips, etc.,—though he insists on being regarded as a recluse; and, wherever he is, nobody is *supposed* to see him there. All the same, he is in great form, really delightful to be with— though he hasn't a good word to say for anyone. I particularly want

[1] Ada Leverson's daughter.

to read him on the subject of Arnold Bennett, of whose *Hilda Less-ways* he said (but will not perhaps put in writing) that it was "like the slow squeezing-out of a big, dirty sponge". He was splendid about a production of Hamlet by William Poel at the Little Theatre. Somebody had taken him to see it, and I asked him what it was like. "Like? Like? It was like Morning Prayers in a work-house!" '

And to Florence:

'I did so wish for you here last Wednesday, for on that day I lunched at the Lewises, and oh you ought to have been there: Henry James was; and so amusing and interesting—nothing much to *repeat*, but delightful at the time. His heart seems to be bad; he looked ill when he came in. And afterwards, when he drove me in a taxi to the Savile, and came in with me to the Savile, he said he must not walk upstairs; so we sat in the billiard-room. All of which gave an additional force of pathos to his remark that "Gosse is a man whom one would prefer to survive!" '

Max also wished Florence had seen the Opening of Parliament. He had never been present at this ceremony before.

'Oh darling,' he exclaimed to her, 'I do so wish you were there with me in the Royal Gallery—you would have loved it so, with your feeling for England. *There* was essence of England, all the history of England, and the charm and wonderfulness that you feel more than I do. The Royal Gallery is just a large hall, leading to the Lords. It is where the royal procession forms and thence passes to the Lords and then passes back. Such a sight! We were admitted—the ticket-holders—at noon, and had to wait till 2.0 before the actual thing, but this wasn't tedious because of the preparations, the gradual gathering of functionaries. Lord Lincolnshire (erstwhile Lord Carrington and "Champagne Charlie") looking on, in a frock-coat, and then retiring and re-emerging with wonderful quickness in ermine and scarlet and with a white wand. All sorts of other peers in their robes fussing around. The Beefeaters lining up along the corridor. The Gentle-men-at-Arms too, led by Colonel Fletcher—these casting back to the Waterloo period, while the Beefeaters exhaled sheer Elizabeth; and the two Royal pages; and the Life Guards; and the Lord Chan-cellor with his train-bearer; and Lord Crewe with the Sword of

State; and Lord Winchester with the Cap of Maintenance; and two trumpeters of the Life Guards stationed outside the doors of the Robing Room that were at last thrown open: then an absolute hush, and a fanfaronade of the trumpets, and then the *very* slowly-passing procession of all the emblems and ornatenesses—the heralds and the equerries and the everything-elses—and at the end of them, hand in hand, the King and Queen. And after they had passed I found myself with tears in my eyes and an indescribable sadness—sadness for the King—the little King with the great diamonded crown that covered his eyebrows, and with the eyes that showed so tragically much of effort, of the will to please—the will to impress—the will to be all that he isn't and that his Papa *was* (or seems to him to have been)—the will to comport himself in the way which his wife (a head taller than he) would approve. Oh such a piteous, good, feeble, heroic little figure. I shall never forget the sight. Darling, I think you would have wept outright. It would have been too much for you, the touchingness of it. So perhaps, after all, it is well that you weren't there.'

Florence replied:

'It must have been a marvellously moving scene—the entrance of the King and Queen. You have given it all to me so that I cannot regret not having been there—only happy that you were. And will you really be content to come from all this interest—all those interesting people—to Rapallo and be again there alone with me?'

This letter shows Florence still nervous lest Max might be bored by life with her. Max gave her no cause. He wrote as often as ever and as affectionately: he worried if he did not hear from her regularly: if he thought she might take some teasing quip of his too seriously, he sought hastily to put things right.

'Darling, after I posted my latest letter, I had a "panic" that you might think I meant *seriously* some sentence I wrote about your "indirectness" in not saying how long your brothers thought you *ought* to stay. I meant the sentence to be written with a *laughing* tone —and in memory it sounded as if it might sound to you *disagreeable* —which was a source of much worry to me—"morbid" worry, I hope. . . . Goodnight, my dear darling love. I am living in the prospect of seeing you. I can't imagine that anything lovelier could

331

happen to anyone than my seeing you and being with you again.'

But nothing he could say could make her feel completely safe. Florence was capable of rapturous moments; she will burst out enthusiastically about the beauty of the sea or the kindness of some fellow passenger or her love for Max. But it is only for a moment. Soon she relapses into a wandering strain in which she passes inconsequently from subject to subject, always with an undertone of anxiety in her voice—about money, about the troubles of the world; and about Max too. Is he sure he is well, is he not doing too much, she asks; how she wishes she could express her feelings better!

'Darling, I must come home for you will grow to dislike me if I continue to write expressing myself always so badly, telling so little of all that is going on, of all that I feel: but I could not love you more however well I might be able to say it.'

All Max could do was to tell her to try to be cheerful and assure her that everything would be right once they were back at the Villino. For himself he longed to be there for every reason.

'Towards the end of my time in London,' he told Reggie after he got back, 'I began to feel as strong a hatred of London as I used to have when I lived there. When first we arrived in London, the place only seemed to me ridiculous and (having to be tolerated only for a couple of months or so) tolerable; but presently it began to oppress me, and the relief of being away from it is immense. All the chatter and clatter and hustle and guzzle—not one single person having a good time, and not one single person thinking of anything *but* the having of a good time.'

These are severe words; but though he had grown more tolerant of individuals, his moral judgements in general were growing more severe. The flippant and sophisticated surface of his personality had always rested on simple and moral foundations: in spite of irony and Oscar Wilde, Max had continued to believe in fidelity and self-restraint and modest contentment. These beliefs began to show more as he grew older; and much more after his marriage and retirement to Italy. It was a good thing: for it was this that made him so considerate and responsible a husband. But it also meant that, if he came back to London, he found himself conscious of a gulf separating him from the people he met there. Pryde and Nicholson, for instance, were both involved in painful matrimonial troubles. Max wrote to Florence that he felt an irrepressible movement of disgust at the spectacle, when he contrasted it with the peace and stability of his life with her in Italy.

'What a ridiculous sort of life those people lead, don't they? I am glad you and I are not ridiculous people. I am glad we are you and I—though the main point, of course, is that you are you and that there is no one in the world to be compared with you, dear sweet pet.'

Fashionable life too had lost some of its charm for him. Max dined one night with Sir Philip Sassoon, a magnificent young patron of the arts, at his mansion in Park Lane. It was an agreeable party and he liked Sassoon: but somehow Max did not feel at home in his house.

'On Wednesday I dined with Philip Sassoon, . . .—Sargent and Lady Essex completed the party—which I found rather dull somehow, though Lady E. is a charming person. I suppose the rooms of the house through which one passes into the dining-room are too many and too perfect. Also the dining-room itself is too big for less than 1000 diners. One little perfect porphyry table without a table-cloth; and a crystal bowl with a lid, and with pink carnations floating inside it, in the middle; and Voisin cuisine—and two automobiles without—it takes the heart out of one—and one only wants to say "I'm glad I'm not rich", and one can't say that, and so one is rather at a loss. . . .'

Rightly or wrongly the England of 1914 seemed to him a worse place than the England of his youth. That spring he wrote sadly to Dora: 'And oh for those old civilized and characterful days! They wring one's heart. But it's well to have lived in them.'

CHAPTER ELEVEN

The First War

(1)

H E was to regret the past far more sharply before the summer was over. Its beginning was unclouded enough. Max found life in Italy doubly delightful by contrast with life in England. Back at the Villino he passed long blissful days on the terrace in a white coat, drawing and writing. He felt inspired to start two new stories during these months—'James Pethel' and 'Enoch Soames'. Then, in August 1914 broke out the first World War. It brought Max's idyllic existence completely to an end, it might be for ever, so far as he could tell. For the time being, indeed, its outward ordering did not change. Italy was not yet involved in the fighting and Max was well over military age: autumn and winter found him and Florence still at the Villino and still occupying their days much as in previous years. But the spirit that had animated their life had fled. Max was not shallow. He could not avert his eyes from the war. He did not try to. It was too tremendous an event and he found himself too deeply concerned in it. For Max warmly espoused his country's cause. He thought the Germans wholly in the wrong and the English right to fight them. That they should do so filled him with pride: all his latent patriotism flooded forth in their support. All the same, he felt profoundly depressed. No rapturous Rupert-Brooke-like sense of glory for him! He saw the facts too clearly.

'What a world!' he cried to Reggie. 'What a period we have been born into! It is very epical and all that; but the horror and sadness and absurdity of it! The horror duly horrifies me, and the sadness saddens, whereas by the absurdity "we are", like Queen Victoria, "not amused". If the whole thing were a sort of *purge* for the human race, if presently the human race were going to feel, and be, *better*, I shouldn't so much mind. But, so far as one can foresee, the thing is not so much a purge as an additional poison: there will be more hatred and bitterness and unrest after the war than there was before; more sulks and scowls, and preparations for other wars, than ever.

It is all very well to talk about beating Germany to her knees, free-
ing Europe from the dread of an insolent hegemony, and so forth.
But not the most bloodthirsty person proposes that Germany shall
be altogether crushed out of existence; and I am sure that whatever
is left of her will have even more recuperative power than France
had after 1870, and a more urgent spirit; so that either she will have
to be crushed all over again (as Bismarck wanted to crush France in
'75), which wouldn't be a very pretty thing to do, nor an epical
thing; or we shall in the not very remote future have the epical
business all over again. All this is assuming that Germany will this
time go under. I live, from day to day and hour to hour, on tenter-
hooks of hope that Germany will in the end be beaten this time. My
breadth and delicacy of mind, and my far-sighted misgivings, come
out only when I set pen to paper. They are but a part of my literary
style. In myself I yield to no one—not to the most rabid of non-
combatants—in the bitterness of my feelings against Germany, in
depression at her triumphs, and joy at the least of her reverses: . . .

Dear England has behaved with all the fineness one expects of her;
and I love to think of her fleet and its magnificent success the world
over, and its superb little raid on the Heligoland ships. She deserves
the good fortune she has in being an Island and safe. But, just as I
haven't the slightest fear that any attempt at invasion would not be
an immediate and ludicrous fizzle, so do I not see how, if Russia
and France fail, she, with the best will in the world, and with all her
Colonies doing all they can, and with America sympathizing to the
utmost, can hope to beat Germany on land. Of course, if Germany
could be starved by the fleet, then . . . but I don't see how Germany
can be prevented from getting enough food through various
channels. Perhaps Germany can be prevented. I am very ignorant.
Anyhow the *spirit* of England is beautiful. Ever since I have lived
away from England I have been growing more and more fond and
proud of England as an *idea*. As such, there never has been or will be
anything to touch her. Florence has always loved her—loved her at
first sight. As soon as I got away from England, and began to see
England with a fresh, a stranger's eye, I began to share and understand Florence's love of her. As you can imagine, Florence has been
much horrified and appalled by the war; all the same, we are two
Jingoes together, tearing open the *Capparo* in the early morning,
devouring the *Corriere* and *Stampa* in the afternoon, walking down

into Rapallo every evening to be exalted or downcast by the tele-grams posted up in the Piazza.'

Max disliked the war all the more because he felt both his work and himself to be out of place in it. It did not shake his ultimate belief in his art; this was too integral and fundamental a part of his personality. But he did have the sense that his was not the kind of art appropriate to the Armageddon of the twentieth century. In December 1914 he wrote to Gosse:

'It seems absurd to write to anyone about anything but the war. It seems to argue a lack of sense of proportion. But if I wrote anything about the war, not less guilty should I seem of that lack. What could I write that would not seem utterly trivial in proportion to this theme? One needs to be Dante at least for any such enterprise.'

As for his proposed exhibition of cartoons in April, Max now thought it out of the question.

'I have been hoping against hope,' he wrote to Brown and Phillips, 'that there might be some gleam of prospect that the world would be at peace soon. But it is now, of course, as positive as anything can be that the war will not be over in the Spring; and probable that it will on the contrary be raging with special ferocity.

Therefore I now write (and I am sure you won't be unprepared for my writing) to ask that the exhibition of my caricatures, arranged for next April–May, may be indefinitely postponed.

If I were a landscape-painter, or a portrait-painter, or anything but a caricaturist, of course I shouldn't think of making a request of this kind. I daresay that my kind of exhibition suffers in war-time; but there is no reason why exhibitions of the usual kind should be postponed. The case of my particular show is on an altogether differ-ent footing. My caricatures, exhibited while England is in the throes of a life-and-death struggle, would not merely fall flat: they would be an offence against decency. In time of peace, they are delightful, no doubt; but imagine a nation being called on, in the midst of a whole world's tragedy of suffering and horror, to enjoy my little jokes about Mr Hall Caine and Sir Gilbert Parker and Mr Bonar Law and Mr Sydney Webb and other people whose foibles, in time of peace, are very good fun, but whose very existence is forgotten in time of war. The idea is inconceivable. So long as the war lasts (and indeed, I think, for some months after peace has been declared) my caricatures must be kept locked up in a drawer. I don't take in any of the English comic papers. Do they still go on, I wonder? Are they publishing funny pictures of the Kaiser? Perhaps they are. It is a chastening possibility. But of course you wouldn't expect me to vie with them.

The war is no laughing matter; and the war is *the only matter* in the present and in the near future.

Of course it is for me a very great disappointment not to have the show to which I had so been looking forward. My only consolation is that you will meanwhile find no difficulty in organizing for April–May some other exhibition that will not, as mine would, be horrible in these days of sadness.'

Max—and Florence too—soon began to realize that they did not like spending these days of sadness at Rapallo. They even felt a sort of guilt at being away from their fellow countrymen. 'I want to be where English is spoken and English thoughts and feelings expressed,' Max told Will Rothenstein. And to Reggie:

'I have been wanting to go over to England with Florence to see my people and also to feel that I shall not have been away from England during the *whole* of England's hour of need. The delightfulness of being here at home has seemed to Florence and me almost oppressive while so many millions of people in England and elsewhere are having such a bad time.'

Accordingly, in the spring, he and Florence left for home: once there, they stayed. Max became much more cheerful once in England. For one thing it was not nearly so changed as he had feared; and for another, now he was, as it were, in the war zone, he now no longer felt himself bound in conscience to think all the time about the war. It turned out to be easier to do this than might have been expected. At first he thought of joining in the struggle itself, and offered himself for clerical war-work. He was directed to Queen Anne's Chambers, where two amiable men, after taking down his qualifications, handed him a card with his enrolment number, which was 131853. 'I gather I am up against a formidable amount of competition!' said Max. Too much competition, it seemed; for he heard no more from Queen Anne's Chambers. Meanwhile, he got a letter from a minister of the Government proposing he should contribute to the war effort by doing some propaganda cartoons. This idea did not appeal to him. Propaganda meant cartoons about the war and Max thought this a subject unsuited to his talent. It was against his artistic conscience to do work unsuited to his talent even in the cause of his country. Further, he judged rightly that, if the work were unsuited to his talent, it would be ineffective for its purpose. He maintained this position throughout the war. In 1917 Colonel Repington asked him to do some political drawings for the Sunday papers. But once again Max refused, and on the same grounds.

This is to anticipate. In the spring of 1915, William Rothenstein, who was living with his family in a farmhouse at Far Oakridge in Gloucestershire, invited Max and Florence to join him there. Since Max had nothing to do in London they accepted. For the next two years Far Oakridge was their headquarters. At first they lived in the Rothensteins' house; later they migrated to a pretty little furnished cottage near by, though they still came up to the Rothensteins' for their main meals. Max never had any country clothes, and every day he could be seen making his careful way up to luncheon and dinner in gloves and spats, carrying an elegant walking-stick, and in winter with socks over his boots to prevent slipping.

These walks were about all the exercise he ever took. Max may have left Italy but he carried his universe with him to his new abode. Once settled in the cottage he and Florence established a mode of life very much like that they lived at the Villino, regular, leisurely and confined. Except when he went up to the Rothensteins', Max only left the cottage to walk the hundred yards needed to reach the neighbouring Nelson Inn where he bought his cigarettes. Florence did not go out much either, for she disliked leaving Max in case he wanted anything. When she did go, however, she enjoyed it. The countryside stirred romantic sentiments in her. Now and again she tried unsuccessfully to make Max share these sentiments. One spring day when she was strolling with Alice Rothenstein near the cottage, she heard a bird singing and asked what it was. 'A lark,' said Alice. 'A lark?' exclaimed Florence excitedly. 'Max has never heard a lark!' And she hurried in to fetch him. The spring air was chilly and Max did not trust himself to it, till he had clothed himself in hat and coat and scarf and gloves. By the time he arrived, the lark had flown.

This, however, was an exceptional excursion. Most of the time he remained in the cottage sitting-room writing or drawing at a little green-clothed table on which were neatly disposed sheets of his favourite drawing-paper, blotting-paper in strips, paints, brushes and a glass of water.

(2)

It was, in fact, the most productive period of his life. The creative flow released by marriage and Italy, checked a little by the outbreak of war, had now started again and more strongly than before. For the fact that the real world was so disagreeable acted as an incentive for Max to absorb himself in the world of his imagination. As has often happened in history, the wish to escape was the goose that laid the golden eggs of art. The quality of his work too was more consistently good than at any other time in his life. Max's art had now attained its full maturity. The last shreds of youthful affectation and uncertainty had dropped away: his technical skill was at its peak: he had found himself completely both in style and subject-matter.

The most important drawings he did at this time were those he afterwards collected in a volume called *Rossetti and His Circle*. It is significant that these were concerned with a past period. Concentrating on them and shutting out the grim present, Max's imagination took flight from wartime England and travelled back fifty years to dwell delightedly in the mid-Victorian London of the Pre-Raphaelites and Carlyle and Whistler and Swinburne, amusing itself in inventing characteristic and imaginary incidents in their lives, imaginary and characteristic fragments of their talk. It had always been a favourite period with him: one of the best drawings in *The Poets' Corner* depicted Rossetti's garden in Cheyne Walk, crowded with strange animals and stranger artists. In his new drawings he explored this vein to the full. He wrote about it too; he started a fantastic tale called *The Mirror of the Past*. The hero of this is an imaginary elderly friend of his own and patron of the Pre-Raphaelites, Sylvester Herringham, who owns a mirror—gold-framed and convex like that on Max's own wall at the Villino—possessed of extraordinary powers, by which it retained the impression of each successive scene that had been reflected in it superimposed one on top of the other like the leaves of a book. Herringham bequeaths Max this mirror, thus giving him a chance to watch the shifting spectacle of the past unrolling itself on the wall of his sitting-room. The main bulk of the story was to consist of scenes and conversations with famous persons of the period. Max never finished *The Mirror of the Past*. He explained later that he had come to the conclusion that to make the device of the mirror plausible to a reader required what he had not got, a science-fiction type of imagination like that of H. G. Wells. But he sketched its outline and wrote various scenes which were intended to be included in it.

The Mirror of the Past was only one of several literary projects. During this period Max wrote a great many of the essays later printed in the volume called *And Even Now*, and also three exercises in fiction, 'Maltby and Braxton', 'A. V. Laider' and 'Savonarola Brown'. These were added to the two pieces already finished before he left Rapallo—'James Pethel' and 'Enoch Soames'—to be published two years later, in the autumn of 1919, under the title of *Seven Men*. In this book Max's art as a writer advances from *Zuleika Dobson* to reach its final and most fully matured expression. Not its most complete: since it is supposed to be a series of his own true reminiscences, *Seven Men* is written in a more realistic convention than any of his earlier tales; with the result that he has less chance in it to exhibit the more flamboyant and flowery strains in his talent. There are none of the sustained flights of decorative fancy that we find in *Zuleika Dobson*, nor is there a touch of sentiment in them, not even the half-ironic sentiment of *The Happy Hypocrite*. Max's comic sense, however, manifests itself in *Seven Men* more subtly and more substantially than anywhere else in his works. More variously too; it shows itself in different ways. 'James Pethel' is a realistic character study, only differing from a story by an ordinary novelist in that it is throughout vigilantly kept in the key of comedy; viewed from the humorist's angle adopted by Max, the more serious implications of Pethel's character and situation are out of sight. 'A. V. Laider' is a whimsical 'tall story', light-heartedly told and with a surprise twist at the end. 'Savonarola Brown' exhibits Max's gifts as a parodist. Introduced by a short satirical prologue, it consists mainly of a play intended no doubt as a parody of the pseudo-Shakespearean verse drama, but rising at moments to be a parody of Shakespeare himself. The two other stories, 'Enoch Soames' and 'Maltby and Braxton', blend satire and fantasy. 'Enoch Soames' satirizes the Decadent movement; 'Maltby and Braxton' satirizes Edwardian fashionable life; and both stories are also exercises in the comic supernatural. The satiric tone is characteristic of Max, not fierce and reformist, but gay, mischievous and, in a curious way, affectionate. Max makes his usual explanation for this. 'I suppose,' he remarks in 'Maltby and Braxton', 'one can't really understand what one doesn't love, and one can't make good fun without real understanding.'

Love and understanding can only come from personal knowledge. *Seven Men* is very much a personal document. Each story is inspired by some phase of its author's history, and involves a description of places and people he had known and lived among. 'Enoch Soames' is the product of Max's *Yellow Book* days. It starts in the Café Royal: William Rothenstein appears there in person, and both Soames himself and his works are a composite picture of the more absurd features of the typical *Yellow Book* writer. The second story, 'Maltby and Braxton', is prompted by Max's excursions into Edwardian high life after his first success. Keeb Hall is Taplow; the Duchess of Hertfordshire, Lady Desborough. Among the other guests, Lady Thisbe Crowborough is probably Lady Helen Vincent, and Lady Rodfitten, Theresa, Marchioness of Londonderry: Mr Balfour, like Rothenstein in the earlier tale, appears as himself. Max is also reported to have said that Braxton, Maltby's social rival, was suggested by Yeats. He can only have been partly suggested by him. Yeats, although aloof and self-absorbed in manner, never set up as a rough diamond as Braxton did. Of the other stories, 'Savonarola Brown' recalls Max's life as a dramatic critic, 'James Pethel' his holidays at Dieppe—its hero was suggested by an acquaintance of his called Hannay—and 'A. V. Laider' Max's solitary visits during the nineties to English seaside resorts out of season.[1] Of course, his previous tales had also been inspired by his personal experience: *Zuleika Dobson* by his Oxford days; *The Happy Hypocrite* by his love for Cissey Loftus. In both these, however, he keeps himself off-stage. *Seven Men* presents him on it and playing a leading part there. Thus

---

[1] It is not possible to date the composition of these stories exactly. But we gather from Max's letters that 'James Pethel' had been written in the summer of 1914, and 'Enoch Soames' between November 1914 and March 1915, 'A. V. Laider' was finished in 1915 and 'Savonarola Brown' and 'Maltby and Braxton' by 1917.

for the first time Max fuses two separate strains in his creative inspiration. Up till now he had appeared in person mainly in his essays. In *Seven Men* the essayist becomes a character in his own fiction. He emphasizes this by his title. The seventh man is Max himself, who both narrates the stories and plays a part in the action. In 'Maltby and Braxton' he makes, as it were, a double appearance. For Maltby, the victim-hero who relates his sad history to Max, is himself a caricature of certain characteristics of Maltby's creator: in laughing at Maltby's social embarrassments in the fashionable world, Max is laughing at his own. So also the character of A. V. Laider telling his tall story to Max comically reflects certain features of Max himself: his love of hoaxes, his tendency to let things slide in order to avoid awkwardness or trouble. Altogether *Seven Men* is the nearest Max ever got to autobiography.

It is not very near. As in his essays, Max gives us no direct self-portrait but a version of himself designed to suit his aesthetic purpose. Broadly speaking, it is the same version. Like the author of *Yet Again*, the narrator of *Seven Men* is Max, the detached observer, surveying the world, himself included, with demure irony. This means that some of the more serious aspects of the real Max are left out, his faith in art for instance, his high-strung nervous system, his unexpectedly stern vein of moralism. A comic artist, he used for his art only the comic aspects of himself. These, however, he passed through the crucible of his creative imagination to be projected with a vividness rarely found in straightforward autobiographies. Max brings himself bodily before us. We watch the characteristic expressions float across his face, note the characteristic idioms of his speech, follow the characteristic movements of thought and feeling, of which speech and voice are the expression.

Max often used to take his finished work—cartoon or manuscript, wrapped up with extreme care—to show the Rothensteins after dinner. Sometimes he read the literary composition aloud: the Rothensteins were enthusiastically appreciative. Once, it is true, when he was reading 'Maltby and Braxton', Alice Rothenstein fell asleep during the reading. Max noticed this and, in order to spare her the embarrassment of waking up after he had finished, began reading the last pages very loud indeed. This ruse was successful; Alice Rothenstein, startled by the din, opened her eyes before the end of the story. She also had her cunning; before risking any comment she remarked that she had found the story so delightful that she hoped he would read it again at once. Max explained that he was too hoarse: he saw through her scheme but was not offended. He did not take offence easily: besides, as he said when describing the scene, he did not take her slumbers as a serious criticism: he knew for certain that the story was good. As a matter of fact, he may have been partly responsible for her feeling drowsy, for he saw to it that any room he was in was hot. Max had a horror of cold; the three Rothenstein children observed that if he noticed a window was open on a winter evening he would wander round the room smoking and talking till he got near it. Then, assuming an absent-minded air, he would quickly shut it. The children also remarked his superstitious horror of crossed knives on a table-cloth. Surreptitiously they would cross them in order to watch Max—once more talking, in order to distract attention from what he was doing—surreptitiously put them straight again.

They found Max delightful as well as comic. He added to their fun. The household at Far Oakridge managed to get a great deal of fun out of life in these years in spite of the war; and Max was responsible for much of it. At once soothed and stimulated by the atmosphere of rural peace, the spirit of mischievous gaiety bubbled up in him once more. The evening was his time. When supper was over and the lamps lit and the night shut out by curtains, the party would settle down to amuse themselves writing communal verses, drawing caricatures, singing popular tunes. Max composed new words for the topical tunes; Max contributed the wittiest lines to the communal verses; and, of course, Max drew the best caricatures. Often they were of neighbours, for the Rothensteins made friends in the neighbourhood. The local worthies would have been surprised and bewildered had they known that the gentleman from London who sat so quietly in the corner was noting their idiosyncrasies with the intention of caricaturing them after they had left. As it was, they liked Max. He entered into local life so far as it came his way and felt friendly to those he met in it. When a rick near the cottage caught fire, Max felt so concerned for the farmer who owned it that he hurried out to help. The farmer was surprised and gratified at the strange spectacle of the middle-aged London dandy, in gloves, hat and overcoat, hurrying hither and thither with a heavy pail of water in each hand.

It was many years since Will Rothenstein had seen so much of his old friend. His eyes agleam behind his spectacles, he observed the middle-aged Max with the same sharp-eyed interest that he had observed Max the youth. He was mellowed now. 'After thirty, one should quarrel with no man,' Max said; and he strove to conform to this principle. All the same, he held some opinions very strongly. He was implacable about the Germans, for example; more than Rothenstein himself was. Nor was there any question of his changing his opinions to suit the changing times: he often found himself disagreeing with the young people about some new movement in art. Yet he got on easily with them just as he got on easily with the neighbours at Far Oakridge; because he liked them—'Young people now are much more polite than in my young days,' he said—and because the fact that people had always liked him gave him an unconscious confidence, so that he felt no need to assert himself. From his side, Max took a fresh look at the middle-aged Rothenstein. He was no longer the brilliant and exotic figure who had flashed down on Oxford in 1893. On the other hand, he was not the occasional source of irritation that he had been during Max's later years in London. Then Will had been irritating because he was touchy; and he was touchy because, beside Max, he felt himself a failure. Max, married and settled, did not make Will feel such a failure as did Max the sparkling and celibate man about town. No longer irritated, Max now looked at Will with affection and a little amusement. He was particularly amused by his passion for generalization. He wrote a rhyme about it:

'How do you do?' Will asked of me.
'Very well, thanks,' said I. Said he,
'Yes, I invariably find
Abundant health in all mankind.'

Next morning, 'How do you do?' asked Will.
I told him I was rather ill.
'Alas,' his voice tolled like a bell,
'Mankind was ever far from well.'

He also noted: 'On Will Rothenstein a generalization has the effect produced on an East-African nigger by rum.' This sentence comes from a notebook surviving from this period, in which Max jots down such thoughts and jokes as casually occurred to him. Some of these are characteristic and entertaining:

'The ant sets an example to us all; but not a good one.'
'It is only when they try to be young that the old seem old.'

CHAPTER TWELVE

'Seven Men'

(1)

MAX did not spend all the time at Far Oakridge. We hear of him in London lunching with Arnold Bennett in December 1915, and in April 1916 at Bognor. This summer found him and Florence for a short time in London staying at lodgings in Southwick Street. Back at Far Oakridge in the autumn, they stayed there till spring in the following year when Max came to London by himself for some weeks. At some time during this period Alice Rothenstein was also away from Far Oakridge. This worried Florence. After seven years' marriage she was as nervously concerned for the proprieties as ever! Was it quite proper, she asked Max agitatedly, that she should stay at Far Oakridge with William, unchaperoned save by the servants and children? Max wrote reassuringly that he was soon coming back.

Max had come to London on family affairs. The year 1917 was an eventful one for the Beerbohms. The first event was happy: in April, Max's sister Aggie remarried. Her husband, Ralph Neville, from whom she had been separated for many years, died; soon afterwards she married Vesey Knox, an Irishman, and went to live in Ireland. In July came misfortune. Herbert Tree, now sixty-four years old, had just returned from a ten-months whirlwind tour round the United States. Though his days were as hectic as ever and his love-life more than usually confused, Herbert was still radiant, bubbling over with projects and reminiscences and jokes. Max, meeting him one morning at Upper Berkeley Street, was amused at his quenchless vitality. A week or two later he fell downstairs and ruptured a tendon in his kneecap. He was operated on for this. Apparently with success: for a few days later he was sitting up in bed laughing, talking and peeling a peach. Suddenly he fell forward dead.

Max had seen little of Herbert in the last seven years. But he could not fail to be moved. Herbert had been the glorious hero of his childhood, his figure associated itself with who knows how many thrilling and precious memories of former days, visits to the theatre from Charterhouse, suppers at the Garrick Club, the tumultuous American tour, his first acquaintance with Oscar, with Kilseen, with Constance Collier. Musing he stood looking down at the dead Herbert.

'His face was both familiar and strange,' he noted. 'Death, that preserves only what is essential, had taken away whatever it is that is peculiar to the face of an actor. Extreme strength of character and purpose was all that remained and outstood now. But at the corners of the lips there was the hint of an almost whimsical, an entirely happy smile.'

The immediate effect of Herbert's death was to plunge Max into an unprecedented amount of practical activity. For he was the only surviving male member of the Beerbohms; and Maud Tree, forgetful of any earlier friction between them, now turned to him for help in everything. The fact was Max tended to avoid practical activities because they bored him, not because he was inefficient. If he had to take action he knew how to do it. He rose to the occasion now. Calmly and competently he made the arrangements for Herbert's funeral, wrote round to various newspapers to ensure that any tributes to Herbert were written by the right people, saw to the disposal of his pictures and posters and spent long hours going through his brother's papers. He destroyed those which were indiscreet to keep and sent on the others to Maud Tree. 'Max has been simply wonderful to Maud,' writes Constance, 'working so hard for her all the time.'

Nine months later, in March 1918, old Mrs Beerbohm followed her stepson to the grave. She had been failing more and more during the last three years, so much so that she had hardly taken in Herbert's death. No one could think her death a tragedy. But for Max it was a landmark that inevitably cast a shadow over his spirit.

'It has been a sad and sorrowful time for my sisters and for Florence and me,' he told Lady Lewis. 'We were all with my dear Mother when the end came; and it is some comfort that she died very peacefully, without any pain.

She had no ailment of any kind. Her heart gradually ceased to beat, merely by reason of her great age. Her memory, and her power to realize things, had been failing during the past three years. But in such years as these have been, in a world so full of horror, one cannot say that this was not a blessing. And, though her memory went, her sweetness and charm of nature was as ever.'

Mrs Beerbohm's friends, as represented by Robbie Ross, spoke her epitaph more lightly but with hardly less affection:

'On Friday I went to dear old Mrs Beerbohm's funeral. There were about 30 people present. Characteristically enough, Viola Tree arrived late, and Lady Tree, plunged in grief and mourning, and a large hired barouche, came after the funeral service was over. I was so fond of the old lady: she reminded me of a fairy godmother.'

By this time Max and Florence had moved from Far Oakridge to London. Their move marks the slackening of that unprecedented creative flow which Max had maintained ever since his marriage. The next two years were spent largely in preparing for publication work done during the creative period; he did little new work. He and Florence lodged in Well Walk, Hampstead, looked after by a landlady called Mrs Hatton, friendly and old-fashioned. So was the atmosphere of Well Walk which, with its line of old terraced houses and empty of noise and traffic, seemed like a fragment of eighteenth-century Bath strayed into twentieth-century London. Max looked an appropriate figure there. A fellow lodger, called Lloyd, used to watch him strolling fastidiously along the pavement. Lloyd also observed Florence, who roused in him the same surprise as she had in Arnold Bennett.

'She was rather tall and slender,' he said, 'with a pallid face and a mass of near-red hair. She wore always in the house a voluminous gown of dead black crêpe-like material that swept the ground, so that she would lift the skirt with both hands as she went up and down stairs. In giving greeting she would move only her lips. I never saw her smile, or look displeased.'

Living out of the world in Italy or Gloucestershire, Max and Florence had not kept up with the changing times: so that now in their middle age they struck people who did not know them with the strangeness of figures surviving from a past age. Max, plumper than formerly and with thinning hair, still exhibited the elaborate gestures and courtly airs of an Edwardian aesthetic dandy; Florence, though a little faded and with her youthful shy eagerness gone, still moved through the world with the mannered grace and dreamy gaze of a Pre-Raphaelite damosel.

Max made some new friends during these War years; in particular Egan Mew. Mew was an agreeable *bon viveur*, who wrote for a periodical called *Every Week*, and had an expert knowledge of old china and a taste in humour which led him both to appreciate Max and to amuse him. They became close friends who went to theatres together, dined together at small restaurants—where the dinner was carefully ordered by Egan Mew—and exchanged letters full of drawings, jokes and pleasant nonsense. At this period also, Max established a memorable literary connection. Six years earlier, lunching one day at the Savile Club, he had noticed a young man, very tall and thin with a square-cut beard and dressed unconventionally in a red tie and brown velveteen jacket. He looked rather like one of the twelve apostles, Max thought, more especially the doubting one who was also called Didymus. He inquired who he was and was told he was a young writer called Lytton Strachey. Max remembered him sufficiently well to be interested when in 1917 Desmond MacCarthy told him that Strachey was bringing out a book about the Victorians which he, Max, was likely to enjoy. This book, *Eminent Victorians*, appeared in April 1918 and made a sensation. Among many of the older generation of readers it was a disagreeable sensation: they thought the book a flippant and irreverent attack on the great and noble dead. Not so Max. MacCarthy had been right, he was delighted as he had not been delighted by a book for many years. It was about his favourite subject, the recent historical past, and it was told in a graceful, civilized, ironical manner which was exactly to his taste—all the more because it was such a contrast to the strident grimness of the war atmosphere. As for Strachey's flippancy and irreverence, they were qualities that had always appealed to Max and added to his pleasure. Further, they gave him a sense of affinity with the author. It was natural they should. For the reader looking back from the distance of forty-six years can now see that Strachey represented a further advance in a movement of which Max had been an originator. Was it not he and his friends who had first made fun of the Victorians? And had not they shocked their elders as Strachey now shocked his? Max felt to him as to a younger brother. He sat down and wrote him a warm letter of congratulation. Strachey, who had long been an admirer of Max's, replied with an equally warm letter of thanks. This interchange led to what was to be the most significant new literary relationship of Max's later life. It was not a personal relationship. Though the two met from time to time they never got the chance to become intimate friends. But Strachey became Max's chief link with the younger generation of writers. He read and re-read his works and admired them extravagantly. Indeed, he went so far as to say that Strachey was a prose writer of the finest quality a far greater wit than himself. This was to overrate Strachey's art which, though deft and lively, is a crude affair compared to that of Max. Max overrated it as he had overrated Oscar Wilde's, and for the same reason; Strachey, he thought, was an artist of the same kind as himself and with the same aesthetic ideal. He thus saw his books through a glow of sympathy which softened their crudities and added a glory to their merits. Fourteen years later, back at Rapallo, he got news of Strachey's premature death; an emotion solemn and regretful rose in him craving to find expression in some ritual gesture. Going to the bookcase, Max took out Strachey's latest volume and wrote in it 'And now Brother for all time, Hail and Farewell'.

(2)

Eminent Victorians appeared in April 1918. In November the same year the war ended. Florence was away at the time and Max alone at Well Walk. Max wrote to her just before the Armistice.

'I have been to the tube for a paper, but there is no sort of official news since the morning, so I didn't wire. I suppose you saw the armistice terms in the *Daily News* this morning. It doesn't seem possible that the Germans (I hope the Censor won't open this letter and assume that I am a traitor for not saying the Huns) should accept unless they really have crocked up militarily; but with the collapse of Austria one is hopeful, for it seems that the Allies could quickly form a new front and invade Germany from the east. Espérons! How nice if Germany really does have to give in at once!'

The tone of this is notably livelier and more relaxed than that of Max's letters at the beginning of the war. Good news was restoring him to normal. Indeed, his armistice-week correspondence with Florence shows him with plenty of attention to spare for other things than public affairs.

'There is a new green-grocer in Well Walk,' he tells her. 'The window shows some real white cauliflowers glaring defiance across the way; I am rather on the side of the newcomers.'

And his landlady has a very trying child staying with her called Lena:

'Yesterday she came in with Annie and asked in a loud voice "Who is that man?" I behaved with all courtesy. This morning she came into my bedroom when I was in a dressing gown. "What are you doing?"—"I am dressing"—"What for?"—"For breakfast"—"What's breakfast?" etc. The child has a squint, which I think was less marked last summer than it is now. . . . She has developed a peculiar laugh, which I often hear on the stairs—very loud, mirthless, and wholly from the throat. I heard her say to Annie, after one of the peals, "I carn't 'elp larfing"—for which I was sorry.'

The next twelve months were restless and uncertain. Max no longer felt it his duty to stay in England. He wanted to get back to Italy as soon as he could. Though, to quote his own words, he might love 'the idea of England', he found this idea when translated into fact growingly displeasing. He hated change. And everything was changing. Changing for the worse too, in his view; the trends he had discerned in 1910 were moving ever faster. England that year grew vulgarer, uglier, more rushed, more given up to commercialism and democracy. Max's distaste was increased by fear. The last years had revealed that the forces of savagery lay just beneath the surface of civilization ready to burst through at any strain and plunge the world into chaos. They still seemed likely enough to do so. Events in Russia showed that the evil spirit of war had called up the evil spirit of revolution. Who knew what country next might get into its clutches! It could even be England; Max read in the papers the bitter speeches of some Labour leaders. Could it be, he wondered, that the English working class were turning into savage revolutionaries seething with hate for their so-called superiors and bent on their destruction? No doubt this would involve their own destruction: but this might not stop them. The war convinced Max that mankind can be possessed by a perverse impulse towards suicide. Seen in the light of later events such feelings look needlessly alarmist; Max's good sense seems to have failed him. But nothing shakes good sense as nervousness does. Max was nervous. The political situation, as he saw it, threatened the foundations on which he rested the philosophy of living. To maintain his chosen attitude of detachment a man had to feel his form of life secure. The idea of revolutionary change shook Max's confidence in his security; and with it his power of balanced judgement. It would, however, be very misleading to represent Max as deeply disturbed by political events or even as thinking about them often. He had been shielded from direct experiences of the horrors of war; with the result that his prevailing mood was calm. All the same he wished he was out of things. He longed—how he longed!—to go back to the Villino.

For the moment, however, he could not do this. Travelling was too difficult and, besides, the Beerbohms did not know what life in Italy was like after four years' absence. It might have grown too expensive for them, perhaps the Villino was no longer habitable. Further, Max had a good deal of work to do before he could leave England. He had to see *Seven Men* through the press and collect the essays he had lately written in preparation for a new volume to appear in the following year. Maud Tree, too, wanted him to edit a volume of tributes to Herbert. With all this to do, the Beerbohms found themselves forced to linger in England for another year after the Armistice. At last, in September 1919, Florence left for Italy. Max would not go with her because he had not yet finished his work on the book about Herbert. Florence also thought it better that she should go first to see what conditions were like in Italy; if they were all right she wanted to be alone to get the house ready for Max. He followed her in December. During their separation he wrote to her every day, so that we suddenly get a small patch of his life emerging from the general twilight to be illuminated in detail.

Unluckily it was not a very interesting patch. Max spent the first weeks staying with Maud Tree in her country house at Glottenham in Sussex, working on the book about Herbert. In September a national railway strike broke out. In Max's present mood this struck him as an extremely ominous event; and he found no comfort in the fact that the English were taking it coolly. Thus had they taken the news of the Archduke's assassination in 1914: they had not realized that this was the prelude to the greatest war in history. Perhaps they did not realize that this strike might be the prelude to a major clash between the forces of civilization and the forces of revolution. Max was all for resisting the strikers. In fact the strike ended in compromise. Max could only hope it was not an ignominious compromise. When he thought the matter over, he admitted that the Government and its leader, Lloyd George, were partly to blame for the trouble. Who could trust a man who had just tricked people into electing him and his party in the recent jingo General Election with its slogan of 'Hang the Kaiser'? Though Max was now so much opposed to the Left, he detested jingo aggressiveness as much as ever.

One other episode, interesting to a biographer, occurred during this stay at Glottenham. Left alone one evening, Max picked up a book, *The Florentine Frame*, by a serious female novelist of the period called Elizabeth Robins. He read a page or two with growing depression at what he felt to be its solemn commonplace wordiness: on an impulse he flung it into the fire. This episode became the basis of 'A Crime', one of the best of all his essays. He did not stick to the facts exactly. In reality the book was successfully destroyed; in the essay, the book put the fire out leaving Miss Robins victorious. This change throws light on Max as an artist. He has made it partly to make a more effective and surprising end to his story and, apparently, because it gives him a chance to make some characteristic fun of himself for his failure to achieve his purpose.

During these weeks he heard frequently from Florence. She had arrived at the Villino to find herself welcomed by her old servants and also by Gordon Craig and his family who, it appears, had settled in a house only a stone's throw away. Florence was not altogether pleased about this, she never liked Max's men friends living near. However, her communications were full of good news. The house was in good condition, the Italians were friendly, living in Italy was still cheap. Moreover, she had found a number of his drawings and was sending them home in case he might want to sell them. Max was interested to get the drawings and delighted to find he thought them good.

'Very odd to see the drawings once more—"Far away and long ago" with a vengeance! The peaceful world they were done in, and the standing desk they were done on, and the sunshine, all come back so vividly! I think some of the drawings are really very remarkable—unberufen—I had forgotten how good especially were many of the designs. I shall take them to the Leicester Galleries. I am not sure that I should like a regular exhibition. But assuredly there must be some money to be made out of them.'

By this time he was in London. He went there in the middle of October to finish going through Herbert's papers. This time he stayed at a flat in Grove Place, Hampstead. He lived there quietly and economically, often lunching at the confectionary shop opposite his lodgings and dining off scrambled eggs cooked by his landlady. Now and again he dined out; mostly with old friends like Mew and the Nicholsons. One evening at the Nicholsons he met W. H. Davies, the tramp poet. Max liked him. He told Florence that he was 'a dear little genial happy person'. For once his perspicacity had failed him: Davies that evening was neither genial nor happy. Personal or social inferiority had made him suspicious; and though he had to admit Max was an amusing talker, he thought him deliberately malicious. Davies had originally been discovered and helped by Bernard Shaw; Max praised Shaw for this. He said that Shaw liked helping lame dogs over stiles. Unfortunately it happened that Davies had a wooden leg and he leapt to the extraordinary conclusion that Max was deliberately mocking his infirmity. This delusion was to cause trouble some years later. The other guests at the Nicholsons that evening were a rich and cultivated couple called Johnson. Unlike Davies, they liked Max very much, and invited him to dinner. He flinched from the thought of adding to his engagements. 'Oh, London!—oh absence of loopholes!' he sighed to Florence—but he went and he enjoyed it.

'The dinner at the Johnsons—or Johnstones—was very pleasant. They have a nice flat in Adelphi House—a tall building facing *along* the Terrace. Barrie lives overhead, and he joined us after dinner. It was odd to see him suddenly appear with his lack-lustre eye and his rolling gait—very *fat* in the figure now, but looking frightfully ill—deep and extraordinarily *black* circles under the eyes. Poor little man! He has neuritis of the right arm—has agonies if he attempts to write. He can't dictate; and he says his brain seems sulky and un-willing to work when he writes with his left hand. The J's appear to be vaguely rich—at least, their drawing-room and dining-room are packed with paintings by McEvoy—which I suppose means riches. Very good white wine and port—but no champagne—I begin to despair of *ever* seeing champagne again—I think I must buy myself a pint before I leave England.'

Florence commiserated with Max about the champagne. In return she invited him to sympathize with her about the Craig family who, it appeared, had tactlessly invaded her privacy. She longed for them to live somewhere else. Perhaps they soon would, Max replied, soothingly. Meanwhile Ted Craig was a very old friend and he must ask Florence to try to be friendly to him.

'Gordon Craig's letter is touching,' he writes on one occasion. 'One *must* be nice to him. I don't see *why* you shouldn't lend him the book with the inscription—but of course don't if you feel you don't like the idea of doing so.'

The book referred to in this letter is *Seven Men*, which was published in the middle of November. Max was very pleased with its recep-tion. He had enthusiastic letters from Lytton Strachey and Walter Raleigh, and had been congratulated on it in person by Lord Balfour. He told Florence about this but added that what pleased him most was that she should like the book. He took the opportunity to pay her a tribute for all she had done for him in the last nine years.

'I am immensely pleased and touched, darling, by what you say of my stories. They would never have been written but for you. I should probably still be doing dramatic criticisms! And besides your advice has always been such a great help to me, and your encouragement. I well remember the *P.M.G.* criticism of you as Rebecca, and I remember the others too. I am afraid I robbed the world of more than I ought to have. Darling love, I hope you will be happy with me. I love you all the world.

Your own
Max.'

Max took pains to be especially warm to Florence because the separation was making her restive and despondent. Why was he so long in coming? she asked. Could it be that he was enjoying himself in England and bored at the thought of solitude with her at Rapallo? To these old questionings Max made the old answers. He did not like London, he longed to be with her, he loved her very much. She was reluctant to be comforted; and for once his patience began to show signs of wear.

'As I have written before, you surely know that I am only dying to get away and haven't wasted a moment in which I could have been working. I only wish I were more efficient and quicker. When you asked me once or twice in letters whether I *wanted* to stay on, I didn't answer because I didn't imagine the question to be intended seriously. But I have all the time been telling you how eager I was to get away, haven't I? . . . Well, darling, I hope you are not annoyed with me—your letters seem rather as if you were. Really I have been doing all that a man could.'

Next day, as if afraid he had sounded a little too sharp, he wrote:

'Darling love, I am hurrying to get away as fast as ever I can. You do understand that, surely. I love you all the world, and you are all the world to me. How lovely to be coming!'

Florence appeared convinced: anyway she had not much longer to wait. By 5 December Max, helped by his sister Aggie, had finished his packing and was ready to start. When she got the news Florence —so she told him—did a little dance by herself on the Villino terrace.

(3)

During these last months in England he had planned and started a satirical fantasy called *The Dreadful Dragon of Hay Hill*. He did not finish it till some years later. It is more appropriate, however, to examine it now. For the mood and thought it mirrors were those of 1918 and 1919. It is a comment on human nature as revealed by the war. This makes it different from anything else Max wrote in two important respects. In the first place it is not inspired by any phase of his own private experience; and secondly, the satire is 'serious' satire propounding a moral judgement on human nature of general application. The story, set in prehistoric London, describes how the

"Hopping in a hat
and a apron"

FLORENCE ON THE TERRACE AT THE VILLINO

Homelanders, a small, discontented and quarrelsome community, are attacked by a dragon. In face of the common danger they make up their differences and are better, and happier, than before. But the hero, Thol, in order to win the love of the heroine, Thia, kills the dragon, with the result that the Homelanders, freed from the fear that visited them, fall back into their old quarrelsome habits, while Thia, now married to Thol, gradually tires of him. In order to regain her love, Thol therefore concocts a hoax by which the Homelanders are persuaded to believe that another dragon is threatening to attack them. The ruse is successful. Thia returns to Thol and together they keep the hoax going. The Homelanders become happy and cooperative once more, till the death of Thia and Thol reveals the truth to them: after which, they relapse for a second time into their original condition. Max writes a concluding comment:

'And thus—does our tale end unhappily? I think not. After all, the Homelanders at large are rather shadowy to us. . . . It is Thol and Thia that we care about. For their sake we wish that the good they did could have been lasting. But it is not in the nature of things that anything—except the nature of things—should last. Saints and wise statesmen can do much. Their reward is in the doing of it. They are lucky if they do not live long enough to see the undoing. It should suffice us that Thol and Thia together in their last days knew a happiness greater than they had ever known. . . .'

Though *The Dreadful Dragon of Hay Hill* is written with the confident accomplishment of Max's prime, it is not from a literary point of view one of his best works. Contrary to his principles, he has for once gone outside his creative range; and he pays the penalty. To be at his best Max had to be personal. Moreover, moral satire of this kind, if it deals, even by implication, with so grim a theme as war, should have a sharper edge to it than is compatible with Max's playful urbanity. Yet *The Dreadful Dragon of Hay Hill* is extremely interesting to the biographer for the light that it throws on its author's view of life at this point in his history. It shows how much the war had confirmed and increased Max's distrust of humanity in the mass. As he wrote to Florence, in the winter of 1919:

'One of the letters that came today is the one in which you describe the loveliness of the aspect of sea and sky, and the contrast of it with the news of mankind. Mankind certainly does come out idiotically, or worse. I never had very great faith in it; but even I am disappointed.'

The story of *The Dreadful Dragon of Hay Hill* illustrates this disappointment. What Max had seen of the world in the war years had convinced him that humanity as a whole was incapable of moral progress. Men are incurably foolish and quarrelsome. Danger and disaster may unite them for a while; by taking them out of themselves, it may even make them happy. But when danger and disaster are past, men forget the lessons they have learnt from them. Yet, as the last paragraph of the story suggests, Max's view was not wholly pessimistic. If he disbelieved in man in the mass, he still believed in man the individual. Saints and wise men did exist; the affection one individual felt for another was a true good, and brought lasting happiness.

Personal affection had always been one of the two things that Max valued most. The other was his inner imaginative life. This, too, he still believed in. Indeed the war had increased his sense of its value; for it had made him concentrate on it, in order to distract himself from the painful outside world. Altogether, disillusioning though the last years had been, Max had emerged from them still able to think life well worth living. But only if it was lived on his own terms: the war had strengthened his determination to keep out of things; more than ever he desired to be back in Italy. Once there, however, he thought he could be happy.

CHAPTER THIRTEEN

Italian Days

H E was right: Max had always understood himself very well. He stayed at the Villino for the best part of the next fifteen years, and for most of that time his life was happy. It was also uneventful. Intermittently he and Florence kept a sort of joint jotting diary. From it and other records we get an impression of their life. Against an idyllic background of lemon trees, olive groves and Mediterranean skies—both Max and Florence refer a great deal to the garden and the weather—the course of their days unfolds itself before our mind's eye in leisurely monotony. The scene is always the Villino. Except in summer when he went down to the sea to bathe, Max hardly ever left its grounds. Florence, when her relations were over in Europe, now and again went for a little trip to see the sights of Italy. Max seldom accompanied her, though he wrote to her every day. Indeed, if he could help it he did not even walk down the hill to Rapallo. Instead, sprucely dressed in a beautifully pressed suit—tweed in winter, linen or flannel in summer —a flower in his buttonhole, and with his hat placed at an angle on his head—he passed his days on the terrace sitting or strolling up and down, now and again pausing to pull a dead head off a plant; or in his study, writing or drawing for half an hour. More drawing than writing; a central feature of Max's life during this phase was the gradual slackening of his creative inspiration. After 1922 he wrote very little. He still went on drawing; he held an exhibition in London every two or three years. But as time passed his impulse to draw also slowed up. There were no exhibitions after 1928.

What was the reason for the failure of his creative impulse? The obvious answer is lack of stimulus: Max was paying the price for cutting himself off from the vital current of his age. There is something in this; but not much. After all, he had said goodbye to the world in 1910; and done his best work in the years that followed. No—the cause of Max's failing power was deeper and more unavoidable. His talent had never been a vital one; with age its vitality declined still more. Further, his writing had always dealt mainly with experiences acquired before 1900—at Oxford, in London, in Dieppe. Like many other authors, only when young had he been sufficiently receptive to experience for it to penetrate into the depths of his personality and kindle his creative flame. By 1920 he had pretty well exhausted these earlier experiences. What then should he write about? Middle-aged writers are often faced with this problem. In order to solve it, most of them try frantically and unsuccessfully to write about fresh subjects that do not suit them: or they vainly attempt to repeat their old triumphs by concocting new versions of their old books. Max was too canny to fall into either of these traps; and too conscientious an artist. If he could not write his best he preferred not to write at all.

In his London days the gap left by dropping his work would have been filled by social and personal activities. This was so no longer. For a year or two the Craigs lived over the way; but after they had gone, the Beerbohms had no close friends established near. They deliberately avoided the local English colony. The chaplain of the Anglican church at Rapallo had called when they first arrived in 1910; but they were out and a maid forgot to give them his card. 'A very good thing,' said Max, 'otherwise I might have had to become a sidesman!' For the rest, once or twice a year, an intimate friend or relation—Dora, it might be, or Reggie—came to stay for a week or two; and throughout the summer a small slow trickle of visitors, stopping at Rapallo on their way somewhere else, passed through the Villino for tea or luncheon. These were often interesting people: a list of the visitors to the Villino between 1920 and 1935 includes many famous names. Max enjoyed seeing them and, for an hour or so, was pleased to provide them with a display of his conversational art. But very rarely did such meetings lead to further intimacy. Max made only two or three new close friends during this period, and these inevitably he saw seldom. However, he did not need them. Sometimes he thought he preferred the company of acquaintances to that of friends. Acquaintances were too much on their good behaviour openly to exhibit their weaknesses.

'I'm so much easier to please,' Max confided to Florence, 'in the matter of acquaintance, than most people are. I wish I were less exigent about *friends*—the Reggies and the Wills e tutti quanti.'

As to keeping up with people by correspondence, Max found this increasingly difficult. He wrote very regularly and often to Florence if she was away and now and again to Reggie or his mother. But for the most part he became a byword for not answering letters. Rothenstein took to addressing his envelopes 'Max Beerbohm, Esq., Villino Chiaro, "Caves of Silence", Rapallo.'

Altogether Max's personal life during these years stagnated as much as his creative did. How then was he happy? By the laws laid down for us by moralists and psychologists he should not have been. Man, they insist, is born to act and construct. If, under the baleful influence of sin or psychological maladjustment, he does neither, the results should surely have been frustration and discontent. In fact, however, people who visited Max during these years were struck by the air of serene gaiety which gleamed in his eyes and made itself softly heard in his laugh. Although he did not laugh quite so often as in his youth, he laughed more than most men of his age. The truth was that he was so exceptional a character that the laws applicable to most men did not apply to him. What was true of him as a boy was true of him in middle life: he was at once older and younger than the average man of his years. Low vitality had combined with extreme sensitiveness to age him prematurely in some respects. Balder and plumper than in the past, Max no longer looked young for his years: he moved with careful deliberation, it was impossible to imagine him breaking into a run. As he appeared, so he was. He tired very easily; to feel well he had to lead a quiet life. His fatigue was nervous rather than physical. We remember that even in 1906, on his first journey to Italy, he had forgone visiting Rome because he knew that he was too sated with fresh impressions to be able to respond to any more. Now when Florence went on one of her occasional sightseeing trips with her family, Max stayed at Rapallo. He had experienced enough new impressions to last him for life; he realized that new ones would merely disturb him. 'I often think of you with envy,' wrote Desmond MacCarthy to him, 'because, as I see your life, it is regulated by so fine a discretion. I have never been able to say it is enough, but have gone on eating till I felt a little sick.' Max's spiritual digestion was so delicate that he felt sick after what most men would have thought a moderate meal of experience. In consequence, in order not to overtax his frail vitality or overstrain his hypersensitive nerves, from the age of fifty onwards he lived the life of a retired elderly man.

Here his gain was negative; his form of life diminished the risk of his being positively unhappy. His positive happiness arose from the fact that in some respects he had remained strangely, startlingly young. From his fifty-year-old countenance his blue eyes still confronted the world with the wide-eyed innocent gaze of childhood. In this, they were the true mirror of his soul. There was much of the child left in Max; he still enjoyed the actual process of living as a child does—putting on a grey suit or a white, choosing a camellia for his buttonhole, sipping his glass of white vermouth before dinner. And the dinner itself too: Max had retained a schoolboy's pleasure in his meals. He kept his taste too for other childish pleasures. Undoing a parcel, for instance: Florence took great care never to undo a parcel addressed to Max; he was so disappointed to lose the excitement of cutting the string and pulling off the wrappings in delighted suspense as to what should be inside. Together with Gordon Craig, also, he liked walking up to a ravine in the hills above the Villino and dropping glasses down it, in order to enjoy the sound of the crash as they shattered on the rocks below. Above all, Max retained the child's power to absorb himself completely in his inner world. Max's terrace was visible from the cottage inhabited by Gordon Craig; and Craig would watch him pacing up and down hour by hour, smilingly lost in private meditation. From time to time he would disappear into his study, where he would scribble down a thought in his diary or on an odd piece of paper. From these scribbles and from his letters we get some idea of his prevailing preoccupations during this phase of his life.

There was nothing very new about them. The range of Max's interests, established so early, was never to change. Max still thought mainly about authors and politicians, and dandies and clothes, and the nineties, about prose style and preciosity. He made a list of books and writers he would describe as 'precious'. They include, we note, his own youthful work. He had grown to like style solider and more restrained and he aspired to modify his own accordingly.

Now and again Max interrupted the gentle flow of his thoughts to do a little reading. Not in such a way generally as to change the current of his meditations: like his preoccupations, his literary taste was much what it had been in the past. If Florence had ever entertained serious hopes of persuading him to study Shakespeare or

Dante, she must have been soon disillusioned. Such poetry as he read was of the romantic nineteenth-century kind that he had enjoyed in his youth: Swinburne, Housman, Byron. One evening he walked unannounced into Ted Craig's cottage declaiming Byron's song 'So we'll go no more a-roving'. At the end, 'Surely the most beautiful lyric in English!' cried Max enthusiastically. He did not take kindly to literary innovation. He was suspicious of Eliot and made an unsuccessful attempt to read Proust. Authors he did like continued the tradition of the nineties, as Lytton Strachey did. Among his older contemporaries he admired Galsworthy and Bennett but, as always, found himself in two minds about Shaw. He admired *St Joan* but not *Heartbreak House*. 'Rather unreadable,' he notes, 'same old mechanism and steel girders without much cement to them, and cold wind just whistling through and around them, and whistling rather vulgar tunes.' Nor could he understand what Shaw meant by professing to write melodious prose; 'It is the music of the carpenter's nail-board,' said Max. Indeed for him Shaw and his works remained a trifle repellent. 'The best brain in England,' he noted, 'but no beauty except that of an engine. . . . He has no reverence, no feeling for father or country or women; he thinks those things absurd.' Impertinent Max was against irreverence; had he not always held that if there was nothing to be revered, mocking impertinence lost its point?

New books, however, formed only a small part of Max's reading. So far as fiction was concerned he stuck mainly to his nineteenth-century favourites: Meredith, Henry James, Trollope. To these he responded as freshly and discriminatingly as ever.

'Apropos of letters, I envy you "wallowing" in Henry James,' he tells Reggie. 'I wrote to Hatchard's for them a fortnight ago, but they haven't yet arrived. Perhaps the postal strikers of Turin are wallowing in them. But I expect they will arrive at length. I long to read them. This craving is in despite of a nasty jar that I lately had. I tried again to read *The Awkward Age*, a book that utterly floored me some years ago. At that time I managed to read on as far as about the middle, where I broke down; and I was much ashamed of my break-down. *This* time I wasn't able to get nearly as far as the middle, and I wasn't in the least ashamed of leaving off—nor even of laying the book down rather violently; nor even of some uncouth words that

I uttered in the act of laying the book rather violently down. As you know, the *A. A.* is by way of being the earliest book in H. J.'s "later manner". And by that manner I have always sworn. And I *will not* believe that *The Golden Bowl* and *The Wings of the Dove* aren't H. J's greatest and richest achievement. But certainly the later manner *began* very inauspiciously. And that beginning seems to me perhaps even worse than it was because I happened, just after I had rejected it . . . , to read *The Adventures of Harry Richmond*. It must be 25 years since I had read those Adventures, and I had only the haziest memory of them; and I feared they might be less golden than the haze made them appear to me. And oh, lo! how much *more* golden they were than I had remembered. What a book! What swiftness and beauty and strength! It is the flight of a young golden eagle high across seas and mountains—beholding which, one likens H. J. to a very old mole burrowing very far down under a very poky back-garden in South Kensington. I mean, one likens the author of the *A. A.* to that mole. I won't hear a word against the rest of H. J's later manner. But I will willingly hear any number of words against G. M's own later manner. For I turned from *Harry Richmond* to *Diana of the Crossways*—a book which had also become dim to me. And oh, the difference!—oh the tedious, crack-jaw, arid intellectual snobbery of *Diana*! Wonderful beauties here too—but coming only in bursts, coming only in *escapes* from the book itself. Meredith ought to have stuck to romance and let who would be clever. But of course a man cannot be romantic in his later age. So the point is that Meredith ought to have died when he was young-ish. Anyhow, I am quite sure it is by his young and young-ish work that he will be remembered. *Diana* is as dead as a door-nail, and I tremble to think what *The Amazing Marriage* and *Lord Ormont* must be as dead as!'

Trollope he loved more and more. For more and more did his solid Victorian geniality attract him by contrast with the insecurity and ill nature of the new age and its representative authors. 'Trollope isn't always turning out his characters' pockets to see what he can find against them,' Max said to a friend.

Max also projected an essay on Johnson. He had come deeply to revere and delight in his personality; and now thought Boswell's *Life* the best book of any kind in the English language. This was partly because it was a biography. Much as Max enjoyed *Harry Richmond* and *The Eustace Diamonds*, he liked reading true stories even better: biographies, diaries, memoirs, especially if they were about periods and people that he himself remembered. It did not matter if they were not very good or about undistinguished characters: if they recalled the past for him Max read them with pleasure, and their title-pages and endpapers were scrawled all over with his comments. These could be caustic, especially if the book was by a professional authoress. Max, unprejudiced in almost every other respect, had an instinctive uncontrollable bias against professional authoresses. He admitted it.

'A "sex war," ' he wrote in an essay, 'we are often told, is to be one of the features of the world's future—women demanding the right to do men's work, and men refusing, resisting, counter-attacking. It seems likely enough. One can believe anything of the world's future. Yet one conceives that not all men, if this particular evil come to pass, will stand packed shoulder to shoulder against all women. One does not feel that the dockers will be very bitter against such women as want to be miners, or the plumbers frown much upon the would-be steeple-jills. I myself have never had my sense of fitness jarred, nor a spark of animosity roused in me, by a woman practising any of the fine arts—except the art of writing. That she should write a few little poems or *pensées*, or some impressions of a trip in a dahabieh as far as (say) Biskra, or even a short story or two, seems to me not wholly amiss, even though she do such things for publication. But that she should be an habitual, professional author, with a passion for her art, and a fountain-pen and an agent, and sums down in advance of royalties on sales in Canada and Australia, and a profound knowledge of human character, and an essentially sane outlook, is somehow incongruous with my notions —my mistaken notions, if you will—of what she ought to be.'

Here is yet another of Max's jesting true words. His outlook was gently but pronouncedly masculine. This made him take a special pleasure in women's company, largely because he felt them to be unlike himself. If a woman did do the same kind of work as he did, the sense of difference was weakened and his pleasure correspondingly diminished. Moreover, authoresses tended to be intellectual and he had never liked intellectual women. 'Women of vision—yes!' he once said, 'but not women of intellect. It is Bertrand Russell's saving grace that he isn't a woman. As a woman he would have been intolerable.' Whatever the cause, his comments on authoresses are severe. Listen to him on the reminiscences of the two lady poetesses who collaborated under the name of Michael Field:

'With all deference to Sturge Moore and Will Rothenstein and with no doubt that Michael Field's work must have been remarkable, what a dreadfully vain, pretentious and provincial couple of frumps they themselves, as revealed in the following pages, were.'

Or in the margin of a book by Mrs Craigie, who wrote fashionable novels under the pseudonym of John Oliver Hobbes:

'This pretty and pleasant little woman of the 1890s was of all climbers the grimmest, of all wire-pullers the most indefatigable and undiscourageable, and of all ladies who ever put pen to paper the most brazenly conceited.'

Or in a volume of literary studies by the learned Vernon Lee:

'Poor dear dreadful little lady! Always having a crow to pick, ever so coyly, with Nietzsche, or a wee lance to break with Mr Carlyle, or a sweet but sharp little word of warning to whisper in the ear of Mr H. G. Wells or Strindberg. . . . What a dreadful little bore and busybody!'

Nor did Max feel drawn to Alice Meynell, overpoweringly cultured and relentlessly refined in taste. She published an essay called 'Decivilized': Max wrote under the title, 'If only she could have been—just a little!' In justice to him, it should be said that he could be equally hard on men. The title-page of Kipling's *A Diversity of Creatures* is thus inscribed in Max's hand:

By R. K. the
Apocalyptic Bounder
who
can do such fine things
but
mostly prefers to stand
(on tip-toe and stridently)
for all that is
cheap
and nasty.

367

He has some disrespectful comments to make about George Moore and Stevenson. George Moore's *Memoirs of my Dead Life* ends with a highly rhetorical passage in which the author declares his belief that time revolves in a circle and that millions of years hence the present moment will recur. 'I believe,' it runs, 'that billions of years hence, billions and billions of years hence, I shall be sitting in the same room where I sit now, writing the same words I am now writing; I believe that again a few years later my ashes will swing in the moveless and silent depths of the peaceful ocean, and that the same figures or the same nymphs and same fawns will dance round me again.' Max was not impressed. He wrote underneath, 'My dear Moore, you don't believe anything of the kind, and the prettiness of the prose is all wasted accordingly.' He complained to Reggie about Stevenson's 'thin little prim little cardboard and tinsel attempts to do something in the manner of Sir Walter'. Reggie sent him *Travels with a Donkey in the Cevennes* to win him over to a more favourable view. Max liked it; but not so much as to make him forget Stevenson's faults.

'Thank you so very much for the Stevenson Cevennes book, which reached me by *grande* vitesse long ago. I enjoyed it greatly. S. hadn't when he wrote it, arrived at his what-a-good-boy-am-I-and-what-a-gallant-suffering-uncomplaining- Scotch- cordial-whimsical-yet-solemn-*best-of-boys*! manner; though even in that quite early volume there are, to the discerning therapeutical eye, visible the seeds of the deep-seated malady. . . .'

The biographer is tempted to quote Max's caustic rather than his friendly comments because they are the more amusing. But it would be misleading to imagine his mood as predominantly caustic; the title-pages and endpapers of his books are as full of praise as they are of blame. He loved Dr Johnson and delighted in Buckle's *Life of Disraeli*. Not, indeed, in its style: 'Buckle,' he said, 'writes like a schoolboy whose father was an Election Agent.' But he had nothing but praise for its matter. Disraeli was a figure after Max's heart. His ironical spirit was enchanted by the contrast between Disraeli's exotic flamboyance and the sober English scene against which it displayed itself; and he loved his zestful flippancy. One anecdote in the book gave him especial pleasure. It related how the seventy-year-old Disraeli, calling on Lady Bradford, was told by the servant that according to her custom she had gone to town on a Monday. ' "I thought you would know that, sir," he added. "I did not," replied Disraeli, "nor did I know this was Monday," and I left him standing.' 'Divinely delightful,' commented Max. 'Seventy years old, Prime Minister, ill, and rejoicing to mystify a butler with the sort of thing that his old friend D'Orsay would have *wished* to say!'

In 1924 William Rothenstein brought out a volume entitled *Twenty-four Portraits* and consisting of drawings of celebrated personages with short appreciations attached. Max knew most of the sitters. Soon the book was scored over with his comments. Opposite the picture of Sir James Frazer, he writes: 'I *must* read *The Golden Bough*—and yet I shan't.' He did not think much of Robert Bridges's work. 'It shows,' he says, 'that the dismallest and driest of creative pedants may be by some dispensation of kindly Fate be set high among poets.' He was much amused by the paragraph about Yeats's compatriot, the Celtic poet and painter A. E. One passage in it ran: 'If he had not written poems, would he have been a better painter? If he had forsworn poetry and painting, would he now be the greatest master of English prose?' Mischievously Max continues in the same vein: 'If he had never met Sir James Plunket, would he be the greatest pianist in Europe? If Mr T. P. Gill had never made his acquaintance, should we be recognizing him as Prince of Entomologists? And so on, and—critically—so forth.' The paragraph had gone on to say that such questions were 'full of intellectual interest'. 'Perhaps not quite full!' noted Max. His sharpest words were reserved for Clutton Brock, a literary journalist and art critic, whose writings were distinguished by a tone of vague, sentimental piety. This was not the kind of thing to appeal to Max. Rothenstein's book praised Clutton Brock for 'speaking quietly of Christian values'.

'I wish Clutton Brock would take Holy Orders and have done with it,' commented Max, '. . . instead of hanging about the vestry "so quietly" with the Vicar and the verger and sexton and then saying— oh so quietly!—to the readers of *The Times* what he has been saying to them. I wish him to go straight up into the pulpit and get Christian values off his chest. It is his eternal "quiet" flatulence I can't stand.'

Rothenstein had included a picture of Max himself in the

collection. The accompanying paragraph described him as 'the wittiest mind in England'.

No!' wrote Max, 'I am not nearly so witty as Chesterton for one. But certainly I have not prostituted and cheapened my wit as he has. How about Lytton Strachey? There's the wittiest mind of the age— and the virtue of it guarded even more strictly and puritanically than I have guarded the virtue of mine.

And I am forgetting G. B. S. He has prostituted his wit certainly and made a drudge of her too. But she can stand it! She's gigantic.'

Once again we are struck by Max's power of estimating his capacities objectively. Instances of this are scattered over his correspondence during these years. It was no good his advising Craig about his work, he told Florence. 'I do wish I had the Rothenstein faculty of deterring people from culs-de-sac and setting them on the broad and shining highroad. I can only offer light hints . . . and my hints are never taken. I suppose I ought to be content with the rather rare faculty of knowing for myself just what I ought and oughtn't to do in work.' Again, writing to Sir Michael Sadler, who had published an article saying he wished that Matthew Arnold had given free reign to his humour like Max, he says:

'Your suggestion that M. A. would have been the better for being the *me* "of his generation" does move me to make stern and spirited protest in his behalf.

You regret that the imp in *him* was "untimely suppressed in his childhood". Suppose it *hadn't* been! Suppose his father had said to him, "Matt, my child, in you I discern the makings of what is called an humorist. Here is a cap-and-bells. Here, moreover, is a wand-and-bladder. Make good practice with these, under God's blessing." What would have happened then? The seriousness that the child had *congenitally* might have saved him from the horrid fate of being just a fribble and a "funny man". I myself have enough seriousness in me to prevent me from being just that—else you never would have honoured me by speaking my name. But oh, how much more amusing I should be if I were much more serious than I am!'

Max was quite right in thinking that there was a strain of seriousness in his own work; and that it is this strain that gives it body and memorable weight.

Paradoxically he took his art more seriously than he took himself. Max was far from growing graver with the years. His favourite activity was still making jokes. Of all sorts too; he still enjoyed practical jokes. Even when he was over fifty he was not above making an apple-pie bed for his wife's young niece. Usually, however, Max's practical jokes were designed to disconcert the mind, not the body. Once he altered the labels in a lady's rose garden, so that when she took some guests out to see the roses, she was bewildered to find them all named after famous criminals: Betty Uprichard had become Dr Crippen, and so on. On another occasion he had got hold of a volume of poems by an unusually solemn author named Herbert Trench. One of these was a romantic dialogue between the god Apollo and some ancient classical mariner. With a penknife, very carefully Max scraped out the aspirates in all the words beginning with 'h' said by the mariner and substituted an apostrophe, so that the classic sailor appeared to express himself in modern Cockney. He then sent the book to Trench, saying that he had not seen this version of his work before. Max had done the work so beautifully that it looked absolutely genuine. Trench was horrified and, when he discovered the truth, a little offended—till Max explained to him that he thought him a true poet, 'Otherwise there wouldn't be any fun in making fun of you.'

Shaw was the object of his most elaborate essay in this kind of humour. Max discovered a volume of photographs of Shaw in youth. Carefully he altered each for the worse; in one amplifying the nose, in another diverting the eyes into a squint. He then had these new versions rephotographed and sent them to various friends in England accompanied by a request to post them back to Shaw along with a letter from some imaginary admirer stating that he had found the enclosed photograph of Mr Shaw and would so much like him to sign and return it. The friends obeyed. Max was delighted to learn that as one monstrous likeness after another arrived by post, Shaw grew steadily more baffled.

The very furnishing of Max's study illustrated his liking for jokes. A visitor inspecting the book-shelves would be struck by unexpected titles: *The Love Poems of Herbert Spenser*, for instance, or a slender volume named *The Complete Works of Arnold Bennett*. Close examination revealed them both to be wooden dummies. Such jokes took time and trouble. Max was prepared to give both! Craig and others who watched him at his endless strollings up and down the terrace noticed that he often broke into fits of laughter at some thought that had crossed his mind. Even when Max is giving his serious views on Shaw or Clutton Brock, he manages to be amusing. But there are more humorous effusions than serious comments among his papers. The drawers of his desk were full of scraps of parody and comic verse and half-finished caricatures. His most typical products of this kind, however, are far from being scrappy or half-finished. With a fine pen, meticulous care and so skilfully that it is hard often to distinguish Max's handiwork from the printed object, he would get to work on a real book 'improving' it, to use his own phrase. This meant altering the title-page, inserting or changing an illustration, interpolating imagined questions, appending absurd and invented press notices, writing a forged dedication or message from the author. He 'improved' his own works in this fashion. His copy of *The Happy Hypocrite* is adorned by a fine flaunting sketch of Lord George Hell, that of *Zuleika Dobson* enriched by a number of elaborate illustrations and also by a letter supposedly written by Zuleika to George Gershwin, the composer.

Dear Mr George Gershwin,

About a year ago, my old friend Mr Beerbohm (if friend he can be called—for I greatly disliked his book about me: it was full of inaccuracies; and besides, why did the silly man hit on three of the least interesting and exciting days in the whole of my brilliant life?) told me, in great excitement, that your and his friend Mr Charles Evans had told him that you wished to write an opera about me. I was much excited and pleased that a musician so gifted and so eminent as you should have this idea. I don't know anything about music really, but I know what I like. Mr Beerbohm is in rather the same rank of critics as I am. He tells me that he has often heard compositions of yours played by orchestras, and heard them with deep delight, and that they have pleased him even through the medium of a horrible thing called 'the gramophone'. He tells me too that he does hope your passion for me has not cooled, and that you will soon declare it through your art to the world.

Yours sincerely,
Zuleika Kitchener.

P.S. I was married, secretly, to the late Lord Kitchener, early in 1915. Being so worried by his great responsibilities at that time, he no longer had the grit to cope with my importunities, poor fellow.

A volume of Ibsen's plays has an inscription in that author's writing:

> For Max Beerbohm
> critic of who
> the writings fills
> with pleasures me.
> *H. Ibsen.*

At the end of Pater's *Renaissance*, delicate gospel of aestheticism, Max has inserted some surprise quotations from imagined reviews:

Some Opinions of the Press

'Something of raucousness but much of virility. . . . Mr Pater does not mince his words.'—*Spectator.*

'Thor's hammer on Vulcan's anvil.'—*Manchester Guardian.*

'At once a scourge and a purge.'—*Wigan Remembrancer.*

On the title-page he has pasted a print of a burly carpenter looking down a plank that is held in a vice and has written in pencil: 'With a portrait of the Author in the act of revising his proofs.'

He was fond of inserting such misleading portraits. Conrad is represented by a picture of a spruce elderly yachtsman, Meredith by one of a plump plebeian countenance winking under a bowler hat. Max turns Tolstoy into a Tartar-looking personage with eyeglass, plumed cap, and a gay, arch leer in his eye; Yeats is transformed into a smiling Victorian paterfamilias with spectacles and side-whiskers. Sometimes his misleading title-pages take other forms too. Beneath the title of Belloc's *The Cruise of the 'Nona'*, Max has pasted a wood-cut of a seasick Victorian couple; under that of *The Common Reader* by Virginia Woolf we find one of a spectacled spinster. Max's masterpieces in this kind are more elaborate. A copy of Oscar Wilde's *Intentions* is adorned all through in a mock-Beardsley style. In one drawing Wilde flies through the air while an outraged John Bull tries in vain to shoot him with a bow and arrow. Even more memorable are Max's additions to Archibald Henderson's biography of Shaw and Queen Victoria's *More Leaves from the Journal of a Life in the Highlands.* Henderson's book was a work of naïve hero-worship: a hero-worship unshared by Max, and not evident in Henderson's book after Max had finished with it. With the aid of an erasing knife, Indian ink and colour wash, he worked at it for more than a year, interpolating passages into the text, superimposing grotesque features or costumes on the various persons portrayed in the illustrations, Morris, Sidney Webb and, of course, Shaw himself. In one picture Max has transformed the youthful Shaw into a Mephistophelean figure with a diabolical smile and wearing a green bowler hat with a feather. There are some explanatory words supposedly by Henderson:

'In the Spring of '91 Eleanor Marx had given to Shaw, as a token of esteem, a green billycock hat which had belonged to her father in his bourgeois days. "It went," says Shaw, "to my head." He feverishly applied himself to the task of dressing "up to" it. Having succeeded in doing this, he offered himself as a candidate for admission to the Marlborough House Set,[1] but was rejected. In deep bitterness of spirit he fell back on the Tivoli Bar, where he perceptibly coarsened. This was a very sad time for all Shaw's friends.'

Rodin's bust of Shaw gives Max a chance to make a little fun of Rodin: 'The bust as conceived by Rodin was to be just a great noble mass of rough bronze with just the tip of one eyebrow protruding somewhere near the summit and several impressions of Rodin's thumb.' Queen Victoria's book is an equally elaborate production and must have taken quite as long to do. All the illustrations are altered with delicate care; and the text is interspersed with comments, imitating the Queen's style and even her handwriting. Beneath a picture of the Queen's dog, Sharp, Max has inserted: 'Such a dear, faithful, noble *friend* and companion, and for whom Albert had the *greatest* respect also. Victoria R.' There is a dedication at the beginning of the book:

> for Mr Beerbohm
> the never-sufficiently-
> to-be-studied writer
> whom Albert looks
> down on affectionately,

[1] The 'fast' set led by the Prince of Wales who lived at Marlborough House.

I am sure—
From his Sovereign
Victoria R. I.
Balmoral, 1898.

More Leaves from the Journal of a Life in the Highlands is a more subtle example of Max's humour than the Henderson's *Life of Shaw*. As always, he is at his best when he is making fun of somebody he liked. He cannot be said to have liked Shaw. He did like the Queen. Sir Theodore Martin in his biography of Prince Albert speaks of her as 'the Great and Good'. Max wrote in the margin 'or at any rate, the Good and Human, the Likeable, the even Lovable; and the Peculiar, the never Uninteresting'.

Max, then, was not unoccupied during these years spent on his terrace or in his study. The odd thing is that he was satisfied to lavish such care and art and wit and fancy on private jokes. But this more than anything else reveals how much there was of the child left in him. He never lost the child's capacity for play. 'Go and play,' says the grown-up to the child; and the child, if it has any imagination, can do so indefinitely. For most people this faculty has gone by nine years old. Max kept it all his life. For this reason he had no need of regular work or varied company. Along with the child's capacity for pure play he kept the child's ability to be completely satisfied by playing. Children are not stopped from building a sand-castle by the sense that they should be doing something more important or something that will make other people admire them. Nor was Max stopped from doodling on a title-page by the desire for fame or glory or the feeling that he should be doing some serious writing. All he wanted was time and place in which to retire to his world of comic fantasy. Nor did he need a companion there. For most people half the pleasure of making a joke comes from sharing it. Not for Max! Florence—in spite of trying—seldom saw his jokes: and only now and again did he get a chance to show his humorous concoctions to anyone else. The audience he played to was himself and he asked for no other. The child does not need an audience. He goes on building the sandcastle even if he knows that no one else will see it. Max was the same. Till the end of his days his inner life retained the happy self-sufficiency of childhood.

Was Florence equally happy? Not quite. She still suffered from

occasional fits of depression. Also of restlessness: two or three times
during these years she was seized with a wish to return to the stage,
at any rate for a short time. She was subject to nostalgic moods too,
when she longed to see her home and her relations. 'My brothers!'
she would exclaim, casting up her eyes as if in ecstatic contemplation
of their shining qualities. She also continued to feel ill at ease in
company, especially in the company of Max's cleverer friends.
Out of nervousness she would interrupt, tell long stories and, when
Max himself was relating an anecdote, stop him in order to correct
him on some small point of fact. The truth was that Florence had a
troubled, unsatisfied nature; and marriage had not cured this. In
some ways it had encouraged it. It had frustrated her creative energy,
for one thing. She could no longer fulfil herself as an actress. And
she had not found a compensating outlet for her energies. Many
women who leave the stage to marry fulfil themselves in family life.
Florence could not for she was childless: nor was Max the sort of
husband who could serve as a substitute child. Childlike in other
ways, he was not, except in purely practical matters, childishly
dependent. Florence realized this only too well. As early as 1914, she
writes to him, 'you would not depend on anything in myself, with
those great resources in yourself for contentment'. She felt him all
the more independent of her because she could not enter into all his
thoughts and feelings. Indeed, she was excluded from some of the
most important. She seldom understood his jokes; she was not even
certain that she approved of them. Surely his caricatures were sometimes rather unkind, she thought, and an unworthy occupation for
a man of his gifts. In the autumn of 1921 Max amused himself by
decorating the little entrance lobby of the Villino with frescoes;
Zuleika Dobson on one wall, and on the other a concourse of his
favourite models, Gosse, Henry James, etc. Florence protested;
satirical grotesques of this kind did not, in her view, make a pleasant
introduction to her home. It needed some weeks of tact and patience
on Max's part before she could resign herself to accepting them.

Marriage had also in some ways intensified Florence's lack of
social self-confidence. As a successful actress in America she had
been helped to overcome her shyness by the sense that she was
recognized as a personality in her own right. Now she was no more
than Max's wife: no one was interested in her for herself. She did
not grudge Max his eminence: she thought him a hero who

deserved all the attention paid him; and she was indignant if he was spoken of with the slightest disrespect. But her eclipse made her more nervous than ever when in company.

None of this means, however, that Florence was unhappier than before; on the contrary, marriage had brought compensations which much outweighed its disadvantages. For one thing, the life at Rapallo suited her admirably. Although she had liked acting, she had always hated the life of the theatre: it was altogether too coarse and competitive for her. Social life too had always been more pain than pleasure for Florence. Life at the Villino, too, provided her with just the right amount of gentle soothing occupations; superintending kitchen and garden and the lives of her dependants. With them she never felt inadequate. The fact that she was in a superior position gave her the self-confidence she otherwise lacked. She delighted to interest herself in the cook's family and the gardener's health: and when this palled she could indulge the romantic side of her nature reading Spenser and Dante under the olive trees. For Florence was as romantic as ever. 'I cannot read poetry any more,' said a visitor one day. 'Oh!' exclaimed Florence in anxious dismay. 'Not even when the soul presses?' Florence's own soul often pressed.

Furthermore, her love for Max made her happy. Even if she could not understand his jokes, yet she continued to be devoted to him. When he was absent and away for long she became restless and anxious, 'Ma—ax' she would be heard calling. It was no wonder. Her melancholy moods made her more dependent on him, not less. It was to him she poured out her troubles: at every turn she asked his advice and sympathy. Not in vain: he could be relied on to be calming, attentive and affectionate. Gordon Craig saw a great deal of the two during these years. 'Was it a happy marriage?' someone asked him. 'Of course it was,' he answered, 'Max was such a dear fellow. He had been a good son; and good sons make good husbands. Any woman would have been happy with him.'

Florence in particular; for happiness communicates itself and Max was happy with Florence. His detachment mingled with his affection, so that her moods did not bother him. Nor was he irritated if she interrupted his conversation or forestalled his stories. Serenely he relapsed into silence; it was the rest of the company who were disappointed. Affectionate but not passionate, Max was the kind of man whose love increased with time. He was a creature of habit and he had become addicted to the habit of loving Florence. This appeared dramatically a few years later in the summer of 1934; it was at a luncheon party at the Villino. Florence suddenly fell to the floor in a dead faint. All Max's usual calm forsook him. Oblivious of the company, he fell on his knees beside her. 'Please don't leave me,' he whispered in anguished accents, 'you can't be so unkind. Please, please come back.'

CHAPTER FOURTEEN

'And Even Now'

(1)

IN most years the blissful monotony of Max's existence suffered some mild interruption. The year 1921 saw the appearance of two books. The volume about Herbert was published in October. In addition to writing a short perceptive appreciation of his brother, Max had been responsible for the general arrangement of the volume; so much so that he had been forced to pay a short visit to England in the summer to give it a last inspection before it was published. It was followed in December by *And Even Now*. This was Max's last volume of essays, and his most important. Its contents are more varied, sometimes more serious; and they tell us more about Max. Indeed, *And Even Now* is a chief authority for his attitude of mind and prevailing mood during his middle years. Not that these were very different from what they had been earlier. In so far as Max had developed, it was in the same direction as before. His manner of writing had continued to grow more sober, his tone softer and more pensive. More tolerant too: in these essays he even goes so far as to say that he had been too hard in the past on popular taste and humour. His actual opinions had not changed any more than his literary taste had. Politically, we have seen, he had even moved slightly to the Right. This shows in the book. The essay called 'Something Defeasible', written in the atmosphere of the 1919 strikes, betrays his nervousness at that time, his odd panicky notion that the British working class might possibly be going to turn into a bloodthirsty revolutionary mob. All the same he had not become a conventional Tory. Max was as incurably against hierarchy as when he was at Charterhouse. His essay on servants shows this. Servants appear to be a dying race, he says, and he is glad.

'Convention (for she too frightens me) has made me accept what servants would do for me by rote. But I would liefer have it ill-done than ask even the least mettlesome of them to do it better, and far liefer, if they would only be off and not do it at all, do it for myself. In Italy—dear Italy, where I have lived much—servants do still regard service somewhat in the old way, as a sort of privilege; so that with Italian servants I am comparatively at my ease. But oh, the delight when on the afternoon of some local *festa* there is no servant at all in the little house! Oh, the reaction, the impulse to sing and dance, and the positive quick obedience to that impulse! Convention alone has forced me to be anywhere a master. Ariel and Caliban, had I been Prospero on that island, would have had nothing to do and nothing to complain of; and Man Friday on that other island would have bored me, had I been Crusoe. When I was a king in Babylon and you were a Christian slave, I promptly freed you.

Anarchistic? Yes; and I have no defence to offer, except the rather lame one that I am a Tory Anarchist. I should like every one to go about doing just as he pleased—short of altering any of the things to which I have grown accustomed. Domestic service is not one of those things, and I should be glad were there no more of it.'

Florence related that he avoided asking hotel servants to do anything for him; he was as shy of them as he had been of his scout on his arrival in Oxford. Time, too, had confirmed his feeling of revulsion against great riches, that he had experienced dining with Sir Philip Sassoon nine years before. In an unfinished essay composed at this time he says that the only good of wealth is to save a man from money worries. Otherwise, from what he had seen, great wealth involved people in a great deal of trouble without bringing them any corresponding increase of happiness. Or of virtue either; no doubt rich men were often bright and good. 'But,' says Max, 'I always felt they would have been brighter and better still on moderate means.'

And Even Now also shows Max as incorrigibly sceptical as ever. He could not believe that any philosophy, especially any contemporary philosophy, had the key to ultimate truth.

'It distresses me, this failure to keep pace with the leaders of thought as they pass into oblivion. It makes me wonder whether I am, after all, an absolute fool. Yet surely I am not that. Tell me of a man or a woman, a place or an event, real or fictitious: surely you will find me a fairly intelligent listener. Any such narrative will present to me some image, and will stir me to not altogether fatuous thoughts. Come to me in some grievous difficulty: I will talk to you like a father, even like a lawyer. I'll be hanged if I haven't a certain mellow wisdom. But if you are by way of weaving theories as to the nature of things in general, and if you want to try those theories on some one who will luminously confirm them or powerfully rend them, I must, with a hang-dog air, warn you that I am not your man. I suffer from a strong suspicion that things in general cannot be accounted for through any formula or set of formulae, and that any one philosophy, howsoever new, is not better than another. That is in itself a sort of philosophy, and I suspect it accordingly; but it has for me the merit of being the only one I can make head or tail of. If you try to expound any other philosophic system to me, you will find not merely that I can detect no flaw in it (except the one great flaw just suggested), but also that I haven't, after a minute or two, the vaguest notion of what you are driving at.'

Max's scepticism went along with a deeply felt and imaginative sense of life's mystery. This finds expression in the essay called 'The Golden Drugget', about a little inn on the road between Rapallo and the Villino.

'By daylight, on the way down from my little home to Rapallo, or up from Rapallo home, I am indeed hardly conscious that this inn exists. By moonlight, too, it is negligible. Stars are rather unbecoming to it. But on a thoroughly dark night, when it is manifest as nothing but a strip of yellow light cast across the road from an ever-open door, great always is its magic for me. . . . I remember that when first I beheld this steady strip of light, shed forth over a threshold level with the road, it seemed to me conceivably sinister. It brought Stevenson to my mind: the chink of doubloons and the clash of cutlasses; and I think I quickened pace as I passed it. But now!—now it inspires in me a sense of deep trust and gratitude; and such awe as I have for it is altogether a loving awe, as for holy ground that should be trod lightly. A drugget of crimson cloth across a London pavement is rather resented by the casual passer-by, as saying to him "Step across me, stranger, but not along me, not in!" and for answer he spurns it with his heel. "Stranger, come!" is the clear message of the Golden Drugget. "This is but a humble and earthly hostel, yet you will find here a radiant company of angels and archangels." And always I cherish the belief that if I obeyed the summons I should receive fulfilment of the promise. Well, the beliefs that one most cherishes one is least willing to test. I do not go in at that open door. But lingering, but reluctant, is my tread as I pass by it; and I pause to bathe in the light that is as the span of our human life, granted between one great darkness and another.'

This passage is unique in Max's work. He had touched indeed on the same theme when he wrote about Maeterlinck's plays: but never before had he written about it with emotion. In *And Even Now*, he several times sounded a similar note. If 'The Golden Drugget' is his first predominantly 'serious' essay, 'William and Mary' is his first predominantly 'serious' fiction. Formally and superficially it is like his other tales, a narrative related by Max in his own person; and in a tone of irony. But the irony is tender not satiric, and Max's aim is less to make the reader laugh than to touch his heart. The story was inspired by the memory of an empty house in the country he visited some years ago when staying with Herbert. He had rung the bell and listened to it echoing forlornly through the desolated rooms. 'I invented a story round the strange emotion caused by the weird ringing of the bell,' he said. What sort of people had lived there? he wondered, and gradually the figures of an imaginary couple had formed themselves in his imagination. The story relates how Max had made friends with a happy young married pair called William and Mary, how the friendship was ended by their death and of his solitary pilgrimage years later to the house, now desolate, where he had witnessed and shared their happiness. Such a subject is untrodden ground for him, and he advances on to it with discretion. Compared with Lamb's, for example, or Sterne's, Max's pathos is a fastidiously restrained affair. But it is true pathos: a sincere and tender sadness pervades the story. This sentiment, like that of 'The Golden Drugget', is associated with a sense of the fleetingness of human existence and human joys. It is as though Max, looking back at his memories over his fifty years of living, was seized by a realization of the melancholy implicit in that sense of the past which was a central inspiration of his genius: and that at the realization an emotion welled up in him to utter itself with an intensity hitherto unknown in his art.

An echo of the same sentiment adds a touch of poignancy to the reminiscence of Swinburne entitled 'No. 2 The Pines', also included in *And Even Now*. Here again Max is attempting something new for him. He who had drawn so many imaginary portraits in words now draws a portrait from life. He employs for it the form he had invented for his imaginary portraits, a personal narrative in which he himself appears as a character. And the piece ends with a little fantasy about Swinburne disporting himself in Elysium which is the verbal equivalent of one of his own more fanciful cartoons. This last collection of his essays is more of a personal manifesto than any of its predecessors. As a comedian's manifesto should, it closed with an essay on laughter. This contains a passage of some interest to his biographer, for in it more fully than elsewhere he seeks to analyse his own particular sense of the comical.

'Many years ago I wrote an essay in which I poured scorn on the fun purveyed by the music halls, and on the great public for which that fun was quite good enough. I take that callow scorn back. I fancy that the fun itself was better than it seemed to me, and might not have displeased me if it had been wafted to me in private, in presence of a few friends. A public crowd, because of a lack of broad impersonal humanity in me, rather insulates than absorbs me. Amidst the guffaws of a thousand strangers I become unnaturally grave. If these people were the entertainment, and I the audience, I should be sympathetic enough. But to be one of them is a position that drives me spiritually aloof. Also, there is to me something rather dreary in the notion of going anywhere for the specific purpose of being amused. I prefer that laughter shall take me unawares. Only so can it master and dissolve me. And in this respect, at any rate, I am not peculiar. In music halls and such places, you may hear loud laughter, but—not see silent laughter, not see strong men weak, helpless, suffering, gradually convalescent, dangerously relapsing. Laughter at its greatest and best is not there.

To such laughter nothing is more propitious than an occasion that demands gravity. To have good reason for not laughing is one of the surest aids. Laughter rejoices in bonds. If music halls were schoolrooms for us, and the comedians were our schoolmasters, how much less talent would be needed for giving us how much more joy! Even in private and accidental intercourse, few are the men whose humour can reduce us, be we never so susceptible, to paroxysms of mirth. I will wager that nine tenths of the world's best laughter is laughter *at*, not *with*. And it is the people set in authority over us that touch most surely our sense of the ridiculous.'

(2)

On 2 January 1921 Max wrote to Messrs Brown and Phillips, owners of the Leicester Galleries.

My dear Brown and Phillipses,

I have been hoping that I should be able to say definitely that I *could* have an exhibition of drawings. But my Muse wouldn't inspire me with the first thing needful: ideas for drawings, and the impulse to draw. She has now suddenly relented. I have done a number of drawings—good ones, I think, *unberufen*. And I could certainly at any moment in the Spring supply you with 30 drawings. Probably 40. What date could you give me, I wonder? I would come over to England 3 weeks or a month before the exhibition, so as to do certain drawings which I can't finish without verifying the features of the subjects. We would, among us, select from among my 1914 drawings (the drawings done with a view to exhibition in 1915) those which stand the test of time, and those which have a queer interest in being so remote from our present time. The *big* room would be essential. (And of course I'd like to have what you promised I should have in the proposed 1915 exhibition—the little percentage on 'gate money'.) Many of the new drawings are of a *generalized* character, rather than personal. Mostly they are political —anti-Coalition, anti-Labour equally. Some of them are rather calculated to make people sit up—not to sit up in anger. I think, but in thought! This sounds like boasting. But you'll find me as modest as ever when you see me.

Messrs Brown and Phillips were delighted with the suggestion: it was settled that the exhibition should be held in May. At the end of March Max arrived in London to prepare it. He came alone. Florence, who had not been home for seven years, was shortly to sail from Italy direct on a visit to America. After a week or two spent in hotels and lodging-houses, Max settled down to stay at Maud Tree's house. But already he was plunged into a whirl of luncheon and dinner engagements. Some of these were with his family. Constance in particular was insistent with her invitations. Past experience made Max accept these with a certain nervousness: 'I hope she won't say that I am always coming and asking for dinner!' he wrote to Florence. At her house and at Maud's he met other relations: Aggie, Dora, and Herbert's daughters. He was also welcomed by his old friends Egan Mew, Will Rothenstein, Gosse, the Lewises, Belloc—'looking oh! so old and weatherbeaten and *blurred*' —and Ada Leverson. Ada Leverson's dining-room made a curious and comical impression on him.

'I don't think you ever went to the house,' he wrote to Florence, 'so you don't remember that very dismal and derelict and yet coquettish dining-room. Yesterday I noticed in it a new feature. On a side-table stood a rather large brass weighing-machine for letters, quite covered with rust. Whence it came, why it was there, I cannot imagine and did not like to ask.'

He spent most of his day discussing the details of the exhibition with Brown and Phillips and later in supervising the hanging of the cartoons. In order to bring his exhibition up to date he drew a few more people, notably Northcliffe and Lytton Strachey. Strachey visited him at his hotel. Max found him extremely pleasant. Strachey's reactions were more mixed. Formed, as he was, by unworldly Cambridge and bohemian Bloomsbury, he was unused to the more mannered and formalized style of social intercourse which Max had learnt from Oxford and Oscar Wilde.

'I went yesterday,' Strachey wrote to his brother James, 'and found him, very plump and white haired, drawn up to receive me. "Let us come out on the balcony, where we shall have a view of the doomed city." He begged me to turn my profile towards him, and for a minute or two he made some notes on the back of an envelope. He was infinitely polite and elaborate; and quite remote, so far as I could see, from humanity in all its forms.'

The exhibition opened on 11 May. A day or two before, the *Daily Express* sent an interviewer to ask Max for information about it. His reply showed that he had retained all his discreet art in putting his personality across.

'I am delighted to see you personally,' he told the interviewer, 'but professionally you are just the man I want to avoid. I am a great disbeliever—an ardent disbeliever—in the "puff preliminary" . . .

For aught I know, these drawings may be quite stupid, and people who see them will be the less indulgent to them if I have a preliminary chat about them. If, on the other hand, there is any cleverness in them, this quality will be less apparent if I have been blowing my own trumpet in the meantime.

You are a young man. You are at the outset of your career. I hope it will be a very successful one. Let me give you one word of advice.

Never blow your own trumpet. If you do that, other people will be so loth to do it for you.'

The event proved the wisdom of his words. London had seen no drawings by Max for eight years. These, bursting upon the world fresh and unheralded, created a brilliant sensation. Most of the critics were enthusiastic; by the time the show closed Max had cleared over a thousand pounds. He was surprised and delighted.

'It's odd that I should be such a commercial success,' he wrote to Florence, 'in drawing and writing, now isn't it? I never expected anything of the sort. I just went on doing my best—and not doing *much* of that; and I think the commercial success is as much due to my leisureliness as to my conscience: I haven't *tired* people. And I have had the rare good fortune of having a wife who never wanted me to tire them!—and who has always inspired me to do just only what I could do best, in my own way, at my own intervals.'

As he had expected, however, he did run into trouble over his cartoons of the Labour party; in particular, over one in which a member of an imaginary Labour Government—there had been no Labour Government as yet in England—was portrayed as refusing financial help to an impecunious poet on the ground that a poet cannot be counted as a worker. Max had been stimulated to this effort by the fact that several young poets had lately joined the Labour movement, explaining that they thought it was more likely to help artists than parties which stood for philistine and materialist capitalism. Max judged this as improbable. He took the Labour party to represent the views of the working class; and his experience as journalist and dramatic critic had convinced him that the English working class had little use for the arts. Further, he had noticed that, whatever lip-service Labour leaders might pay to culture, in practice they seemed to be exclusively concerned to obtain material benefits for their supporters. Were they likely to change if they came into office? Max thought not; he depicted the typical Labour leader as a coarse, beery-looking individual, and he dedicated this particular cartoon to

'those of our young poets who, not knowing very much—why *should* they know very much?—about politics and the deplorable part which human nature plays in politics, imagine that under the domination of LABOUR the liberal arts might have quite a decent chance.'

The idealistic Left were distressed by Max's words and still more by his tone. The *Daily Herald*, in an article signed by J. Q. X., treated him to a solemn lecture on the shocking lack of taste he showed in suggesting that the British working man was uncultured. Its tone was more sorrowful than angry: how could so distinguished an artist, it implied, stoop to such vulgarity? 'Vulgarity is the only word,' proclaimed J. Q. X. severely. Max was sufficiently interested to write a letter in answer to the *Daily Herald*:

Sir,

This morning as I sat in an attitude of the utmost refinement surveying that restrained sea the Mediterranean, my attention was drawn to a criticism written by J. Q. X., and published in your issue of May 18th, accusing me of having been guilty of vulgarity in a prophetic drawing of a Labour Minister of Education scoffing at a penurious poet who, declaring himself a 'worker', has applied to him for aid. I am not a young man; and my work has in the course of years met with a certain amount of adverse criticism. But never till now have I been called vulgar. It has been reserved for J. Q. X. to call me that. I must say I feel the epithet inexpressibly refreshing—all the more because it is not undeserved. The drawing in question is distinctly vulgar and so is my inscription on it.

Vulgarity has its uses. Vulgarity often cuts ice which refinement scrapes at vainly. And I like to think that some of the Labour leaders who have read J. Q. X's account of my shocking little draw-ing will visit the Leicester Galleries and be shocked themselves—

shocked even into realizing, as they do not seem to have realized—that the well-being of skilled and unskilled manual workers is not quite all that matters.

Yours obediently,

Max Beerbohm.

Max had been fortified in his anti-democratic sentiments by his visit to London. The war had brought a great change in its appearance; and in those West End streets and squares, where in Max's youth the ladies and gentlemen of England had spaciously sauntered, there now pushed and elbowed a motley mob drawn from the humbler classes of society. Max found it an unpleasing spectacle.

'Where are all the gentlefolk of the world gone to?' he wrote to Florence. 'Not a sign of them in London (barring in the private houses one went to). Not a sign of them in the train or on the boat or anywhere. Only this rabble of dreadful creatures—who aren't of course dreadful at all, except from the standpoint of a carefully-brought-up person who remembers the days when enjoyment of life was a thing reserved for a few other carefully-brought-up persons. However, that is the sort of talk that depresses you, darling, and makes you angry, and sets you conscientiously rejoicing on behalf of the rabble (which you really like much less than I do); so no more.'

Meanwhile, back in Italy, he made a selection of his cartoons to be published in September in a volume called *A Survey*. It opened with a preface in which he makes his final statement about the offending drawings.

EPISTLE DEDICATORY
TO
BRITANNIA

Madam,

I venture to dedicate this volume to you because you have always been very kind to me, and because I cannot think *why* you have always been so kind to me.

You have never, since you came to woman's estate, smiled much on caricaturists, or on satirists, in general. During the eighteenth century you were indulgent enough to them; but then you were still a headstrong girl: there was still a strain of brutality in your nature, to which caricature and satire were agreeable. That strain worked itself out of you long ago. You had become mild and buxom long before I had the honour to behold you. And the recent War has left you as mild as ever; though less buxom.

That is the kind of remark which in my childhood on your shores I was taught, very rightly, not to make about any one. It is the kind of remark which, so soon as I was grown up, I began to make about every one. For, after all, what is a caricaturist but a man who says, 'A, you're too fat; B, you're too thin; C, your nose is too large'—and so on? Such a man, alas, am I. And what is a satirist but one who says, 'D, you're a fool; E, your character and motives won't bear looking into; I see through *you*, F'—and, very jarringly, so forth? Such an one am I. I jar even on myself. I hold no high opinion of the satiric temperament. I despise Thersites and the whole lot of which I happen to be one. I have to go on being rude, because that is (a part of) my nature. But O Britannia, whenever I sail from my home in Italy, across your neatly-ruled waves, and step with a new sheaf of drawings on to those yellow sands where you sit enthroned, I do feel all the more guilty because your eyes are invariably so benign to me from beneath the brim of your lovely golden helmet.

You say that you have always frowned on *some* of my drawings? True, Madam; and thank you for reminding me. Over some in every batch you have frowned, murmuring a fine and favourite phrase of yours: 'Not in the very best of taste.' And I seem to find in all the drawings at which you have gently drawn the line a common denominator. In my youth, and indeed until quite recent years, the Court was a very dominant factor in your life. A satirist, instinctively, goes for what is very strong: the weaker things he derides with less gusto, or not at all. But you, Madam, have a great respect for strength, and it is the weaker things that are aptest to tickle your sense of humour. I myself have a respect for strength, but also I am inclined, in my fallen nature, to look for the weak points that all strength has, and to point them rudely out. I used to laugh at the Court and at the persons around it; and this distressed you rather. I never laughed with you at Labour. Labour didn't seem to me quite important enough yet. But Labour is very important now, very strong indeed; as you have found. And I gathered, this year, from a certain mild downward curve of your lips when I laid out for you on the yellow sands those of my new drawings which referred to Labour, that you thought me guilty of not the very best of taste in failing to bow my knee to your new Baal.

Perhaps I ought to exclude these few drawings from a book dedicated to you. Do I compromise you by their inclusion? I hope not. I *think* not. You have but to say to Labour, 'O honoured and darling and terrifying Sir, *I* know you're perfect. Don't blame *me* for some drawings done by an utterly absurd man who lives ever so far away in a country shaped like a jack-boot.' But if such words avail not, and you deem it expedient to reject the dedication, then reject it, dear Britannia: I shall not be thereby the less affectionately your old servant,

Max Beerbohm.

Max was speaking no more than the truth. He had always made fun of what was especially revered at the time. Equally characteristic is the frankness with which in his letter to Florence he talked about class distinctions. His detachment always had the effect of removing the inhibitions imposed by the predominant prejudices, moral and emotional, of the society in which he lived. This had appeared years ago at the time of Oscar Wilde's trial. Then, homosexuality had been a taboo subject. Most people felt too embarrassed to speak openly about it. They thought anyone who did so must be so grossly insensitive as to be called vulgar. Max—who felt no moral disapproval of homosexuality—spoke to his friends about it with the same blithe frankness that we should nowadays. By 1921 sex had begun to disappear as a taboo subject and class was taking its place. Now it was those who talked frankly of class distinctions who were called vulgar. Max was as impervious to the new taboos as he had been to the old. Though not a snob—Max attacked grossness and stupidity as readily in a prince as in a Labour leader—he was also no egalitarian. He approved of aristocracy and the kind of culture and manners it produced, and he saw no reason why he should not say so plainly.

He did this with the more ease because it did not upset him if people spoke plainly about him. In the previous October Gordon Craig had been sharply criticized in the newspaper by St John Ervine, playwright and dramatic critic. Craig was very much upset and poured out his wounded feelings in a letter to Max. Max comforted him in a letter which reveals his own reactions to similar attacks.

My dear Ted,

I haven't the faintest notion who 'St John Ervine' may be. I infer that he is a Saint; and I infer also, from his manner of writing, that he is an Ass. And I am delighted to hear of him from you, for it is a sign that you are splendidly convalescing. Perhaps your annoyance at St John has quickened your recovery. If so, go on being annoyed till you feel *quite* well. But not a moment later. What do the St Johns of this world matter? I cast no aspersion on the memory of that charming singer, Florence;[1] nor on the memory of the rugged but gifted Baptist. But Ervine . . . no, I refuse to bother about Ervine. I am glad to see that the 'correspondence is now closed'; otherwise perhaps you, in your unworldly way, would be rushing in and giving Ervine an advertisement that would waft him into the seventh heaven. Never take any notice of what Ervines say. That is a golden rule. I have been something of an Ervine myself, in my day. When I started writing, I delighted in being rude to eminent elder men. And oh, my delight when (as frequently happened) I 'drew' them! Never be drawn, I repeat.

I certainly shan't tell you the name of anybody on the staff of *Punch* who might make fun of Ervine and thereby make him permanently happy and temporarily important. As for your own feelings in the matter—well, well! I remember Gosse told me years ago a pretty and touching little story about Hans Andersen, whom he met once in Copenhagen. H. A. was already of course an old man at that time, and one of the glories of Denmark. He complained to Gosse that there was an attack on him in some newspaper—some quite obscure newspaper. 'But surely, Master,' said Gosse, in Danish, 'such a trivial thing can't vex *you*?' Hans Andersen stroked his beard: 'A little, my dear,' he answered.

Well, don't let Ervine hurt *you* even a little, dear Ted.

Such detachment made Max an impartial satirist. The *Daily Herald* need not have taken his cartoons on Labour so much to heart. For near them hung other drawings which revealed him just as ready to make fun of their opponents—nonconformist Liberals and Tory

[1] Florence St John, actress and singer of Max's youth.

militarists, go-getting supporters of Lloyd-George and grim pro-
moters of scientific warfare. Nor was Max enamoured of the modern
capitalist. One drawing shows a boorish and ferocious-looking
Captain of Industry, declaring to a nervous cleric 'that the desire of
the manual workers to be paid exorbitant wages for doing the least
possible amount of work is a sure sign that they have lost their faith
in a future life'.

The Leicester Galleries held another show of his work in October
of the same year. This time it was smaller and confined to those
drawings of imaginary episodes in the lives of Rossetti and his
friends which he had made at Far Oakridge during the war. These
are the most exquisite of all his cartoons: no others combine so
perfectly the satiric, the fanciful and the decorative; and they enhanced Max's reputation still further. Indeed, he had now become a
sort of living classic. It was an indication of this that Heinemann that
summer proposed bringing out a book about Max's life and works,
to be written by the author and cartoonist John Bohun Lynch.
Lynch wrote to ask Max's approval for the book and also that he
should write an introduction to it. He suggested coming out to Italy
to talk the matter over. Max, who knew and liked Lynch, invited
him to stay. He agreed to his requests but imposed certain conditions.
He proposed to state these in his introduction which took the form of
a letter to Lynch.

'I shan't offer you the slightest assistance,' he said, 'except of the
purely negative and cautionary kind that now occurs to me. I won't
supply you with any photograph of myself at any age, nor with any
scrap of corrected MS., nor with any caricature of myself for a
frontispiece (you yourself have done several brilliant caricatures of
me, and I commend these to your notice), nor with any of the things
you seem to think might be of interest. You must forage around for
yourself. I won't even try to prevent you from using anything you
may find. I eschew all responsibility whatsoever. I disclaim the horrid privilege of seeing proof-sheets. I won't read a single word till
your book is published. Even if modesty didn't prevent me,
worldly wisdom would. I remember several books about men, who
not yet dead, had blandly aided and abetted the author; and I
remember what awful asses those men seemed to me thereby to
have made of themselves. Two of them were rather great men.

They could afford to make awful asses of themselves. I, who am 100 miles away from being great, cannot afford such luxuries. My gifts are small. I've used them very well and discreetly, never straining them; and the result is that I've made a charming little

MAX BEERBOHM, SELF-CARICATURE

'They call me the inimitable and the incomparable, and the sprightly and whimsical. . . . I wonder if I *am*.'

reputation. But that reputation is a frail plant. Don't over-attend to it, gardener Lynch! Don't drench and deluge it! The contents of a quite small watering-can will be quite enough. This I take to be superfluous counsel. I find much reassurance and comfort in your phrase, "a little book". Oh, keep it little!—in due proportion to its theme. Avoid such phrases as "It was at or about this time that the young Beerbohm" etc. My life (though to me it has been, and is, extremely interesting) is without a single point of general interest.

Address yourself to my writings and drawings. And surtout pas de zèle, even here! Be judicial. Make those reservations without which praise carries no weight. Don't by dithyrambs, hasten the reaction of critics against me. Years ago, G. B. S., in a light-hearted moment, called me "the incomparable". Note that I am not incomparable. Compare me. Compare me as essayist (for instance) with other essayists. Point out how much less human I am than Lamb, how much less intellectual than Hazlitt, and what an ignoramus beside Belloc; and how Chesterton's high spirits and abundance shame me; how unbalanced G. S. Street must think me, and how coarse too; and how much lighter E. V. Lucas' touch is than mine; and so on, and so forth. Apply the comparative method to me also as caricaturist. Tend rather to underrate me—so that those who don't care for my work shall not be incensed, and those who do shall rally round me. . . .'

Max's attitude to his public reputation was complex. It was not a matter of supreme importance to him. On the other hand, he disliked people getting a wrong impression of him; and took pains to avoid this happening. The fact was that he—it was one of the paradoxes of his character—had always been both showman and recluse, desirous to escape from the world yet enjoying cutting a figure in it. As he grew older the recluse had gradually come to dominate in him. But the showman was not dead; and, if circumstances brought him before the public he was still concerned about the image he created in the eyes of his audience.

Much more did he mind about the impression made by his work. As much as ever he paid extreme attention to the way his work was presented. Every detail of mounting or presenting or binding was designed carefully to contribute to the effect of the whole. For this reason, once a work was completed Max objected to altering it. When his American publishers wanted him to illustrate *And Even Now*, Max said that the very idea made his blood freeze and his tongue cleave to the roof of his mouth. As for allowing pieces of his work to be cut out and selected, the suggestion filled him with horror. In 1923 a lady wrote asking him if she might extract some paragraphs from an essay in *And Even Now* to be included in an anthology. Max refused with a vehemence which showed how strongly he felt in such matters.

Dear Madam,

I am very sorry (for myself) that I cannot have the honour of appearing in your anthology on children and childhood. All best wishes for the anthology, which I have no doubt will be charming— if it doesn't contain many such extracts as those which you have made from my essay about the sand-castle. I don't mean that you haven't made as good extracts from that essay as could be made. I mean merely that *any* extracts would be (saving your presence) damnable. My essays have many faults, but they have the virtue of being very closely written. Every paragraph in any one of them depends on every other paragraph; and every sentence on every other sentence. This is what gives them the modest quality of *life*, of *movement*. A dead bird can be carved acceptably: a bit of the breast, a leg, a liver—wing, and so on. But oh, don't mutilate a live bird. Let it fly, let it sing. Don't chop off bits of it. Don't hand such bits round. They aren't good to eat. The look of the bits you have sent me makes me feel slightly sick. I enclose them in this envelope, with many thanks and regrets, and am, dear Madam, yours truly,

Max Beerbohm.

Lynch came and went. Florence did not get back till August. In his letters to her Max gaily traced the idyllic course of his summer days: told how he dined on the terrace, frugally but deliciously, on a single dish, some fruit and a glass of wine: how he visited the Craigs three times a week, entertained callers, bathed at the neighbouring *spiaggia*, drew cartoons, read the newspapers and took notice of what was happening in the garden. For example:

'Further local news: the chimney plant has begun to re-issue those flame-coloured blossoms which I and everybody but you admire so greatly. One of the camellias has issued a queer affair resembling a large tight pink cherry with a sort of thread hanging out from it. I hope this is all in the course of nature and not a sign of the approaching end of the world.'

Florence had come back and the two settled down for a quiet winter together. Little happened in 1922 to break the quiet. The Rossetti drawings were published by Heinemann in a volume called *Rossetti and His Circle*: and Max also agreed to the issue of a standard edition of his works. He was characteristically concerned about its form and also that this should not be incongruously pompous and official. There must be no gilt and calf: he said he wanted each volume to be bound in a different shade of linen and with a plain white label on the spine.

The winter had seen the arrival of Florence's brother Mannie, his wife Nell and his daughter Dody. In the spring these took Florence off on another short tour of Italian towns including Rome, Florence and Pisa.

'*Appuyez-vous,*' wrote Max gaily, 'on the lovely calm blank classic clear dear aged smug gloom of Pisa; but don't lean on the leaning tower: it is such a broken reed to lean on.'

Her stay in Florence caused Max some moments of anxiety. Reggie Turner was living there: Max thought Florence ought to go and see him; she did not want to. Florence, it seems, did not much care for Reggie. She seldom liked Max's great friends and had little taste for humour. Some people also thought she disapproved of Reggie and, indeed, his amorous habits were all too like those of his friend Oscar Wilde not to shock Florence if she knew of them. They did not shock Max. But he could sympathize with some of Florence's other complaints. For Reggie had lately become moody again. Granville Barker and his wife had come to call, and Reggie for some unknown reason was morose and silent throughout their visit. Nor, in Max's view, had he thanked Florence sufficiently when he went away. All the same, Reggie was his oldest friend; he owed him a great deal; and he was still very fond of him. Max felt he would be extremely hurt if he learnt Florence had been in the same town as himself and had not called. Max besought her to do so.

Meanwhile, Max had not been lonely at the Villino. An international conference was being held at Genoa; so that in addition to the ordinary summer visitors there were many people from England and America in the district who knew Max or wanted to know him. Letters of introduction in hand, they arrived on the terrace to be received by Max dressed in his best and offering them a glass of Marsala. More rarely a visitor called in order to see Florence. When this happened Max hastened to tell her about it, in order to encourage her self-confidence.

'There was an "invasion" this afternoon,' ran one letter, 'a large solid sandy-haired man, whom I supposed to be a Conference journalist, and accompanied by a rather pretty woman who I thought might also be a journalist, suddenly sprang upon the terrace. . . . They turned out to be Dr and Mrs Kirkpatrick from Genoa. And great was my disappointment for them that you and Nell and Mannie and Dody weren't here to welcome them. I did all I could in the way of welcome: tea, milk, sugar, cake, Marsala, "Yes, practically due south", "Yes, it's a pleasant little room to write in", "Yes, it *is* a good blue: my wife chose the colour", etc. etc. And I liked them both immensely, and I think they liked me, and they stayed some time, but mainly talking of *you* and all *your* kindness to Kp. . . . insomuch that I felt inclined to say "But, *I'm* kind too"—to which the reply would have been "Yes, but you aren't *they*!!"

Kp. said at one moment impressively: "Mr Beerbohm, I never met a woman whom I so . . ." and then, remembering that we were both of us married men, continued: "*respected* as Mrs Beerbohm." '

Florence returned early in May. In October she and her family went on another trip; this time Max accompanied them—to Bologna, Carrara and Lucca. From Lucca he wrote to Gordon Craig:

'We came hither 2 or 3 days ago from Carrara, having utterly failed to understand the place: it consists almost entirely of cafés: there is only one little hotel, and not a single restaurant but the restaurant of that hotel; there is one chemist's shop, one draper's, no grocer's, no butcher's, one shop where they sell very small ornaments of marble rimmed with red or blue velvet; and all the rest of the town consists of large cafés. The mystery is the more baffling because one never sees anybody tipsy. "Perhaps," you suggest, "the Carrarese have very strong heads." They may have, or they mayn't. One doesn't know. They never drink. The multitudinous gleaming great cafés are all quite empty, day and night. It is good to be here, in a place that one can more or less understand. The churches here are almost as many as the cafés out yonder. But there are worshippers in them. It is good to see San Michele again; also the Duomo; but especially San Michele, with the wonderful way that its façade and its campanile have of taking the light and looking lovelier in the afternoon than in the morning, and lovelier still in the evening, and lovelier always today than yesterday.

(3)

Drawings had been accumulating during the last eighteen months. In 1923 Max decided he had enough for an exhibition. Florence and he went to London in the late spring to prepare for it; but went away before the opening which took place in June. It met with a more mixed reception than his earlier exhibitions had done. Not only did some critics begin to say that his art was out of date, but he was, for the first time since *Yellow Book* days, the subject of a violent attack by the Press. It is impossible for a satirist not to annoy someone. This time it was right-wing opinion that took offence. The exhibition included some cartoons dealing with his old subject, the Royal Family. Among them was one depicting Edward VII as a fat angel playing a lyre in Heaven: it was inspired by Max's amusement at the idealized version of the King's character presented to the public since his death.

In the past Max had often been thus disrespectful to the Crown without creating any great stir. But times had changed since the gay and graceless days of Edward VII. His successor had carried out his duties with so unsparing a conscientiousness as much to increase the reverence in which the Crown was held: and this reverence had been reinforced by that new conception of monarchy as an embodied national ideal, a living symbol of English virtue, which was to make the Crown more venerated, if not more powerful, than ever before in its history. All this created an atmosphere in which Max's flippant little fantasy struck a discordant note. The newspapers were quick to respond to the mood of the time. Accordingly, Max opened his paper the day after the exhibition startled to find himself the object of a barrage of journalistic moralizings. 'Teutonically brutal,' thundered *The Times*; 'A scarifying exhibition,' proclaimed the *Daily Chronicle*; 'The end of Max Beerbohm,' declared the *Daily Graphic*; and another journal announced that it had come to the conclusion that the author of such enormities as these drawings must be 'either a shameless bounder or a stealthy Bolshevist'.

It is not to be supposed that Max minded such attacks any more than he had in the old *Yellow Book* days. But no longer did he think it seemly to be involved in a public row; he had no intention of appearing before the world in the role of an elderly *enfant terrible*. All the more because it gave a wholly misleading impression of his opinions; for by this time Max was a firm supporter of the monarchy: it stood for the kind of things he believed in. Was it not traditional, picturesque and a bulwark against revolution? He therefore rang up the Leicester Galleries and suggested that they should withdraw the offending cartoons from the exhibition. 'I know the Press,' he said, 'they won't stop till they've had their way': and he enclosed a letter to be printed in the papers explaining his action.

My dear Messrs Ernest Brown and Phillips,

Away down in the country, I have yet seen only three of the newspapers. From these I gather that certain of my drawings in your galleries are likely to shock the susceptibilities of the general public. You, who are on the spot, will be better able than I to judge whether or not these drawings should vanish or remain. I take no stand in the matter. No question of principle is involved. The question is one of taste merely, and I cannot strike a dignified attitude and say to the public in solemn tones: 'My taste, believe me, is perfect.' The drawings objected to were conceived, as you know, in a spirit of light-hearted fantasy; but if the public is likely to read any shadow of seriousness into them, and accordingly to regard them as unkind and even 'disloyal', I think it would be as well to avoid this misunderstanding of my disposition (in which, as again you know, there is no unkindness and certainly no disloyalty) by removing those particular drawings from the exhibition.

Yours very sincerely,

Max Beerbohm.

Florence must have approved his action. For, in a letter to him written apparently before the opening of the exhibition, she shows herself distressed lest King George V should be hurt by Max's drawing of King Edward VII.

'If only kings had humour! But even if King George were so gifted, he could not tolerate the cartoon since it would show a want of respect for his father. They seem such good people, they might not like it. I should be sorry if it hurt them. And of course it seems a cynical and rather unkind view of them.'

She added, resignedly: 'However, you must do as you think best.' We know he did; but the incident must have confirmed Florence in her suspicions of the dangerous art of caricature.

'If only kings had humour! . . .' so Florence had said. It must be admitted that George V and his Queen would have had more than their fair share easily to have appreciated Max's jokes. He made unsparing fun of them as well as their relations. Another cartoon, exhibited some years earlier, had depicted the King heavily inspecting an infant school: Max had also composed a ballade, mischievously mocking the royal conversational powers. There was, of course, never any question of this being published. But—so Max told Behrman in later years—some audacious person did show it to the King and Queen. 'How did they like it?' asked Behrman. 'They were vexed,' replied Max, looking demure.

As before, the exhibition led to a book, *Things New and Old*, which appeared in October of the same year, and offered, though omitting the royal cartoons, a representative selection from Max's work during the last years. It shows him trying his hand at some new models like Aldous Huxley and the Sitwell brothers, and includes some topical political drawings, notably a series illustrating the relative positions of France, England and Germany *vis-à-vis* of each other during different phases of the last three hundred years. The book leaves us with an impression that Max, though still pessimistic about politics, had continued to grow more tolerant about them. The John Bull of the new cartoons is still a John Bull whose greatness is in decline: but Max presents him no longer as the cringing, ignominious philistine of the 1900 series, but rather as an ageing, well-meaning, bourgeois-looking person, roused sporadically to action during the 1914 war, but afterwards relapsing into anxious, weary waiting on the will of other nations more vital than his own.

Max spent some time in the autumn and winter making a selection from his dramatic criticisms to be included in the new standard edition of his works. Otherwise nothing much happened in 1923. The year 1924, on the other hand, opened with a squall. Frank Harris caused it. In February Grant Richards published a volume of *Contemporary Portraits* by Harris; it contained an essay on Max. In general this was complimentary and perceptive. But Harris could not for long control his propensity to tell sensational lies: and, to brighten up his picture, he inserted a malicious little anecdote about Max's courtship, painful to Florence and wholly at variance with the facts which he professed, unplausibly, to have heard from

Max's sister Agnes. Agnes, or some other person, complained to Max about it. The effect was surprising and formidable. Forgetting all his long-cherished habits and preferences, he immediately left for England in order to get redress. Once there he went off to interview Grant Richards, Geoffrey Russell the lawyer, and, a little later, Bruce Richmond, the editor of *The Times Literary Supplement*. All three heard him with sympathy. Grant Richards also apologized: inadvertently he had failed to notice the offending passage. Now he offered to withdraw the whole issue and republish the book with the passage left out. Max accepted his offer but felt withdrawal was not enough. He proposed writing a letter to the newspaper publicly denying the story. Russell was against this. For one thing, he thought it would attract attention to the matter and so do more harm than good: for another, he feared lest Max's letter might lead Harris to sue him for libel. Max was unmoved. Not to deny the story would, in his view, be to admit its truth. As for the risk of libel, he was confident he could compose a letter which should make his point without giving Harris any ground on which to sue him. To avoid too much publicity he suggested, after talking things over with Richmond, that the letter should appear only in *The Times Literary Supplement* and then in an inconspicuous place in the middle of its correspondence column. It ran:

Sir,

I have only just seen a copy of Mr Frank Harris' book *Contemporary Portraits*, which was published about a month ago with a drawing of mine reproduced on the cover.

In the course of what he writes about me in this book, Mr Harris tells an anecdote which he says was told to him about me by one of my sisters, many years ago. The anecdote is utterly untrue; and it was not told to Mr Harris by one of my sisters. I wonder that he, knowing me, could have supposed that it was true, and not palpably false; and I wonder that he could have supposed that any sister of mine would have told it. I impute no malice to him; merely a deplorable lapse of memory in regard to my sister, and of sense of character in regard to both of us.

Mr Grant Richards, who published the book, has agreed that in all copies that leave his premises, henceforth, the passage shall be eliminated, the type being reset for that purpose.

I hope you will be so good as to publish this letter on a matter that has caused me deep annoyance.

Yours obediently
Max Beerbohm.

Harris did not attempt to reply: no more was heard of the matter. Max had demonstrated once again that when he thought it necessary he could be a man of action. We see too what kind of thing it was that forced him into that unusual, unwished-for role. He had reacted very much in the same way as he had twenty-five years before when he thought that Maud Tree had spoken rudely to him about Kilseen. In so far as Harris's words reflected on Florence, they outraged Max's sense of chivalry; in so far as they reflected on himself they outraged the sense of his own honour. The impact of these two outrages was to make him lose his temper. Loss of temper made him take action.

Max stayed only two or three days more in England after this, in excellent spirits. It had been a very satisfactory visit. He had succeeded triumphantly in his aim and enjoyed the opportunity to see his friends and family, especially Dora. Dora, it appeared, had just written the words of a music-hall song. The Mother Superior of her convent had given her permission to get it published provided she did so anonymously. She showed Max the song. Its refrain began thus:

Left right, left right,
The girl that I left
Is the girl that is right.

Dora certainly was an unusual kind of nun. Certainly, too, she was the most like Max of all the family.

She kept up with him more than the others did. For, as a nun, she had no opportunity to create new personal relationships which might wean her mind from the past. Alone in her convent cell she let her fantasy hover whimsically round his figure:

'At the foot of my bed there are uneven marks on the green wall, and one of them makes a picture of you—*older* than you are—your eyes and forehead, surmounted by a rather small hat—and close to it is a picture made by these marks too—also you, but about three years old—with a large sad eye in profile, and a tiny mouth—*very* sweet— and I lie and look at these two pictures and love them.'

DORA BEERBOHM

Every year still Dora came out for her fortnight's holiday to the Villino, where the brother and sister would pass the sunny hours sitting on the terrace by the camellia tubs recalling old days, playing nonsense games and—a new-found enjoyment—doing crossword puzzles. Dora had taken to making patchwork quilts out of old scraps of stuff, to sell for the benefit of the Convent charities. Max interested himself in these. Dora and he, their heads bent together over her sewing basket, used to sit attentively matching the coloured scraps. Dora had a high opinion of Max's taste in these matters. She found it far harder to compose the quilts without him, so she wrote after she had got home. Indeed, the only trouble about her holiday was that she missed him so much when it was over. She told him so: 'My thoughts are with you;' wrote charming Dora, 'how I envy my thoughts!'

Max enjoyed her company as much as she enjoyed his. People noticed his excitement before her arrival. 'Dora is coming!' he would exclaim with brightening eyes. He was always thinking of how to please her and would even, unasked, walk down to Rapallo, which was a thing he disliked doing—to get some wool for her quilt. His manner changed in her company: once more he was the younger brother leading about his elder sister by the hand to show her things in the garden he took pride in. Together, too, they would gently tease Florence, who did not quite understand but was too happy with them to mind.

She was as fond of her brothers as Dora of Max; and she had not seen any of them except Mannie for over two years. In the autumn of 1924, therefore, she went over to America for a few months. As before, Max remained behind 'improving' title-pages, pacing the terrace, doing an occasional drawing and desultorily reading the novels of Dickens and Disraeli. Though the season was waning Max had occasional visitors. Among these were Rothenstein's eldest son John, who stayed for a week or two—most pleasant and intelligent, Max told Florence—and later in the year Ada Leverson and the Sitwell brothers, who stayed for some weeks in Rapallo and several times came up to the Villino for a meal. Gently triumphant, Max called Florence's attention to the fact that they and everybody else who visited the house particularly admired his frescoes.

CHAPTER FIFTEEN

'A Variety of Things'

(1)

I N March 1925 the prospect of another show took Max to London, to be followed a few weeks later by Florence. He first stayed at the Charing Cross Hotel and then in a studio in Apple Tree Yard lent him by William Nicholson. This last was a welcome economy. But he had much enjoyed the Charing Cross Hotel; Max had during his last few visits to England acquired a taste for staying at station hotels. Was it not noisy and restless? asked one of his relations. 'Not at all,' replied Max, 'I never notice individual noises in these admirable hotels. I derive real pleasure for a little while from the railway hotel atmosphere—of life and of ever-changing activity. One of my most potent reasons for staying in station hotels,' he went on, 'is that I delight in seeing my luggage up straight from the platform. No bother with taxi-cabs—delightful!' Max continued to cultivate solitary pleasures even when he was on his visits to London. He was often tempted not to tell his friends and relations that he had arrived, so that he could alone savour the delights of life at the Charing Cross Hotel. He would lunch by himself at the Holborn Restaurant off a dozen oysters and a cup of coffee, consumed to the agreeable sound of selections from *Pagliacci* or *Iolanthe* played by the restaurant orchestra; and dine in solitude at Gatti's 'which', he wrote to Florence, 'has a common charm about it—not XX century commonness, commonness entirely Victorian. You will be glad to hear that I had mulligatawny soup and afterwards stewed steak—in honour of the genius loci.'

This time his exhibition provoked no hostile reactions. Max had drawn some of the cartoons since he came to London and from new models: Bertrand Russell, Walter de la Mare, and a group of politicians, including Baldwin, Ramsay MacDonald, Austin Chamberlain and Duff Cooper. Max saw most of them at a debate in the House of Commons in which official tributes were paid to the memory of the recently dead Lord Curzon. He told Florence about it.

'After luncheon, the H. of C. Tributes to Curzon. I knew I should like Baldwin, but not so much as I *did* like him. Had expected something rather muzzy and rough; whereas he has a pleasant voice and *admirable* articulation—without any loss of obvious honesty, etc. Speech very well phrased, in a humdrum way. Quoted M. Arnold's 'last enchantments'—with a preliminary glance at his notes. Whole thing very carefully prepared at Chequers, because Curzon was a theme not to be scamped, and because Curzon did such themes so finely. Altogether a great darling. Ramsay MacDonald not so attractive—but no Scotsman ever was so *attractive* as a person of other nationality. Seemed slightly conceited and self-conscious. I liked him better in his speech about Singapore. John Simon (on Curzon) frightfully prosy and trite and non-conducting, as always. I sent in my card to A. Ponsonby, but he wasn't there. Also, to Duff Cooper, who came to me, and we walked about the lobby together. He wanted me to stay and dine, but—I know not why—I didn't want to, and said I was dining out (as indeed I was: at Gatti's). He is as nice as ever; and less fat.'

A few days later he dined with the Duff Coopers and went with them to *Hamlet*, where the past rose to recall itself to him in the shape of Constance Collier who was playing Gertrude to the Hamlet of John Barrymore. As the weeks passed the invitations began to pour in and he was less and less alone. We hear of him lunching with Arnold Bennett to meet Somerset Maugham, and dining with Mrs Tickell to meet Belloc. On each occasion he made an extremely favourable impression. The guests at Mrs Tickell's dinner were entertained by the quiet mischief with which Max teased Belloc alternately with paying him compliments. 'Of course,' he said, 'I can only speak for man; but Mr Belloc knows God's point of view.' Arnold Bennett was chiefly struck by the unobtrusive originality of his conversation, his odd, modest, individual philosophy. He asked Max whether he wanted a Turkish or a Virginian cigarette. Max replied it did not matter, he took whatever came; 'I don't care about many things,' he added. 'As soon as I own something that I have wanted, it ceases to please me.' The conversation also turned on London. Max said he could not feel romantic about it because he had been born there: 'the smuts fell on my bassinet', he explained. Bennett was surprised how little Max seemed to mind growing older. He said he did not envy young people in the least; in fact he felt sorry for them. For they might die any day, and if they did die—what a suck-in for them! How much they would have missed without knowing it!

Max made some new great friends this year: the most important were Sydney Schiff, who wrote under the name of Stephen Hudson, and his wife Violet. Since Violet was Ada Leverson's sister, Max must have met her often before. But it seems to have been during this time that he got to know her and her husband very well. About this time, too, he made friends with Ellis Roberts, the critic and journalist, and his American wife. Warm-hearted, appreciative and with something homely about them, the Ellis Robertses had the additional and rare gift of making Florence feel at ease in their company. Theirs was a house to which she could go without feeling shy, even if Max was not with her to keep her in countenance. From this time on, whenever Max and Florence were in London, they spent a good deal of time with the Schiffs and with the Ellis Robertses.

In this year Max made the acquaintance of another Roberts, Cecil Roberts, the novelist. The circumstances of their first meeting were sufficiently curious and characteristic to be worth recounting. It took place in Italy. Cecil Roberts, accompanied by a friend, arrived at Rapallo with letters of introduction to Max and to Gordon Craig.

'My friend and I,' he related, 'thought it prudent to rehearse our visits to the neighbours, so two evenings previous we walked along the Via Aurelia, out of Rapallo, in search of their villas. Somewhere we went wrong; the result, after hours of climbing through olive groves, was that we emerged on an enchanting small piazza, with dark cypresses, that rewarded the wanderers with the whole bay of Rapallo scintillating before us. But, alas, the villas we sought were far away below. It must have been almost midnight when we found ourselves lost on a wide road. There was a light in a villa above and a figure near a balustrade. I hailed it for information, asking whether we were anywhere near the villa of Gordon Craig. A gentle but very precise voice said—"Mr Craig's villa is over there—but if it is Mr Craig you want, he is not there. He has gone into Turin, which is hot and noisy, in order to be cool and quiet, to write."

We thanked him for the information. "That," I said, as we journeyed on, "must be Max." '

It was. And then Roberts sent his letter of introduction and two days
later was invited to a luncheon at the Villino, which laid the foundation of a subsequent friendship.

For the third time an exhibition was followed by a book. *Observations* appeared in October. It was to be the last collection of
cartoons Max ever published, but it was a remarkably up-to-date
one. In fact, it was largely concerned with the new world; how it
developed from the old and how it would be likely to develop in the
future. During the last two years Max had meditated much on these
matters. Escapist in fact, he was not escapist in thought: for all that
he chose to live out of the world, he was vividly and intelligently
aware of it. His view of its future was, if possible, more pessimistic
than ever. One cartoon shows us an animated Principle of Evil
conversing with a plump lethargic-looking Principle of Good. 'How
is it that you always seem to get the best of it?' asks Good. 'Because
I'm *active*, my dear,' replies the Principle of Evil. Max feared that
this activity was growing more effective each year; and had an
alarmingly shrewd idea what forms it might take. In another cartoon
called 'Recurrent Alarms' he portrays himself as a tiny figure be-
seeching the English not to take refuge in complacent confidence:
surely before long it is only too likely that they may find themselves
either the slave of a totalitarian system or blown to pieces by bombs.
Even if it was not going to turn out catastrophic, Max did not feel
happy about the future. For, surely, everything was getting uglier
and more and more were people losing their sense of style. A cartoon
called 'Class-Consciousness' depicts a seedy-looking proletarian
youth gazing yearningly at a magnificently arrogant aristocrat of the
Regency period. 'Now, that's the sort of class-consciousness *I*'d like
ter have,' he says. Egalitarianism, thought Max, encouraged vulgarity. But not only egalitarianism; so also did commercialism and
advertising: there are cartoons attacking these. So also did the
modern journalist-politician; another drawing contrasts a statesman
of the past spending his leisure translating Virgil for nothing with his
successor snatching a minute to dictate a piece for the popular Press
to be paid for at the rate of seventy-five pounds a line. So most of all
did the new industrialism. In 'Civilization and the Industrial System'

Max depicts Industrialism as a monster, half-naked and horribly fat, who thus addresses his dejected wife, Civilization: 'No, my dear, you may've ceased to love me; but you took me for better or wuss in younger and 'appier days, and there'll be no getting away for you from me, ever.' This drawing is unique in Max's work. For once it does deserve the epithet 'savage'. The figure of Industrialism is hideous and repulsive in a way which is true of no other figure by him. Hatred was never an inspiration to Max, as a consequence the cartoon is artistically a failure: compared with the work of Goya or Daumier in a similar mood it looks strained and feeble. Like *The Dreadful Dragon of Hay Hill* it shows Max working outside his natural range and failing in consequence. But it too throws an important light on his feelings and thought. Its very unbridled and untypical violence shows what really frightened him; the threat to civilization from industrialism and from the coarse, soulless and ruthless forces of mechanization and mass production which were its offspring.

It is the only cartoon in the book in which Max loses his urbanity. Otherwise, even when he is warning England against totalitarianism and bombs, he somehow manages to appear detached and lighthearted. Though he felt civilization might be decaying, he did not allow the feeling to obsess him, but retired into the security provided by his irony and his curiosity. The book concludes with a series of drawings called 'The Old and the Young Self' in which nineteen persons now in late life are confronted by themselves in youth, so that they see the difference between what they are and what in those days they expected to become. The series, which contains some of Max's favourite subjects, Gosse, Kipling, Shaw, Bennett, etc., is the best thing in the volume. Max is on his home ground dealing with individuals not abstractions, and with an extraordinary penetration. No wonder that he did not envy the young. Why should he, when advancing years were so full of interest to the observer of the human comedy? Who would have thought that the bohemian young Rothenstein would grow into such a pillar of respectability and the serious Asquith into a *bon viveur*; that Lloyd George should have changed so much and George Moore so little! During these years the ironies of time loomed large in Max's thoughts—not always to be perceived so gaily as here. They were all too easily associated with a sense of mortality to be untouched by sadness. Looking through the back pages of his jotting diary one day

Max found them scrawled with sketches of people now dead; 'How very odd and remote this book is,' he noted, 'with its sketches of people no longer alive . . . and I going on still; skipping through the pages occupied by these corpses!'

Max did not include a cartoon of himself in the series 'The Old and the Young Self'. Perhaps he realized that in his case there was not enough difference between them to make it worth while. So far as tastes and opinions were concerned, the fifteen-year-old Max would have found little to surprise him in Max at fifty. There was some change in him, however. He was a quieter, ampler, more rooted personality than in his youth; and much more considerate of others. This last appeared in an incident which disturbed his tranquillity towards the end of 1925. Like his trouble with Harris, it was caused by a book. W. H. Davies published an autobiography. In it he described his meeting with Max in 1919 in which, so he alleged, Max had alluded disparagingly to his success as a poet and made a joke about his wooden leg. Max saw the passage referred to in a review and sent for the book. He did not get angry, as he had over Harris's book, because he did not feel his honour insulted; but he was seriously distressed. Apart from the fact that he liked both Davies and his poems very much, he was horrified to have been thought rude and cruel. Once more he had recourse to *The Times Literary Supplement*; and wrote it a letter, giving his version of the meeting in such convincing terms and revealing such genuine concern that he should have caused Davies pain, however involuntarily, as to persuade any unprejudiced reader that he was speaking the truth.

'Mr Davies,' the letter ended, 'thought my words were a blow deliberately aimed at him. He thought me capable of that. I do not think that even the nastiest little street urchin nowadays mocks at the infirmity of lameness. In the Middle Ages such mockery, even from adults, was common enough, I believe. What sort of a creature did Mr Davies imagine me to be? I can assure him that at the time I was wholly unaware of anything amiss. Let me further ask him to believe that the pain I caused him by my careless use of that phrase cannot have been greater than is the pain I feel at his misjudgement of me. And let me express the hope that in any future impressions or editions of *Later Days* he will either emend or omit his painful account of me.'

Max's hopes were vain: Davies did not omit the passage in subsequent editions. However, the story was too preposterously out of character for people to believe it, especially after Max's letter. The episode is interesting though for the light it throws on Max at fifty-three. The gadfly of the past has come to have a peculiar horror at the idea of hurting people's feelings. As Rothenstein said, writing of Max two or three years later, 'The pitiless satirist has become the most humane of men.'

This change of Max's temper had an important effect on his work. Caricature and good nature go ill together: a caricaturist must have a certain ruthlessness. Max had now lost this. It was not only that he disliked hurting other people's feelings. He was no longer quick to notice their ludicrous features; he liked them too much. The result was he found it hard to caricature them. The picture he did of Noël Coward for his *Bitter Sweet* cartoons in 1930 is not a caricature but a portrait done with sympathy, even pity. Max remarked on this himself; in consequence he thought he had better give up caricaturing. 'I have lost my zest for cartooning,' he told a friend. 'It is a young man's hobby—you get kinder as you get older.'

Alas, moral improvement meant aesthetic sterility. Soon he was drawing almost as little as he wrote. His failure of inspiration does not seem to have worried him. Max was always ready to be idle. Besides, he was not sure if satirical caricature was a seemly occupation for one of his advancing years. 'Nothing is more admirable,' he noted in his commonplace book, 'than Eld inexhaustibly imparting scholarship or great ideas or creative dreams, but an octogenarian, with just a light touch, a spritely impertinent Nestor, pulling faces at his juniors, and drawing caricatures of them on the brink of the grave—oh no! please no, not that!!' Max was not an octogenarian yet: but in his late fifties he judged it wiser to do nothing than to present himself before the public in the deplorable role of an ageing Puck.

His growing considerateness showed itself in small incidents. For example, in 1929 he met the young Evelyn Waugh for the first time at a luncheon party. Mr Waugh, silent in the presence of his august elders, made little impression on Max, so that when next day he met him in the hall of his club, Max mistook him for someone else. Afterwards he discovered his error, went to some trouble to find Mr Waugh's address and write him a letter deeply apologizing. He remembered, he said, being taken for someone else when he was a young man and how much he had minded it. This growing social sensitiveness had some disadvantages. For Max a social slip had come to assume the proportions of a serious disaster. Once he mistook the time of a luncheon party and arrived half an hour late: in consequence, he became uncontrollably agitated. Twenty minutes were spent explaining and apologizing and, by the time he had finished, the party was two-thirds over. Even then Max was hardly himself again. This was not just because he feared he might be thought ill-mannered. It was also due to a growing tendency to nervous agitation. Here was another change. As he grew older Max grew more nervous. A visitor to the Villino noticed that when a door banged he jumped right out of his chair and for an instant looked angry.

Advancing years also made Max more frankly orthodox. This was a change of tone rather than opinion. Max had always had a natural bias towards the orthodox: as he often said, he made fun of established institutions largely because he respected them. Now, in middle age he was ready to express this respect openly. The big event of 1926 in England was the General Strike. As might be expected, Max was disturbed by this portent of possible revolution; and all the more because, living away from England, he fancied it as much more dangerous than it was. His feelings appeared in a letter he wrote after the strike was over to his old friend Henry Arthur Jones, who was now living in retirement in Buckinghamshire, a vociferous exponent of conservative opinions.

'My dear Henry Arthur,' wrote Max, 'I have been thinking of you much during the past horrible week or so—and now I write to say how glad I am with you that England has done well. I suppose there may be difficulties yet, but they won't matter so much: the long-impending big fight has been fought and won. England has all sorts of faults—dullnesses, stupidities, heavy frivolities, constantly pointed out by you. But in politics somehow she always is—somehow slowly, dully, but splendidly—all right. I have often thought, in reading your brilliant and violent rebukes of her, that you hadn't quite as much faith in her as she deserves. You didn't overstate her dangers; but I felt that you believed not quite enough in her power to meet these and deal with these successfully in her own fumbling and muzzy way, by her own dim (damnably dim, you would say) lights. You are a die-hard, and she is a die-soft. She says mildly, "No violence, pray! I quite see your points of view, dear gentlemen all! I'm full of faults. Really I rather doubt whether I deserve to survive. Yet I hope, I even intend, to do so" . . . and she *does*—the dear old thing! *Brava, bravissima*, dear silly old thing!

Dear Henry Arthur, I know how happy you are feeling—and I write to add my happiness to yours. The past week has made for my wife and me 'a goblin of the sun', and the big roses in our small garden look horrible. In writing to me at about Christmas-time, you said I did well to be out here, because of all the trouble brewing in England. But really out here, in this alien golden clime, one feels more acutely any dangers to England. What a relief it was to us both, my wife and me, when, early in 1915, we settled down into England! And Civil War is of course much more distressing to the heart and to the imagination than war with any number of more or less natural enemies. And oh, what paeans our hearts sing that the wretched affair is, to all intents and purposes, over—and that the right side has won.

I think King George's Message to the people very finely composed. I read it with emotion. Had you been he, the message would have been still finer, and I should have read it with still greater emotion. But it wouldn't have been so exactly right for the occasion. For the purpose of interpreting the deepest feelings of the British People, I back Hanover against Bucks every time!—though I sometimes wish Hanover had a little of Bucks' sparkle, all the same.

Your affectionate,
Max Beerbohm.'

Max, an Englishman, proud of his country and affectionately moved by his King's message to the English people—this is a different figure from the *jeune féroce* of twenty years earlier, mercilessly mocking John Bull and his rulers!

But for the General Strike, the year passed in unbroken tranquillity. Max continued to prefer it so. At the beginning of the year an American impresario had written offering him a large fee if he would give a lecture tour in the United States. Though he was always short of money, he refused at once and enthusiastically:

Dear Mr Reid,

I thank you for returning to the charge. But you don't charge hard enough. Or at any rate you don't seem to think I shall charge high enough . . . $12,000, minus 35 p.c., for 'hard travel', plus the horror of 'widespread newspaper publicity' in your 'beautiful country' for a 'period of three or four months'—oh, dear Mr Reid, how little you know me!

If you will guarantee an absolutely smooth Atlantic (forfeit of $500 to be paid by you for the least ripple observed by me) and will build an exquisite little marble hall on Ellis Island, a hall warranted not to hold more than twenty-five persons, to whom, on one night only and for not more than twenty minutes, and for a fee of twenty-five million dollars, I shall utter very quietly whatever nonsense may come into my head, do let me hear from you again, and meanwhile believe me yours very truly,

Max Beerbohm.

Max was no more tempted by ambition than by money. A new caricaturist had lately risen to eminence in England: Low was now as famous as Max. Some men would have been spurred to activity by this. Max, on the contrary, was only moved to admiration. As he had felt about Lytton Strachey the writer, so he now felt about Low the cartoonist. How splendid to find an artist working on the same lines as himself! Max admired Low so much that he even bestirred himself to write a letter to him.

Dear 'Low',

You will have heard of me as a caricaturist, and will probably have seen reproductions of my drawings here and there, and will therefore not think it very impertinent and irrelevant of me to sit down and say how very grateful I am to you for these drawings of yours in *The New Statesman*.

I wish you lacked some of the qualities that go to make a great caricaturist; for then I shouldn't seem to myself so presumptuous as I do seem to myself in praising you. But I can't for the life of me see what qualities you do lack—alack! You have the primal quality: sympathy. Without sympathy there can be no penetration. Without penetration there can be no fun. A caricature is no good unless it makes one laugh; it can't (unless one is an ass) make one laugh unless the subject has been seen through and through; and the subject can't be seen thus without tolerant good-will towards it. . . . But this sort of analysis is dreary. All I mean by it is that you are all right! . . .

In *St Loe Strachey* and *Joynson Hicks* I thought the clothes were rather heavily treated, detracting from the faces above them and the limbs inside them. I throw in this adverse criticism so that you shan't think I can't keep my head.

Yours sincerely and thankfully,

Max Beerbohm.

This relationship, so auspiciously begun, ran into trouble later. Low commented on Max publicly. 'Although he is still alive, he has ceased to create,' he said. Max took offence at this remark. It is odd that he should have done so considering that he usually paid little attention to hostile criticism. What displeased him was that he looked on Low as a friend; and he considered that a man should not speak of a friend in such a contemptuous tone. Low, who clearly did not realize that he had done anything to be ashamed of, made things no better by asking Max to luncheon. Max accepted because he thought it more dignified to ignore Low's words. 'But,' he said, relating the incident later, 'I have not forgiven him. It was too crude, too coarse.'

Even less happened to Max in 1927 than in 1926—except for one incident. For the second time Will Rothenstein was to have a decisive effect on Max's history. He came out to stay on a visit to the Villino. Gerhart Hauptmann, the distinguished German dramatist, was at this time living in the neighbourhood. Rothenstein had not lost his taste for the company of famous persons or his talent for making their acquaintance. Already he knew Hauptmann: now he took Max over to see him. It was not an interesting interview, for neither Max nor Hauptmann knew a word of the other's language; so that their intercourse was limited to bowing and smiling at one another in dumb good will. But there was another member of the Hauptmann's household who did know English, his secretary companion, a thirty-year-old lady of German–Jewish parentage called Elisabeth Jungmann. Tall, vigorous and handsome, with dark hair, a ready smile and a warm exuberant manner, she threw herself into the task of entertaining the Beerbohms with great success: before the evening was over the three had made friends. By the end of the year she seems to have become a regular visitor at the Villino. In theory she was equally a friend of both Max and Florence; and it is true she was one of the few people to thaw Florence's shyness

ELISABETH JUNGMANN

sufficiently to be on intimate confidential terms with her. For herself, however, there was no doubt that Max was the chief attraction. He had struck her as old at first sight; within a short time, however, she was only conscious that he was fascinating. As a matter of fact his age actually added to his fascination. Under a normal exterior Elisabeth Jungmann concealed an unusual temperament. The adored and adoring daughter of a well-known Jewish Breslau lawyer, she had passed a happy childhood and early youth, in which she had flung herself energetically into the pleasures, social and sporting, appropriate to her age. With maturity, however, a more individual strain revealed itself in her; highly charged, romantic hero-worshipping, instinctively seeking to fulfil itself in dedication to the care and service of some individual human being whom she admired. Further—and this may well have been the result of the peculiar devotion she had felt for her father—her idea of a hero was a distinguished man of an older generation than her own. Ardent and intelligent, she had the qualities to achieve her aim; with the result that her subsequent career was to consist of a series of such dedications. At the time when she enters our story Hauptmann was her hero; her feeling for him was filial and platonic. Five years later she was to leave him in consequence of a more passionate attachment to another older man, the poet Rudolf Binding. But her sentiment for neither was so exclusively compelling as to make her insensible to the charms of others; and from 1928 onwards she kept a very soft spot in her heart for Max. After leaving Hauptmann in 1933 she frequently came back to stay for a week or two with the Beerbohms. Florence was much occupied with household affairs; meanwhile Elisabeth kept Max company on the terrace, where he used to draw cartoons for her and pick her a camellia to wear in her dress. His manner, she noted, was often delicately flirtatious. For the first time for many years the Max who had enjoyed himself with Kathleen Bruce and Bettina von Hutten reappeared on the stage. Elisabeth gaily responded to Max's gay attentions and—though hardly more ironical than Florence herself—had enough straightforward sense of fun to laugh heartily at his cartoons. She had a natural eye for fine quality in human beings; and this, increased by much experience of remarkable people, led her to appreciate Max to the full. On his side, he sunned himself in her sympathy, her vitality and her youth. It was true that she was not yet very perceptive of those finer nuances of refinement in manner and speech of which he was a professional exponent. But he did not mind this in her any more than he had in the youthful Kilseen. People remarked that Max, in general so horrified by what he thought to be colloquialisms of language, never corrected Elisabeth Jungmann when she said 'boy-friend' or 'bye-bye'. To him this was part of her robust rejuvenating charm. One must not exaggerate the strength of their feeling for each other at these earlier stages in their acquaintance. Apart from anything else, Elisabeth's heart, most of the time, was elsewhere. But their pleasure in each other's company was intensified by the fact that it was sweetened by a waft of playful sentiment.

This is to anticipate. The year 1927 saw only the start of the friendship. Meanwhile, in 1928 appeared the last volume of the definitive edition of Max's works: *A Variety of Things*, a heterogenous assemblage of pieces hitherto uncollected. Most of them, like *The Happy Hypocrite* and the essay on Beardsley, dated back to the beginning of his career: but three were relatively new and had not appeared before in a permanent form: *The Dreadful Dragon of Hay Hill*, *T. Fenning Dodworth* and *Walter Argallo and Felix Ledgett*. These had been written, or at any rate finished, after his return to Italy. *The Dreadful Dragon of Hay Hill* has been considered earlier. Of the two others, *T. Fenning Dodworth* is an imaginary portrait of a successful fraud. Not successful in any obvious sense, Dodworth is a man who has failed as lawyer, journalist and politician. But he had contrived to persuade people that his failure was somehow to his credit, that he is a brain and wit of too fine a quality to be appreciated by the vulgar public. *T. Fenning Dodworth* is a sketch. *Argallo and Ledgett* is a more considerable work, of the same type as the tales in *Seven Men*; a realistic fantasy related by Max in person. It describes how a noble and sombre novelist of genius, suggested by Conrad, after years of neglect, achieves the fame which is his due. Later he is persuaded by Max to praise from motives of kindness the worthless work of the futile little man of letters called Ledgett, possibly suggested by the dramatist Alfred Sutro. In consequence, the public transfer their admiration to Ledgett; so that after Argallo's death his works once more sink into oblivion. Both pieces show Max the satirist at his sharpest; indeed, *Argallo and Ledgett* is one of his masterpieces. They are interesting to the biographer because they indicate that Max, during his later middle age, was preoccupied with the subject of fame and success. It struck him that they were not worth much. Admiration was worth little, even from the supposedly intelligent and educated. They were just as likely to praise frauds like Dodworth and Ledgett as a true genius like Argallo. Max did not feel bitter about this; the tone of both pieces is one which is of impish gaiety. But they do make us realize why their author felt no need to go on working, just to maintain his reputation. From what he had seen of the world, even posthumous reputation was no certain proof of merit.

For the rest, 1928 was a year of deaths; during it a number of the great names of Max's youth took their departure from this world: Hardy, Ellen Terry, Gosse. This was not a cause of great grief to Max. Gosse had been his only personal friend among them, and for many years he had seen little of him. But the fact of their passing increased still more his sense of the transience of things human. He came over in November for another exhibition: it is significant that he called it 'Ghosts', and that it consisted mainly of cartoons of persons he remembered from an older generation. He stayed on in London till well into 1929 and, as usual, saw a great many people. Records of the time supply us with one or two characteristic fragments of Max's talk. He dined with his old flame Kathleen Bruce, now married for a second time, to Hilton Young, the politician. The talk turned on public speakers, and especially on Asquith's hesitations, as he fastidiously searched for the exact word, however unimportant this might be. Max said that when he was listening to him he wanted to call out, 'Don't worry, sir—the word you are looking for is "*the!*"' At Arnold Bennett's he was more controversial and attacked the Russians as a thoroughly inferior race chiefly to be distinguished for their inefficiency. This might seem unexpected; but Max had always been as prejudiced against Russians as he was against professional authoresses. They stood to him for a blend of earthy barbarity and unintelligible mysticism, two phenomena he particularly disliked. He said he found all their writers, except Tolstoy, unreadable, and that he thought their ballet was ludicrously overpraised. No doubt Nijinsky could jump very high, but, said Max, so did the demon king in the pantomime: and the fact that the demon king was propelled by machinery and not by his own muscles was no reason for thinking his performance less satisfactory from an aesthetic point of view.

(2)

March found Max back at Rapallo, full of memories, he said, of charming people and things. The latter part of the year was to provide him with some more, for 1929 was marked by the appearance of two names not yet mentioned in this story. The first, Siegfried Sassoon, had met Max before and had long been an admirer of his art. He came this autumn to Rapallo and presented himself at the Villino. He was all an admirer should be, uniting youthful enthusiasm with mature discrimination, and he pleased both Florence and Max very much. Thereafter Siegfried was a member of the inner circle of their friends. The second name was more unexpected. In November Max got a letter introducing the Very Reverend H. R. L. Sheppard, Dean of Canterbury, who was staying at Portofino convalescing after a sharp attack of asthma. Max went over to call. He arrived at the villa at which Sheppard was staying, tired from his climb, and was ushered into the Dean's presence. With surprising results:

'Hardly had I beheld my host and exchanged greetings with him,' Max related, 'than I felt perfectly fresh and in the best of health. On men of my age, a man who seems very young is apt to have the effect of making him feel older than his years. The Dean looked worn and pale but he radiated a youthfulness that was less that of an undergraduate than of a schoolboy. Nevertheless he made me feel younger than my years. And better than my character. Generous, unselfish, altruistic—I might even have felt a little clerical, if he had seemed less signally lay. In fact I was under the wand of the enchanter.'

Subsequent meetings did nothing to weaken Sheppard's spell.

'The pen,' writes Max to him a few months later, 'makes me so garrulous as to say that it is not often that a man after he has reached the age of 30 or so feels that he has made a new friendship. New acquaintances are formed constantly, with the greatest ease, up to the eve of one's ninetieth birthday. But new friendships are apt to be the prerogatives of one's young days only. And I am 57 years old, and had long ago thought I shouldn't meet again a man of whom I could say to myself, "A new friend." '

It was odd that he should have said it of Sheppard; for besides being a clergyman—and one does not associate Max with clergymen—he was also an idealistic reformer with left-wing leanings. But he had other qualities extremely attractive to Max: spontaneity, humour, and a gift for perceptive, affectionate intimacy. On his side, Max was the man to appeal to Sheppard. His tranquillity of spirit and light-hearted flippancy were qualities Sheppard loved and had looked for in vain in clerical circles. Now he responded to them with characteristic enthusiasm. 'Max Beerbohm,' he told a friend, 'is by far the most attractive person to meet and talk to that I have ever met.' Though they were never to have a chance to see much of each other, the friendship between them had a special place in the lives of the two men.

Max spent the last part of the next year in England. Edinburgh University wrote offering him an honorary doctorate. He went over in the summer to receive it. Florence did not accompany him, presumably because it cost too much; he wrote to her describing the ceremony in detail. It was Max's first public honour and he enjoyed it very much; the spectacle, the company, the crowds, the speeches—including his own—the red silk gown and black velvet hat which he had to wear, above all the reception he received. For when he rose, the hall reverberated with a thunder of applause from the five hundred people present. Max felt his eyes pricked and his throat constricted by a sudden onrush of emotion. He had meant to go straight back to Rapallo afterwards. But possibilities of work made him change his plans. He was offered six hundred pounds to do ten cartoons of eminent persons, mainly sportsmen; and he received a proposal, from C. B. Cochran, to do some pictures of the author and characters in his successful new production, *Bitter Sweet* by Noël Coward. These two assignments kept Max in London for the rest of the year. Florence joined him in September. Before she came he established himself in Upper Berkeley Street with his family. As usual he thought London had changed for the worse. 'The English people are going to have the sort of capital they deserve in return for their crass indifference,' he wrote to Florence. 'Let them have it. And damn them!' Members of the Labour Government, now in office for the second time, displeased him as much as the appearance of London. Will Rothenstein took him to an art school where George Lansbury was giving away the prizes. 'His speech,' said Max, 'delivered in wildest and weakest Cockney, was beneath the level of anyone's mentality anywhere, and depressed me greatly. It is a dismal thought that a great nation should be ruled by such creatures.' These ominous symptoms of national deterioration did not prevent Max from settling down to enjoy a lively social season. He saw all his old friends, in particular the Rothensteins, the MacCarthys, George Street and Egan Mew. And he also encountered the world of fashion at the tables of Lady Colefax, Maurice Baring and Sir Philip Sassoon. He stayed a weekend with Sir Philip Sassoon at his exotic residence at Port Lympne. Once again the magnificence of Sassoon's mode of living roused mixed feelings in Max.

'This place seems very *restless*,' he wrote to Florence. '. . . But it is of course beautiful to the eye. Extraordinary elaboration of Persian fantasy, controlled by Etonian good taste. Wonderful successions of gardens with flowers blazing in seemingly endless vistas. Endless steps ascending steeply between walls and towers of clipped yew. Etc., etc. How awful it would be to *own* them! My bathroom is walled with little bricks of rough white marble. Black and white dado of r.w.m. And there are 2 steep steps of white r.w.m. into the vast bath. The door is of some kind of pale discoloured gold. Not *real* gold, of course (though why "of course"?), but of some strange and no doubt priceless material. And the water is of course very hot and very cold.'

His sporting assignment brought him into contact with the racing world, his work for Cochran with that of the theatre. This last he found an agreeable experience. Max took a great liking to Noël Coward himself and was enchanted with his play. Its nostalgic evocation of the Victorian and Edwardian epochs chimed deliciously with his own backward-looking daydreams. He liked its music, too. In his later years Max got a great deal of pleasure out of music, especially from that of Puccini, Sullivan, and the operettas of his youth. The score of *Bitter Sweet* now joined the circle of his especial favourites. Max's musical taste was not elevated; nor did he demand a high standard of performance. As in previous visits to London, he liked to take his solitary meals at a cheap popular restaurant where there was an orchestra that played selections of his favourite melodies.

This agreeable experience he was not to repeat for some time.

Except for a few days in 1931, Max remained in Italy for the next three years. They do not seem to have been quite such happy years as those preceding them. Two causes account for this. He was anxious about money, for one thing. On the face of it Max's financial position was better than when he first married; for he had inherited some money from Herbert; and this, added to what he had already and what he earned from time to time from exhibitions and royalties on books, would before 1914 have been enough to maintain him in the modest style of living which was all that he aspired to. But now prices had gone up and the value of money declined. By 1930 there are signs the Beerbohms were feeling the pinch of poverty. This, it would seem, was why Max stayed in Italy; he could not afford journeys to England. He also talks in his letters of applying for a Civil List pension and of letting the Villino and retiring to the little annexe behind it. Things did not in fact ever get bad enough for him to try to put these ideas into action. But the fact that he mentioned them at all shows that he must have been anxious. A more powerful cause of gloom was the international situation. In 1933 Hitler came to power and from this time on the Fascist danger cast an ever-darkening shadow over Europe. Italy, indeed, had been Fascist for some years, but without much bothering Max. At first he had even thought it a movement which—though unthinkable in England—might do some good in Italy. When it showed itself in its true colours, he felt differently; if he mentioned it, a gleam of cold ferocity revealed itself beneath the suavity of his usual manner. As for Mussolini himself, Max once caught sight of him driving by on the way to Genoa; he was not attracted. 'He looks like a larger and darker Horatio Bottomley,' he told Osbert Sitwell. About German Fascism Max had never had any doubts; brutal and fanatical, the Nazis represented all that he loathed most, and their treatment of the Jews was especially horrible to him in view of the fact that Florence was a Jewess.

Further, Hitler's dreadful spirit seemed infectious. Max was shocked by the growing amount of ill will in the world. Human beings seemed actually to wish to hate each other: even the small towns of Italy were at daggers drawn. 'I read *The Times* eagerly each morning,' he said to Dick Sheppard once, very sadly, 'and then I try to shut Europe out of my mind. What can you hope for when even the people of Rapallo think the people of Santa Margherita all devils!' In fact Max did not succeed in shutting these things out of his mind. Though he still appeared cheerful, a cloud of melancholy hovered in the further reaches of his spirit. A cloud of anxiety too; for surely such a situation was likely to lead to war. We recall that as early as October 1914 Max had prophesied that Germany, if defeated, would want to start another war in revenge. It looked now as if his grim prognostications would soon be realized.

Florence had always been more easily cast down than Max. She tended to be very depressed during these years. For this reason, and also because it might be a means of making money, she was pleased when in 1931 she had a letter from the impresario who twenty years before had arranged for her appearance in *Rosmersholm*, suggesting that she should come to England to act in a play by Pirandello, to be put on for a short season at Huddersfield. Max encouraged her to accept: in March she went over. Max followed in time to be present at the first night. Some leading London critics were present and Florence's performance received respectful praise. Max soon went back to the Villino. Florence stayed on in England looking for other parts. In vain: after some months she went back to Italy. She made two more appearances on the boards, one at the Old Vic as Åse in *Peer Gynt* in October 1935, and one with the O.U.D.S. at Oxford in March 1935, as the Duchess of Gloucester in *Richard II*. Max took his usual interest in both performances. He was enthusiastic about that in *Peer Gynt*; 'Her performance is one of the utmost loveliness,' he told Reggie. During the rehearsals for *Richard II* he stayed in Oxford. Florence liked him to sit in the audience during any scene she appeared in: she used to stop after every speech to ask his opinion as to how she had done it. Whether his opinion was trustworthy is uncertain, for this time Florence's performance met with a mixed reception. Older critics praised it for its distinction and moving sincerity. Those of a younger generation thought her style mannered and old-fashioned to a comical degree. In particular they were amused by her habit of accompanying every phrase with an illustrative gesture. If she spoke of her heart, she pointed a finger at her left breast; at the mention of a spear, she flourished an imaginary weapon in the air. This practice tended to slow down the pace of every scene in which she took part. Florence herself was not happy about her performances and, in fact, after this year she did not appear on the stage again. The atmosphere of the theatre had never suited her shrinking nature; it suited it even less at fifty-nine than at thirty.

Between March and September 1935 the Beerbohms were back at the Villino. The summer was made memorable by a visit from Dick Sheppard. Max and he had kept up the friendship. Sheppard was too hard-worked a man for them to see each other often, but he had visited Rapallo in 1929 and they had met occasionally in London. Now in May 1935 he came to stay for the first time. A publisher had offered to pay his fare to Italy in order that he might persuade Max to write his autobiography. In this he failed: but he took the opportunity to make some notes on Max, rather in the manner of Max's own impressionistic notes on personalities.

'Max met me,' he says, '—a little older—cheeks redder but same blue eyes that gaze into vacancy and see everything—same inside chuckling that comes out suddenly—smart as ever—shirt coming below coat, and over part of his wrist—cane with white ebony top. . . . Max's stained fingers—bad Italian—thick boots—well-pressed trousers—legs like the King's—stoops. . . . He uses old words, amanuensis, stylographic etc.'

Sheppard found Max just as likeable as before and just as good company. 'I don't know whether I love or hate Shaw the more,' he remarked to Sheppard. 'Will you join my Kickshaw Club? There will be a good deal of genuflecting for members.' Max put himself out to entertain Dick, especially in the evenings.

'He spoke of the Kaiser's visit to the Castello, and acted his arrival. He acted several other of his stories, with exquisite gestures of his trim deliberate hands (cuffs coming right over his wrists), he glanced shyly at us as he acted, looking almost chubby with joy at his own success, and then suddenly bursting into gurgles of laughter. I was delighted to see that Mrs Max could hardly contain herself with pleasure; she is very intelligent, and Max often deferred to her authority, especially in matters of history. She told me he was the best conversationalist she had ever met. He pretended to be shocked, but was really glad.'

On the subsequent evening he kept Sheppard in fits of laughter as for twenty whole minutes he acted imaginary scenes showing, first, a young actor entering the smoking-room of the Three Arts Club carrying a love-letter, and, second, the same man ten years later, now mature and famous, entering the Garrick Club with a very different demeanour. Max was as amused by his performance as was his audience. Sheppard heard him after it was over laughing with delight at his own success in the next room and then saw him emerge with tears of mirth in his eyes.

The visit had its more serious moments. These revealed to Sheppard how enigmatic and paradoxical Max's character was. Though delighting in gossip about the great world, Max was yet conspicuously unsnobbish; loyal to the Crown, he still enjoyed making fun of Royalty. Sheppard also noticed that he was both nervous and even-tempered, and that his gaiety went along with a very melancholy view of life, especially modern life. Once the two found their voices drowned by the roar of a passing petrol-tanker. Max grew grave and angry; 'I refuse to take a hand in making the world safe for machinery,' he shouted above the din. However, he did not let machinery or the modern world get him down. 'He obviously enjoys his lazy, quiet, undisturbed life,' noted Sheppard. The tone of this remark is not censorious; but it is a little mystified. How could it be otherwise when Sheppard's view of life was so profoundly different from that of his fascinating friend? His own beliefs would have made it impossible for him to adopt Max's mode of living. What then were Max's beliefs? As a priest Sheppard found himself wondering more and more what Max thought about religion. He brought the conversation round to the subject. Max responded with a proper reverence but with nothing else: the subject clearly meant little to him. Human life in his eyes was merely a fleeting space of light between two tracts of impenetrable darkness. 'It was "The Golden Drugget" all the time,' commented Sheppard. Though Max professed to feel guilty at never having made the acquaintance of the local Anglican clergyman, Sheppard perceived that he still had no intention of doing so. He told Sheppard frankly that he thought the Church of England a poor affair, merely national and conservative. With mischievous brilliance he gave an imitation of a typical, empty, ecclesiastical public statement.

Sheppard became conscious of the gulf between himself and Max. It did not cool his affection. 'You will always remain in my mind,' he wrote after he got back to England, 'as the most interesting and delicious man I have ever met.' Max's feelings remained equally warm. This made it all the sadder that it was their last meeting. Within two years Sheppard was dead and there had been no chance of his seeing Max in the interval. Max wrote of him:

'It is a truism to say that he was irresistible. At any rate I never heard of anyone who didn't find him so. His rays went circling round always, in all directions. At the end of Portofino there is a lighthouse. I often watch it at night across the distance. And if at any time of night I wake from my sleep, I am aware of a faint silvery recurrence of light on the walls of the room; a friendly intrusion—"Ah, there you are!" Dick wore himself out with his years of far-reaching radiance in this world. Dick is gone. But the lighthouse remains and reminds me of him.'

To return to 1935; Sheppard's visit marked the end of a phase of relative tranquillity for Max. In the late summer Mussolini invaded Abyssinia. The English, led by their Foreign Secretary, Anthony Eden, opposed this as a violation of international law and urged the League of Nations to apply sanctions in order to force Italy to desist. It soon looked as though England and Italy might be at war with each other. The foundations on which Max's life rested began to shake and crumble. If war broke out he was likely to forfeit his home and possessions and himself might be interned. It might be best to leave the country while it was still easy to do so: in any event the future was ominous and uncertain. As a matter of fact Max and Florence had already arranged to go to England in September for the production of *Peer Gynt*. The political situation steadily deteriorated as the autumn progressed. By October it looked so bad that Max was recommended not to leave England for the present. He stayed for nearly a year, longer than at any time since 1919. For the second time international events had broken up the peaceful pattern of his life and forced him back into the world. Though he concealed his feelings under his accustomed manner of humorous serenity, he felt it a considerable blow. At sixty-three years old Max clung more than ever to his chosen and tranquil mode of living. He also minded leaving his home because it seemed a terrible proof of the growing strength of those forces that threatened the destruction of the civilized world. Nor was he fortified to bear his apprehensions by a conviction that England was doing the right thing. The ageing and tired Max was not the man to understand the ruthless necessities of twentieth-century international politics. No doubt, he thought, Italy might be wrong about Abyssinia, but was it worth quarrelling with her about it? The Italians were old friends and lovable people, even if for the time being they had got into the hands of a ruffianly leader. Besides, the quarrel with them might throw them into the arms of the sinister Germans waiting under Hitler for another chance to plunge the world into bloodshed. Max could believe that Eden—'the graceful, well-meaning, but deleterious Anthony,' as he called him—was an agreeable person and actuated by high motives. All the same he wished he was not Foreign Secretary.

He wrote to Reggie:

Ever dearest Reg,

How long since we have done aught but telegraph! And the fault has been mine, of course; for my unwillingness to write letters (which I know will be 'literary' and would-be-remarkable) has grown more and more pronounced with the passing years. But you know that you are constantly in my thoughts, and are always the dearest to me of all my friends. You held out hopes that you would be coming to Rap. But you never came. I hope you have been having a happy time and good health in the midst of this troubled universe. How odd it seems that we once lived in a time when the world was quite gay and careless, and its ways smooth—and there was nothing for one to worry about but one's own affairs! What a lot we shall have to talk over when we meet, dear Reg! I hope that will be soon. . . . I hope all will go well in the crisis. I think it likely that there won't be any really serious trouble between the countries of our respective birth and adoption. You, living in a city, are a much better judge than I. If you have any doubts as to the immediate future, you will of course, won't you? hasten forthwith to some land where it won't be unpleasant for English people. If things didn't turn out well, it would worry me to think of you being here. Alfred Burney was here recently, and the talk hinged continually on you and your wit and your lovely character. He is a great dear. Chesterton was also here lately—*enormous* as compared with what he was; but delightful. But it is absurd to touch the fringe of news, after all this time! Word of mouth is what's wanted. Let us have it soon. Meanwhile, here is the devotion of Max.

Reggie replied:

My dearest Max,

It was a great thing for me to get that letter from you, and when I got it and 'signed' for it as it was registered I went for a walk before I opened it to get into a quiet mind. Let me begin my answer by saying that to be so placed in the category of your friends is to have been a success in life and made it worth living, and far indeed beyond my deserts. . . .

He went on to say how much he agreed with Max about the Italian situation but added that he found consolation for the present discontents by reading Max's essays. He ended:

'Your letter, dear Max, was wonderful. My answer is quite inadequate and I do think that I shall never waver in doubt as to whether you have forgotten me.

Lovingly
Reg.'

These two letters are revealing. Max's words are more demonstrative than any he has written to Reggie for years. In the dangerous present, he turned instinctively back to the happy past and to those he had known and loved when he was young: more than ever did he feel that the affection of one individual for another was the single unquestioned good in a disillusioning universe. Reggie's weaknesses were forgotten; Max only remembered how fond he was of him; he wanted to tell him so before it was too late. Reggie responded at once. His affection had never died. A word from Max and its flame burned up again, bright as when the two of them strolled the antique quadrangles of Merton nearly fifty years before.

CHAPTER SIXTEEN

On the Air

THE year 1935 was a very important one in Max's life. For towards its close an event took place which unexpectedly and
almost by chance was to inaugurate a new chapter in the history of
his art. At the end of October he got a letter from Mr Moray
McLaren of the British Broadcasting Corporation saying that he was
producing a new series of talks to be entitled *Revisited*; and that he
wondered if Max would give one about revisiting London. Max
was extremely interested. He was not so consistently opposed to
modern mechanical inventions as he sometimes made out; and of
late he had got a good deal of pleasure out of listening to the
radio.

'The B.B.C. is a wonderful triumph of variety and soundness, isn't
it?' he wrote to Reggie. 'Did you hear G. B. S. and the Girl with the
Golden Voice? It was very well done—G. B. S's acting quite
capital. But he's no good in a "talk", much too loud and quick—too
platformy and grimly determined to be a vigorous hefty youth.
G. K. Chesterton *very* good, don't you think? The right technique.
A friend in one's room, pensively and quietly monologizing. The
best voice I've heard is D. S. MacColl's. Next to his the King's. I like
Gracie Fields' also. I have only heard one of the "What is the Law"
series. It was exquisite. Almost to be mentioned in the same breath
with your reproduction of two English clergymen conversing in an
Italian railway-carriage. . . . I have a deep regard for the Announ-
cers. They seem to be a lesson to us all—morally, intellectually, and
in every way.'

The idea of himself trying his luck as a broadcaster appealed to him.
He was interested in the aesthetic possibilities of this new medium
and he was also attracted by it as a way of making money. Before
finally accepting Mr McLaren's proposal, however, he laid down
certain conditions.

Dear Mr McLaren,

Thank you for your kind and very courteous letter.

The idea that I should radiate on the subject of London interests me much, and gratifies me much; but also terrifies me rather—not because I haven't known London fairly well, nor because I haven't definite views about the present edition of London, but because I am essentially a private, a non-radiant person, by nature and habit. Only a rather heavy bribe would tempt me forth to speak urbi et orbi.

I should want—I was going to say £100, but won't grossly say that: I will delicately say £90.

Do you think this outrageous? If so, tell me so; and have no fear that my feelings will be hurt; and invite instead of me one of the obviously many men who could 'take' the subject of London just as well as I or much better than I, and would be more modest in the matter of finance. And don't bother to read the rest of this letter.

But suppose that you *aren't* outraged, and are reading this page 3, I must lay down a further condition. Read on.

I am not the sort of man that does a thing unless he knows that he could do it well. Before agreeing to radiate, I should ask you to be so good as to let me read something for 3 or 4 minutes to the microphone, with you 'listening in', and with my wife doing likewise. If you and she concurred that the quality of my voice and of my enunciation was such as would not irritate the public and shame the B.B.C., then—and only then—would I make my invisible bow to the world.

In ordinary private life my voice and enunciation aren't, I fancy, bad. But on the radio, that rather incalculable instrument, they might be, for aught I know. You would have to judge.

And now, dear Mr McLaren, forgive me for writing at such length and so tediously.

Yours sincerely,
Max Beerbohm.

Mr McLaren agreed to Max's terms and suggested a date for the trial and proposed they should meet beforehand at the Langham Hotel which, he thought, still exhaled an Edwardian atmosphere likely to attract Max. It did so: the Langham Hotel, Max said, was a bit of old London surviving amid a waste of modernist horrors. When the day came, he arrived for the rehearsal making a great profession of feeling timid at the thought of the ordeal before him. In fact he struck Mr McLaren as remarkably self-assured; surely the professed timidity was an act. But it was not an annoying act; for Max performed it with charm and did not appear to expect it to be taken seriously. When he came to reading his piece he showed himself admirably gifted for the medium. Also fully prepared: there were no hesitations. Clearly Florence and he had gone through it many times. This did not prevent Max asking for six or seven rehearsals, far more than most speakers required. He was rewarded for his trouble. The performance, which took place on the evening of 29 December, was a triumph. Enthusiastic letters poured in, and the chiefs of the broadcasting system, headed by the great Sir John Reith, asked if they could meet him. This he politely refused—from fatigue or from fear of boredom, who can tell? But he was delighted by his fan mail, and when it was suggested he should do some more broadcasting, he accepted at once. Max gave two other talks during the following year, one entitled 'Speed' on 19 April 1936, and on 26 July a second about his childhood enthusiasm for statesmen entitled 'A Small Boy Seeing Giants'. In both he repeated the success of his first talk. He had insisted on just as many rehearsals as for the first. He was always to do so: some of the tapes[1] recording his rehearsals still survive: they give a vivid and comic impression of the scene. Max shows himself courteous and anxious to cooperate. But he is also tense, nervous and meticulous. He seldom gets going without one or more false starts; now and again he stumbles over a word. When this happens we hear an agitated cry followed by an apology and a request to be allowed to begin afresh some way back. Before beginning Max then intones in a marked slow rhythm the words 'rumpity tumpity' in order to remind himself of the tempo in which he is intending to speak. It is only after a number of such attempts that he succeeds in going through each part and finally the whole piece with the varied smoothness and appropriate expression at which he aimed. Max brought to his new art of broadcasting the same craftsman's conscience as he had brought to his old arts of writing and drawing.

He said that he found the new art easier. Certainly in one way it suited his talent better; in it he had the chance for the first time to

---

[1] These are of his later broadcasts, but Max's habits were the same throughout his broadcasting career.

make professional use of his gift for acting. Up till now this had shown itself only in private conversation. Now he had found an art form in which it could be employed and he took full advantage of it. Max's broadcasts are models of the art that does not so much conceal art as make it seem easy. We appear to be listening to a leisurely, effortless improvisation. In fact every effect is calculated at once to convey the speaker's exact meaning and to beguile his listener's ear and attention. He goes slowly enough for the listener to appreciate his words without strain, but saves his discourse from monotony by subtle variations of pace and emphasis. Now and again he indulges in a direct piece of acting, impersonates a celebrity, imitates a Cockney singer. But, of course, the chief character he projects before us is his own.

For—and this is why the form suited him so particularly well—a broadcast talk is a projection of a personality and, what is more, a private, informal, intimate projection, designed to be heard not by a large audience but by an individual listener alone in his room. Here it resembled Max's chosen form, the occasional essay; in fact, formally speaking, his broadcasts do derive from his essays. They are different, however, in two significant respects. For one thing Max modifies his style in them to suit a different medium. Since his words are meant to be spoken, his writing is looser in structure, simpler and more colloquial in diction.

The talks are also different from the essays in that the personality projected in them is different. Max has assumed a new mask. His old mask had been the creation of youth and the Edwardian period. Now after a long interval of absence and silence he had returned, a man on the verge of old age, to be confronted with a world which had suffered revolutionary changes and from which the last trace of the Edwardian period had vanished. The old mask was clearly inappropriate; and it was no good at his time of life trying to make himself an up-to-date and modern one. Max resolved to profit by what might have been thought his disadvantages and to stress, even to exaggerate, the fact that he was elderly and anachronistic. He made his reappearance on the public stage as an ancient *revenant*, a sort of elegant Rip Van Winkle, gazing with curiosity at an unfamiliar world, or turning away from it to contemplate his memories of past days. He made no bones about the fact that he preferred the old days. In 'A Small Boy Seeing Giants' he suggests that no modern politician could appeal to the imagination in the way the great statesmen did in Queen Victoria's time: in his two other talks he goes further. The London of 1935 he describes as 'a bright, salubrious hell'; and most of his discourse on speed consists of a racy account of the horrors let loose on mankind by the invention of the internal-combustion engine. Max found it easy to sustain his new role. He had started his literary career posing as an old man and throughout his life he had gone in for looking back at the past. All he had now to do was to learn to restate old sentiments in his new character. This he did with gusto. Indeed gusto, a delicate Maxian gusto, was the outstanding characteristic of these talks. So much so that though the views expressed in them were pessimistic, the effect they made was cheerful. The truth was that Max was enjoying himself very much when he was giving them: and through his gloom-laden prognostications and grandfatherly head-shaking airs there bubbled irrepressibly up a youthful spirit of gaiety.

It was an unusual combination; but it gave his talks a piquant, unusual charm which largely accounted for their success. This success was on a bigger scale than any he had had before. For since he was using a popular medium, Max's admirers were for the first time not confined to a limited and sophisticated circle. The consequence was that at the age of sixty-three he became a national figure. This was the more sensational because during recent years his fame had begun to fade. If you turn your back on the world, the world will soon turn its back on you. The result of Max's long silence was that by 1935 he was thought of as belonging to the past. Indeed, most of his books were out of print. Now he made three broadcasts: and his whole position changed. His voice and manner were a living reality in every house in England that contained a wireless set. And they remained so till he died.

During their stay in London the Beerbohms lodged in rooms in Tavistock Square, Bloomsbury. It was Max's first sojourn in Bloomsbury. He delighted in the spacious eighteenth-century houses with their broad flights of steps and elegant fanlights: but he did not take to the new type of bohemian youth, male and female, who frequented the district. Seedy and despondent-looking, with cigarettes hanging vertically from their unsmiling lips, they lacked the panache of the Chelsea bohemians of his youth. Moreover, he was out of sympathy with their opinions; their taste for the ugly and the austere—'tricksy snippets of dry prose,' so he described their attempts at poetry—their glum hostility to tradition and convention. Max had not enjoyed public-school life much; all the same, he was so much irritated by the Bloomsbury attack on the Old School Tie that he took action about it.

'It had never occurred to me,' he writes, to 'exercise my right to wear such a tie. But now, here, in the heart of Bloomsbury, I felt that I would belatedly do so, and I went to my hosier and ordered two Old Carthusian ties. Do you know the colours? They are three: bright crimson, salmon pink, and royal blue. They are dangerous to the appearance of even a quite young man. To that of an old man they are utterly disastrous. Nevertheless, I, without faltering, wore one of my pair until my sojourn in Bloomsbury came to its end.'

The turn of the year was marked by the death of two men who had figured conspicuously in Max's art, Kipling and King George V. He had made merciless fun of both in his time. His heart was still hardened against Kipling. But he had learnt to feel differently about the King.

'I am told,' Max wrote, 'that Mrs Kipling (née Balestier) very much resents the death of the King at so solemn a moment.

For my part, I very genuinely mourn that transcendently decent and lovable King, and wish he could have lived as long as I. I'm sadly doubtful of the future effects of Edward VIII. But of course he *may* turn out all right.'

Max showed prescience about Edward VIII. He had doubted his fitness for his office since he had heard rumours of his appearing at Sunday lunch in an Italian hotel dressed in shorts: he should have realized, Max thought, that the Italians would not approve of such a costume on such an occasion. Nor did Max himself. In his view a prince owed a duty to aesthetic decorum just as much as an artist did. He applied the principles strictly to himself. Some time during these years Cecil Beaton, now in the first flush of his triumph as an *avant-garde* photographer, asked to be allowed to take a portrait of Max. Max agreed, but only if it was in a straightforward and traditional manner. He thought it unseemly for a man of his age to be the subject of one of Mr Beaton's more fanciful and freakish creations.

His foresight showed itself again one evening in the following spring. In April 1936 a new three-act dramatization of *The Happy Hypocrite* by Clemence Dane was produced at His Majesty's Theatre by Ivor Novello, who himself took the leading part of Lord George Hell. The first night was a brilliant affair; a distinguished audience gave the piece an enthusiastic reception. Only Max stood apart from the crowd; looking, it was said, 'in it but not of it', and wearing the air of a man who did not expect the play to have a long run. He turned out to be right. The play failed to attract the general public.

To Max's biographer this production of *The Happy Hypocrite* has another and more sentimental interest as the occasion of the last appearance in this history of the forgotten figure of Kilseen. Nothing is known of her between 1911 and 1936 save for a rumour that she was at one time very poor. Now we find a letter from her to Max saying how interested she was to hear of the production, since it reminded her of long-ago days—*The Happy Hypocrite* had been published in 1897 when she and Max were together—and that she hoped it would be a success. The fact that she wrote at all suggests that her memories of Max meant much to her. But her tone is tentative, modest and a little formal: no one would guess from the letter that she and Max were once engaged to be married. Max's reply to her does not survive: nor do we know if the two ever communicated with each other again. Apparently, soon after this, Kilseen died.

Meanwhile the tension between Italy and England had temporarily relaxed. In October, therefore, Max and Florence went back to the Villino. They stayed there for two years more. Though their life was outwardly tranquil, they felt more insecure than in earlier days. For one thing, the international situation continued to get worse—every year Hitler grew more menacing—and for another, Max had by now arrived at the evening of life when the days were inevitably darkened by bereavement. George Street died in November 1936—Max wrote a warm obituary notice about him for *The Times*—and in August 1937 Maud Tree. Max had grown fond of her in his later years. Anyone he connected with his youth now stirred affection in him: his memories of the past were suffused with a rosy glow. He wrote wistfully to Reggie referring to Henry James's story *Daisy Miller*, 'I have been reading the story again, with pangs of longing for the dear, delicate, un-panic-stricken world of sixty years ago.'

In July 1937 Max and Florence went for a month's holiday to Montreux in Switzerland. 'I wonder if you will like Switzerland,' wrote Dora to Max. 'There is a snugness about its smugness, though when you come to the mountains, there is no snuggedness about their ruggedness!' Max was happy enough there to judge by the only letter we have of his from Montreux—though, indeed, he says little about Switzerland in it. It is written to Siegfried Sassoon thanking him for sending him the diary of Parson Woodforde, that most placid and reassuring of eighteenth-century characters. Max read it with extreme pleasure. His letter begins with a paragraph of parody, and then goes on:

'But this is enough, dear Siegfried, to show you how steeped I am in Parson Woodforde. Ever so many thanks for sending him to me. Your doing so showed as much insight as kindness. You were, as usual, right: he's the man for me: I'm devoted to him. The relief of being wafted far away out of the accursèd modern bounds of cleverness!—of finding oneself in the company of a quiet, decent, loveable, unpretentious fool, in Arcadia. You may object to the term *fool*. But, after all, isn't he one? He seems never to have had an idea, he seems never to have even *seen* any one or anything: he just takes people and things dimly as a matter of course. He leaves one to see them *for* him. And one leaps to the occasion. One's imagination is hot and active. One is *there*, on the spot, in Arcadia, all the time. When he does—as all too rarely he does—describe somebody, one is rather mystified. But even so, one hugs the mystery. How about Miss Anne Thomas (May 30, 1786)? What manner of girl was she? The eldest daughter of the Thomases "is very reserved and not handsome—Miss Betty is very agreeable and pretty—Miss Anne very still and coarse". To my dying day I shall wonder about Miss Anne. The undescribed multitudes of gentle and simple who figure in the Parson's pages are clear to me: I see them living their Arcadian lives and going their Arcadian ways quietly, rather clumsily, day after day. But Miss Anne? She is my favourite.'

Mr and Mrs Ellis Roberts were with the Beerbohms at Montreux. The two couples saw much of each other during these later years; more than once the Ellis Robertses came to Rapallo. With amusement Mrs Ellis Roberts noted Max's idiosyncrasies. His extreme care for appearances, for instance; Ellis Roberts, impulsive and unself-conscious, thought nothing of showing himself in public with a large irregular piece of plaster stuck across his face to cover a cut made while shaving. Max was shocked. Mrs Roberts learnt after-wards that once at the Villino when he had a very small boil on his neck with a very small plaster on it, Max said, 'I don't think I had better go up on to the terrace this morning.' Equally Mrs Roberts was struck by Max's concern for other people's feelings. He told her that he thought his early caricatures had been much too cruel; and he would not show her one he had done of a friend of hers, lest it should cause her pain. In later years somebody else showed it to her; it turned out to be inoffensive and delightful.

The Beerbohms passed most of the next year at the Villino, save for one or two short visits in the neighbourhood to stay with some Italian friends called Pio. Dora paid her annual visit in May. As the years went by her thoughts, like Max's, tended to turn to past days, especially to those days they had spent together.

'My darling Max,' she writes to him on his birthday, 'Many many and much much love for your birthday, when I shall be thinking of you early in Chapel and so often in the day. I am sending this very early, as I think it possible you may be away, I want so much for my wishes to reach you on the day.... Strange, how as one gets old, the things of one's childhood start into clearness. A day or two ago I re-called a black and white picture of yours drawn I should think sixty years ago. It was called "A Dream or a Nightmare". One saw quite at the bottom of the page a little man lying in bed, and all around and right very high above him soared figures cloaked and veiled, very sinister, like the Brothers of the Misericordia—or worse the people in the gas-masks of this time. Rather a haunting picture—do you remember it? Another memory sprang up yesterday—this one cosy and cheerful—something I had forgotten entirely—the pattern of the tea-service at Aunt Lucy and Miss Forster's tea-parties in Tyr-whitt Road, Lewisham—a very bright pink china, covered with gold wriggles—just the right dishes for the hot-house grapes, and the Dundee cake brought by Buzzard's weekly cart—Aunt Lucy pour-ing out the tea—and Miss Forster's exclaiming to Mamma "Law! Eliza you have no appetite." Law! darling I hope you have one, and feel well, and will have a very happy day, and many many afterwards. I had no birthday-card but thought you might like this of me outside the Chapel you love, and I know you love me too as I do you.

Your ever loving Sister
Dora Mary.'

Dora's mention of a gas-mask was all too topical. By the end of the summer the international situation had become more critical than ever. It was the year of Munich. Before the crisis had reached its peak, Max decided to go back to England. War seemed imminent and who knew if Italy might not be involved? Anyway, to the prospect of war Max reacted in the same way as he had in 1915: 'When England is in danger, I like to be there,' he told a friend.

This time Max and Florence took up residence in rooms at No. 62 Inverness Terrace, Bayswater. Max liked Bayswater better than Bloomsbury; 'The inhabitants all look so clean and fresh and respectable and happy,' he told Reggie, 'a great contrast to the fauna in and around Tavistock Square.' Bayswater, too, had pleasant associations for him, for his childhood had been passed there. The Munich crisis passed; and though the political atmosphere was still ominous, the London social scene had soon become as animated as ever. Max and Florence were swept into its turmoil. 'A great deal of sullen yet suave hospitality has been offered us,' Max wrote to Egan Mew. The phrase was more picturesque than accurate. London society welcomed Max as warmly as ever. One hears of him with new friends and old, with the literary, the intellectual, the fashionable; with the Rothensteins, the Schiffs, the Ellis Robertses, lunching with the fashionable Lady Colefax, dining with the artistic Miss Ethel Sands. Here he sat next to Virginia Woolf who has left her impressions of him.

'Max like a Cheshire cat. Orbicular. Jowled. Blue eyes. Eyes grow vague . . . all curves.'

She noted down some of his talk. He said among other things:

' "It takes all sorts to make a world." I was outside all the groups. Now dear Roger Fry who liked me, was a born leader. No one so "illuminated". He looked it. Never saw anyone look it so much. I heard him lecture on the Aesthetics of Art. I was disappointed. He kept on turning the page—turning the page. . . . Hampstead hasn't

439

yet been spoilt. I stayed at Jack Straw's Castle some years ago. My wife had been having influenza. And the barmaid, looking over her shoulder, said—my wife had had influenza twice—"Quite a greedy one aren't you?" Now that's immortal. There's all the race of barmaids in that. I suppose I've been ten times into public houses. George Moore never used his eyes. He never knew what men and women think. He got it all out of books. Ah I was afraid you would remind me of *Ave atque Vale*. Yes; that's beautiful. Yes, it's true he used his eyes then. Otherwise it's like a lovely lake, with no fish in it.'

Max spoke of his own writing:

'Dear Lytton Strachey said to me: first I write one sentence: then I write another. That's how I write. And so I go on. But I have a feeling writing ought to be like running through a field. That's your way. Now how do you go down to your room, after breakfast— what do you feel? I used to look at the clock and say oh dear me, it's time I began my article. . . . No, I'll read the paper first. I never wanted to write. . . . What you said in your beautiful essay about me and Charles Lamb was quite true.[1] He was crazy: he had the gift: genius. I'm too like Jack Horner. I pull out my plum. It's too rounded, too perfect. . . . I have a public of about 1500. Oh I'm famous, largely thanks to you, and people of importance at the top like you. I often read over my own work. And I have a habit of read-it through the eyes of people I respect. I often read it as Virginia Woolf would read it—picking out the kind of things you would like. You never do that? Oh you should try it.'

Another authoress, Miss G. B. Stern, gave a party especially to celebrate Max's return. All her life she had passionately admired his works. Now she had met him she found herself equally delighted by the man. There was something so amiable about him as well as so entertaining. The two discussed a well-known writer, a friend of Miss Stern and an old acquaintance of Max. Max's tone about him was lukewarm. 'I don't believe you really like him,' said Miss Stern. Max paused. 'Does anybody?' he asked, gazing at her with unfathomable eyes. Miss Stern burst out in defence and then apologized a little for her violence. 'Never mind,' Max reassured her, 'when

[1] Max considered Virginia Woolf the best living critic: he had written to tell her so in 1927.

two people disagree over a third person, the one who likes him is always right.' Miss Stern's party was a big affair and was reported in the *Daily Sketch*. Max cut out the report and sent it to Egan Mew.

In Max's Honour

Probably there has been no more interesting dinner party this month than that given by novelist Miss G. B. Stern in a private room at Quaglino's.

Guest of honour was Mr Max Beerbohm. There were more than fifty other guests seated at the round tables. Naturally the party was largely literary. In fact the room was filled with celebrities. H. G. Wells was at a table near the door. In the centre of the room was Miss Tennyson Jesse. John Van Druten, who produced some superb remarks, was at a table near the wall.

It was Max who underlined the phrases 'near the door' and 'near the wall'. 'The new school of topographical journalism,' he commented. 'Interesting!' Max's reactions to such festivities were mixed. He usually enjoyed them at the time and all the more by contrast with the quiet of his previous months. But he found he did not look forward to them as much as when he was young, and that they left him tired. It was partly that social life had become so much more rushed than it used to be. 'People now have no time to eat!' he once said to Miss Eiluned Lewis. 'You turn to your neighbour and when you look back the food has been taken away. No time to talk either. Soon the young people say "We must get back to work. Goodbye." They all *work*!' This last was a dreadful thought: even to hear of it made Max feel jaded. Furthermore, he professed to be less and less pleased by his own conversation on these occasions.

'I have become aware that in my later years,' he wrote to Sydney Schiff, 'I talk too much, *and* that not enough of what I say is interesting.

I heard a sad story, the other day, about a man who went to consult a "nerve specialist". He said, "One of the things that worries me, and makes me afraid, is that when I am alone I can't help talking to myself." "Oh, well," said the consultant, "many people do that. It's not at all a dangerous sign." The patient, leaning forward, said, "But, doctor, I'm *such an awful bore*."

That's rather how I feel in company.'

The winter was to be a sad one for Max. Viola Parsons, Herbert's eldest daughter and his own favourite niece, died in November; to be followed early in the next year by his sister Constance. A few weeks before, Reggie Turner had died in Florence. This could not be the grief it would once have been; for it was many years since Max had seen Reggie often. All the same he was moved: he could never forget that Reggie had been his closest friend. Moreover, as we have seen, the troubles of the time had brought the two closer together again during the last years. Only three weeks before Reggie's death Max had been writing to him to expatiate on his pleasure in some magnificent handkerchiefs which Reggie had given him. The sexagenarian Reggie still sent Max presents of clothes and the sexagenarian Max still enjoyed getting them. He ended the letter, 'Well, dearest Reg, forgive a dull letter because, with all its dullness, it does carry to you our devoted love, your affectionate old Max.' Now with sorrow and tenderness he meditated on his memories of Reggie.

'I had known him so long,' he wrote to Sydney Schiff; 'he was the earliest of my great friends, and remained always the greatest—and will always remain so. . . . I think his life had been on the whole a happy one, full of interest and fun. Of course he had been too sensitive an observer and feeler of things to be genuinely and uninterruptedly happy in such a world as this. But he had had a good share of happiness. And now he is beyond the reach of the other thing, and is at peace, dear fellow.'

Sydney and Violet Schiff had themselves been friends of Reggie and could enter into Max's feelings about him. They also noted that Max and Florence were finding London life a strain. The Schiffs owned a country house near Dorking; in its garden was a *cottage ornée*. They now offered the Beerbohms the use of it for as long as they liked. Max and Florence accepted with enthusiastic gratitude and went down there in February. It was to be their home for several years. From time to time Max went up to London to see his sisters and to visit Broadcasting House. For there was some talk in the spring of 1939 of Max's giving a wireless talk on the subject of men's clothes. This fell through. But three of the stories out of *Seven Men*—'Enoch Soames', 'A. V. Laider' and 'Savonarola Brown' —appeared on the air in dramatized versions. The producers consulted Max about them; he wrote back very fully, discussing what would be appropriate incidental music and what kind of voice would be suitable for each character. These performances were a good thing for him from the worldly point of view. They earned him money and spread the knowledge of his earlier work. His reputation continued to increase. In June 1939 it was crowned. Max received a letter saying that the King offered him a knighthood. He accepted.

Certainly Time is an ironical spirit. We recall Max's essay on literary knighthoods and his cartoons of Edward VII, and the ruthless satirical fun which animates both. It is not to be supposed that he himself had forgotten them. But, since he was the most confirmed of ironists, the recollection must have added to his pleasure. He was very pleased. 'I shouldn't have liked it when I was younger,' he writes in answer to a congratulation, 'for it would have cramped my style. Now it's all right': and to Alice Rothenstein:

'I knew you would be pleased about my little knighthood—though why do I say "little"? It seems very large to me really! It seems to me Great Fun. And when I say Fun, I don't mean vulgar side-splitting Fun I mean Fun of a steadying and ennobling kind. When next we meet you will see no superficial change in me but I think you will discern a profound spiritual alteration, which I hope will be permanent.'

His gratification was further enhanced by the fact that the knighthood was, by implication, an honour paid to a lucid and graceful ideal of art. One day a young writer showed Max a copy of James Joyce's *Finnegan's Wake*. Max turned over the pages; and then, 'I don't think that he will get a knighthood for that!' he said with satisfaction. The ceremony of the accolade took place on 13 July. As might be expected, Max did not neglect his appearance on such an occasion. He would as soon have presented himself before his Sovereign in his underclothes as in a hired or a ready-made garment; and poor though he was, he went up to London to order his tailor to make him a new morning coat. It required several fittings but proved to be worth them.

'My costume yesterday,' he wrote to Mrs Schiff, 'was quite all right, after all. Indeed, I was (or so I thought, as I looked around me) the best-dressed of the Knights, and quite on a level with the Grooms of the Chamber and other palace officials. I'm not sure that I wasn't as presentable as the King himself—*very* charming though he looked. He has a smile and a look in the eyes that are most endearing.'

Meanwhile the twentieth century proceeded inexorably on its unpleasing course. On 1 September Hitler entered Poland and another major war had begun.

CHAPTER SEVENTEEN

The Second War

(I)

THE Beerbohms' life during most of the Second World War repeated the pattern of their life during the first. As then they had
lived in a cottage at Far Oakridge on the land of their friends the
Rothensteins, so now they lived in a cottage at Abinger on the land
of their friends the Schiffs. Once again Florence spent her time cooking, looking after the house, and enjoying the beauties of nature; as
before, Max wrote a little, doodled a lot and went for short slow
walks, carefully dressed and with walking-stick and gloves. Social
life was rather more varied than in 1916; for Surrey was less sequestered and rural than the Cotswolds. Abinger was the scene of a
small society of intellectual and artistic persons. Max and Florence
were welcomed by this society and made friends with its members;
more especially with Max's old schoolfellow, Vaughan Williams,
and with Cecil and Sylvia Sprigge, a husband and wife of refined
tastes and liberal sympathies, who had lived much abroad and with
whom Max and Florence could share memories of Italy.

Florence and Max did a little modest entertaining at Abinger in
the Villino tradition; asking people to light meals, delicately cooked
by Florence, and sometimes followed by paper games in which
Max took the lead. Abinger society found these gatherings an agreeable change from the war news. London was not very far and so the
monotony of Max's days was also varied by visits from friends there,
and more especially from his sisters Agnes and Dora. Alas, Dora was
not fated to go very often. Early in May 1940, during the worst days
of the war when the Germans were sweeping over France, Max
wrote to Siegfried Sassoon from London.

'Florence and I have been here for a week, for a sad reason. Darling
Dora fell down a flight of stairs at the Priory, and broke her arm.
She was taken at once to the London Hospital. She does not seem to
have had any internal injuries; but of course she has always been

delicate, and is now old, and it is hardly to be expected now that she can survive. Her mind is perfectly clear, and she talks exactly in her own delightful way. She does not at all wish not to die. She feels that she has had a very happy life, and she has of course a firm belief in life to come. . . . Her voice is weak, but, like her mind, perfectly clear—and happy, like her face.'

Dora lingered on till 13 August. After her death, at the request of the Mother Superior of Dora's Sisterhood, Max wrote an account of her for the little magazine of the Order.

'Her knowledge,' ran its last paragraphs, 'of life, and of all that was going on in the world, was so remarkable as to be almost puzzling: it seemed to spring from intuition. There was nothing she didn't know of the latest fashions in politics, in social life, in all kinds of life; and on all these points she had a quiet, sane little opinion of her own, gently Tory, and profoundly English.

But such matters, doubtless, were but a small thing in the glow of her inner, her spiritual existence. In the few weeks that passed between her last illness and her death, her mind was as clear as ever. She insisted on knowing all the news of the war. Though it was mostly bad news, and worse news, she was perfectly confident of victory for her darling England, and would have liked to see it. But she was entirely glad that she should die soon, if it were God's will. And so it was willed.'

It will be noted that Max only touches tentatively on Dora's religious faith. It was the one thing in her experience he could not share. Yet this had not created a gulf between them. Max loved Dora for what she was, and did not ask for her to be different. She felt the same about him. Now and again she had spoken to Florence about religion and said that she wished that Florence who lived so Christian a life would one day partake of the Christian hope. So far as we know, she never mentioned the subject to Max. But she admired and loved him too entirely to doubt that he would in his own way attain divine salvation.

Abinger, though quiet, did not turn its back on the war. On the contrary, there sprang up there a number of mild wartime activities suitable for elderly people. Max and Florence took part in these. Florence entertained to tea members of the troops stationed near and gave simple lessons to some of the children evacuated to the district. Max found employment for his pen. Sprigge and others started a magazine, *The Abinger Chronicle*, whose profits were to go to help the war effort. Max contributed to this periodical and took as much pains over his contributions as if he were composing a broadcast to be heard by millions. He also took great interest in the war news. Before hostilities had broken out he had dreaded them as yet another and fatal blow to civilization. This fear combined with age to make him, in spite of his horror of Hitler, favour Chamberlain's appeasement policy. But when appeasement failed and war broke out, Max changed and became as militant in support of it as he had been in 1914. All his strong patriotic fervour surged into aggressive life. The worse the war went the firmer he became in favour of going on with it and the surer he professed himself that England would win in the end. He responded enthusiastically to Winston Churchill's 1940 broadcasts, and all the more because they were so eloquent. How heartening to be led by a Prime Minister with a sense of style! When two years later Harold Nicolson misquoted one of those broadcasts in an article in *The Spectator*, Max could not contain himself, but wrote at once in protest.

Sir,

Not being a Member of Parliament, I cannot rise to ask the Prime Minister whether he can forgive the Hon. Member for West Leicester for quoting him as having said that 'never in the long history of human conflict have so many owed so much to so few'. But, as a devoted admirer of Harold Nicolson's own prose, may I not ask him whether he can forgive himself for not having written 'has so much been owed by so many to so few'? For this has a noble and a classic cadence: whereas the other is joggety-jogget and tumpty-tum.

Yours obediently,
Max Beerbohm.

Anyone or anything that seemed to be criticizing the Government for taking strong action roused Max's opposition: he thought it would weaken the country's will to battle. *The Abinger Chronicle* published an article implying that the Government was treating aliens living in England with unnecessary harshness. Max wrote at once to the editor to say that if it was going to print this sort of thing, he could no longer contribute to it. He was so indignant that it took two days and a good deal of explanation before he calmed down.

These feelings did not prevent him from assisting any individual enemy alien he thought unjustly treated. Oscar Pio, a son of his Italian friends, was in England and very much on the English side: recommended by Max and others, he had been allowed to join the allied forces. There was suddenly a hitch; a countryman of his, wishing to curry favour with the authorities, warned them against Pio on the ground that as a boy he had been a Fascist. When Max heard of this, he went immediately up to London to make a protest. Using all the influence he possessed, he obtained an interview with some person of importance at the War Office. So formidable did he show himself at this interview that Pio's wrongs were immediately put right. Max in his old age showed himself still the same man who had journeyed from Rapallo to London to tackle Frank Harris for his words about Florence. Max also came forward to write a letter vouching for Elisabeth Jungmann when she had to appear before a tribunal dealing with aliens.

'Do let us know,' he wrote to her, 'as soon as possible after your visit to the Tribunal that all went easily and well (as I'm sure it will). I think the mere look and manner of you will enslave the Chairman and every member of the Committee.

Of course don't bother to answer *this* letter. Or no! after all, please send a postcard or "ring up" to say that the documents have reached you quite safely. Florence sends you her love, and so do I, you very dear friend.'

In fact Elisabeth Jungmann had little difficulty in convincing the tribunal. As a Jewess, she had several years before come under the ban of Hitler's anti-Jewish legislation. This had led first to her breaking with the poet Binding and then to leaving Germany for England where she had made friends with the Schiffs, the Rothensteins and other members of Max's circle. After the Beerbohms had come to England she often came to see them. For she now lacked a hero to worship; and Max did something to fill the role. All through the war the friendship grew closer. Elisabeth Jungmann was one of the most frequent visitors to Abinger: and when she was away she poured out her feelings in a series of tumultuous and affectionate letters. In 1942 she heard that her mother had died in Germany.

'Dearest Lady Beerbohm,' she wrote to Florence, 'You say "words seem useless", but I assure you: I loved yours and to read them did me so much good, as well as I constantly feel your good thoughts like healing and warming rays, so bitterly needed in this grim life.

The more I read and hear of those inconceivable horrors, inflicted on the poorest of the poor, and the most helpless of the helpless, the—so self-centred I admit to be—easier I feel and as though a terrible, wounding, narrow iron band round my chest, painfully festering it day and night, had been released: to know a beloved Mother exposed to these horrors would certainly drive one mad.

Still, in spite of all endeavours to regain my balance and at least some of that serenity without which certainly is of no use either to oneself or to anybody in this world—as our old great minstrel Walter von der Vogelweide says:

"NIEMAND TAUGT OHNE FREUDE"

—well, in spite of striving for it, the successes are, so far, blameably poor.

All the more, dearest Lady Beerbohm, do, please, tell Sir Max that what I did not expect even any god could achieve in a time like this for me—*he* contrived to do: the irresistible supreme delight of his *Zuleika Dobson* (I found "her" at last in my Paddington Library) not only absorbed me entirely (oh, what a blessing!)—I dare say not often have I read a novel where actually every sentence is a gem!—but I, really and truly, heard myself several times laugh so heartily that the sound of it rather woke me up out of that happy spell—but just to be only more grateful for its power. . . . How wonderful to know that, loaded with so much sorrow, deep sadness and distress, one's battered soul yet has not grown listless altogether and not become too heavy not to be carried away and to be uplifted into more serene and brighter spheres by the wings and the grace of a genius!

May God bless you and him!

Yours lovingly

Elisabeth.'

Max was touched by her message to him. He wrote:

Dearest Elisabeth,

My thoughts have been constantly with you since the news of your sad, sad loss; and my heart is deeply stricken for yours. I know how brave a creature you are, and just how you will have been bearing your sorrow. Time will gradually lighten the load for you, I am sure.

We live in a tragic age; insomuch that the loss of those whom we love is, in a way, less bitter than it used to be. Those whom we have loved and lost are unconscious of this pitiable world; blissfully unconscious of it. . . .

How I wish I could send you a copy of *Z.D.*! I haven't any copy of my own, except that illustrated one, which I can't part with. I hate cheap editions; otherwise *Z.D.* would have been reprinted long ago.

Ever so many thanks for the glorious praise that you bestow on it. I am so proud that you admired it. I certainly did put a lot of work into it. . . .

Yours affectionately
Max.

Max speaks sadly here; how could he do otherwise in a letter of condolence! But in general he did not make a sad impression during these war years. On the contrary, people who met him for the first time were struck by the fact that in a collapsing world he appeared to remain serene and immaculate. Camille Honig, a young Polish admirer, knocked uninvited one evening at the door of the cottage. He was impressed to find Max sitting by himself, as elegant, he thought, as his prose style, in a perfectly cut grey suit and wearing a dark tie with a pearl pin in it. Lady Vaughan Williams, too, was awe-struck when she went to call, to find Max at the bus-stop, stylish in snuff-colour and standing right in the middle of the road, apparently oblivious of the fact that the bus was just about to start and might run him down. Not even a wartime bus could make Max hurry.

Nor the threat of danger: on the one or two occasions when Max was in danger during the war, he maintained an imperturbable demeanour. Hesketh Pearson describes meeting him in London at the Savile Club. They talked of old days at His Majesty's Theatre, then the alert sounded. Max rose; 'Tis the voice of the siren. I hear her complain,' he said smiling, and then, waving a graceful hand, went out into the exposed streets to stroll to his hotel. On another occasion an ammunition dump blew up close to the cottage. The Sprigges ran across to see how the Beerbohms were. They had thought it was a bomb and were hiding under the table. On learning the truth they emerged, Max still very tidy and very calm. The Sprigges stayed for an hour or two, talking and drinking cups of tea. Meanwhile, the dump continued to explode at intervals making a deafening roar each time it did so. Without appearing to notice it, Max conversed in his usual manner. Only once, after an especially loud explosion, he paused to say, 'This is designed to make conversation a little difficult.' He sought to take mental shocks equally impassively. Sylvia Sprigge related that if she met him walking on a day when the news was especially bad, he would look at her gravely and say, 'Well . . . there it is!' and after a short pause turn the conversation serenely enough on to other topics. At such moments Max's serenity was assumed. More often it was not. His smiling and unruffled demeanour was in some degree an expression of the spirit within. Considering his age and the times he lived in, Max still continued to get a surprising amount of enjoyment out of existence. Even under the immediate shock of the outbreak of war he could be amused.

'Dearest Violet,' he writes to Violet Schiff a few weeks after hostilities had started, 'Thank you for your delightful note. It has made us both laugh so much. Thank Heaven that Hitler himself cannot drive laughter out of Europe!'

Certainly Hitler did not succeed in driving laughter out of Max. Such creative work as he did was no more serious than it had ever been. His contributions to the *Abinger Chronicle* consisted of squibs and skits.

Max did not need anyone to laugh with; he retained his faculty of self-sufficient amusement. Mrs Schiff used to watch him out of her window pacing up and down the lawn hour by hour: often, just as in old days at the Villino, he would stop to laugh at some thought that had occurred to him. For him, even a practical joke lost nothing by being private to himself. Every day after they had finished reading *The Times*, the Schiffs used to send it down to Max, who later, in his turn, sent it on to the local schoolmistress. Before doing so he often 'improved' the illustrations. The poor schoolmistress was bewildered. 'What a strange kind of football they play now!' she confided to a friend. 'With two balls: I saw a picture of it in *The Times*.' Max did not hear her make this remark; and he could not witness her bewilderment. But for him it was enough to imagine it.

He told the Schiffs about these secret pleasures. He also sent them a great many of his 'improved' advertisements—also cartoons and fragments of parody. Together with Elisabeth Jungmann they had come during these years to take first place among Max's friends. They were peculiarly equipped to appreciate his flavour, Mrs Schiff in particular. She delighted in humour and was, besides, an accomplished connoisseur of personalities, with an eye to discriminate the fine, the rare and the odd in her fellow human beings. In Max she found an object worthy of her study; and during the years at Abinger took full advantage of her opportunities to investigate him. She noted that what pleased him most was a small perfection. This was what he aimed at in his own art. But he liked it in everything; he got more pleasure, for instance, out of a small Rembrandt drawing than a large Rembrandt picture, felt happier in a small house than a big, however beautiful. He once said to Elisabeth Jungmann, 'The great English country houses are built for gods; an exaggerated conception of the human being led to their scale. It is nightmarish to think of living in those terribly big rooms.'

In time Mrs Schiff penetrated below Max's surface idiosyncrasies to examine the moral nature beneath. Her conclusions about this were extremely favourable. She was wont to apply three moral tests to character: behaviour to women, to servants and about money. Max passed all three with flying colours. Mrs Schiff found him honourable about money, chivalrous to women and very considerate to servants. Further, Mrs Schiff, like others, was struck by his extraordinary self-dependence. It was, she noted, spiritual. Max might be at sea in practical matters and would offer a conductor sixpence for a penny bus fare: but in a deeper sense no one was necessary to him. He did not need companions, he did not mind whether or not people agreed with him, he was indifferent to public opinion. Nor was this because he was blind to the value of success and popularity. On the contrary, he recognized it; but with detachment. It was one of Max's outstanding characteristics, said Mrs Schiff, that he combined an accurate appreciation of worldly values with an ultimate indifference to them.

An unusual combination! But Max's character, as Mrs Schiff saw it, was full of such unexpected blends. He was civilized yet simple, modest yet self-confident, pessimistic yet cheerful, sensitive yet somehow invulnerable. His detachment armoured him against the wounds inflicted by vanity on the one hand or, on the other, by entangling affection for other people. In consequence, for all his apparent helplessness and hypersensitiveness, Max was less likely than most people to be hurt by life. 'Max,' said Mrs Schiff, 'is not a man to be pitied.'

She turned her investigator's eye on to Florence too. Here she found more to criticize. She recognized the qualities in Florence that had led Max to marry her; her gentleness and refinement, the romantic glance in her pensive dark eyes. But she also thought her self-dramatizing and self-deceiving. These qualities showed themselves when she came down to help look after the evacuated children. Sinking gracefully to the floor, she would gather them round her with a gesture and then in theatrical tones proceed to tell them a story. The children were embarrassed; so was Mrs Schiff. She could not feel that Florence was really interested in the children. The next day convinced her she was right in this: for Florence, returning to the children, did not remember who any of them were. Mrs Schiff was also amused by Florence's extraordinary capacity for being shocked. When she discovered that the servant girl who came to help them at the cottage was going to have an illegitimate child, she was so dismayed that she felt unable to see her again. She was also distressed by some of Max's 'improvements' in the newspapers. 'Oh, they are too horrible,' she would exclaim, averting her eyes.

Mrs Schiff was not the only person to criticize Florence during these years. Others complained of her interruptions and attempts to dominate the conversation—'The only thing wrong with Florence,' said Sylvia Sprigge, 'was that she did not let us hear enough of Max'—her agitations and her puritanism. Once when Max insisted, against her wish, on opening a second bottle of wine when they had a friend to dinner, she left the table and did not appear again. On another occasion, he was describing an Oxford friend who, he said, was very uninteresting. 'But I liked him,' he explained, 'because he was the best-dressed man in Oxford'; and he started drawing a caricature of him. Florence, apparently because she thought the conversation trivial and flippant, seized the paper from Max's hands and tore it up. It would be a mistake to think of these incidents as symptoms of any deep disturbance in Florence. She was the same woman as she had always been, with the same love for Max: Mrs Schiff noticed that if he was away from her for more than a short time, Florence grew uncontrollably agitated. But war and ill health —Florence was often ill during these years—had united to impose an unusual strain on her, had exasperated her nerves and weakened her self-control. Further, she was away from Italy and her own home and forced to move in a society where it was again and again brought home to her that people wanted to see Max more than they wanted to see her. This roused her latent self-distrust, making her tense and uneasy and now and again betraying itself in sudden emotional outbursts.

(2)

The Beerbohms did not spend all their time at Abinger. We hear of Max staying with the Sassoons, addressing a literary society at Eton; and, in August 1941, spending some weeks at Hampstead with Dr Leo Rau. Dr Rau was a German who had fled from Hitler in the thirties and set up in London. He met Max in 1937 and became his doctor. Max himself took no interest in his own health, but he worried a good deal about Florence's and used frequently to consult Dr Rau about her. They became personal friends. Dr Rau liked Max very much. It was extraordinary to meet an artist so unegotistic, he thought. When Dr Rau came back in the evening from work, Max began questioning him with interest about what he had been doing and never seemed to want to talk about himself. Meanwhile Dr Rau observed Max's mode of living during the visit. He remarked that he seldom had lunch, but, dressed with his customary care, would go over to the public house opposite to eat a sandwich and converse with the publican. Five years before Max had told Dick Sheppard that he had not been into a pub more than ten times in his life. Now he was becoming an habitué, and a popular habitué too. 'A very nice gentleman,' said the publican. 'Who is he?' Even Max could not help changing with the times. Even Max was growing socially, if not politically, more democratic. Dr Rau accelerated the process by taking him to Whipsnade on Bank Holiday, and he enjoyed the crowd. He enjoyed Whipsnade too: 'It was a pleasure,' he wrote to the Schiffs, 'to see not one of the strange and enchanting animals showing the faintest sign of awareness that there is a war on.'

Max also came up to London to visit Broadcasting House. In 1942 he gave two more broadcasts. He had been approached to do so in the previous autumn. At first there had been some difficulties about choice of subject. It seems that even in his new role of grand old man Max could not help making established authorities nervous lest he should say something shocking. He suggested speaking on 'Eating and Drinking'. Would not this create a bad impression in the austere days of war? asked the B.B.C. Max wrote back in a conciliatory vein to Mr Salmon of the Corporation.

'I fully agree that the "Eating and Drinking" idea would be in-opportune. I had been thinking insularly. People aren't at all irked by the rationing system; and the Christmas ration for this year is to be raised. But I had overlooked the fact of which you remind me: the danger of starvation in other countries. . . . I wonder how a broadcast with some such name as "Glimpses of Royalty" would do. Not in the sense of "Monarchs I Have Met"!—but rather in that of illustrious persons I have set eyes on from the kerb. I have always taken great delight in Monarchy and felt it to be a thing to be thankful for. I have often (in writings as well as in drawings) mocked at it, as I do at all things of which I am fond. But I don't think any mockery would creep into my broadcast. Please let me know your thoughts.'

Mr Salmon's thoughts were unfavourable. Had not Max once been famous for making fun of the Royal Family? It seemed only too likely that, justly or not, he would now be suspected of making fun of them once more. After some more discussion it was agreed that he should speak on the less inflammatory subject of old music halls. The performance took place on 18 January. Max dared to sing some of the old music-hall songs himself. He had only a whispering quavering thread of a voice, but in the event this added a comic charm to his discourse. The broadcast was an even greater success than its predecessors: Max got more letters than ever, including some from schoolboys and private soldiers. He was very pleased:

'The pleasure of praise is, if anything, more acute as one grows older,' he said.

The second broadcast took place on 18 September. It was about advertisements. Once more the B.B.C. authorities had shown themselves a little nervous. Afraid lest Max might offend the professional advertisers, they had wanted him to talk about his memories of the *Yellow Book* period. However, Max did not want to risk wearying his public with too many reminiscences.

'I daresay I might be quite fairly good,' he said,' on the theme that you suggest; the *Yellow Book* time. But here again I am averse. Last January I seemed to be generally liked in the character of dear old gentleman. But I think it would be a mistake to repeat those effects. There are other elements in me. There is for instance some "snap" in me still, and I should like to give that a turn.'

In fact he did stick to the role of old gentleman. But he was a more sharp-tongued old gentleman than in his last broadcast; and more up-to-date. As sometimes before, Max showed himself less behind the times than he professed to be. In fact he was ahead of them; Max was one of the first persons publicly to attack that arch-enemy of the modern intelligentsia, the commercial advertiser. He did it on different grounds; less because he thought that advertising corrupted the innocent masses than because he found the advertisements themselves ugly and vulgar. He certainly showed his 'snap' in pointing this out.

'Meanwhile,' he announced, 'if I were endowed with wealth, I should start a great advertising campaign in all the principal newspapers. The advertisements would consist of one short sentence, printed in huge block letters—a sentence that I once heard spoken by a husband to a wife "My dear, nothing in this world is worth buying." But of course I should alter "my dear" to "my dears".'

During the war years, to add to his exiguous income, Max did a little occasional journalism: reviews, articles, and so on. Of these the only one of interest to the biographer is an article composed in February 1940 for *John o' London's Weekly*; and this is interesting only for its last sentences. The article was designed to inaugurate a series entitled *My Ambitions*, to be written by various authors. Max discusses ambition in general: just at the end he turns to his own. 'I never had any,' he says, 'I had merely some modest wishes—to make good use of such little talent as I had, to lead a pleasant life, to pass muster.' Max was more master of his fate than most of us: if these were his wishes he had achieved them all. Nor had he been disappointed with the result. Max was a pessimist about human affairs in general: but looking back over his own life, he judged it had equalled his hopes. A journalist who came to interview him asked him if he thought he had been lucky. 'Once,' replied Max. 'Only once?' queried the journalist. Max answered, 'Once is enough—when I was born!'

Max fulfilled one more important literary engagement during 1943. In the autumn of 1942 he got a letter from Cambridge inviting him to give the Rede Lecture for the following year. He accepted and made it the occasion to pay a tribute to Lytton Strachey, partly because he admired Strachey so much, and partly because he thought that he had upheld classical standards of writing in a chaotic age. The lecture was delivered in the Senate House at Cambridge in May. In itself it is not among Max's most memorable works. His intimate style was cramped by the formal public occasion. Moreover, he had little new to say about Strachey. But in his peroration Max turns from the particular to the general: and, taking advantage of the fact that he was on a public platform with all the authority of the university behind him, proceeded to speak his mind about art and about the times he was living in. Once more he proclaimed himself a confirmed aesthete to whom beauty must always be the first aim of the artist; and he offered a final Puckish affront to democratic sentiment by mocking at the new and fashionable cult of the 'Common Man'.

'If I were asked what seemed to me the paramount quality of Lytton Strachey's prose, I should reply, in one word, Beauty. That is perhaps a rather old-fashioned word, a word jarring to young writers, and to young painters or musicians, and by them associated with folly, with vanity and frivolity. To me it is still a noble word, and I fancy it will some day come back into fashion. I believe that the quality it connotes is essential to all the arts. The stress and strain, the uncertainty of life in the past thirty years has not, I think, been favourable to the arts, though in those years a great deal of admirable work has of course been done (mostly, alas, by men of maturish years). Nor do I suppose that in my time, or until long after my time, will very propitious conditions supervene. There is a spate of planning for the future of many things. Perhaps some people are at this moment strenuously planning for the future of the arts. But I doubt whether in the equalitarian era for which we are heading—the era in which we shall have built Jerusalem on England's smooth and asphalt land—the art of literature, which throve so finely and so continuously from Elizabethan to paulo-post-Victorian days, will have a wonderful renascence. We are told on high authority, from both sides of the Atlantic, that the present century is to be the Century of the Common Man. We are all of us to go down on our knees and clasp our hands and raise our eyes and worship the Common Man. I am not a learned theologian, but I think I am right in saying that this religion has at least the hall-mark of novelty—has never before been propagated, even in the East, from which so many religions have sprung. Well, I am an old man, and old men are not ready converts to new religions. This one does not stir my soul. I take some comfort in the fact that its propagators do not seek to bind us to it for ever. "*This*," they say, "is to be the Century of the Common Man." I like to think that on the morning of January the first, in the year 2000, mankind will be free to unclasp its hands and rise from its knees and look about it for some other, and perhaps more rational, form of faith.'

The lecture was warmly received by a large audience and ten thousand copies of it printed by the Cambridge University Press were sold. This was an extraordinary number for a university publication of this kind, and indicates that Max's reputation had reached its highest peak yet. This showed itself in the number of honours conferred upon him during these years. The invitation to deliver the Rede Lecture had been one of them. It was preceded in 1942 by an honorary degree at Oxford, and a year later by an invitation—which he refused—to give the Romanes Lecture there. His old college of Merton made him an honorary fellow in 1945. Max came up to Oxford in 1942 to receive his degree. He had not seen his old university in wartime or since it had become a centre of industry. He did not like it. 'It looked,' he said, 'like the innermost circle of Hell.' He went through the degree-giving ceremony with inscrutable composure. Meanwhile, in August 1942, a group of his friends had united to celebrate his seventieth birthday by founding in his honour the Maximilian Society, a select body of distinguished admirers of his work. Its inauguration was marked by a dinner in London at which Desmond MacCarthy proposed his health and Max himself replied with a few words.

(3)

So passed the years 1940 to 1944. Then came a succession of events which broke up the pattern into which the Beerbohms' life had temporarily formed itself. First of all, one day in August, a flying bomb fell in the Schiffs' grounds close to the Beerbohms' cottage. The neighbours hurried over to see if Max and Florence were all right. They found them alive and apparently unperturbed. But, as it turned out, the explosion had rendered the cottage uninhabitable. A few hours later Max was observed in elegant tweeds directing a chauffeur in leisurely tones to put some luggage into a car. He and Florence were going to stay with some friends, the Whitworths, who had offered them temporary shelter. The cottage proved to be too much damaged for them to return to it. During the next few months they remained in the district, staying with various other friends. Max made little of the actual bomb incident but he was sad to leave Abinger. 'What horrible years of history to have lived through!' he wrote to the Schiffs. 'And yet for Florence and me how vast an amount of happiness there was in the dear cottage!' During the next few months two more events occurred to bring home to him still more the impermanence of things human. Sydney Schiff died in November, and in February 1945 Will Rothenstein. Both deaths were sources of sorrow, Rothenstein's was also a landmark in Max's life. He had been the one great friend of his youth left alive. Moreover, none had played so crucial a role in determining the course of his history. The relationship had not been without its troubles, but in the last years these had been forgotten. A memorial service for Rothenstein was held in St Martin-in-the-Fields in February and it seemed right and natural that Max should give the address.

The year was a melancholy one for Max. Nor did the end of the war in 1945 do much to cheer him. Private pleasures and affections had enabled him to keep up his spirits fairly well while the conflict lasted. But he had always looked on the war itself as nothing but a disaster which, though inevitable, must leave the world even worse than before. With a bitter-sweet emotion he found his mind lingering more and more on the memories of the irrevocable past.

'You and I,' he had written to Will Rothenstein in the summer of 1944, 'were very fortunate in being born so long ago—in having had our young days in beautiful days of peace and ease and civilization—auspicious and nutritive days, days before the world was ruined by science and machinery and other things darling to the Devil. I caught a glimpse of those days this morning, here. You remember the plots of grass with the white posts and black chains around them. The grass has been growing very long and high in these days. A labourer came to-day from Raike's farm in a small old cart drawn by a large old brown cart-horse, accompanied by a son aged six. The father was very active with his scythe. So also was the son, with a sickle small enough not to be out of proportion to him. They have now returned to the farm, the father leading the horse, and the son perched aloft on the hay (for some of the grass-plots had been shorn a week or so ago). Have you seen the photographs in *The Times* and elsewhere of the "prefabricated" homes which will presently arise all over England? I suppose these homes will be congenial enough to generations flourishing in the altogether prefabricated world which lies ahead. Well, well, let the future take care of itself. Though really it need hardly trouble to do that. It's going to be taken such a very good care *of*. Meanwhile you and I have the past to revel in.'

And to Sydney Schiff:

'As a child, I was a believer in Progress. Perhaps children still believe in it!? Adult believers in it have been extinct for a long time. At any rate I have met none.'

Max's general view of the historical situation was summed up in some sentences he wrote in his private notebook:

'Those whom the gods loved died in July, 1914.
Those whom the gods liked died very soon after Armistice Day, in November, 1918.
Those whom the gods hated lived to see the War's effects.
Those whom the gods loathe will live to see the effects of this War.'

460

Now the war was over and as the months passed its effects began to show themselves. Max found them just as bad as he had feared. Surely post-war England was a distasteful place. All its characteristic features displeased him: the shortages, the ill temper, the huge featureless crowds, the Woolworth shops he noted springing up in every town. Even the lack of domestic servants; for though Max did not like having servants himself, he had a sentiment for the ancient country houses of his land, and thought them dreadfully depressing places without servants to run them. The advent of a Labour Government, too, filled him with foreboding; was it not likely to continue the regime of drab austerity? So far as he could see, the only remaining institution that gave a touch of splendour and style to the dreary scene was the Royal Family. Max had grown to be more thankful than ever for the presence of the Royal Family.

With England as it was, both he and Florence longed to get back to the Villino. They also hoped that they might live more cheaply there. The rise in prices and taxes since the war had made Max very poor again; and this in spite of the fact that he had been left three thousand pounds by Reggie Turner. His friends worried about it and one of them had got into touch with a member of the Government to see if Max could not be given a grant from some public fund. The Labour Government proved to be less insensible to the claims of culture than Max had feared. He got a letter from the Prime Minister, Mr Attlee, offering him two hundred and fifty pounds to help him out of his present difficulties. Max thanked him warmly but refused the offer. He was not, he said, so poor as to be a deserving object of charity. At the same time he thought he should give up smoking, since the tax on tobacco was so high. He could not complain of this, he said, as it would be good for his health. It did not look as if it would be possible to go back to Italy for some time. Things seemed unsettled there and Max had received no information as to whether the Villino was in a fit state to be lived in. For two years after the end of the war, therefore, the Beerbohms stayed in England.

At first they had no settled residence. After the bomb fell at Abinger they moved about, staying sometimes with friends, sometimes in lodgings. In August 1946, however, Ellis Roberts, now in America, wrote offering to lend them a house near Stroud in

461

Gloucestershire. This was to be their home till they left England. From Stroud they made occasional excursions into the world. We hear of them at Malvern, where Florence took a cure—'If you have never been to Malvern, remain strange to it,' wrote Max to Christopher Salmon, 'it's the ugliest little town I ever saw'—at Heytesbury with Siegfried Sassoon, and, in December 1946, spending a weekend at Faringdon with Lord Berners, to meet Desmond MacCarthy and his daughter and son-in-law. The impression he made there showed that neither his age nor the Labour Government nor the deplorable state of the world had succeeded in weakening his mind or dimming the sparkle of his spirit. Every evening he favoured the company with an exquisite display of his conversational art. Great talkers was one of the topics discussed. 'What do you think we should have thought of Coleridge's talk?' someone asked. 'A little too much of the Third Programme about it I am afraid,' said Max slyly. He went on to give vivid verbal portraits, illustrated with imitations, of the distinguished talkers he himself had known: Meredith, George Moore, Oscar Wilde. He showed himself extraordinarily observant of voice and movement; George Moore, he said, had a gesture while talking of waving his hand round and round, beginning at the lips as if drawing the words out of his mouth in a spiral: with a deft expressive movement of his hand Max suited the action to the word. He had preserved, too, his delicate sense of conversational timing. Lord Berners mentioned Lady Cunard, with whom Max had spent an unenjoyed weekend long ago in Edwardian days. 'I haven't seen her for years,' he said, with an innocent air. 'Has she changed at all?' 'No,' answered Lord Berners, warmly. 'It's wonderful, she's exactly the same.' Max did not answer for a moment; then, still looking innocent, 'I am very sorry to hear that,' he said.

This remark shows that he was still mischievous. There are other instances of it about this time. One day he got a letter asking him to contribute to a symposium by various authors about capital punishment. It was a solemn letter: Max's answer was not solemn. He wrote: 'I can only say that for the sake of that large public which takes an absorbing interest in trials for murder, I should like capital punishment to be abolished; for then there would be so many more murders.' A little later he was asked to send a message to Shaw complimenting him on reaching the age of ninety. Shaw always roused a devil in Max. He replied:

'I suppose that the world itself could not contain all the books that have been written about G. B. S., and I think it is high time that a book should be written *to* him. I wish I could be among the writers of it. But I think that no great man at the moment of his reaching the age of ninety should be offered anything but praise. And very fond though I am of G. B. S., and immensely kind though he has always been to me, my admiration for his genius has during fifty years and more been marred for me by dissent from almost any view that he holds about anything. I remember that in an interview published in Frank Harris' *Candid Friend* G. B. S., having commented on the adverse criticisms by his old friends Archer and Walkley, said "And Max's blessings are all of them thinly disguised curses." I remember also a published confession of my own that I was always distracted between two emotions about him, (1) a wish that he had never been born, (2) a hope that he would never die. The first of those two wishes I retract. To the second one I warmly adhere. Certainly he will live for ever in the consciousness of future ages. If in one of those ages I happen to be re-incarnate I shall write a reasoned estimate of some aspect of him and of his work.'

The tone of his talk at Faringdon was mostly playful. But not always: he had his graver moments. He spoke with loving veneration of Thomas Hardy's character; his noble simplicity, his beautiful modesty about his own work. With less approval he spoke about H. G. Wells. His interlocutor thought that this was because Max identified Wells with the scientific advances now manifesting themselves in the disagreeable guise of air warfare. 'You mean,' he suggested, 'that he is partly responsible for our present ills.' 'He was responsible for himself,' said Max crisply, 'and that was one of the worst of them. He was at once a man of real genius and a mean bounder. It is a rare combination.' As Max spoke, his voice changed, a new and incisive severity came into his tones. Suddenly he sounded formidable.

In 1945 he gave one more broadcast, entitled 'Playgoing'. Reminiscent and genial, it recalled his talk on old music halls. It was inspired by memories of his days as a dramatic critic: but there is no trace in it of himself as a militant supporter of the new serious drama. This had been his role when he had started work on the *Saturday Review* in 1897. He had largely abandoned it, however, during the years that followed. Now, looking back from a distance of forty years, he stated openly that, like the aesthete that he was, he thought the object of the theatre was to delight.

'I have a notion,' he said, 'that the drama is, after all, essentially a vehicle for action, is essentially, or at least mainly, a thing to cause the excitement of pity and awe, or of terror, or of laughter, rather than to stimulate one's ratiocinative faculties. The theatre, I would say, is a place for thrills.'

'Playgoing' is the last of Max's second series of broadcasts. There were enough now to make a book. In the autumn of 1947 this came out with the title *Mainly on the Air*.

Otherwise Max did no more writing during these last years in England. He was too old and too tired. He drew very few cartoons either. Instead, as at Abinger, he went for short strolls or sat indoors reading and listening to the radio and gramophone. The gramophone added a great deal to the pleasure of his life, and he was particularly delighted by a record of Noël Coward singing 'Don't put your daughter on the stage, Mrs Worthington': during the summer of 1946 he played it again and again. Sometimes Elisabeth Jungmann came to stay. When she was away, she wrote and sent presents. Max thanked her with the especial and flirtatious affection he reserved for her alone.

Dearest Elisabeth,

The pears are delicious. And so are the cigarettes. BUT how more than naughty, how wicked of you to go spending all that money on me! You certainly will not go to Heaven—unless you promise never to do it again. And I had so hoped we should meet there. So please make that promise, and keep it. I was telephoning to Florence early this afternoon, and I told her about the gift, and she echoed my strong disapproval of you.

Yours affectionately
Max.

Florence was as intent on getting back to Italy as Max was. Early in 1947 she decided to go out herself and see how things were there. She left in April and was away the best part of two months. As in the past, Max wrote to her almost every day. These letters have a special interest; for, since the two were never to be parted again for any length of time, they are almost the last he ever wrote to her and the chief evidence of their relations to one another at the end of their life. Much of them is about practical matters, Florence's journey, and the arrangements to be made for their return to Italy. But Max also takes pains to tell her any little piece of news he thinks may interest her—Purcell, the cat, spends all the time with him, he says, and seems to worship his shoes fanatically; Alice Rothenstein is much offended with some male friend because he dared to receive her at five in the afternoon wearing an ornamental blue dressing-gown; Max has heard the cuckoo for the first time that year—'but without the accustomed thrill,' he said. 'Somehow these wild uplands make the cuckoo seem impersonal—unlike his intimate old self in such places as dear little Abinger.' More significant than anything that Max says in these letters is their loving tone, the endearments with which they are scattered, the anxiety he shows about Florence's health, his repeated wish to see her again. Melancholy and uncontrolled though Florence may sometimes have shown herself in these last few years, Max's affection for her was unchanged. After she got back she left him for a weekend to stay at Abinger. He wrote to her:

'Darling sweet, I hope you are not tiring yourself at all. I was glad to hear you say you had *plenty* of help. I wish I were in Abinger with you. I always wish I were wherever you are! Take great care of your dear self.

Your very own loving
Max.'

Florence found everything much better at the Villino than she expected. The house was undamaged, the furniture intact and the population friendly. There seemed no reason why she and Max should not go back. She returned to England in June; the two prepared to get ready for departure. Before he went, Max took another journey. The widowed Agnes Knox was now the only one of Max's immediate family left alive. He had always been fond of her and during the war had managed to see her regularly. She used to come and stay at Abinger. Looking like Whistler's portrait of his mother with her white hair and dark sweeping skirts, she would sit by the fire while Max hovered about her, ministering to her wants. Later she went to live at Newcastle in Northern Ireland in order to be near to her husband's family. Now, in 1947, Max heard that she was failing. He determined to visit her before he went back to Italy: if he did not, he feared he might never see her again. Early in September, Elisabeth Jungmann saw him off by the night mail. He was too poor to travel anything but third class; but the journey turned out to be less of an ordeal than he had expected, for—and this, he said, made him realize how old he must look—everyone in the carriage came to his assistance, helping to settle him in his seat and to carry his luggage. The visit was a success; he found Newcastle a pleasant place, reminding him a little of Rapallo, in that it was situated on a bay with hills rising picturesquely around it. Agnes seemed very pleased to see him. Though her mind wandered for much of the time, there were still lucid intervals when she could recall old days and lovingly recognize a figure she associated with them. Max stayed for three days and then said goodbye. As he had half-expected, it proved to be a last goodbye. Agnes died six months later. Max felt her death deeply. The B.B.C. were about to broadcast a recorded talk of his; Max wrote asking them to explain at the beginning of the programme that the recording had been made at a date before Agnes's death. He could not bear people to think him heartless enough to be entertaining the public during the first days of his bereavement.

To return to 1947: back in London Max took another final farewell. He and Florence left England at the end of September. They were never to see it again.

PART IV

CHAPTER EIGHTEEN

Latter Days

M AX had nine more years to live. They were as uneventful as most of his Italian years. More so, indeed; for now he was too frail to travel. The Leicester Galleries held two exhibitions of his cartoons during this period, the first in 1947, the second in 1952. But there was no longer any question of his going to England to arrange them as he had in the past. The time was at an end, too, for those occasional excursions to other Italian towns which had in former days diversified his life. Twice a year, however, he did sleep out of his own bed. He had begun to feel the need of a change of air after the winter and also to get away from the intense heat of August. At these times Max and Florence took to going for some weeks to Montallegro, a little place high up in the mountains above Rapallo and celebrated in the neighbourhood for a shrine to which people came to be miraculously healed. It consisted mainly of a wide pavement leading to a flight of steps at the top of which rose a large tawdry marble church. At the side of the pavement stood a little hotel where Max and Florence stayed, and which commanded a sweeping view of coast and sea and mountains. Unexpectedly Max delighted in the mountains; 'They give me a sense of power,' he used to say in mild tones. On his first visits he used to take short walks among them: later he found it enough to stroll up and down the stretch of pavement between the hotel and the church. For the rest he sat on the terrace taking his meals there or in the little hotel restaurant. Later the hotel built a larger, handsomer restaurant looking towards the Mediterranean, but Max, it was observed, remained faithful to his accustomed and humbler table. It was its modesty that attracted him to the hotel. He wrote in the visitors' book: 'This is the least vulgar hotel in Europe, so far as I know, and one of the cheapest; cheap to the purse though dear to the heart.'

At the Villino life resumed its old pattern, though with some inevitable differences. For one thing, Max was now incapable of doing any work that required sustained effort. In the first two years after he got back and because he needed the money, he did a few reviews for English Journals, notably one of a reprint of Henry James's *A Little Tour of France*. In this he took occasion to criticize Henry James's habit of rewriting passages in his early works in his later manner—'A process,' Max said, 'akin to patching grey silk with snippets of very thick brown velvet . . . a strange sad aberration and a wanton offence to the laws of art.' After 1950 there are no more reviews; clearly he found they imposed too great a strain on him. As for writing letters, he had pretty well given it up by this time. Max's correspondence after 1947 comprises a thin sheaf of papers and these consist mostly of necessary letters; of refusal and thanks or relating to his negotiations with the Leicester Galleries or the B.B.C. Only once or twice does a special cause spur him to a special effort. In 1948 he had got a letter from Shaw in which he criticized Gordon Craig in a manner Max thought unjust. He was as fond of Craig as ever: and felt he must protest.

'In the whole history of marksmanship,' he wrote, 'were ever so many shots fired in quick succession so wildly wide of the mark as those which you, for my benefit, have fired at the E. G. C. target? Never, I do believe.

You allow that his writing has "cleverness and subtlety". There never, however, was a less clever[1] or less subtle fellow than Craig. The qualities that his writing has, and has from the outset had, are a lovely freshness and vivacity and luminousness; "magic is about"—with a lot of nonsense, and much artlessness, and sudden splendid beams of wisdom and rightness. Cleverness never is there, believe me, nor subtlety. You should read Craig. *The Art of the Theatre—Books and Theatres—Nothing and the Book-Plate*—I fancy they and various others are still in print. But to return to your shots:—

You think he "cannot control his drawing to an end". Yet you may remember, if I remind you, that his drawings have had rather an effect on European scenography. His etchings and his woodcuts are (to my mind) much finer works than his drawings on paper, and they are admired by the connoisseurs (of whom I don't pretend to be one) as very satisfactory specimens of mastery in two exacting forms of art. You should study some collection of them (but not from the standpoint of a ready-made connoisseur).

[1] Good heavens!—what a rhymer I am!

MAX BEERBOHM, SELF-CARICATURE, 1952

You hold that 'the Lyceum, that little hell of ignorance and egoism, aborted' the soul of Craig. I should have supposed rather that (despite his great and in-many-ways right veneration for Irving) the Lyceum acted just as a spring-board for his leap into the void and in quest of an Ideal Theatre. (If you imagine, as you imply, that he is an egoist in his work or in his mind, let me assure you that you might just as well say that Blake—whose work and mind his somewhat resembles—was egoistic).* . . .'

*And why *shouldn't* you say so? What *wouldn't* you say to make somebody sit up?

Max was also spurred to take up his pen on matters relating to the presentation of his own work. It was proposed in 1947 to make a radio version of *Zuleika Dobson*. Max wrote several letters about this, making suggestions. Could not each character, he said, be introduced in the Wagnerian manner by a leitmotif, all, that is, except the mean and uncouth Noaks: 'Noaks is too dreary a character to be given a motif,' wrote Max, 'no lyre should be struck for Noaks.' And he felt so passionately about the correct pronunciation of his heroine's name that he sent a telegram to London about it. 'Zuleika speaker not hiker' it ran. The B.B.C. managed to persuade Max to do some more work for them. They wanted him so much that, since he could not go to England, they told him that they were ready to send out an apparatus to Rapallo to record him. Max agreed. In his last years he broadcast eight times; in May 1949, on Nat Goodwin, an acquaintance of Edwardian days; in October 1950, on George Moore; in May 1951 he paid a tribute to Marie Lloyd who had just died; and another in 1952 to Desmond MacCarthy. He spoke about his memories of Yeats in 1954 and of H. B. Irving in January 1955. In December 1955 came some extracts from his unpublished and unfinished tale, *The Mirror of the Past*, with its hero Herringham rechristened Hethway. This was followed in January 1955 by a short anecdote about Henry James. None of these talks represented much creative work on Max's part. The two tributes and the story about James were very short, while the longer pieces had all been written many years before, and needed very little adaptation to make them suitable for the microphone.

Life at the Villino had changed too. Fewer people came to stay there than in the past. Now that she was old, Florence found it too tiring to minister to guests: anyway, most of the old habitual visitors like Dora and Reggie were dead. The one regular visitor surviving from the past was Elisabeth Jungmann. It had been a great blow for her when the Beerbohms left England. She wrote to them:

Dearest Florence,
Dearest Sir Max,
    This is exactly the mood I was foreseeing and dreading for a long time: leaning against a tree in Kensington Gardens (which, by the way, are utterly disfigured and turned into a huge tent laager, or kraal, looking almost like one of those scurrile film ideas of Walt Disney's), on a grey and lonely Sunday, the yearning thoughts still directed towards lovely Abinger which, though, has, to my great grief, lost that strong magnetic power that attracted not only the thoughts but 'every scrap of the body' irresistibly, gave it wings and made it fly until it came to rest and revel near you, with you.
    'Why hast thou forsaken me'?! . . .
    May all be lovely and pleasant for you, my very beloved Friends! Will I ever hear??
    I hardly dare to ask: can one ever come near you? But I do feel forlorn, and the world looks different in these our bereft spheres——
                                        Yours ever devotedly
                                            Elisabeth.

She need not have worried. Max and Florence were only too pleased she should come near them. As before, she spent her yearly holiday at the Villino, listening sympathetically to Florence's confidences and gossiping on the terrace with Max. Other frequent visitors—though they generally slept at the hotel—were two new friends, Selwyn Jepson and his wife Tania. Selwyn Jepson, a son of a writer of the nineties called Edgar Jepson, was already acquainted with Max. But it was only now that he and Mrs Jepson got to know him well. Lively, intelligent and sympathetic, they were soon close friends; and helpful ones too. In spite of his enhanced reputation, Max did not make as much money as he should out of his books and drawings.

Selwyn Jepson, who had a professional understanding of the book trade, helped to get his work republished, and both he and Mrs Jepson also assisted to arrange the exhibitions at the Leicester

Galleries. The result of their efforts was to make Max better off. This was something to be thankful for, since when they first got back to Italy both he and Florence had found it hard to make both ends meet. Dr Rau, visiting Rapallo in the cold winter of 1949, discovered his old friends in very reduced circumstances, eating exiguous meals and huddling round a minute fire, the only one in the house. When he got home he wrote to a friend in an influential position asking him to see if anything could be done to get Max a pension. He got a reply saying that money had been offered to him and refused. It is not clear whether this referred to his answer to Mr Attlee. In fact, Max did not like taking money except for work done, and done specifically with the purpose of making money. Three years later when Desmond MacCarthy died, Max paid a tribute to him on the wireless, but he refused to be paid for it. The tribute, he said, had been a gesture of affection to an old friend. He did not think it right to make money out of a gesture of affection. Another time he returned part of his fee on the ground it was more than the broadcast was worth. With such opinions it was no wonder that he was hard up, and lucky for him that he met Mr and Mrs Jepson.

Though few people came to stay in the house, Max's life was not solitary. Daily visitors abounded—more, to judge by the records, than ever before. Here we come to a chief difference between Max's life in Italy before and after the second war. During his absence he had achieved the position of a national figure, an august and ancient monument; and he retained it after he came back. Monuments are objects of pilgrimage. So now was Max; if not to the mass of ignorant tourists, yet to the choicer spirits, intellectual and artistic, of the English-speaking world. Thornton Wilder and Somerset Maugham, John Gielgud and Laurence Olivier, Robert Graves and Truman Capote—these are only a few of Max's visitors during these years: and besides these came many with less famous names, children of old friends, humble students.

Max was aware of his position and, like the actor he was, played up to it. For all he did so little work, the creative impulse was not dead in him. It had always expressed itself in his person as well as in his art. Indeed, Max the man was one of his masterpieces. Conspicuous during the Edwardian age, it had been, as it were, withdrawn from exhibition by its creator when he retired to Italy. But now the public were prepared to come to Italy to see it: for it had the added

attraction that it was now historical, a surviving relic of the picturesque past. Max the man was not only an exquisite *objet d'art*, but
also a fascinating period piece and the work of an Old Master. The
Old Master was ready and willing to display his handiwork. Max's
creative instinct still showed itself in the performance he put up for
visitors.

It was admirably staged. Now he was so old, Max liked a little
time to prepare himself before making the effort to meet a new
person. Generally the visitor was introduced into the drawing-room
where he was met by Florence. She then took him up to the terrace
where Max was waiting. He was dressed with all his old care:
Florence arranged with a little Italian tailor to copy his old suits at
small cost. We hear mention of one in white linen and one in prim-
rose-coloured tweed, with a double-breasted, broadly lapelled waistcoat. His appearance still mattered to him. Cecil Beaton visited him
during these years and took some more photographs. After he had
finished, 'You'll let me see them?' Max asked. 'And you'll destroy
any horrors?'

As a matter of fact there were no horrors. Max was too photo-
genic. He looked wonderful but not wholly human: 'resembling',
said Mr Michael Lloyd, one of his youthful visitors, 'a very old, but
beautifully exquisite, quite big fairy'. After he had greeted his guests
he sat down, carefully adjusting his cuffs as he did so. Then the
conversation would begin. His mode of speaking, like his style of
dress, was that of his youth. He pronounced Café Royal and waltz
in the French fashion, interspersed his talk with the phrase, 'Don't
you know,' and started an inquiry with 'Tell me'. He inquired often.
For in spite of his old man's air, Max remained youthfully curious
about the world around him. The visitors, however, had come to
hear him talk, especially about the past. Readily he would answer
their questions and relate anecdotes—about Wilde and Beardsley
and Mrs Patrick Campbell, and himself when young, ornamenting
his descriptions with quips and fancies and pretty phrases. He did it
with an obvious pleasure in language and an accomplishment so easy
as to seem negligent. 'He speaks his remarks,' said Mr John Russell,
'as Pachmann at the end of his life would play an encore waltz and
with the same indifference to mere effect.'

Yet he made his effect all right. No pilgrim went away disappointed. Max's performance could be depended upon to be

brilliant. But it cost him a considerable and growing effort. For after he went back to Italy Max did begin noticeably to age and more so with every year that passed. His mind remained alive and quick. But not his body; he looked shrunken and transparent. His long hands had grown to resemble beautiful bird's claws, sheathed in freckled pale parchment: he spoke slower and more faintly: he tired quickly. The Beerbohms seldom asked people to dinner now. Max liked to go to bed about 9.30. This frailty, this weariness, subtly modified the impression made on his visitors. His performance was as finished as it had ever been and as unforced, in the sense that Max seemed equally and freshly responsive to his audience. But there was something fatigued about it, as if he could only keep it going for a short time and that by vigilantly husbanding his resources. In this, its last manifestation, Max's mask still appeared exquisite. But the delicate enamel of its surface was worn so thin that it seemed as if, at the slightest jolt, it might crack.

Time was telling on Florence and in a more cruel fashion. Though younger than Max, she had always been more sickly. All through the war years she had suffered from rheumatism. Back at Rapallo her health continued to decline. This affected her spirits and her efficiency. For the first time Max's clothes were sometimes frayed and unmended. Florence grew confused too. Beneath an appearance of tidiness was disorder. She tied up papers neatly in bundles but arranged them under no system. This made for chaos; all the more since she had a horror of throwing anything away, even old invitation cards or advertisements from shops. After her death a cardboard box was found among her things labelled 'For pieces of string too small to be useful'. Ill health also made her depressed. She worried about their finances more than necessary; in the summer of 1950 she persuaded Max to forgo his visit to Montallegro for fear the cost might ruin them. More than ever she suffered from fits of gloom. 'I am a most unhappy woman!' she cried to Elisabeth Jungmann, gazing out at the sea from the terrace. She took care not to worry Max about her depression: so that to him she appeared courageous and contented. However, he did realize that she was ill. It preyed upon his mind. For if she became an invalid, who was to look after her?—and if she died, who was to look after him? When Elisabeth Jungmann was staying at the Villino in the summer of 1948, Max asked her for her address and telephone number. She told him, and he pencilled it on the flyleaf of a copy of Siegfried Sassoon's poems. 'We won't tell Florence about this,' said Max, as he put the book back on to the shelf. On each of Elisabeth's subsequent summer visits Max took the volume out of the shelf again. 'Will this address still find you?' he would ask. She said, 'Yes.' 'For if anything should happen . . .' he began. 'If I am at the North Pole or the South Pole I will come,' said Elisabeth. In 1950 she received a warning that she might soon have to keep her promise. She arrived on her annual visit to find Florence looking much the same. But almost at once she took Elisabeth round the house and, pointing at various possessions, gravely gave her instructions as to what she wanted done with them, should she die. She seemed to have a premonition of approaching death.

It was a true one. Early in January 1951 she became very ill indeed. Max telephoned at once to Elisabeth Jungmann. Throwing up her work, she left by the first train. She arrived to find that Florence had died two hours before. Immediately Elisabeth took command of the situation and arranged for Florence to be cremated in Genoa as soon as possible. Meanwhile she saw to it that Max did not see the corpse or the coffin, or come to the cremation. Instead, she herself followed the cortège to Genoa. As it pursued its slow way along the winding coast road, Elisabeth was bewildered to find herself possessed by a curious feeling of excitement. When she got to Genoa she found that owing to some hitch in the arrangements the cremation could not take place till next day. However, she came back and told Max all was over: on the following morning, pretending that there was still some formality to go through, she went back, returning in the afternoon with an urn containing Florence's ashes. This was placed on the terrace. The Italian servants protested: the sight of it filled them with a superstitious fear. Accordingly, a few days later, bearing the urn, Max and Elisabeth were rowed out by the young gardener, Agostino, into the bay of Tigullio. When they were some way out, he rested his oars, rose and dropped the urn into the still, sky-reflecting waters. Erect and baring his head, Max watched, and then paused to pay a last silent tribute to the 'dear little friend' of long ago, the human being who, ever since he married her in 1910, had been the most important figure in his life. Never, it may be, as important as some wives are to their husbands: Max's spirit was too incurably self-sufficient for this to be possible. But he had given her as much of himself as he had to give; and all his memories of her were tender. 'I wish she could have lived as long as I,' he wrote to Katie Lewis. 'But I am grateful for the forty whole years of happiness that she gave me.' Meanwhile, Agostino had rowed the boat to the shore. When Max got back to the Villino, he took the copy of Siegfried Sassoon's poems from the shelf and carefully rubbed out Elisabeth's address from the flyleaf—'For I won't be needing this any more, will I?' he said to her.

There was no need to wait for an answer. Elisabeth stayed with Max for the rest of his life. Indeed, she had attained her heart's desire. She must not be blamed for feeling a little exhilarated as she followed the dead Florence to the crematorium. How could she help it? All her mature existence she had been looking for an older man of genius to whom she could dedicate herself. Up till now her quest had been disappointing. Hauptmann had not needed her enough and Binding had died in 1938. During the war years her empty searching heart had turned more and more towards Max. For the more she saw of him, the more she loved him. Moreover, she felt that there was much she could do for him. Elisabeth took the view that the ageing Florence was an inadequate wife. If only she could look after him herself she would, she was sure, make him twice as comfortable without spending a penny more. She longed for such a task. For Elisabeth's vital temperament needed scope for action. She wanted the man of her heart to be one she could look after as well as look up to, one to whom she could be nurse as well as disciple. Max filled this role perfectly. Wise and charming, he was also frail and unpractical—more than ever, now that he was seventy-nine years old. How could Elisabeth feel other than exhilarated? Here at last was a worthy and willing object on which to lavish all the enthusiastic devotion of her intense nature.

So intense was it that some men might have found her overpowering. Not so Max; he was not very different from what he had been at thirteen. With a child's physical dependence he still retained the child's inner detachment. Besides, Elisabeth's devotion was too genuinely unselfish to be a burden to him. 'The Angel', 'the Darling' —it was thus that she always spoke of him in her private diary; and to make him happy in the way that he best liked was the sole object of her life. From the moment she arrived at the Villino, she took all the weight off his shoulders. His clothes were mended, his papers put in order, his money affairs were established on a better basis. There was no more question of his being too poor to go to Montallegro. Unless he was unwell he went there every year for the rest of his life. Elisabeth also acted as his secretary; and she managed his social life. Better than Florence had done, at least during his last years: the food was as good, the hostess younger and more cheerful. Nor, unlike Florence, was Elisabeth ever tempted to interrupt Max or correct him on small matters of fact. Her sole wish was to display 'the Angel' to the best advantage without letting him get tired.

She had plenty of opportunity to satisfy it. The pilgrims continued to throng to Max's shrine. Most were content with one visit. A few stayed in the neighbourhood and saw more of him. Among these was his niece Iris, Herbert's youngest daughter, with whom he spent agreeable hours joking and recalling old music-hall songs, and Cecil Roberts. Roberts called at the Villino in February, 1952, after many years of absence. Max, to his surprise, behaved just as if he had seen him recently. 'My dear boy,' he began, 'where have you been? We have just been talking of you.' It was the first of several visits. Max professed himself much interested by the thought of Roberts's active existence spent largely in travelling all over the globe. 'You have had a busy life,' he said, 'it must have been fun!' This did not mean he envied him. During one of their talks Roberts asked Max what he would do if he had the chance to live his life over again. Max thought a moment; then he said, 'Forgive me, just what I have done—and with the same good fortune.'

To these friends from the past a new one added himself. Mr S. N. Behrman, the celebrated American playwright and biographer, had always been an admirer of Max's work and had long wished to make his acquaintance personally. He resolved to go to Rapallo for a week or two for this purpose. In June 1952, armed with an introduction, he presented himself at the Villino. Genial, clever and voluble, he made an excellent impression and was asked to come again as often as he liked. 'I don't remember,' said Max, 'having met in my later years anybody who appealed to me as this charming magnetic man has.' Elisabeth Jungmann liked him too. She noticed that Mr Behrman had the art of drawing Max out in such a way as to leave him cheerful yet not tired. It was true that he had a propensity to smoke between the courses at meals, a practice Max thought barbaric: but

this might be overlooked in view of the fact that he was so entertaining. Mr Behrman was more tolerant: he found nothing to
criticize in Max. Never did hero prove less disappointing to hero-
worshipper! Behrman's visits were the beginning of a close friendship, the last Max was ever to make. He paid three more visits to
Rapallo, in 1953, 1954 and 1955: each time he stayed several days. In
1954 he introduced Max to a very different figure from himself in
the shape of Mr Edmund Wilson. Very different from Max too;
blunt, radical and with a very different approach to literature. 'What
does he write about?' Max had asked Mr John Russell, who replied
that Wilson had written lately about Marx and Vico and Michelet.
'Ah, I see,' exclaimed Max, 'he is the henchman of the unreadable.'
The two kept off Marx and Vico when they met. Instead they talked
of Henry James. Wilson asked Max what he thought of the theory
that *The Turn of the Screw* was a study in neurosis, that all its events
were supposed to be taking place in the governess's mind. Max said
he thought it nonsense, the creation of 'some morbid pedant, prig
and fool!' Wilson confessed that he was the author of the theory.
Politely but firmly Max stuck to his point. He instinctively disliked
elaborate and fancy explanations of simple literary phenomena.
Moreover, he had a prejudice against the new psychology in literature or anywhere else. He felt it a threat to the privacy of spirit on
which he set a supreme value. Nor did he believe in its healing
powers. 'What would they do to me?' he once said to Behrman. 'I
adored my father and mother and I adored my brothers and sisters.
What kind of complex would they find me the victim of? Oedipus
and what else?' He reflected a moment. 'They were a tense and
peculiar family, the Oedipuses, weren't they?'

In spite of Wilson's regrettable propensity to take the new psychology seriously, Max liked him. The liking was returned. Wilson had
always thought highly of Max the satirist, especially Max the satirical
cartoonist: he enjoyed the steely strain in Max's art. This he found
also in Max the man. Indeed, Max was a more forceful and formidable figure than Wilson expected. He even looked bigger, with his
Germanic head: and he gave an impression of fundamental self-
confidence that was much to Wilson's taste.

'He's quite sure of himself,' Wilson told Behrman afterwards, 'he
knows the value of what he has done, both as a writer and as an

MAX BEERBOHM

artist. He doesn't give a damn about having all his caricatures collected and published, as I suggested to him they ought to be. He doesn't even know where many of them are. He knows very well that somebody else will have to worry about all that some day.'

Indeed, Max was as indifferent to public opinion or fashionable taste as ever. It was partly because he realized that his was not the type of art ever to appeal to a wide audience. In these later years an American publisher once asked him if he could include one of his essays in an omnibus volume of contemporary work. Max refused. 'I don't care to be omnibussed,' he wrote. The publisher wrote again urging that he might gain four hundred thousand new readers by this means. Max knew better. 'There are fifteen hundred readers in England and a thousand in America who understand what I am about,' he replied.

Behrman wrote down much of what Max said to him: so did several of his other visitors. From them and from notes kept by Elisabeth Jungmann we get a clear impression of his talk during this the final phase of his life, and of the thoughts and preoccupations that inspired it. These were mostly about people and the arts. Max no longer seems to have been interested in politics as he had been during the inter-war period. He did, it is true, in 1954 sign a petition against the hydrogen bomb: but this seems to have been because he had been asked to do so and on general grounds of principle, not because the subject stirred him deeply. For there is no other record of his mentioning it. But he continued to keep up to date with the non-political news and got a great deal of entertainment out of it. He was much amused to hear that Bertrand Russell should have married a fourth wife at the age of eighty, and still more that George Robey should have been given an official memorial service in St Paul's; would that Reggie had been alive to improvise an appropriate sermon for such an occasion! The news of Lord and Lady Bath's divorce, too, caught Max's attention: 'That is what comes of throwing Longleat open to the public,' he said. To show your home for money struck him as vulgar. 'But then,' as he said to Elisabeth on another occasion, 'no one mentions vulgarity any more, they take it for granted.'

He was equally caustic on the subject of modern painting and sculpture. Sir Edward Marsh wrote to ask him if he would sit for his portrait to Graham Sutherland: Sutherland, he said, now ranked with Henry Moore, who had put English sculpture on the map of Europe. 'If so,' Max replied, 'Pitt would no longer wish to roll up the map of Europe, it would be squashed for ever!' As for sitting to Graham Sutherland, Max had seen a reproduction of his portrait of Somerset Maugham and he thought he would prefer not. 'Maugham,' he said, 'looks as if he had died under torture.' Modern artistic photographs pleased him as little as modern paintings. 'They don't keep their place,' he said, 'they are too big. Something mechanical should not be so important.' We note that Max uses the word mechanical as a word of disparagement. Machinery and the science that produced it remained a bugbear to Max. This was as true of past science as of modern. Elisabeth Jungmann was reading about Newton and said to Max that she thought it would have been delightful to meet him. 'I wouldn't have understood him,' Max replied. 'He would have liked you,' said Elisabeth. Max was amused by this. 'I would have taught him the Law of Levity,' he said. He was less opposed to modern writing than modern painting, though he did not much approve its more serious manifestations. Nothing could make him enthusiastic about D. H. Lawrence's books.

'Poor D. H. Lawrence,' he once said. ' . . . Although his prose style was slovenly, he was a man of unquestionable genius. But then he became afflicted with Messiahdom. Now, what equipment had poor D. H. Lawrence for Messiahdom? . . . He had a real feeling for nature and in this he was at his best. But through his landscapes cantered hallucinations.'

T. E. Lawrence pleased Max no better than his namesake, at least not as a translator. 'What did he mean by calling the *Odyssey* "pastiche and face powder"?' said Max. 'He confused the *Odyssey* with his translation of it.' Max had read this translation some years before and 'I would rather *not* have been that translator than have driven the Turks out of Arabia,' he wrote to Will Rothenstein. He had reservations too about Virginia Woolf. He did not care for her diary. 'I have never understood,' he told Elisabeth, 'why people write diaries. I never had the slightest desire to do so—one has to be so very self-conscious.' Surely, too, it was deplorable to mind hostile criticism as much as Virginia Woolf did. She could have learnt from Turgenev in such matters.

'Turgenev,' Max said, 'appreciated that criticism is a delightful pastime for the critics—that, even, it may be delightful to their readers. But, he says, it has nothing whatever to do with the artist, nor with the process by which art is achieved. A pity poor Virginia couldn't have remembered that!'

Ezra Pound came in for severer condemnation. Max thought him crazy—fancy believing in Fascism!—and too obstreperous to be a comfortable companion. In the thirties he had settled near by, but Max had declined to see much of him.

'He seems out of place here,' he told their common acquaintance, Miss Phyllis Bottome. 'I should prefer to watch him in the primaeval forests of his native land wielding an axe against some giant tree. Could you not persuade him to return to a country in which there is much more room?'

Further, Max detected in Pound a vice he found peculiarly distasteful, namely, envy.

'He would start out to rave about some friend,' he said, 'and you thought you were in for a paean of praise. And then the qualifications would creep in. And then you realized that he had begun with the paean in order to conclude with the denigration. The treacle of admiration, don't you know, was always strongly tinctured with the vinegar of envy.'

Max did like some modern books however; the poetry of Robert Graves and Siegfried Sassoon, Gertrude Stein's autobiography of Alice B. Toklas, and the work of Thurber, both writings and drawings. 'His people are ugly,' said Max, 'but not in an unpleasant way.' He was also impressed by Hemingway's *The Old Man and the Sea*. 'It's a poem,' he said. 'I must read more of what I suppose I ought to call old man Hemingway.' In general, he cared less for novels than he used to. 'I have lost the power,' he complained, 'of being illuded by a novel, of being held in that state of mind when it matters terribly if they live happy ever after.' Biographies, on the other hand, absorbed him as much as ever: Rupert Hart-Davis's life of Hugh Walpole—'that lovable, pitiable and enviable fellow Hugh

Walpole,' Max called him—Sacheverell Sitwell's life of Liszt, Peter Quennell's life of Ruskin, and especially the section in it dealing with Ruskin's unfortunate marriage. Max found this a mystifying story. For all his sophistication, he was in some ways strangely ignorant of human aberration and he could hardly believe that a man would dare to marry unless he had reason to know he was not impotent. 'Surely Ruskin behaved very badly,' Max said to Elisabeth. She replied that such things often happened. 'I don't know another case of a man being impotent and marrying all the same,' said Max incredulously.

Much of his talk ran on authors of the past. He continued to read his old favourites, Henry James, Thackeray, Trollope; 'Trollope reminds us that sanity need not be philistine,' he said. He re-read his favourite old poems too, sometimes aloud to Elisabeth. Sitting on the terrace he would intone 'La Belle Dame sans Merci' or Henley's 'Invictus'. Romantic poetry remained his favourite. He liked it better than Shakespeare's. Max is among the few persons of taste who have failed to enjoy Shakespeare's sonnets. One afternoon sitting out with Elisabeth, he noticed a procession of coloured caterpillars wriggling along the sunlit balustrade. 'They remind me of Shakespeare's sonnets,' Max said. 'Each so beautiful and each a little unpleasant.' Elisabeth protested against this. 'Well, crawling is always a little unpleasant,' insisted Max. 'Normal human beings crawling may be unpleasant,' said Elisabeth, 'but here it is a demigod who loves and with passion!' Max was unconvinced. His point of view had the limitations of its virtues. His smiling detachment, his fastidious reserve, meant he could not enter sympathetically into so complete and self-surrendering a love as Shakespeare's.

More reasonably and predictably, Max remained hostile to the works of Kipling and William Morris and Shaw. He wrote to Behrman about Morris: 'Of course he was a wonderful all-round man, but the act of walking round him has always tired me': and of Shaw he said, 'He has a bad influence on his disciples and even on himself.' His feelings about Kipling were more complex. He disliked his work and all it stood for far more bitterly than he disliked that of Shaw or Morris. But this very bitterness made him feel guilty. For by now Max thought it morally wrong to feel bitterly. One day Behrman brought up the subject of Kipling and Max's opinion of him: Max became silent and changed the subject. Some minutes later he suddenly returned to it, and rather agitatedly. He explained that in the past he had often wanted to make it up with Kipling. 'But I didn't. Why didn't I do it? Why didn't I unbend? Why did I go on persecuting him? And now he is dead and it is too late.' He paused and then, 'But it had to be so, I had to do it. He was a great genius, who didn't live up to his genius, who misused his genius. . . .' Indeed, Kipling's work stood for too much that Max thought evil for him to soften towards it even in the mellow sunset of his extreme old age. Elisabeth Jungmann once found him in his chair murmuring angrily to himself; 'Damned balderdash!' he was saying. She asked what he was thinking of: it turned out to be some work of Kipling's.

People often asked Max about his own work. He was willing to tell them; how the idea of *Zuleika Dobson* had been originally suggested to him by a paragraph in the paper, that he thought 'A. V. Laider' and 'Enoch Soames' were his best stories, about the enjoyment he got from the actual process of colouring a cartoon—'It is a sensual pleasure to prepare a wash,' he said, 'and fill it in and make it a shade deeper.' Who had influenced him? inquired an admirer. He replied that Wilde and Thackeray had—'Thackeray gave me an ideal of well-bred writing'—but not, as critics had suggested, Lamb or Montaigne. He had read Lamb very little as a boy and without pleasure; Montaigne he had not read at all. To Michael Lloyd Max summed up his view of his own capacities and limitations. 'I have no great intellect,' he said, 'in fact rather less than the next man. What I have is intuition and a sense of humour, sense of fun and sense of beauty.'

The sense of fun had always come first with him. More than ever now: the aged Max did not care even for beauty if it suggested sadness. 'I dislike moonlight,' he said, 'and the moon, that dead companion'; and he found it hard to admit that an overcast sky could be beautiful at all. 'That yellow-grey is so ugly,' he complained. On the other hand, he was, if possible, readier than ever to be amused. Visitors noticed how spontaneously Max could still laugh; his laugh sounded like a schoolboy's, said Michael Lloyd. Nor was it mainly heard in company. Elisabeth and he were often in fits of laughter as they talked and played games in the evening together. They also entertained themselves by singing. In summer the terrace, in winter the drawing-room, was sometimes the scene of a comic and pleasing spectacle; the octogenarian Max and his middle-aged companion trolling out snatches from *La Bohème* and *Ruddigore* and *The Belle of New York*. If he did not know the words of a song Max whistled the tune instead. Besides singing and whistling he enjoyed hearing music on gramophone and radio. 'It makes me feel serener and lighter,' he explained to Elisabeth. Mendelssohn concertos, *Cavalleria Rusticana*, popular ballads—he got pleasure from them all, especially if they had old associations. It was often a sentimental kind of pleasure. Max realized this, but without shame. 'Of course it's sentimental,' he said to Elisabeth, 'why shouldn't it be sentimental?' Indeed, during the little time that remained to him he was determined to make the best of what life should offer. Sitting with Elisabeth one day he suddenly remarked, 'Let's be happy! There is much to be happy about—let's be happy!' He sought to extract happiness from the very fact of existence. Once at the end of a long day Elisabeth overheard him murmuring to himself with satisfaction, 'I am here, I am here—I am alive!'

Such words are evidence of a fighting spirit. But was it not a spirit too consciously cheerful to be wholly convincing? Thoroughly happy persons take their happiness for granted: they do not say, 'Let's be happy.' Nor does a man in whom the pulse of life beats high need to remind himself that he is alive. Max said these things because at times he felt his happiness threatened, found it hard to keep his mood consistently serene as of old. Moods of gloom succeeded moods of gaiety. Once or twice Elisabeth noticed with a shock that his face wore a weary, strained, grim expression. The causes of his troubles were physical. Max was a victim of his own ageing body. He tired more and more quickly—'I feel so weak!' he lamented—he began to suffer from asthma, indigestion, anaemia, gout. Physical ills reacted on his nerves, particularly at night-time. Asleep or half-asleep he was unable to summon reason to help him dispel the troubled feelings brought on by feeling ill. He suffered frequently from nightmares. Max's nightmares were curiously characteristic, in that they were more concerned with embarrassment than with horror. Once he dreamt about getting lost in the streets of London when on the way to dine with Edward VII; and on another occasion that he had arrived at Broadcasting House to give a talk, only to find he had left his script behind. Considered in the rational light of day such fancies do not seem so very dreadful. When he was feeling better Max realized this and could smile at his dreams. He announced to Elisabeth one morning, 'I have had a pleasant, noble and dignified nightmare about Queen Victoria and Mr Gladstone.' More often, however, the dream was shrouded in an inexplicable cloud of horror, which remained after he woke up and cast a shadow over his thoughts. Even when he did not have nightmares, Max slept restlessly. Elisabeth in the next room would hear him groaning and sighing; 'God save me!' he would ejaculate

His days were far better than his nights, but they were not always free from nervous troubles. Elisabeth thought he was like someone born with a skin too few, so that what to an ordinary man might seem a light touch was to Max a bruising blow. Loud noises like the telephone bell startled him violently: he was disturbed by any alteration in routine, a stranger arriving unexpectedly or a guest at the wrong time. 'Max doesn't like surprises,' noted Elisabeth. And he was worried by the fact that he got confused and could not remember things as he used to. 'My dilapidated mind will not work,' he said. Worse than this, he was liable to sudden fits of acute groundless apprehension, generally about Elisabeth. Once she went to open a window and did not come back immediately. Max was transfixed with horror; he thought she had fallen out of the window. Another time he called to her in the night and got no answer; he was seized with a fear that she might be dead. His sense of security was inextricably bound up with her presence.

Such childish apprehensions showed only too clearly that Max had begun to enter his second childhood. His childishness was not mental—Max's mind had not deteriorated—but emotional; it showed itself in irrational fears and agitations, and in the way he oscillated between high spirits and despondency. His relation to Elisabeth, too, was growingly childlike. For the first time in his long life he may be said to have become spiritually as well as physically dependent. He found it harder to hide his feelings than in the past and, when distressed, turned instinctively in search of someone to whom he could pour out his troubles and cling for support. Elisabeth perfectly filled the role: she had by now taken complete charge of the way his life was ordered. The day followed a regular routine. She called him herself and he spent most of the morning in bed reading and doing *The Times* crossword. After a leisurely toilet he rose to lunch at twelve-thirty; indoors in the winter and in the spring and summer on a little terrace in front of the annexe, which Max called 'the vining-room', because it was protected from the wind by a vine trellis. He remained out for the rest of the afternoon reading or, if he felt inclined, doing a little drawing. Dinner was early; afterwards he listened to the gramophone or radio till he went to bed at half-past nine. Elisabeth had moved him into what had been Florence's bedroom. It was not luxurious—Max never lived luxuriously—but it was larger and warmer than his old bedroom had been. Neat, pale and clean, with a narrow well-sprung wooden bed and plain table beside it, it suggested a secular, comfortable monk's cell. Out of it opened a smaller room where Elisabeth slept so that she could be ready if he wanted her. He often did. She did everything for him now, helped him to dress and wash and get into bed. At night especially she had to be on the alert. If he was disturbed by a nightmare or insomnia he would call and she would come in and soothe him. This happened regularly, it was rare for her to have more than two hours' uninterrupted sleep. In the day-time, too, she watched vigilantly over his health, his spirits and his appetite. Tirelessly and attentively she coaxed him, and cheered him up. He accepted her attentions easily. In some respects Max had never grown up; now he was old and weak he found no difficulty in resuming the role of a child again. But, as of old, he was a good child—affectionate, sweet-tempered and grateful. He was always thanking her for what she did for him and apologizing for any trouble he might cause. He strove to express his gratitude in action as well as word: Elisabeth noticed how very considerate he grew in this last phase of his life. She was touched when with feeble eyes and trembling fingers he tried to find her spectacles for her. When she had an attack of gastritis, he sat by the hour by her bed, holding her hand and seeking to make her laugh with his stories.

Meanwhile, in England his name was kept before the public by exhibitions and broadcasts. Max still took a great interest in his exhibitions, in what cartoons were chosen and how they were arranged; especially was he anxious that nothing should be shown that might give offence to anyone. Before the Retrospective Exhibition in 1952 he wrote a careful letter about this to Oliver Brown of the Leicester Galleries. The Galleries possessed many of his drawings. Max divided them into three categories; those he would like exhibited, those—mostly of old friends—which he wanted locked up and shown to nobody, and those he thought unsuitable for public exhibition, but which might be shown privately down-stairs to any clients likely to be interested.

'There are a great many drawings which I have suggested would be suitable to be shown to appropriate clients from portfolio down-stairs. Some of the King Edwards,[1] for example: it wouldn't do to have many of him *on the walls*. I remember the "Unforgotten" one; I think this is rather too cruel to be hung. . . . As I mentioned to you, I want the series of Shaw and Mrs Campbell kept *downstairs*. They are (1) The Campbell Tartan and the Cockney Fling. (2) "The Babes in the Wood". (3) The Bar Saloon. (4) Mrs Campbell and Mr Shaw as they respectively appeared to themselves. (5) Mrs Campbell and Mr Shaw as they respectively appeared to each other. (6) "But why do you call me Joey? I'm only the pantaloon". . .

By the way, it should be explained to any likely client that the drawings were done by me in disgust at Shaw's ridiculous pseudo-love-letters published in Mrs Campbell's autobiography.'

To the day of his death Max had his knife into Shaw.

His broadcasts continued to be a great success. Since they were either short tributes or composed of material already written, the composition did not involve Max in much work. On the other hand, now that he was old and frail he found delivering them a con-siderable strain. The records of the rehearsals reveal him as speaking more slowly than before and with many interspersed sighs and groans. He had to stop and start again more often too. At intervals he would pause to recover himself and then 'rumpity tumpity' he would gasp out hoarsely. The effort it cost him made him nervous lest he should be losing his skill; and it is true that his voice did sound weaker and more forced than in the first talks. But the art of his discourse was as finished as ever, and its charm just as great. Max had no difficulty in maintaining his reputation as a broadcaster. So high had this become that in 1952 the B.B.C. asked him if he would introduce the Queen in her first Christmas broadcast. Max politely declined this offer. But he was amused that he should have been considered an appropriate speaker for such an occasion. 'So far as I can see,' he said, 'my only qualification is to have caricatured Her

---

[1] He also refused permission for his harsher caricatures of King Edward to be reproduced in a new selection from his early drawings published by Rupert Hart-Davis.

Majesty's ancestors.' He meditated on what he might have said if he had accepted the assignment. 'I should have ended it like this,' he remarked to Elisabeth. ' "And now everybody's mind will in this moment be turning in gratitude to one, but for whom we should have a King on the Throne. I refer to Mrs Simpson!" '

Even more unhesitatingly, he declined to appear on the television screen. In 1955 Behrman passed on a proposal from The National Broadcasting Company of America offering Max three thousand dollars to take part in a series of television talks. Numbers of famous people, including Bertrand Russell and Robert Frost, had already agreed to take part: and the National Broadcasting Company proposed to send a representative to see Max. Max, however, offered no hopes of accepting.

'I am, alas, quite incorrigibly opposed to any idea of being televised. Mr Davidson Taylor was here recently and wished me to revoke the unwillingness I had expressed last year to Miss Marconi even after she had shown me on the wall the immensely mobile features of Bertrand Russell amplifying the artful modulations of his voice.'

Notwithstanding this discouraging reply, an envoy came and pressed the company's case. 'You see, Sir Max,' he said, 'it will be very simple. Our people will come and arrange everything. You will sit, if you like, as you are sitting now. You will simply say, "My dear friends, I am very happy to be here addressing you." ' 'Do you wish me to start with a lie?' Max asked politely. After this no more was heard of the proposed television programme. Later Max explained to Behrman his reasons for refusal. A talk, he said, was a piece of verbal art. There was no doubt about this in sound radio; the listener was forced to concentrate on the words because he could not see the speaker. On television his attention was diverted from the words to the speaker's face. The result was that the talk ceased to be a work of art and became the naked unedited exhibition of a personality. 'Television,' he said, 'is not literature, it is actuality.' To the end of his days Max was true to his youthful aesthetic principles. The artist, he still thought, should wear a mask. He did not think he could do this on television.

Further, his natural conservatism gave him a bias in favour of sound radio: he had known it first. 'Some people dislike the microphone,' he told John Russell; 'I welcome it into the house as a friendly animal.' He was grateful to it, moreover, as an animal especially friendly to himself. The B.B.C. made him a present of the records of his own talks. Curious and delighted Max sat up till long after his usual bed-time playing them over and over again: and for the rest of his life, along with music-hall songs and selections from Puccini's operas, they were among the records he played oftenest. He enjoyed them partly because he liked to observe his own art in action and from the audience's point of view; partly, too, because they reminded him of his past. Max, who had always loved recalling his past, loved it still more when he was old. His records were to him what old photograph-books and diaries are to others, a means by which he evoked vanished days. So too were his other works. The B.B.C. put on a dramatized version of 'Enoch Soames' in December 1954. Max listened to it. 'To think,' he said to Elisabeth, 'that I wrote it before this grate; and now here I sit forty years later listening to it!' 'Enoch Soames' took his mind further back than forty years—to the London of the nineties which had been its inspiration, the gay gas-lit London of the Café Royal and the Crown bar and the *Yellow Book* and the Diamond Jubilee. Summoned from oblivion by his own words, the ghosts of his delightful youth came to gather round Max eighty-two years old and sitting pensive in the shadow and flickering firelight of the little Villino drawing-room.

Some months earlier there had entered it a flesh and blood *revenant* from his past. A letter arrived for him in August from his old flame Constance Collier, saying that she was motoring through Italy to Venice and would like to call in on the way. Max wrote a polite letter of welcome; but he awaited her arrival with mixed feelings. He entertained only friendly sentiments towards Constance: on the other hand, remembering her flamboyant personality, he feared that in his present frail state he might find her company exhausting. He did. At four o'clock in the afternoon, Constance, still looking remarkably young, swept into the drawing-room having driven for eleven hours and intending to drive for nine more. She greeted Max with theatrical rapture; he had not changed at all, she said, from the days of their love. What wonderful days those had been! Max showed her a snapshot of himself and her together at Dieppe: 'Is that *us*?' she cried. 'Are they really *us*?' After an hour and a half spent in enthusiastic reminiscence she took her farewell.

Before she left, she led Elisabeth aside to explain how much she liked her and how little she had liked Florence: she added that Max was the only man whom she, Constance, had ever really loved. Two days later Elisabeth got a letter from her in which she said that Florence had taken away Max from all his friends. Elisabeth repeated this to Max who was amused. 'What impudence,' he exclaimed. 'I *wanted* to be away—that's why I came to Italy.'

We do not know whether Elisabeth also told him that Constance had said he was the only man she had really loved; nor what he would have thought about it if she had. As it was, he spent part of the same evening entertaining Elisabeth with lively anecdotes about Constance's romances with other men.

CHAPTER NINETEEN

The End

MAX lived for two more years after Constance's visit. Gradually he grew weaker. He tired more easily, slept worse, suffered more fits of asthma. His spirits remained much the same. He was intermittently attacked by moods of anxiety and depression, but not very often. He still enjoyed reading and listening to radio and gramophone; he could still make himself agreeable to friends and pilgrims. Eiluned Lewis called early in 1956. Max talked enchantingly, warming his fragile hands before a crackling fire of olive and pine wood and with a skull-cap on his head to keep off the cold.

This was in February; on 10 March he took a sharp turn for the worse. Elisabeth was spending the night away for the first time for fifteen months. It was to see a performance at the Scala in Milan of a ballet founded on Max's *Happy Hypocrite*. She came back on the 11th to find the house in some disorder; Max had suddenly been taken with a bad attack of rheumatic asthma. Elisabeth sent for their usual medical adviser, Dr Bacigalupo of Rapallo, and also for Max's old friend Dr Rau, who happened to be staying in the district.

It was soon clear that he was too ill to be nursed at home, and on 26 March he was moved to Dr Bacigalupo's clinic at the Villa Chiara in Rapallo. Meanwhile, Dr Rau, thinking that Max might have some arrangements he would like to make before death, had warned him that he was unlikely to recover. Max took the news calmly: but at once his mind flew to Elisabeth. What was her financial position likely to be if he died? As a matter of fact he had some years earlier made a will leaving her all that he possessed. But he had learnt that Italian law laid great stress on a man's obligation to bequeath his property to his relations. Max thought, therefore, that his will would go through more easily if Elisabeth was his wife. He had wanted her to be for some time; but had refrained from asking her for fear she might think it embarrassing to appear before the world as the bride of an octogenarian. She on her side, though she longed to be married to the man of her heart, shrank from suggesting

494

it lest she should be suspected of marrying him for his money. The prospect of death swept the scruples of both away. Lying in bed with a serene look on his face, Max suddenly said to her, 'What do you think of the idea of getting married?' After a pause she broke out, 'I adore you more than anything else in the world. I think it would be a good idea.' 'I am so delighted you think it *is* a good idea,' he answered.

The next step was to send for David Balfour, the British Consul at Genoa, to ask him to make the arrangements for the ceremony. Max wanted it to be done secretly: otherwise he was afraid that Elisabeth would be pestered by journalists and Press photographers. Balfour explained that it was not possible legally to keep the wedding a complete secret. But he promised that everything should be done to keep it as secret as possible. Certain formalities had to be gone through before it could take place: Max grew worried lest when the time came he might be too ill to sign the documents and that in consequence Elisabeth might not get her money. All was well, however. On 20 April the Mayor of Rapallo arrived at the clinic to perform the ceremony. The other witnesses were Balfour, Dr Bacigalupo and Mrs Jepson, who had come out to be with Elisabeth at the beginning of April when she heard of Max's illness. They stood watching the bridal pair; Elisabeth dressed in her best but looking lost, Max in bed and unusually pale. When the ceremony was over it was noticed that he turned to Elisabeth with a radiant, devoted smile. Soon they were left alone together. 'I think Elisabeth Beer-bohm is a wonderful combination,' he said affectionately.

It was a moment of sunshine, but a brief one. Max was very ill by now. Throughout the last weeks his condition had been deteriorat-ing, and not without suffering. Now this grew worse. Max, lucky all his long life, was not to be granted the final good fortune of an easy death. He did not, it is true, endure much actual pain; nor was he in the least frightened of dying. But from time to time he was racked by fits of suffocating asthma; he was afflicted with bed-sores; and his wasted aged body became agonizingly sensitive to the slightest pressure or friction. The effect was that he was frequently in acute physical distress. This in its turn reacted on his worn-out nerves. Even Max's self-command was not ultimately proof against the combined and relentless attacks of old age, infirmity and death. At times a black cloud of misery engulfed him which uttered itself uncontrollably in lamentation. Elisabeth, watching by his bed, would hear him moaning to himself in broken half-conscious tones, 'Why did I fall into this world . . . I never knew there could be such misery . . . I saw my mother die and my sister but not like this . . . there is no part of my body that has not betrayed me.' At such moments he could only long for all to be over as soon as possible. 'You could not want me to live like this,' he said to Elisabeth. 'You can't blame me if I long to die. Though I would love to live with you serenely, as before.' Prostrate on his bed he murmured to himself those tolling, chiming lines of Swinburne which, in the pride and glory of his youth, he had loved only for their beauty, but which now all too truly expressed the utter weariness which possessed his spirit.

> From too much love of living,
> From hope and fear set free;
> We thank with brief thanksgiving
>   Whatever gods may be
> That no life lives for ever;
> That dead men rise up never;
> That even the weariest river
>   Winds somewhere safe to sea.

His distress was intensified by the fact that he felt guilty at not concealing it better, he who had always made it a point of honour to present a pleasing and imperturbable face to the world. 'I have no capacity for bravery,' he said pathetically to Elisabeth, 'the nurses will soon lose patience with me; I am a horrible patient.' Or, looking at the concern on her face, 'Poor Elisabeth,' Max said, 'the strain is too much for you.' It almost was. Her suffering was more unrelieved than his: she could hardly bear to watch him and feel herself unable to help. She was mistaken in feeling this. It was noticed that however wretched and restless Max seemed, if Elisabeth came into the room, buoyant and benignant, at once he was soothed. He hated her to leave him for a minute: once she stayed in the sickroom for fifteen hours on end. After a spasm of asthma he recovered his breath to gasp out, 'I love you, I love you.' In his brighter moments, too, it was to Elisabeth he turned that she might share his revived spirits. For he had brighter moments. When the phases of acute discomfort passed, Max's lifelong habit of enjoyment reasserted itself; and soon he would be trying to make Elisabeth laugh by giving a comic imitation of the doctor's voice or affectionately teasing her about the fact that she was bigger than himself. 'I am glad I can never call you my sweet *little* wife,' he said. He also made fun of himself and his symptoms. Once he found himself turning away from his food with a faint involuntary grunt of distaste: 'How different from the sound made by the lions at feeding time!' said Max.

The aesthete in him was still alive too. Elisabeth used to hear him drowsily repeating fragments of Virgil that he had learnt to love when he was a boy at Charterhouse: or watched him lying contemplating with pleasure the decorative pattern made by the shadow of the blind against the yellow wall. 'It was Gordon Craig who taught me to appreciate the beauty of shadows,' he told her. Nor had he wholly lost his wish or his ability to please. On hearing of his illness, Iris Tree had come to Rapallo. She went up to see Max. Eighty-three years old and dying, his personality, she noticed, still exhaled a waft of the old charm. She said impulsively, 'You are very much loved, Uncle Max. Everyone loves you.' A look of pleasure came into his fading eyes. 'Well, my dear,' he answered, with an effort, 'I was always—er—a well-wisher.'

The days passed: the thin feeble flame of Max's life flickered lower and lower. On 18 May the doctor paid his usual visit. As he left, Max gathered his failing forces, '*Grazie per tutto*'—thank you for everything—he whispered. Was it a last effort of his customary politeness? Or did something tell him that it was time to take a final farewell? For the end was at hand. After this Max sank into unconsciousness. On the next day, he woke for a moment to see Elisabeth bending over him. 'You had a good sleep, didn't you?' she said comfortingly. 'No,' he answered: even in this dark moment Elisabeth could not help smiling at his determination not to come to terms with his illness. Her presence soothed him as always: clasping her hand he sank into a calm sleep. A few hours later, still holding her hand, he died. On 22 May, on a brilliant Italian spring day, the funeral took place, at the little chapel of San Giorgio in Rapallo. The body was then cremated and the ashes sent to England, where on 29 June they received the honour of burial in St Paul's Cathedral.

It is pleasant to speculate about what Max would have thought had he heard that this was to be the ultimate destiny of his mortal remains. He might well have been amused; as he had been amused to hear that an official memorial service had been held in the same place for George Robey. Was it not equally incongruous that he, the impish ironist, should lie with Nelson and the Iron Duke beneath the grave and monumental arches of the national pantheon? But he was also a patriot, with a romantic taste for the historical and the ceremonious. And he would have been gratified too.

Index

Abinger Chronicle, The, 447, 451

Acland, Sir Henry, 66, 67

Admirable Crichton, The, J. M. Barrie, 188, 261

Adventures of Harry Richmond, The, G. Meredith, 365–6

aesthetes, 103, 248

aesthetic movement, the, 24, 44, 59, 60–1, 69, 130, 140, 150

  burlesqued by Max, 100

Alexander, George, 120, 295, 297–8, 317

America, Max visits, 113–20

  Max asked to lecture in, 413–14

And Even Now, Beerbohm, 340, 379, 382–3, 394

Archer, William, 189

Arnold, Matthew, 49, 140, 370

  Max's opinion of, 370

Asquith, H. H., 329, 409

Autobiography of a Boy, The, George Street, 130

Awkward Age, The, Henry James, 364

Bachelor, Crouch—mock House of Commons, 140–1, 143

Bagnold, Edith, 326–8

Baldwin, Stanley, 405–6

Balfour, Arthur, 68, 205–7, 263–4, 318, 320, 341, 355

Baring, Maurice, 205, 422

Barker, Granville, 396

Barrie, J. M., 188, 260–1, 354

Barrymore, John, 223, 406

Beardsley, Aubrey, 65, 85, 92, 96, 98, 103, 105, 137, 149, 183–4, 320–2, 475

  death of, 196–8

  impresses Max, 95

  memorial article by Max, 197

Beardsley, Mabel, 198

Beaton, Cecil, photographs Max, 435, 475

Beerbohm, Agnes, b. 1865, 6, 12, 56, 385, 401, 445

  death of, 466

  marries Vesey Knox, 346

  visited by Max, 466

Beerbohm, Constance, b. 1852, 6, 11–13, 56, 126–7, 162–3, 253, 296, 328, 385, 442

Beerbohm, Constantia, *née* Draper, 5

Beerbohm, Dora, b. 1868, 6, 12, 23–4, 30, 253–4, 298, 385

  affection of Max for, 402, 404

  becomes postulant Sister of Mercy, 89–92

  illness and death of, 445–6

  takes final vows, 134

  visits family and Max, 134, 310, 361, 438

Beerbohm, Eliza, *née* Draper, mother of Max, 5, 6, 23, 35, 42, 46, 126–7, 225, 252, 295–6

  extravagance of, 162–3

  failing health and death of, 328, 347–8

Beerbohm, Ernest, b. 1850, 6, 7, 19

Beerbohm, Florence, *née* Kahn, 228–31, 240, 306

  affection of Max for, 337–8, 465

  death of, 477

  dislikes Max's friends, 396

  engaged to Max, 288–9, 292–4

  ill-health of, 376, 424, 454, 476–7

  letters from Max to, 232–40, 246, 259, 266, 270–91, 308–10, 330–3, 464–5

  marries Max, 3, 300, 303

  Mrs Schiff criticizes, 453

Beerbohm, Florence, stage career of, 275–6, 285–7, 290, 424
  travels of, 324, 352, 404
Beerbohm, Herbert—see Tree, Herbert Beerbohm
Beerbohm, Julius, b. 1854, 6, 9, 10, 19, 21, 22, 55
  death of, 254
Beerbohm, Julius Ewald, father of Max, 4–6, 12, 23
  death of, 57, 63, 102
Beerbohm, Max:
  Broadcasting, 472, 489
    attacking advertising, 456
    Max invited to, 430–1, 455–6, 463
    stories, 442
    success of, 432–4, 490
    television, refusal to appear on, 491
  caricatures, Max's, 32, 47–8, 57, 71, 73, 77, 101, 103, 147, 191, 272, 283, 328, 376, 411
    Beardsley admires, 95
    exhibited, 242, 307, 319, 336
    lose ruthlessness, 411
    published in book form, 136, 198, 339
    Rothenstein's appreciation of, 66–7
  comedian, as, 218, 371
  conversationalist, as, 266–9
  dandy, as, 15, 19, 32, 34, 40, 60–3, 130, 232, 233, 300, 349
  Defence of Cosmetics, A, 97–9, 101–103
  Doctrine of the mask:
    as exponent of, 61–3, 73, 87, 126, 140, 151, 204, 232, 244
    discards, 303
    reassumes, 433
  drama, standards of judging, 184–8, 248–9
  drawings, early, 19, 32, 137, 139
  essayist, as, 135, 145–8, 150, 190–2, 244, 324, 340, 353, 365, 379, 383, 394

  fantasy, love of, 27, 32, 49, 228, 304, 356, 375
  humour, views on, 181
  illness, last, 487, 488, 494, 496
  imagination, 27, 60, 61, 73, 89, 131
  knighthood, offered, 443, 444
  laughter, essay on, 383–4
  luxury, dislike of, 422
  moralist, as, 251–2
  music, enjoyment of, 422, 479, 486, 487, 492
  painting, modern, views on, 482
  parody, 34, 145, 316, 317
  playwriting, dabbles in, 188
  retirement, 303, 304
  scepticism, 381
  style, literary, 26, 39, 40, 363
  wealth, revulsion against, 333, 380
  women, relationships with, 218–19
  writer, as, 101–3, 126, 140
  writing, modern, views on, 483–4
Beere, Mrs Bernard, 20
Beggarstaff Brothers, 131
Behrman, S. N., 151, 215, 479, 480, 491
Belloc, Hilaire, 50, 54, 180, 261, 373, 385, 394, 406
  Max's liking for, 201, 262
Bennett, Arnold, 258–9, 330, 346, 364, 406, 409, 419
  describes Florence, 318, 348
Benson, Arthur, contributes to *Yellow Book,* 98
Bitter Sweet, Noël Coward, Max's cartoons for, 411, 421
  music of, 422
Blanche, Jacques-Émile, 184, 223, 237
Boer War, Max opposed to, 179, 180
Book of Caricatures, A, Beerbohm, 242
Brock, Clutton, 369, 372
Brough, Lionel, 113–15
Bruce, Kathleen, 277–81, 417, 419
  marries Robert Scott, 281
Burnand, Francis, Editor of *Punch,* 20

Café Royal, 93, 98, 105, 263, 321, 325, 341

Campbell, Mrs Patrick, 12, 188, 287, 329, 475

Cardigan, Lady, 265–6

Carfax Gallery—see exhibitions

Caricatures of Twenty-five Gentlemen, Beerbohm, 136–7, 147

Carson, Murray, 162–3, 188

cartoons, Max's, 41, 166, 338, 400
  political, 386–7, 391–2
  published, 178–9, 189, 319, 388, 408

Chamberlain, Joseph, 17, 68, 180

Chesterton, G. K., 54, 180, 182, 199, 258, 307, 370, 394
  meets and describes Max, 200–1

Christmas Garland, A, Beerbohm, 145, 195, 316, 317

Churchill, Lord Randolph, 17, 30, 47, 207

Churchill, Winston, 207, 263, 295, 308, 447

Clown, The, 57

Cochran, C. B., 421

Collier, Constance, 221, 223, 227–8, 231, 240, 271, 284, 291, 347, 406, 492
  Max engaged to, 224–6

Common Reader, The, Virginia Woolf, 373

Conder, Charles, 65, 133, 162, 183–4, 199, 225, 305
  death of, 259

Conover, Grace ('Kilseen'), 117, 129, 136, 159, 160, 231, 240, 271, 272, 315, 347
  death of, 436
  disliked by Beerbohm ladies, 126–129
  Max unofficially engaged to, 119, 126, 183, 125, 219, 200
  Max breaks engagement, 211, 224–5

Contemporary Portraits, Frank Harris, 400–2

Cooper, Alfred Duff, 405–6

Coward, Noël, 411, 421–2

Craig, Edward Gordon, 130–1, 199, 258, 304, 310, 328, 390–1
  in Italy, 353, 355, 361, 363–4, 377, 407

Cunard, Sir Bache, 264, 265

Curzon, Lord, 205, 207, 263–4, 405–6

Daily Herald attacks Max, 387, 391

Daily Mail, 139, 189, 245, 306
  Max writes on Italy for, 247–8, 277
  Max writes weekly commentary for, 140–1, 157

Davidson, John, 133, 134, 260

Davies, W. H., 354, 410, 411

De Profundis, Oscar Wilde, 124, 125

Decadents, the, 92–3, 103, 105, 125, 161

Desborough, Lady, 205, 207, 264, 297, 341

Diana of the Crossways, George Meredith, 365

Disraeli, Benjamin, 190, 368, 369

Diversity of Creatures, A, Rudyard Kipling, 367

Douglas, Lord Alfred, 58, 68–9, 73–5, 79, 85, 107–8

Dreadful Dragon of Hay Hill, The, Beerbohm, 356, 358–9, 409

Eden, Anthony, 427–8

Eden, Sir William, 157–8

Edinburgh University, Max offered doctorate by, 421

Edwardian era, Max's attitude towards, 178, 180, 232, 270

Edwardyssey, The, Beerbohm, 137

Elcho, Lady, 205–7

Eminent Victorians, Lytton Strachey, 349, 350

Era, The, 143–4

Essay Society, the, 50, 51, 59

exhibitions, 405, 419, 489
  at Carfax Gallery, 189, 242, 307
  at Leicester Galleries, 297–8, 319, 354, 384–5, 387, 469, 474, 489

Fifty Caricatures, Beerbohm, 319
Fry, C. B., Max interviews, 102

Gallienne, Richard Le, 92–3, 137, 145, 199
Galsworthy, John, 248, 261–2, 364
Garden of Proserpine, The, A. C. Swinburne, 208, 496
Garrick Club, The, 54, 347
General Strike, 1926, 412
George IV, essay on, 102–4
Germans, Germany, Max's views on, 344, 350, 423, 424, 428
Gershwin, George, 372
Gissing, George, 261–2
Gladstone, W. E., 16–19, 30, 137, 207
Godwin, E. W., 19, 21
Gorki, Maxim, 180, 187
Gosse, Sir Edmund, 3, 97, 258, 317, 330, 336
  caricatured, 320, 376, 409
  criticizes Max's work, 193, 194
  death of, 419
  meets Max, 152–6, 208, 329, 385
Graves, Robert, poetry of, 484
  visits Max, 474
Grenfell, Mrs—see Desborough, Lady
Gridiron Club, 58, 77

Haldane, Lord, 207, 263
Hamilton, General Sir Ian, 264, 265
Happy Hypocrite, The, Beerbohm, 121, 131, 280, 312, 340–1, 372
  analysis of, 150–1
  as one-act play, 188–9
  published in book form, 148–9
  three-act dramatization by Clemence Dane, 436
Hardy, Thomas, 92, 135, 260–1, 419
  Max's veneration for, 422–3
Harland, Henry, 92, 96, 97, 105, 199
Harmsworth, Alfred (later Lord Northcliffe), 157, 245, 385

Harris, Frank, 163–6, 188, 324, 326, 328
  committed to Brixton, 325
  publishes *Contemporary Portraits*, 400–2
Heartbreak House, G. B. Shaw, 364
Hichens, Robert ('Crotchet'), 107–8, 130
Hilda Lessways, Arnold Bennett, 330
Holland, Vyvyan, 329
Holt, Maud (later Mrs Herbert Beerbohm Tree)—see Beerbohm, Maud
Housman, A. E., 261–2, 364
Hutton, Baroness von, 281–3, 285, 295–6, 417

Ibsen, Henrik, 49, 100, 180, 189, 275, 373
Idler, The, publishes memorial article on Beardsley, 197
Importance of Being Earnest, The, Oscar Wilde, 71, 120
Intentions, Oscar Wilde, 373
Irvine, St John, 390, 391
Irving, Henry, 19, 50, 70

Jackson, Holbrook, Max's letter acknowledging dedication of book by, 320
James, Henry, 49, 97, 209, 258, 260, 307, 329, 480
  admires *A Christmas Garland*, 317
  caricatured by Max, 242, 376
  contributes to *Yellow Book*, 98
  Max meets, 152–5
  Max's enjoyment of work of, 321, 364–5, 485
Jepson, Selwyn, 473–4
Jepson, Tanio, 473–4
  witnesses Max's marriage to Elisabeth, 495
Jerome, Jerome K., 140, 250
John, Augustus, 204–5, 261, 263
Johnson, Dr, Max's proposed essay on, 365

Jones, Henry Arthur, 129, 130, 192, 412

Jungmann, Elizabeth (later Lady Beerbohm), 415, 417
dependence of Max on, 477–9, 488–9
friendship with Beerbohms, 448–452, 473
Max marries, 494–5

Kahn, Florence—see Beerbohm, Florence
Kahn, Mannie, visits Italy with his family, 396, 397
Kahn, Morris, 297
Keppel, Mrs George, 205, 206
Kilseen—see Conover, Grace
Kipling, Rudyard, 92, 270
caricatured by Max, 147–8, 409
death of, 435
hostility of Max to, 139, 147, 180, 251, 320–2, 367, 485–6
Max meets, 116
Knewstub, Alice—see Rothenstein, Alice

Land of Heart's Desire, The, W. B. Yeats, 96
Lane, John, of the Bodley Head, 65, 67, 92, 101, 134, 201
conceives idea of Yellow Book, 96
lacks appeal for Max, 93
Lang, Andrew, 154–6, 166
Later Days, W. H. Davies, 410, 411
Law, Andrew Bonar, 318, 320, 336
Leicester Galleries—see exhibitions
Leverson, Mrs Ada, 121–2, 199, 258, 287, 328, 385
interviews Max for The Sketch, 103–4, 152
Lewis, Eiluned, 441
Lewis, Katie, 258
Lewis, Lady Elizabeth, 258, 329, 347, 385
Life of Disraeli, Monypenny and Buckle, 368

Life of Shaw, Archibald Henderson, 373–5
literary style, Max's, 26, 39, 40, 363
Little Tour of France, A, Henry James, reviewed by Max, 470
Lloyd George, David, 353, 409
Locrine, A. C. Swinburne, 193
Loftus, Cissy, 100, 105, 119, 149, 299, 341
Max falls in and out of love with, 80–8
Low, David, Max's admiration for, 414–15
Lower Depths, The, Maxim Gorki, 187
Lucas, E. V., 394
Lynch, John Boheen, 392–4

MacCarthy, Desmond, 258, 349, 362, 422, 459
death of, 474
MacDonald, Ramsay, 405, 406
Maeterlinck, Maurice, 49, 223, 310, 382
high opinion of Max for, 187–8
Mainly on the Air, Beerbohm, 464
Marinetti and 'Futurism', 249–50
Masefield, John, caricatured by Max, 320
Maugham, Somerset, 53, 212, 225, 248, 406, 474
Maximilian Society, founding of, 459
Memoirs of My Dead Life, George Moore, 368
Meredith, George, 49, 100, 208, 258, 373, 462
death of, 260
Max's opinion of, 209, 211, 214, 260, 364–5
parodied in A Christmas Garland, 145
Mew, Egan, 349, 354, 385, 422, 441
Meynell, Alice, 145, 191, 367
Mirror of the Past, The, Beerbohm, 340

Modern Society edited by Frank Harris, 324-8

Moore, A. K., 20-1

Moore, George, 204, 212, 265, 329, 368, 409

described by Max, 202, 462

Moore, Sturge, 261-2, 367

More, Beerbohm, 191, 192, 244

More Leaves from the Journal of a Life in the Highlands, Queen Victoria, 374-5

Morris, William, 320, 322

Max's hostility to work of, 485

Munich crisis, 439

music halls, 55-6, 80, 93, 105, 181

Max broadcasts talk on, 455

Myrmidons, the, 51, 52, 78

Napoleon of Notting Hill, The, G. K. Chesterton, 201

Nevill, Lady Dorothy, 107, 157

Nicholson, William, 131, 133, 161, 199, 223, 258, 285, 295, 305, 308, 328, 333, 354

Max stays at Portofino with, 281-3

Nicolson, Harold, misquotes Max, 447

Northcliffe, Lord—see Harmsworth, Alfred

Observations, Beerbohm, 408

Old Man and the Sea, The, Ernest Hemingway, 484

Old Wives' Tale, The, Arnold Bennett, 259

Opening of Parliament, Max describes, 330, 331

Pain, Barry, 98

Pall Mall Budget, Max contributes to, 102

Parnell Commission, the, 38

Passing of the Third Floor Back, The, J. K. Jerome, 250

Pater, Walter, 44, 47-9, 60, 65, 149, 373

Pearson, Hesketh, 268

Pelligrini, Carlo ('Ape' of *Vanity Fair*), 137, 190

Peter Pan, J. M. Barrie, 178, 261

Pick-Me-Up, Max publishes drawings in, 102

Picture of Dorian Gray, The, Oscar Wilde, 71

Pinero, Arthur, 130, 250

Poets' Corner, The, Beerbohm, 189, 193, 242, 339

Pound, Ezra, 329, 484

practical jokes, Max's liking for, 371-374

Pre-Raphaelites, 13, 24, 321, 339

Princess of Wales, Max meets, 266

Pryde, James, 131, 326, 333

Punch, 16, 137, 149, 391

attacks *Yellow Book*, 98-9, 103

Max's early liking for, 18-20

Rau, Dr Leo, 454, 474

Raven-Hill, Leonard (*Punch* artist), 137, 139

Rede Lecture, Max gives (1943), 457-8

Renaissance, The, Walter Pater, 150, 373

Roberts, Cecil, meets Max, 407, 479

Roberts, Ellis, 407, 437, 438, 439

lends Max house near Stroud, 461

Rodin, 261-3, 277

Rosmersholm, Ibsen, 285-6

Ross, Robert, 85, 159, 198, 258, 348

Kilseen warns Max against, 125, 161

Max writes to, 109-10

member of Wilde circle, 107, 125

writes article on 1913 exhibition, 319

Rossetti and His Circle, Beerbohm, 339, 395

Rothenstein, Alice, 195, 196, 338

Rothenstein, William, 77, 162, 183, 225, 254, 304, 308, 314, 329, 342, 367, 409

Rothenstein, William, at Oxford, 64–7
  brings out *Twenty-four Portraits*, 369
  death of, 459
  edits supplement to *Saturday Review*, 161
  importance of to Max's career, 92, 93, 95, 107, 133, 415
  invites Beerbohms to Gloucestershire, 338, 343–4
  marries Alice Knewstub, 195–6
  Max's letters to, 77, 85, 167, 194, 306
  Max quarrels with, 256–7
  warns Max against Alfred Douglas, 108–9
Routledge, Edmund, 19, 20
Royal Family, Max's affection for, 444, 461
  objections to Max's cartoons of, 398–400, 443
Ruskin, John, 247, 314
Russell, Bertrand, 367, 405, 482

Sadler, Sir Michael, 370
St Cyres, Lord, 52, 59, 66
Salome, Oscar Wilde, 71
Sargent, John Singer, 204, 258, 329, 333
  Max describes, 205
Sassoon, Sir Philip, 333, 380, 422
Sassoon, Siegfried, 420, 437
Saturday Review, 104, 123, 463
  Max contributes to, 141, 145, 147, 157, 161, 183, 296
  Max dislikes working for, 269, 290
  Max as dramatic critic to, 163–7, 248–50
  Max resigns from, 297, 299
Savoy, The, 147, 321
Schiff, Sydney (pseudonym, Stephen Hudson), 407, 441–2
Schiff, Violet, 451–3
  criticizes Florence, 453
Scott, Clement, 141–3, 156

Scott, G. R., Max's tutor, caricatured, 47
Second Childhood of John Bull, The, Beerbohm, 178, 189, 307
Seven Men, Beerbohm, 340–2, 352, 355, 418, 442
Shaw, George Bernard, 70, 92, 180, 201, 248, 261, 270, 326, 354, 370–2, 374, 409
  caricatured by Max, 242, 320
  criticizes Gordon Craig, 470, 472
  dramatic critic of *Saturday Review*, 163–4, 167
  hostility of Max to, 166, 187, 262, 328, 462, 485, 490
  plays of, 364
Sheppard, Rev. R. L. ('Dick'), 420–1, 425–7, 454
Sickert, Walter, 56, 107, 129, 158, 183, 184, 204, 223, 308
Sketch, The, 102, 103, 152
Smithers, Leonard, 136, 147
Social Success, A, Beerbohm, 317, 318
Society, Edwardian, 205–7
  Max's part in, 261
'Souls, The', 205–7
Spirit Lamp, The, 75, 148
Sprigge, Cecil and Sylvia, 445, 447
Star, The, Max writes his first paragraph for, 40
Steer, P. W., Max describes, 204
Stern, Miss G. B., 440, 441
Stevenson, R. L., 209, 316, 368
Strachey, Lytton, 349, 350, 355, 364, 370, 385, 414, 440
Strand, The, 57, 102
Street, George, 130, 199, 258, 308, 328, 329, 422, 436
Sturt, Lady Féo, 205–6
Survey, A, Beerbohm, 388
Swinburne, Algernon Charles, 135, 141, 193, 208, 339, 364
  death of, 260
  described by Max, 208, 209, 383
Symons, Arthur, 92, 93, 98
Syrett, Netta, 107

Terry, Ellen, 260, 263, 329, 419
Thackeray, W. M., 13, 33, 35, 40, 58, 245, 316, 485
    influence of works on Max, 486
Things New and Old, Beerbohm, 400
Times Literary Supplement, The, 324, 410
Times, The, 98, 205, 322, 369, 451
Todd, M. Alexander (master at Charterhouse), 33
Tree, Felicity, 252, 385
Tree, Herbert Beerbohm, b. 1850, 9, 10, 13, 18–19, 22, 38, 50, 54, 104, 211, 308
    assumes name of Tree, 7
    death of, 346–7
    Max's admiration of, 21–2
    success of, 254
    tours America, 113–17
    tributes to, 352, 379
Tree, Iris, 252, 385, 479, 497
Tree, Maud Beerbohm, *née* Holt, 22, 127–9, 254, 257, 347, 352
    death of, 436
    dislikes Florence, 299
    Max stays with, 384
Tree, Viola, 252, 305, 348, 385, 422
Trilby, George du Maurier, 116
Trollope, Anthony, 316, 321, 364, 365, 485
Turner, Reginald, 52, 54, 109, 110, 184, 195, 223, 254, 295, 304, 308, 328, 396, 442
    becomes jealous of Max's friends, 74, 79, 159
    generosity of, 256
    Kilseen's friendship with, 160
    letters from Max to, 57, 59, 63, 68, 71, 78, 86–7, 100–1, 107, 115, 117, 121, 123, 157, 282, 299, 313, 428
    visits Max, 361
Twenty-four Portraits, W. Rothenstein, 369

Vanity Fair, 33, 137
    Max contributes caricatures to, 242
    Max writes essays for, 115
Variety of Things, A, Beerbohm, 418
Vaughan Williams, Ralph, 32, 445
Victoria, Queen, 44, 139, 190, 373
Vincent, Lady Helen, 264, 341

Waugh, Evelyn, Max meets, 411
Wells, H. G., 145, 180, 244, 251, 252, 270, 367, 441
What's Wrong with the World?, G. K. Chesterton, 307
Whistler, James Abbott McNeill, 19, 44, 65, 154, 156, 305, 339
    Max's admiration for, 157
    Memorial Exhibition, 262
Wilde, Oscar, 19, 20, 58, 70–1, 92, 161, 198, 320, 347, 373, 462
    death, 123–4
    influence on Max, 60, 75, 107, 124, 486
    leader of aesthetic movement, 49, 217
    praises Max's work, 68
    scandal threatens and breaks, 108–9, 119
    trials of, 119–23, 390
    writings, Max's high regard for, 73, 350
Wilde, Willie, 85, 104
Wilkinson, Mr, day-school kept by, 25–6, 33, 38
Wilson, Edmund, Max meets, 480
Wings of the Dove, The, Henry James, 245, 365
Woman of No Importance, A, Oscar Wilde, Max attends first night of, 68
Woolf, Virginia, 74, 373, 439, 483, 484
Works of Max Beerbohm, The, 148–9, 151–2, 191
World War, First, 334, 349, 350
World War, outbreak of Second, 445

Yeats, W. B., 61, 96, 147, 261, 310, 329

Yellow Book, 105, 107, 125, 149, 183, 199, 321, 341
  first produced, 96–7
  Max writes for, 98–101, 147–8
  Punch attacks, 103
  scandal caused by, 98–100

Yet Again, Beerbohm, 244, 342

Zuleika Dobson, Beerbohm, 116, 195, 310, 340–1, 372, 376, 486
  acclaimed, 313, 317, 449
  inspiration of, 312–13
  Max complains about printing of, 315
  radio version proposed, 472
  writing of, 295, 307–8

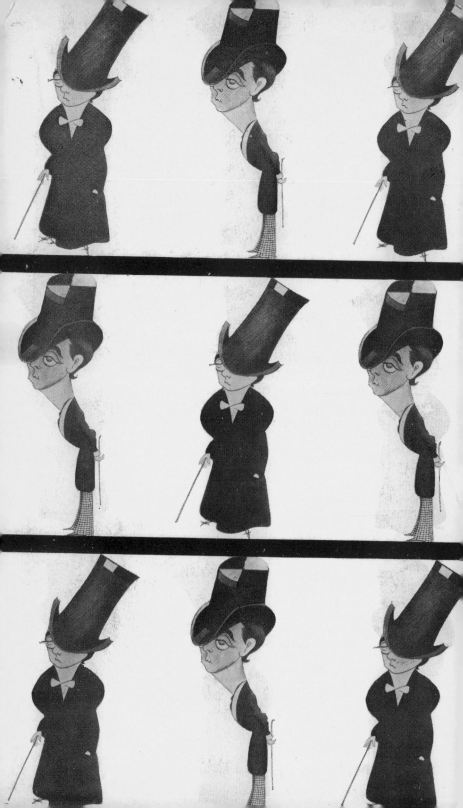